WHY GENDER?

Why is a focus on gender so important for interpreting the world in which we live? Sixteen world-famous scholars have been brought together to address this question from their respective fields: Political Theory, Philosophy, Medical Anthropology, Law, Geography, Islamic Studies, Cultural Studies, Philosophy of Science, Literature, Psychoanalysis, History of Art, Education and Economics. The resulting volume covers an extraordinary array of contexts, ranging from rethinking trans* bodies, to traumatized tribal communities, to sexualized violence, to assisted reproductive technologies, to the implications of epigenetics for understanding gender, and yet they are all connected by their focus on the importance of gender as a category of analysis. The publication of this volume celebrates the anniversary of the launch of the Centre for Gender Studies at the University of Cambridge, and features contributions from the Diane Middlebrook and Carl Djerassi Visiting Professors to the University.

Jude Browne is the Jessica and Peter Frankopan Director of the University of Cambridge Centre for Gender Studies, Head of the Department of Politics and International Studies, and Fellow of Social and Political Sciences, King's College, University of Cambridge.

WHY GENDER?

Edited by

Jude Browne

University of Cambridge

CAMBRIDGE
UNIVERSITY PRESS

University Printing House, Cambridge CB2 8BS, United Kingdom

One Liberty Plaza, 20th Floor, New York, NY 10006, USA

477 Williamstown Road, Port Melbourne, VIC 3207, Australia

314–321, 3rd Floor, Plot 3, Splendor Forum, Jasola District Centre,
New Delhi – 110025, India

103 Penang Road, #05–06/07, Visioncrest Commercial, Singapore 238467

Cambridge University Press is part of the University of Cambridge.

It furthers the University's mission by disseminating knowledge in the pursuit of education, learning, and research at the highest international levels of excellence.

www.cambridge.org
Information on this title: www.cambridge.org/9781108833370
DOI: 10.1017/9781108980548

First published 2021

A catalogue record for this publication is available from the British Library.

ISBN 978-1-108-83337-0 Hardback
ISBN 978-1-108-97036-5 Paperback

From all the contributors to this book, we dedicate it to the next generation ....
And from me personally,
to Etta & Martha.

Contents

Figures

Tables

Contributors

Bina Agarwal Professor of Development Economics and Environment at the Global Development Institute at the University of Manchester.

Akbar Ahmed The Ibn Khaldun Chair of Islamic Studies at American University.

Sara Ahmed Feminist Writer and Independent Scholar.

Seyla Benhabib The Eugene Meyer Professor of Political Science and Professor of Philosophy at Yale University.

Rosi Braidotti Distinguished University Professor, the Centre for Humanities at Utrecht University.

Jude Browne The Jessica and Peter Frankopan Director of the University of Cambridge Centre for Gender Studies and Fellow of King's College, University of Cambridge.

Judith Butler The Maxine Elliot Professor in the Department of Comparative Literature and the Program of Critical Theory at the University of California, Berkeley.

John Dupré Professor of Philosophy of Science and Director of the ESRC Centre for Genomics in Society (Egenis) at the University of Exeter.

Nancy Fraser The Henry A. and Louise Loeb Professor of Political and Social Science and Professor of Philosophy at The New School for Social Research.

Jack Halberstam Professor of Department of English and Comparative Literature and the Institute for Research on Women, Gender and Sexuality at the University of Columbia.

Sandra G. Harding Distinguished Research Professor of Education and Gender Studies at the University of California, Los Angeles.

Patricia Hill Collins Distinguished University Professor, Department of Sociology, University of Maryland.

Marcia C. Inhorn The William K. Lanman Jr. Professor of Anthropology and International Affairs at Yale University.

Cindi Katz Professor of Geography in Environmental Psychology and Women's Studies at the Graduate Centre of the City University of New York (CUNY).

Catharine A. MacKinnon The Elizabeth A. Long Professor of Law at the University of Michigan and long-term James Barr Ames Visiting Professor of Law at Harvard University.

Juliet Mitchell Emeritus Professor of Gender Studies, Fellow of Jesus College, University of Cambridge and Founder Director of UCCGS

Mignon Nixon Professor of Modern and Contemporary Art at University College London.

Jacqueline Rose Professor of Humanities and Director of the Birkbeck Institute of Humanities at the University of London.

A Prefatory Note

I need to start with a simple observation: this extraordinary and excellent collection demonstrates how complex and difficult is the subject at hand – gender. Each of these sixteen intellectually brilliant, world-renowned scholars have held (or are very soon to take up) the Diane Middlebrook and Carl Djerassi Visiting Professorship in the University of Cambridge Centre for Gender Studies. Two things: first, it is a very special Chair endowed by two remarkable people – Diane, an extraordinary author, literary scholar and feminist, and Carl, an eminent scientist, novelist and playwright, whose development of the contraceptive pill in the late 1950s has changed hundreds of millions of women's lives. Together they were wonderfully participant and supportive of the Centre's activities. Second, the Chair is held in turn by each visiting scholar, yet here in this book is a conversation between them on the question of why gender is important for understanding the world we live in, as though they were all together at the same time. This is the result of their expertise and the unifying nature of the subject. Outstandingly edited by Professor Jude Browne, the Jessica and Peter Frankopan Director of the Centre for Gender Studies, we have not only first-rate, fascinating, individual and powerfully *different* essays but a united euphony of voices. The result is profound: it is its diverse and collective profundity that we must celebrate – and read!

When, after nearly ten years of hard informal work, we established the Centre for Gender Studies, 'Women's Studies' alone was on the academic agenda, and it had been a time of unmitigated backlash against feminism, prompting us to regroup and rethink. However we are gendered, transgendered or ungendered, we will always need the longest revolution. Feminism is a process of uneven gains and losses. Gender is everyone who wants to join. The Centre's original aim of arguing how completely gender everywhere 'queers' the world has come of age with this book. But 'everyone and everywhere' is not diffuse, quite the opposite; by claiming it as fundamentally a 'category of analysis', the book demonstrates how scholastic rigour comes first and foremost and is always at a premium. Yet there must always be a creative contradiction in play: to become, unbecome and re-become, the thrust of what 'gender' means, like the feminism which coined its popularity, must always work against the grain.

There is here also a political aesthetic. A book which opens and continues with highly original analyses of the gender concept to both endorse it and use it to challenge received wisdoms concludes with a paeon to Yoko Ono's project for peace and love. Bed Peace is reexamined in the last chapter of the book to combat the old chestnut of how women's and gender struggles must wait till a 'more important' fight is won. This proposition, tediously repeated in every liberation struggle, should never again see the light of day once the implication of these essays sinks in; just as there is no 'before' women's oppression, so too is there nowhere in time or place which is not gendered and in need of 'ungendering'.

Juliet Mitchell

Acknowledgements

Enormous thanks to all the Diane Middlebrook and Carl Djerassi Visiting Professors at the University of Cambridge Centre for Gender Studies of the past and near future. It has been a great pleasure to collaborate with you all.

Very special thanks too, to John Haslam, Cambridge University Press Executive Publisher for his vision, wisdom and excellent guidance, and also to Toby Ginsberg and Claire Sissen, Cambridge University Press, to copy-editor Llinos Edwards and to research assistant Clemi Collette for all their really hard work and invaluable help in putting this edition together.

Finally, I'd like to warmly acknowledge Diane Middlebrook, Carl Djerassi and their family for supporting such an extraordinary Visiting Chair at Cambridge, to David and Primrose Bell and finally, to Jessica and Peter Frankopan whose support to Gender Studies at Cambridge across the years has been vital.

Professor Jude Browne
The Jessica and Peter Frankopan Director,
University of Cambridge Centre for Gender Studies

Introduction

Why Gender?

Jude Browne

WHY IS GENDER SO IMPORTANT FOR INTERPRETING the world in which we live? In this volume, sixteen world-famous scholars address this question from their respective fields: political theory, philosophy, medical anthropology, sociology, law, geography, Islamic studies, cultural studies, philosophy of science, literature, psychoanalysis, history of art, education and economics. Inevitably, questions of race and sexuality run through the volume as authors grapple with the consequences of gendered social orderings. The chapters cover an extraordinary array of contexts, ranging from rethinking trans* bodies, to traumatized tribal communities, to sexualized violence, to assisted reproductive technologies, through to epigenetics, post-humanism and post-anthropocentrism, and yet they are all connected by their focus on the importance of gender as a category of analysis.

What better place to start than with a defence of the term 'gender' and of 'gender theory' against dissenters? In Chapter 1, *Gender in Translation: Beyond Monolingualism*, **Judith Butler** begins by focusing on two particular types of criticism. The first is demonstrated by public statements made by prominent political and religious leaders who see gender theory as challenging heteronormative and traditional family forms – what the Vatican has called for example 'a gradual process of denaturalization'. The second comes from those who claim that 'gender' is an imperialist term – a cultural export from the Anglophone first world – that ought to be substituted by local vernaculars. Butler's response is to question monolingualism – the singular interpretation of a term, its relationship to culture and its generalizing tendencies. Instead she asks us to think about the question of gender in translation. She argues that the fear of gender as a 'destructive cultural imposition' manifests in attempts to 'purify' language along nationalist lines and attendant cultural intolerances. Butler observes that gender complexity is with us whether we accommodate it linguistically or not. She therefore concludes that when the term gender is not used merely as a scapegoat for global anxieties or a placeholder for new challenges to family and religion, it remains a powerful category that raises fundamental questions about freedom and norms. Indeed, as all the authors in this book agree, without it we undermine the capacity to understand what is at stake in converging and conflicting legal and social frameworks for thinking about difference, power and embodiment.

A greater recognition of those who seek to live without stigma or threat of violence in virtue of their gender or sexuality, is also a central theme of Chapter 2, **Jack Halberstam**'s *Gender and the Queer/Trans* Undercommons*. Here, Halberstam argues that most discussion around trans* bodies has focused on making bodies and selves rather than the 'unmaking' of how we think about them. Akin to Butler and other authors in this volume, Halberstam suggests we ought to construct new forms of knowledge and different narrations of life that are not limited to fixing or stilling gender. Halberstam brings his argument to life through four examples: the poetry of June Jordan; a *New York Times* story relating to the death of a black gender queer body which defied identification and was lost to an undocumented trans* and queer history; the purposefully bewildering work of the artist, Kent Monkman; and the performance art of the trans* artist boychild. Through these examples, Halberstam illustrates how trans* bodies should not be thought of as reifying the normative body by comparison but rather be understood as 'fragmentary and internally contradictory bodies that remap gender and its relations to race, place, class and sexuality'. Halberstam ends with a call to unbuild the worlds in which bodies are wrong or right.

In Chapter 3, *Gender and the End of Biological Determinism*, **John Dupré** continues with the theme of bodies and gendered orderings but this time in the context of scientific epistemology. Dupré argues that the biological determinist argument that gender is an expression of the dichotomous genetics of sex – what he calls the 'Biological Big Picture' – is no longer scientifically defensible in light of advances in biology over the last half-century. In examining the biological and ontological assumptions of the sex/gender distinction, Dupré explains that the '*exhaustive* division of people into two sexes' is not a reflection of how things really are in the world but rather of a categorizing gender order: 'We have been encouraged to think of the genome as something static and fixed, a programme or recipe that guides or directs the development of the organism. This is quite wrong.' Dupré takes us through some key elements of the history and philosophy of science behind the relationship between sex and gender, and argues that sex must be understood developmentally. This does not mean merely a developmental process predetermined 'in the genes', but rather including epigenetic development as a process of interaction between the developing organism and its environment. Here, the profound implications of this perspective on sex and gender are explored and Dupré concludes, in line with both Butler and Halberstam albeit from a very different field, that diverse expressions of sexuality are 'leading the way for our interpretations of sex'.

Like Dupré, **Sandra G. Harding** focuses on the importance of gender to new philosophies and histories of science. In Chapter 4, *Gender, Sexuality, Race, and Colonialism*, Harding challenges dominant international philosophies of science with the example of an alternative anti-colonial theorizing emanating from Latin America and focusing, in particular, on the Iberian colonizers of the late 1400s onwards. Harding argues that this example gives us a different interpretation of gendered and racialized colonial practices than the more common post-colonial theorizing associated mainly with British colonization of India and Africa approximately 300 years later. In so doing, Harding draws out some of the interwoven gender, sexuality and racial issues in these Latin American histories – asking what will philosophies of science look like that can recognize the present-day residues of these still oppressive histories, and can figure out how to move past them?' Central to this question is the colonial exploitation of racialized women and the infliction of hierarchical and rigid gender, sexual and racial categories on the Americas. These included, for example, the narrowing of sexual identities, the destruction of distinctive family forms and the de-humanization of the colonized. Such practices, argues Harding, were not only exported back to Europe but still serve to shape the world today. In response, Harding argues that philosophers of science ought to be inspired by the new work emanating from Latin America which interprets the world in such a way that is anti-racist, non-heterosexist and post-androcentric.

In continuing to explore forms of de-humanization and resistance to unjust hierarchies, **Rosi Braidotti** takes us to the very different context of post-humanism and post-anthropocentrism. In Chapter 5, *Posthuman Feminism and Gender Methodology*, she provides a cartographic account of 'meta-patterns in contemporary knowledge production processes, using gender as the navigational tool'. She begins by illustrating the feminist, post-colonial and critical race critique of the humanist tendency to construct an idealized 'Western Man' as the universal representative of humanity, citizenship, rational thought and culture: 'the measure of all things'. As Braidotti explains, humanism has deployed epistemic and social violence against those who were other to 'Man', and who consequently became 'disposable and unprotected [which raised] crucial issues of power, domination and exclusion'. Alongside these post-humanist insights, the rejection of species hierarchy and the environmental degradation associated with anthropocentrism requires a de-centring of the *bios* (the 'exclusively human life') as the ultimate priority of human action. Braidotti argues that as anthropocentrism inevitably declines, questions of social justice remain ever pertinent in the context of *zoe* (non-human life), *geo* (planetary and environmental) and *techno* (science-derived, non-living) forces. Gender-driven critical cartographies, intersectionally co-produced with anti-racist, environmental and disability theorizing, are well equipped to understand the post-humanist and post-anthropocentric condition from a situated and historical perspective of marginal subjects already excluded from full humanity, devoid of the benefits of new technological advances and subjected to the worst effects of environmental degradation. Such perspectives are what Braidotti describes as the 'embodied and embedded understandings of the knowing subjects'. In building on such a powerful critical-theory tradition, Braidotti, while acknowledging the challenges, calls on feminism to sharply focus on the emancipatory potential in both post-humanism and post-anthropocentrism for resisting the suppression of pluralistic human and non-human flourishing.

With a similar emphasis on transformation, and especially transformation through technology, in Chapter 6, *Gender, Sperm Troubles, and Assisted Reproductive Technologies,* **Marcia C. Inhorn** takes us to the transnational 'reprohub' of Dubai in the United Arab Emirates. Inhorn explains how rising numbers of infertile men and their partners from all over the world travel to Dubai to seek the assistance of *in vitro* reproductive technology, in particular intracytoplasmic sperm injection (ICSI), in the hope of becoming parents. In cases where sperm are low in number, immotile or unusually shaped, the ICSI technique enables a single sperm to be collected and injected directly into an egg, thereby taking on the function of fertilization and enabling growing numbers of infertile men to become biogenetic parents along with their partners. Central to what Inhorn describes as 'reprotravel' are the various cultural, religious and legal restrictions on assisted reproductive techniques in patients' home countries. Inhorn argues that men's role in reproduction has been neglected by gender scholars despite the fact that sperm-related infertility contributes to more than half of the world's cases of involuntary childlessness and that 'sperm quality' is in decline globally. Based on in-depth ethnographic research, Inhorn explores the ICSI treatment quests of infertile men travelling to Dubai. Drawing on the case of Hsain, an infertile British-Moroccan man, Inhorn illustrates why ICSI is a particularly compelling technology for infertile Muslim men. Inhorn concludes by arguing for increased gender scholarship on men and reproduction as a key element of how we think about the future of society.

Linking biological reproduction to social reproduction, **Nancy Fraser** argues in Chapter 7, *Gender, Capital, and Care,* that a gendered crisis of care is intrinsic to capitalism. By 'social reproduction', Fraser means both affective and material labour, largely performed by women without pay. Social reproduction, she argues, is essential to the functioning of society: 'Without it there could be no culture, no economy, no political organization.' And yet, it is often overshadowed by a greater focus on other societal challenges such as the ecological. Fraser takes us through a history of the crisis in social reproduction generated by what she calls 'the social contradiction of capitalism', and ranging from the liberal competitive capitalism of the nineteenth century, through the state-managed capitalism of the twentieth century, to the present-day financialized, globalizing neoliberal form of capitalism. In this contemporary era, Fraser argues, feminism and other emancipatory movements have been folded in with marketization to undermine social protection. While espousing gender equality in the workplace for example, she argues that states simultaneously disinvest in public social services alongside the stagnation of wages even though the cost of living continually rises. The result is a frantic struggle to transfer carework to others or postpone it. As emblematic of the contemporary crisis in social reproduction, Fraser cites new practices such as assisted reproductive technologies, in particular the commercialization of egg freezing, not for the infertile, as Inhorn writes about in the previous chapter, but for the fertile who fear that the combination of parenthood and employment might not be feasible in the near future. What we are witnessing, argues Fraser, is a '*dualized* organization of social reproduction, commodified for those who can pay for it [and] privatized for those who cannot'.

With a similar focus on crisis and social reproduction to that of Fraser's chapter, in Chapter 8, *Aspiration Management: Gender, Race, Class, and the Child as Waste,* **Cindi Katz** looks at the gendered and racialized politics of what she calls 'aspiration management' in increasingly privatized, commodified and financialized economies. By 'aspiration management' Katz means the 'anxious strivings and affective relationships . . . seen in the everyday practices of social reproduction', especially those of motherhood. She focuses on the ways in which aspirations for the future are defined, managed and reached through the family and children's education. Drawing on three examples – the best-selling book *Battle Hymn of the Tiger Mother,* and the films *Waiting for Superman* and *Race to Nowhere* – Katz examines the ways in which middle-class and wealthier parents have been painstakingly (sometimes aggressively) crafting their children's education and life experiences in preparation for 'the imagined niche markets of the future' in which they will compete for the highest salaries and status networks. These children are set against a backdrop of others, the vast majority of children, who suffer the consequences of a disinvested public sphere, the rising costs of living and the stagnated social wages of their parents. These children, Katz argues, are treated as 'waste that must be managed and contained' much like, as Fraser also explains, the other waste products of contemporary capitalist societies. In the context of increasing economic precarity in which millions are faced with insecure employment, Katz concludes that the gendered and racialized social reproduction of the next generation is increasingly characterized by a growing human detritus of commodity production and marketization.

In Chapter 9, *Gender, Race and American National Identity: The First Black First Family,* **Patricia Hill Collins** continues with the theme of precarity and asks us to consider the central place that gender and notions of the family inhabit in racial politics and national identity at a time of increasing economic insecurity. In particular, she analyses how the first African American President, Barack Obama and his wife, Michelle Obama, worked together in operationalizing the American Dream to underpin the public policy objectives of the Obama Administration (2009–2017): 'hard work, commitment to family, and fairness – can achieve an adequate standard of living and societal respect'. Hill Collins argues that Barack Obama consciously navigated a narrative course away from negative stereotypical accounts of black American families and instead, promoted responsible fatherhood as an ideal form of masculinity for men, and for women, a work–family balance centred in dynamic motherhood as epitomized by the First Lady. Accordingly, the Obamas not only perpetuated a highly traditional gendered account of national identity but one that was dependent on a 'colorblind ideology' which addressed racism by adopting 'wilful blindness' in a promoted culture of inclusion. Hill Collins demonstrates how Barack Obama used 'colorblind' gendered family rhetoric and the personal stories of his own childhood and that of Michelle Obama's to signal a successful route to economic security wrapped up in the American Dream. However, Hill Collins argues that because the idealized family is in fact a moral discourse operating in an increasingly precarious economic context for many, it 'misrecognizes the interdependence of macroeconomic and macro-political forces and family outcomes'. This, in turn, serves to cast families who live in poverty as '*causing* their own disadvantage by ostensibly rejecting dominant norms'. Through these observations, Hill Collins brings into focus the ways in which gender and racial inequality as well as economic insecurity are intricately intertwined in constructions of national identity.

In Chapter 10, *Gender and the Collective*, **Bina Agarwal** considers an alternative to the forms of marketization discussed by Fraser, Katz and Hill Collins, through an analysis of economic collectives and their impact on gender inequality. Here, Agarwal explores the power of women's presence in collectives not only in terms of enhancing social justice but also for improving economic and environmental outcomes. As Agarwal explains, collectives – groups of people united by a common purpose – are central to human society and come in many forms including political assemblies, village councils, trade unions, clubs and cooperatives. Agarwal's analysis of collectives moves beyond the usual questions of why women have historically been excluded and asks instead, what is the impact of women's inclusion? In addressing this question, Agarwal considers several others: how does the presence of women in collectives impact on families, communities, markets and the state? To be effective, how large a presence of women is needed to form a critical mass for change? How does the heterogeneity within collectives, class, caste and ethnicity impact on cooperation? Do the collectives need a gendered consciousness? Agarwal offers answers to these questions by drawing on her extensive empirical research of the many thousands of economic collectives in South Asia. In particular, Agarwal focuses on two types of collectives: community forestry collectives and farmers' collectives. The community forestry collectives, who work in partnership with governments, manage and conserve local forests which are vital to them for firewood, food and building materials. The farmers' collectives are constituted by rural women who pool land, labour and other resources to farm and share their costs and returns. Agarwal concludes that an understanding of the gendered dynamics of collectives is vital to capturing the potential they offer as a progressive, environmentally effective and economically productive alternative to the state–market dichotomy.

In **Sara Ahmed's** *Willfulness, Feminism, and the Gendering of Will*, Chapter 11, she, like Agarwal, explores the implications of resisting traditional gendered social orders. Ahmed explains gendering as a dynamic social process that is illustrated by a history of those who are willing to obstruct – a history of wilfulness. Drawing on a range of cultural materials such as the Grimm story of *The Willful Child* and George Eliot's *The Mill on the Floss*, Ahmed discusses the figure of the 'willful girl' whose wilfulness is judged as a character fault that must be corrected or quashed. These cautionary tales of moral instruction are designed to urge obedience and become part of the gendering of the will. Ahmed reflects on what the wilful girl who refuses to submit her will, might tell us about feminism. 'To be willful is, here, to be willing to announce your disagreement .... Feminism we might say is the creation of some rather disagreeable women.' These disagreeable women Ahmed calls 'feminist killjoys', those feminists who complain or who are 'willing not to go with the flow', those who go the wrong way, are understood as being *in* the way where it takes stamina to remain wilful, to resist. In this sense, Ahmed reclaims wilfulness as a form of political action. By connecting wilful subjects with feminist killjoys, Ahmed argues that feminists are understood as being wilful in their refusal to go along with a gendering social order. In so doing, she shows how gendering operates to cast 'female disobedience' as a problem to be solved and how the history of wilfulness helps us to make sense of the pathologizing of feminism.

In Chapter 12, *Gender and Emigré Political Thought*, **Seyla Benhabib** writes on two famously wilful women, Hannah Arendt and Judith Shklar. In particular, Benhabib considers why gender as a category of analysis is important for understanding the lives and work of these distinguished political theorists even though neither of them identified as feminists – despite the important place that sexuality and family held in their work. Benhabib explores the subtle ways in which the public and the private, the political and the personal are imbricated throughout the considerable contributions these two women have made to political theory. One of Benhabib's central observations is the curious shift in Shklar's assessment of Arendt's work from the wholly admiring piece 'Hannah Arendt's Triumph' (1975), to the deeply derisive 'Hannah Arendt as Pariah' (1983). Benhabib sets out to account for this turn of opinion and in so doing, tells us something of the biographies of two of the world's most formidable women theorists, and how their personal experiences and their work interlocked. It is a story of women scholars in exile, their intellectual journeys, their Jewish backgrounds, their place in the academe, sex discrimination and Arendt's highly controversial relationship with her lecturer, the philosopher Martin Heidegger, who later became a Nazi Party member, and whom many, including Shklar, held in deep contempt. Benhabib draws out these details in such a way that gender becomes a key category of analysis for understanding the anxiety and influence bound up in the complex relationship of the younger scholar, Shklar, to the imposing figure of Arendt.

Jacqueline Rose, like Benhabib, is fascinated by the work of Hannah Arendt from a gender perspective, and in Chapter 13, *Feminism and the Abomination of Violence: Gender Thought and Unthought,* Rose puts Arendt in the intellectual company of Melanie Klein to explore the topic of violence against women. Rose argues that violence against women is not an aberration, but central to the gendered dynamics of human society and therefore a key issue for feminism. Rose argues, however, that the feminist discourse on violence has tended to be appropriated by radical feminist thinking which, she argues, fails to understand violence as part of psychic reality: 'feminism has nothing to gain by seeing women solely or predominantly as the victims of their histories'. By way of an alternative approach, Rose turns to the work of Arendt and Klein, both of whom engage in various ways with the entanglement of social and psychic violence and subordination. Rose considers Arendt's writing on the dynamic relationship between dwindling power and violence as a thoughtless human act. For Rose, 'violence against women is a crime of the deepest thoughtlessness' driven by impotence and frustration, and without compassion. Through Klein, Rose explores violence as a consequence of psychotic anxiety which she places at the core of the inner mental life of the child. Here, Rose argues that to address violence against women, the darkest urges must be brought to the surface, encountered and challenged in order to bring about compassion for others. Crafting these analyses together, Rose offers a new psychoanalytic interpretation of violence against women for contemporary feminist theorizing and practice.

Catharine A. MacKinnon's focus is also violence and gender in Chapter 14, *Trafficking, Prostitution, and Inequality: The Centrality of Gender.* Here, MacKinnon argues that gender inequality is at the core of the sex industry. Beginning with what has largely become a polarized debate, MacKinnon sets out its two major positions. The first is the 'sex work model' which calls for sex work to be institutionalized like any other form of employment and through which sex workers have substantive agency: 'this means freely choosing, actively empowering, deciding among life chances' and compensation 'for what is usually expected from women for free'. This model is rejected by MacKinnon as liberating for women: 'There can be nothing equal about it.' Instead, she advocates the 'sex exploitation model', which focuses on the limitations of choice that prostituted people have within the sex industry. This is an abolitionist position pioneered in Sweden in 1999. Its legal form has three primary components: the first is the criminalization of those buying sex – 'the driver' of the sex industry; the second is the criminalization of the third party – the 'sellers, the pimps and traffickers'; the third, and equally important, is the non-criminalization of those whose sexual services are for sale, whom MacKinnon calls 'the sold'. For these people, predominantly women and girls, the sexual exploitation model provides support and resources not least for exiting the sex industry. Drawing on a range of empirical studies and her own extensive research, MacKinnon concludes with the argument that prostitution is a violence against 'the sold' who, with few exceptions, exercise little choice in their provision of sexual services despite the claims of the sex industry advocates.

In Chapter 15, *Gender, Revenge, Mutation, and War,* **Akbar Ahmed** also focuses on the gendered dynamics of destitution and violence in the context of the 'war on terror'. Ahmed argues that after the events of 9/11, the US and other nations intensified their hunt for terrorists in the so-called 'ungoverned spaces' of tribal Muslim communities often situated at the peripheries of states around the world. Ahmed argues that the intensive and lethal conflict that ensued, including the deployment of drone strikes, helicopter gunships and heavy artillery as well as the movement of large numbers of refugees and very high incidences of sexual harassment and rape, has profoundly traumatized many communities. Ahmed argues that the turmoil of these conflicts has led to the breakdown of the traditional structure of Muslim tribal society and has resulted in a mutation of tribal codes as well as Islamic custom and law. Ahmed argues that as a result of ongoing violent chaos, women in Muslim tribal societies have adopted suicide bombing to avenge the wrongs they believe have been inflicted on them and their families. Ahmed illustrates his argument through a range of examples of women suicide bombers in the context of conflicts such as those in Chechnya, Kurdistan, Somalia and Nigeria. These women's acts are in contradiction to Islam's prohibition on 'suicide and the killing of innocents' and, as Ahmed shows, must be understood in the context of revenge, despair and changing tribal identity. Ahmed concludes that an understanding of the gendered impact of the global fight against terrorism in Muslim tribal societies is key to finding future solutions.

Finally, in the last chapter, we turn from the gendered dynamics of war and violence to those of peace movements. In Chapter 16, *Bed Peace and Gender Abnorms,* **Mignon Nixon** considers how the gendered social order can be challenged and reworked through art to create an innovative feminist political perspective. By way of example, Nixon focuses on the work of avant-garde artist, filmmaker and composer Yoko Ono and her husband, John Lennon. Nixon argues that their famous 1969 peace protest *Bed-In for Peace* demonstrated how gender equality was integral to the social process of eventually bringing the American war in Vietnam to an end and looking towards a peaceful future. Nixon describes the anti-war movement at that time as riven with sexism and dominated by the view that women's liberation was not only 'trivial, but dangerously diversionary'. Feminists who rejected what they saw as a growing misogyny in the anti-war movement were treated with contempt and sometimes public violence within the movement. Set against this backdrop, Ono and Lennon planned to make their honeymoon a feminist political statement that embodied gender equality, commonality, freedom from sexual violence, reproductive freedom and a communal space, where visitors could come and join the newly-weds in their expression of peace witnessed by millions through relentless media. Nixon closes with the observation that as we face new cycles of militarism, war and conflict in the world today, we have to work against our norms to achieve peace in the context of both war and gender inequality – 'as long as our war and gender norms align, we struggle to conceive of peace'.

Together, the authors in this volume demonstrate why gender is so important for understanding the world in which we live. Gender is perhaps the oldest social ordering of human society. Its complex relationship to other social characteristics such as race and socio-economic status is vital to understanding social processes and imagining alternative societies. Its meaning is both a source of misunderstanding and of new epistemologies. It is a process, both in the social sense as well as in the biological. It is an axis of violence and exploitation, and it is a form of disruption, protest and resistance. It is a device of colonial and patriarchal politics, and yet without it, politics fails to become progressive. Why gender? The authors in this volume make it obvious.

CHAPTER 1

Gender in Translation: Beyond Monolingualism

Judith Butler

IN THIS CHAPTER I CONSIDER HOW DANGEROUS AND DISTURBING the term "gender" has become in the minds of those who fear its power and influence (Gallo, 2017). The stated concern about "gender" as a foreign term, an English term, acting on local or national cultures as if it were a foreign element or, indeed, a foreign power is matched by a presumption within feminist and LGBTIQ theory that "gender" can function as a generalizable concept no matter the language into which it enters. The aim of the following chapter is, thus, twofold: first, to establish that there is no "gender theory" without a problem of translation, and second, the fear of "gender" as a destructive cultural imposition from English (or from the Anglophone world) manifests a resistance to translation that deserves critical attention. As much as the resistance to cultural imperialism is surely warranted, so too is the resistance to forms of linguistic nationalism that seek to purify its language of foreign elements and the disturbance to syntactical ways of organizing the world that they can produce.

Let us start with the proposition that gender is, from the start, a foreign term, that it was devised first by sexologists and then reappropriated for feminist purposes, then renewed in light of queer and trans studies. The term has a history, and it never fits easily into any language it enters. One reason has to do with how

This chapter was presented in adapted form as the inaugural Simone de Beauvoir lecture at the World Congress of Philosophy in Beijing in August 2018. It benefited greatly from audience response at the Gender Institutes at Cambridge University and the London School of Economics in 2016. A longer version was published first in Butler (2019).

biologically enmeshed the notions of women and men seem to be, but also how the binary framework for understanding gender seemed to function as defining one for understanding sex.

As the contributions to this volume illustrate, gender has never been without its controversies and it has never operated without resistance. Sara Ahmed, for example, argues that perhaps "to resist the demands of a gendered social order; we might need to be willful, creative, bold, daring, and imaginative." Even within the history of feminist philosophy, gender appears as a recent phenomenon, confounding the Euro-Atlantic debate for decades, and now taking on the status of a global disturbance. For instance, "gender" is not a term that Simone de Beauvoir used. It would have been, for her, a foreign term in French. And yet, arguably, her own writings pointed the way toward the development of one strain of the philosophy of gender. Beauvoir argued in *The Second Sex* that one is not born a woman but rather becomes one. That formulation became the basis for the feminist theoretical distinction between sex, understood as a biological reality, and gender, understood as the cultural or social meanings that that biological reality assumes in a specific time and place. In the 1970s and 1980s, the distinction was important for many reasons, chief among them the claim that there is nothing in the sex of a woman that determines what kind of work she should have, what kind of life she should live, who or how she should love.[1]

The problem, in fact, was never biology as such, but a certain account of biological sexual difference governed by natural teleology (see John Dupré's chapter in this volume). The clear separation between the two was important for making the claim that no

[1] See Anne Fausto-Sterling (2012). There she argues that sex and gender are in part social constructs. Because both take place in the body, they are also biological. She calls for a dynamic systems theoretical perspective in order to highlight the link between the social – which always impinges on the developing body – and the body itself. Conversely, she shows how cultural experience has physiological effects and so is engaged in a reciprocal action. Her views show how the biological can be taken seriously at the same time that natural teleological models are rejected and replaced with more dynamic models.

natural teleology governs the development of a woman from a biological condition of being female. A social man could emerge from someone assigned female at birth; a social woman could emerge from someone assigned male at birth. For some, Beauvoir's contention that one "becomes a woman" established that gender is a choice, but others interpreted that "becoming" as a form of reckoning within what she called a "situation." That "situation" included sex, but understood neither as a natural fact nor as a natural teleology. The interdisciplinarity of *The Second Sex* showed that a category such as "woman" was established through political, social, psychological, and economic influences. Beauvoir never denied natural facts, but she insisted that such facts are organized by the situation in which they occur, and that their meaning could not be understood outside of this complex situation.

Some scholars of Beauvoir, such as Alice Schwarzer (2000) or Toril Moi (2008), insist that the category of women was surely more important to Beauvoir than any potential idea of gender. It was the category of "women" that she sought to empower by insisting that no causal determination or natural teleology governs the kind of work a woman can and cannot do, the kind of thinking she can and cannot pursue, her relation to reproduction, kinship, marriage, and sexuality. The radical lesbian challenge of Monique Wittig (1992), disputing the category of woman itself, in some ways followed from Beauvoir, but also highlighted the tension among her followers. The tremendous theoretical and political challenge of trans theory was one that was not anticipated, even though the notion of "becoming" suffuses trans studies, especially in the work of Kate Bornstein and the public discourse of Laverne Cox, but also among those working within the critical tradition of Gilles Deleuze. As Jack Halberstam argues in this volume, trans* bodies "remap gender and its relation to race, place, class and sexuality." The contemporary life of the category of gender is perhaps nowhere more important than it is in trans studies (Aizura & Stryker, 2013; Stryker & Whittle, 2006).

RESISTANCE TO GENDER, RESISTANCE TO TRANSLATION

Let me foreground two points that will prove central to my argument. The first is that sex cannot be fully separated from the linguistic formulation that establishes it as a fact. The linguistic formulation of sex as a fact is, in my view, part of what is meant by gender. Second, gender is a foreign word. Gender always produces a problem for translators. Indeed, gender only arrives in any language as a result of a difficult translation. As a result, it never quite carries the same meaning in different languages. In effect, my thesis is that translation is the condition of the possibility of gender theory in a global frame. The resistance may be to the tasks of translation that emerge for global conversation and scholarship on the part of Anglophone cultural imperialists who do assume the universality of all that is thought within English (as both Sandra G. Harding and Jack Halberstam argue in different ways in this volume) but it may also be the result of a fierce defense of patriarchal power, the heteronormative family, the natural character of both sexual difference and hierarchy, and the pathology of LGBTIQ lives.

Sometimes the resistance to the term "gender" is syntactical, as if to start to use the term in language would challenge, or even defy, the basic syntactical structures that govern sense-making within a given language. This produces a different kind of linguistic disturbance at a basic level. At first the problem appears to be one of usage: How does one use the term? Does a person belong to a gender? Is gender a predicate of a person? How does one use the term "gender" in a sentence? Other times, the problem seems to be the introduction of a broader set of cultural practices where the use of the term is presupposed and put into play. The debates about whether "gender" can be translated focus on what is lost and gained, lost from English, but also traditional terms vacated from the language into which "gender" enters. But perhaps we need to ask: What kind of disturbance does the entrance of that foreign word into a language produce?

When the term "gender" enters into another language, English itself enters, or rather, enters again (certainly "gender" does not introduce English for the first time). It seems fair to assume that English has been entering for a long time. That clearly happens when the term "gender" is preserved in the second language in its English form; it happens differently when a new word is devised in the second language to approximate the term. Of course, as important as it is to consider specific responses to the various arrivals and incursions of English into other languages to the term "gender" or to gender theory and analysis, that will be only a partial task (though it is related and is surely a worthy project, raising as it does, and from the outset, the question of cultural influence, even cultural imperialism).

My question is slightly different: Why is it that debates about gender as a term do not very often consider the presumption of monolingualism at work in such debates? For instance, when in the US, the UK, or Australia we approach gender as a category or a concept, we tend to set aside the fact that we are referencing an English usage. We assume in romance languages that it will be relatively the same – *le genre, el genero* – or that it should be, and that in principle the discussions we have in English are generalizable to an indefinite number of contexts. Indeed, when we argue about "gender" – and here I mean the term – elaborating its meaning or its conceptualization, we are already operating within a monolingual field, unless of course we are arguing in another language and "gender" is a foreign term. But even then, when gender enters as a "foreign term," it remains oddly foreign in languages other than English; it burrows into another language as a foreign incursion. As such, it raises all the usual questions: What is the foreign doing here? Is it welcome? Has it been invited? Is gender the sign or instrument of an imperial takeover?[2]

[2] See Theodore Adorno (1958: 290–91), where he notes the importance of the breakdown of the organic and pure idea of language: "The power of an unknown, genuine language that is not open to any calculus, a language that arises only in pieces and out of the disintegration of the existing one; this negative, dangerous, and yet assuredly promised power is the true justification of foreign words."

In English we make various generalizations about gender as if we were referring to a concept and not a specific linguistic usage; generalizations of that sort might include gender as performative or relational, intersectional or processual. For the most part, in English the presumption is made that what we are arguing about is easily, if not fully, translatable by virtue of its inherent generalizability. Although gender theorists in Anglophone contexts may not always recognize it, they invariably take up an attitude toward translation when they are arguing about gender. There are several senses in which this turns out to be true. First the term "gender" within feminist, queer, and trans theory, and throughout the social sciences, comes to us from other sources, both grammatical and sexological. So we are working with a received coinage, and we coin it further all the time. Second, in practicing theory as we do, our assumptions about the generalizability of our claims rest on a tacit conviction that there will be no disturbance or blockage when "gender" is translated into other languages: in fact, the political uproar about the entry of the term into non-English-language contexts has only intensified in recent years – I will give some indication of that. Third, gender assignment is a discursive and institutional practice that works upon the body at the time that an assignment is made, but it continues to work on the body through time. Gender assignment operates according to translation, since the infant who is gendered, called into life as a boy or as a girl, must undertake the work of translation from the adult world into the infant's own universe of meanings.

So first, then, let us consider whether when some of us debate in English about what gender is, or should be, we rarely ask whether the terms we are using are translatable even though the generalizability of our claims presumes that they are. Of course, some of us who work in English may not care whether the key terms are translatable – that is, after all, a problem for translators, and though we are glad to assist them with their struggles, we do not always consider that the generalizability of our claims actually depends on establishing a conceptual equivalence between the terms used in different languages. Further, the very possibility of establishing that equivalence depends upon such a term existing in those other languages. Thus, in order to establish the communicability of our theories across languages, translation or, rather, translatability, is a precondition.

When there is no correlative term or when conceptual equivalence cannot be established, a different problem emerges. Of course, one can avert the problem by simply assuming or asserting that "gender" is not readily translatable, because, in fact, it properly belongs to English, or has come to belong to English. With this rather smug monolingual presumption, Anglophones invite everyone into English as the established contemporary linguistic frame or lingua franca, or they export that frame in a beneficent spirit. Generous imperialists, we! Alternatively, it may be that philosophically we maintain that gender names a concept and that the language we use to name or to describe the concept is quite incidental to the concept itself, and that we are engaging in a purely conceptual analysis, not a linguistic one. According to that kind of argument, linguistic usage neither generates nor sustains concepts. Concepts are generally presumed to be relatively independent of linguistic usage. Gender is one such concept; therefore, gender can be analysed conceptually without regard to the language in which it is used or, indeed, the language in which it gains its sense.

This last view, however, cannot take into account the problem of conceptual non-equivalence that emerges in the practice of translating gender. Sometimes this emerges as a grammatical problem: how to use the noun-form of gender in a language, for instance, that only inflects gender through verbs or adjectives. But sometimes it is a syntactical disturbance, meaning that the very joints that hold a sentence together cannot operate, challenging sense-making itself. That happens in languages that describe actions or states, and inflect the verb to indicate whether it is he or she who is acting or in a state. Gender in those cases is not self-standing and is certainly not a noun. Even in English-language contexts, the noun-form accorded to gender does not quite grasp its social meaning. For anthropologist Marilyn Strathern, for instance, categories such as "man" and "woman" are abbreviations of social relationships, and they do not have an independent ontological status outside of those relationships. The noun-form of gender poses serious problems not only for translators but also for theoretical description.

What I have tried to name so far as a problem is certainly familiar to those who regularly work among languages or for whom English is a second language (or third or fourth!). But I have yet another point to make that may not immediately appear to follow, and that is simply that translation is the condition of possibility of gender as a useful category of analysis. The problem of translatability is an unmarked presumption of a monolingualism that pervades the discourse on gender as it crosses academic and popular life. Derrida refers to "monolingual obstinacy" to describe the "resistance to translation" in his monograph *Monolingualism of the Other* (1998). There he describes the conviction that strengthens as one enters ever more deeply into one's own language to argue a point or to hone a description. One not only inhabits that particular language as one's home, but one becomes convinced that only in that language can one make sense and communicate the sense of things. So I not only speak this language, but this language is my way of inhabiting the world and the very essence of who I am, and the very condition of the sense I make of the world and, hence, of the sense of the world itself.

Derrida counters this conviction first by claiming that one's own language is never really one's own, surely not a possession, but already, and from the start, a sphere of non-belonging. Language has its life before we utter any word, and it always precedes us, arriving from elsewhere. That spatiotemporal elsewhere, in Derrida's view, is there at the inception of the speaking subject, and it never really goes away. And yet, monolingualism – or what we can call monolingual conviction – not only covers over this originary dispossession but intensifies the sense that whatever we utter or write in this language is immediately generalizable. Derrida ventriloquizes the defensive posture of the monolinguist when he writes:

> Not only am I lost, fallen, and condemned outside the French language, I have the feeling of honoring or serving all idioms, in a word, of writing the "most" and the "best" when I sharpen the resistance of my French, the secret "purity" of my French ... hence, its resistance, its relentless resistance to translation; translation into all languages, including another such French. (1998: 56)

The intensification of monolingualism produces a paradox (if not a full-blown aporia): the language one inhabits as one's own is precisely where one is dispossessed from the start, for in the language in which one speaks or writes one has no rights of ownership. And yet every refinement of thought within that language intensifies the sense that this is one's own language, resulting in a resistance to translation. Translation threatens the monolinguist with a loss of place and property in language, but that dispossession has always taken place and was, in fact, the condition of speaking and writing themselves. In one's own language, one is already dispossessed.[3] In fact, what occurs in one language cannot be completely or adequately translated into another language. Thus, Derrida argues that every translation founders on moments that cannot be translated. The "untranslatable" haunts every translation, not only as a small problem here and there, but as a structural condition that makes itself known in those moments of grammatical faltering and syntactic disturbance that happens nearly every time, for instance, the English "gender" enters into another language.[4]

[3] For a further reflection on dispossession, see my cowritten volume with Athena Athanasiou (2013).

[4] There is much to be said about this topic, recently pursued first in French by the philosopher Barbara Cassin and the topic of a rather enormous volume, *The Dictionary of Untranslatables: A Philosophical Lexicon* (Cassin, Apter, & Lezra, eds., 2014), in which numerous concepts are thought – or rethought – in relation to the problem of translation. An earlier version of this paper appears there under the category of "Gender."

Translation opens up the productive potential of errancy and coinage, challenging ideas of linguistic mastery, offering a path of linguistic humility for English, and a possibility for encounter that preserves the untranslatable dimension of any language. The untranslatable dimension of gender opens up the question of how to cohabit a world when conceptual non-equivalence is part of the increasingly global feminist and gender conversation.

GLOBAL DEBATES ON GENDER

There was a time not so long ago for example, when one could be engaged in conversations in France with scholars and activists who were trying to make sense of "gender" and "queer" – two imported terms that were variously celebrated and condemned in various publications, both popular and scholarly. Of course, the term "genre," which refers in French to types of literary writing or as a function of definite and indefinite articles, had to be stretched to accommodate a new set of meanings for the debate over "genre" to begin, and the resistance to translation was evident. The willingness to adopt new usage, especially from English, could hardly be taken for granted (Rennes, 2016; Agacinski, 2012). The paradox of accepting and rejecting the term emerged quite forcefully when one historian said to me, "There is no place for *gendaire* in French." She had not only given it a place, but she had even made it French, resisting its translation as genre. The resistance had left- and right-wing variants. Some feared that this was the "McDonaldization" of academic theory. Of course, the problem of American cultural influence was often cited. For many, "gender" or "*la theorie du genre*" signifies no less than the breakdown of the unity of the French nation, the increasingly porous national boundaries across which anything, and anyone, can pass, and so at issue as well is migration, minorities, racial mixing, ever more vague forces of cultural destruction, but also debates on religion and secularism (or *laicité*), focusing the cultural primacy of Catholicism to the nation, natural law, patrilineality, normality and pathology, family, homosexuality, gay marriage, and queer kinship. Very often the popular use of the term "gender" is abbreviated shorthand for a wide range of social practices and freedoms: access to reproductive technology by single women, trans men, single parent parenting, lesbian and gay parenting, gay marriage, trans rights. All of the debates on these topics are haunted by migration, the loss of national identity, and the dissolution of the founding presumptions of the nation, and they take different forms when gender and race are considered inextricably linked. Yet, "gender" is understood either to threaten to destroy a version of natural law that holds family and nation together or to challenge cultural or symbolic laws or norms that hold the family and nation together and without which post-national chaos is understood to ensue (Perreau, 2016). In announcing his candidacy for the French presidency in 2016, Nicolas Sarkozy named the opposition to "gender" as one of his first priorities, and subsequently sided with Pope Francis when he announced that "the theory of gender" should not be taught in schools and should be considered a "diabolical ideology" (Reilly, 2016). More recently in 2019, the Vatican released a document which described gender theory as a "gradual process of denaturalization" (Vatican, 2019). The term "gender" now signifies in a wide range of ways: depending on the context, it can signify women, women's rights, or women's equality, and so feminism, but also transgender, gay, bisexual, and lesbian life, love, associations, partnerships, and marriages, reproductive freedoms, rights to adoption. In some religious objections, "gender" simply is the same as, or is a cover for, homosexuality. One finds that presupposition operating in many countries, including Brazil, Poland, Hungary, and Greece, as well as in UN debates on gender, violence, and autonomy.

For some, this theoretical notion of gender is unreadable and not just because the language is difficult or the theory is abstruse. It raises a problem of translation and even translatability. On the face of it, the problem seems to be one of semantics, but it emerges from a broader sense that the syntactic organization of sense-making within a national language and religious framework is imperiled. When people rail against gender or gender ideology for religious reasons, we are not always in the realm of thoughtful debate or the presentation of evidentiary claims; something socially significant is happening that calls for some thoughtful reflection, a cultural reading, or even a redefinition of the task of theory in light of its detractors.

Why has "gender" become such a proscribed term? In Brazil, Italy, and France, the teaching of gender in schools as part of a state-approved curriculum is no longer allowed. Hungary's Prime Minister, Viktor Orbán, has expressed his intention to ban gender studies courses at Hungarian universities, and there are bitter debates in Poland, Turkey, and Serbia as well. In Spain, the Real Academia Española refuses to accept "gender" into the language because it is apparently a Puritan deflection from simply saying sex. In this way, sex and sexuality are conflated while gender is prohibited. Whatever the term "gender" might once have meant is for the most part quite transformed through translation as it becomes a specter to be fought and defeated. Those of us who sought to craft precise meanings for the term have found ourselves surprised by the public appropriations and translations, the phantasms that have replaced our formulations.

Gender – the academic term, the debates on gender – is now bound up with the question of whether the word, the theory, the politics for which it is imagined to stand, can be let in, or whether it should be barred at the border, and all this as a result of religious, social, sexual, and political fears and anxieties. The life of the term has exceeded and confounded any original intentions or animating aims it may once have had in the English language context. The term has entered into other zones than the one in which I live, and it takes me with it, challenging my monolingualism. Now no one owns this term, but the truth is that no one ever did. The implications of this primary dispossession have taken on heightened significance as the anti-gender ideology gains global traction, since we cannot exactly take gender back into a purely academic world nor can we exactly let it go in its public form with critical opposition.

Quite contrary to feminist and queer appropriations of the term, the original deployment of "gender" was in the service of gender management programs with strong and cruel normative plans. John Money, the sexologist who established "gender" within medical scholarship in the late 1950s did so with the aim of identifying and "correcting" people with intersexed conditions understood as mixed primary sexual characteristics that produced the question for him of how such a body could possibly conform to gender norms. Mixed or ambiguous anatomy posed for Money a serious problem of social adaptation: How could such a child come to live a happy or "normal" life as a woman or a man?[5] The category was bound up with a restrictively normative imaginary of a livable life. Money expected gender to mirror sex, for sex to be identifiable, and for gender to follow a normative developmental sequence. He expected that an infant would develop along normal lines, so he thought that gender should follow from sex, and that on the basis of sex an expectation of social roles would follow. Over and against those who imagined a natural teleology for sex to unfold as a specific kind of gender, Money understood that there could be a disconnect, and sought to repair it in his effort to secure the reproduction of a heteronormative social order.

In the view of sexologists at his clinic, and still in many places in the world, intersexed children constitute "a disturbance" to be "managed" in order to realize a normal developmental trajectory

[5] John Money and Anke Ehrhart (1972); Robert Stoller (1968); Katrina Karkazis (2008). Money's dissertation, "Hermaphroditism: An Inquiry into the Nature of a Human Paradox," observed past surgical interventions as problematic because of their exclusive focus on gonadal tissue (Karkazis, 2008: 48). He sought to underscore the psychological dispositions of the person and physical developments at puberty, both of which he understood to be malleable. According to Karkazis, "Money did a comparative analysis of 248 published and unpublished case histories (from 1895 to 1951) and patient files, as well as an in-depth assessment of ten living individuals classed as hermaphrodites" (2008: 49). His version of social constructivism has been criticized for ushering in, and justifying, social engineering and corrective surgery, but the idea that gender could change does not necessarily lead to those brutal conclusions. The counter conclusion is possible on the basis of the same premise: the idea that gender can change also leads to greater claims of autonomy for those who seek to change gender assignments. See also Terry Goldie (2014).

for the child. It was this perceived failure to conform to the expectation of what a sexed infant was supposed to be that first brought about the notion of gender: developmental expectations were not met, or could not be met, or they were confounded; there was a deviant beginning that called to be corrected before the future of the child could be realized.[6] In this context, gender named a problem, an errancy or deviation, a failure to actualize the developmental norm in time.[7]

Of course, the origin of the contemporary use of "gender" in the work of Money and others was taken up by feminist anthropologists and sociologists in the 1960s, including Sherrie Ortner and Marilyn Strathern. We might think that they made a mistake by taking up this word, or that their own efforts were tainted by the sexologists who came before them. But they entered into this genealogy to effect a very different set of changes. For anthropologist Gayle Rubin, whose work continues to investigate the history of sexology, other histories of sexology offered more promising trains of thought, especially those that sought to establish the variable character of human sexuality, which included the intimation that sexual variance was not sexual deviance – and that something similar could be said of permutations of gender. Rubin realized, of course, their limits: "sexualities keep marching out of the diagnostic and Statistical Manual and onto the pages of social history" (Rubin, 2011: 287).[8] What feminists of that generation (the 1960s, 1970s, and 1980s) sought to do with the category of gender was to shift the term away from a developmental norm, marking instead the cultural variability of what it means to be a man or a woman. When anthropologists such as Ortner and

[6] The expectation of the normal life involves the imagining of the future life of the infant; intersex was considered a block against that imagining of the normal life – indeed, as a term it emerged at about the same time as the films of Douglas Sirk, who, in films such as *Written on the Wind* (1956), documented the various errancies that confound the normative imaginary of development for sex and sexuality.

[7] See Jack Halberstam (2011) for a further elaboration of this idea.

[8] See Gayle Rubin (2011: 127–233), "Thinking Sex" and essays written as reflections on that essay.

Rubin started to work with the category of gender, they disputed the normative dimension of that developmental model. Their argument was that the cultural and historical process by which a sexed infant becomes a gendered being is variable, and that it depends on language and culture, history and kinship. The thesis of gender variability opposed the claim that there is an inherent developmental teleology to be found in "sex," one that unfolds naturally or normatively into one kind of gender or its other.

As the historian Joan W. Scott puts it,

> When American and English feminists borrowed the term gender from the writings of John Money and Robert Stoller they could be said to have performed its second translation. Translation here means moving a term from one context to another and thereby altering its meaning. Money and Stoller had previously taken the grammatical category to distinguish between anatomy (sex) and social role/social identity (gender) in order to resolve the dilemmas faced by intersex children and to justify medical intervention that would assign them to an appropriate male or female identity. (Scott, 2016: 358)

Feminists took up the term in order to refuse the dictum that biology was destiny; the motivation was political, not medical, and it troubled (rather than accepted) the normative male/female dichotomy with which the endocrinologist and the psychiatrist had worked. Biology was left to feminist historians and philosophers of science to pursue, showing how natural teleology was an Aristotelian notion that consistently displaces the history of sex, and the dynamic interrelation between sex and gender as categories.

Scott rightly points out that Stoller and Money made a distinction between sex and gender, and that meant that whatever the perceived sex of the infant, the gender could be acquired through behavioral technologies. Only a few of those feminists who critically appropriated the sex/gender distinction from the sexologists returned to the original scene of the naming practice to consider the cruelty of sexology and the brutal treatment of intersexed kids. Of course, in recent years, many have done that, and now contemporary writers such as Paul Preciado (2013) and Catherine Clune-Taylor (2010) have given important consideration to this dimension of the genealogy of gender as a term. And some of them, like Alice Dreger,[9] write extensively on the practice of gender assignment and sought to lend support to some intersex groups, but have also, in the meantime, agreed to the diagnosis in the DSM-5 as a disorder of sexual development (or DSD).[10] Terrible echoes of John Money are to be found in that recently adopted formulation. One reason to be adamantly opposed to that diagnostic category is that it forgets the earlier feminist criticisms of developmental models and proves complicitous with its pathologizing cruelty.

GENDER AS A FIELD OF DISTURBANCE

Perhaps the previous discussion suffices to affirm that there is no referent we might call "gender" that belongs to a pure order of being or even a translinguistic concept. No one language has the exclusive power to define gender or to regulate its grammatical usage, and that means that every way of referring to gender has a certain contingency – the emergence of the singular "they" is a case in point. We may individually feel urgency and necessity about being referred to in one way rather than another; we may understandably feel disrespected if we are referred to in the wrong way. Those may be moments of monolingual obstinacy or failing to see that the work of translation is obligatory. But it can also be an occasion for feeling humility about the particular language we use, whether it is English, French, Chinese, Japanese, Spanish, or Tagalog. There is no one language that can monopolize that referent, no one mode of representation, no one medium, so sometimes those various versions of gender clash depending on the language. Of course, this can be hard, since if we understand

9 See Alice Dreger (2007).

10 For critical commentary, see Cynthia Kraus (2015: 1147–63).

our gender to be part of who we are, and if we seek to refine the language of who we are in the monolingual context, drawing on the lexicon and grammar of that language in order more precisely to specify the identity, translation becomes all the more difficult, and it would seem then that one can only get recognition for who one is within a monolingual frame – perhaps within a specific set of language users within that monolingualism.

The proliferation of noun-forms for gender and sexual identity raises specific problems for translation. Consider the fact that there is no noun-form for gender in Japanese, Chinese, or Korean. There are words for women and for men, but not for the concept of gender itself. In Japanese, for instance, linguistic self-reference is gendered: the terms *O-re* and *Bo-ku* are informal ways of referring to the first-person singular "I" of a man while *Atashi* and *Watashi* are first-person references for a woman. The use of each of these terms, however, is inflected by social class, educational background, cultural conventions, and, importantly, the relation to the one who is addressed. Although what in English we could call "gender" operates in complex ways, implicated in formal and social modes of address coordinated by power, there is no single term for this "gender." The closest Japanese gets to approaching this non-translatable word is *jen-daa,* which is not unlike the French coinage, *gendaire,* by seeking a phonetic echo with gender. Where gender cannot enter, it is coined, suggesting that it was, and remains, a coinage, a historical matter of linguistic use, if not an approximation of translation.

TOWARD LIVABILITY

Some feminists and gender theorists have argued about whether there can be genders that go beyond man and woman, or whether gender itself should be transcended, and we should live in a world without gender categories at all. My own view is that we should seek to bring about a world that is more livable for the many relations to gender that exist, the many languages for gender, and the many ways of doing or living a gendered reality. Some people very much like the binary framework for gender and want to find their rightful place either as a man or as a woman and to live peaceably, if not joyously, within its terms; for them, gender is a prerequisite for inhabiting the world. They have struggled to name themselves with the category and to recognize themselves and to feel at home in the language of gender that they speak, and to find themselves acknowledged in the name by which they are addressed. Ethically considered, such claims are to be honored – radically and without qualification. At the same time, there are others who cannot live very well, cannot find a livable life, within those binary terms, including trans people who understand "trans" to exist at a critical angle to the binary, and for them other gender vocabularies are required for inhabiting the world, feeling at home, or relatively at home, in the language they use, or in refusing the language that is used; that refusal is also an opening onto a habitable world. And so, reasonably enough, there are some who ask for new lexicons, or for ways of living outside the category of gender altogether, as nonbinary, for instance: they press coinage to a further extreme and for another purpose, refining their vocabulary for self-reference within a monolingual frame, or they abandon the practice of naming, undertaking a linguistic and embodied strike against gender as we know it.

In fact, all of these are legitimate positions because each of them tells us about a group of people who are searching for livable lives within the language that they find or make or refuse. Indeed, one cannot be "against" any of these positions, if each of them opens up a different trajectory of hope for living a livable life. Given that not everyone finds the same terms to enhance livability, we have to be careful not to impose a new gender norm that generalizes the conditions of livability, or that decides without consultation what someone else should be called (some of the debates about whose perception defines "cisgender" bring this to the fore). We have to be prepared to translate between a language in which we live and another language that dispossesses us from that sure sense of things that comes with monolingual conviction. After all, some find life and breath by escaping the terms by which gender recognition is conferred, others find life and breath precisely through finally feeling recognized by existing terms, and some welcome or make the foreign term as a way of busting open the naturalized function of language (Theodore Adorno found hope in the foreign word precisely for that reason as he sought to unsettle the connection between monolingualism and nationalism in Germany).

If the task is not to generalize a way of life but to become attuned to the various vocabularies that make life more livable, then a transphobic feminism is out of the question. Indeed, a transphobic feminism is no feminism, and it allies with forms of coercive gender norms. An anti-feminist trans position also has to rethink the history of feminism, allowing for the profound alliance among those who seek to have their claims for political recognition registered and honored. Those who should be most enraged by my argument are those who believe that the gender binary is mandated by a version of natural law referenced or occasioned by the Bible. I have seen my own name become synonymous with a diabolical power in some of these debates, a particularly interesting and disturbing way of being dispossessed in language.

If I try to counter that form of dispossession in order to give a more just presentation of who I am, then I have to remember that the alternative to defamation is not mastery. The language I use to declare who I am turns out fundamentally not to be my own, but that does not mean that I cannot, or will not, enter into the contest over its signification. Gender introduces a problem of translation under the best of circumstances, but it can also be the source of skepticism for those who fear another imperial incursion of English into contexts that understandably resist the syntactical disturbances it introduces. The answer, however, is not to recede into national languages untouched or untransformed in the course of linguistic exchange.

Translation allows us not only to affirm the contingency of the language we speak, seeing it as only one way of making sense of the world, but also to be affected by those with whom we are in some kind of exchange based on translation. And that means that something foreign enters into language, destabilizing the smug assumption that, for instance, the grammatical structure of English is the very structure of reason. Experiments with grammar, riddled with foreign words, produce an impure language, potentially disrupting national identity at the level of language use where we are always stumbling to find the right words, and allowing ourselves to feel less sure, less certain than we can when we live in a world of shared grammatical and syntactical assumptions or presumptive monolingualism.

At the moment one has to explain one's gender in another language, one sees that one's own language is but one way of trying to present who one is, and that one becomes someone slightly different once one enters into a new language. If we insist that we can only be who we are in the primary language in which we speak, then we will become defined by this resistance to translation. Indeed, we may find ourselves increasingly unable to communicate who we are across languages, defending identity and monolingualism against anything foreign in a world whose multilingualism is irreversible.

The deep fear guiding the campaign against gender is that once gender is delinked from sex, any life trajectory can become possible – single mothers, gay parents, queer households, trans identities and communities, women who choose abortions, women who divorce or leave their families, trans women legally and socially recognized as women, or trans men who elect pregnancy, top surgery, or legal change of status. It seems that all of these are choices that are shut down once we know that sex implies a reproductive future constrained by heterosexual marriage. Is it true that gender signals a future of freedom? Gender is not simply freely decided. If and when it is an exercise of freedom, it is one undertaken within a scene of constraint and within what Beauvoir called a historical situation. To claim that trans people deserve the freedom to live freely as trans does not mean that they experience trans identity as freely chosen. The deeply felt character of gender identity or, indeed, of sexual orientation can qualify as the unchosen dimensions of life, the ways of being that are fundamental, intractable, indispensable. Yet, it is hardly a contradiction to affirm and articulate gender as a condition of life that is largely or partially unchosen and to insist on the right to affirm that condition in public life without discrimination or threat of violence. Significantly, the language in which I affirm my gendered life is not always one that I myself have made. I am, as it were, dispossessed, even in the language that makes my life possible.

I seek to say who I am within a language that proves to be untranslatable or that is, in important respects, already foreign to me. Only by seeing the matter this way can we escape the intensification of an ever more refined monolingualism as we seek to make ourselves known. As much as we seek to own and master the language of the self to contest the assignments we refuse, we are still dispossessed within the very language that gives us our sense of mastery. So the double task, as it were, is to break out of monolingualism by suffering the humilities of translation, to refuse the implicit nationalism of the national frame, the singular and dominant language, to reach, and be reached by, a broader world, multilingual and multi-syntactical. Thus, the most treasured of our self-proclaimed nouns may well come apart as we come to value translation and the important possibilities that loss of mastery opens up for the making and sustaining of a livable world.

The paradox involved in all acts of public claiming is what we call performative. That does not mean that all gender is chosen, or that it is a voluntaristic expression of individuality. The performative act by which gender is claimed communicates the conditions of livability for the one who claims it. This is perhaps the more important sense of gender performativity to be preserved for the present.

For Jean Laplanche, gender poses a problem of translation from infancy on. These lifelong efforts to decipher and translate a demand imposed by the categories and names do nothing more than open up a zone of provisional freedom where we claim or coin a language of our own in the midst of a linguistic dispossession for which there is no remedy and no exit. For what we call our language is and is not our own; the terms by which we seize ourselves may or may not be translatable, even to ourselves. The untranslatable may be another name for the desire that exceeds every effort at lexical capture and normative control. It may constitute that pause or break in language that calls us to attend ethically to one another across languages. It may also, for those of us who live in English, point to the value of faltering in a foreign language, ceding the mastery of monolingualism for a world in which we are, luckily, dispossessed together, fathoming gender, as we can, through terms we both find and make, in order to find a more livable way of inhabiting the multilingual world with all its promising disturbances.

REFERENCES

Adorno, Theodore W. 1958. On the Use of Foreign Words in Writing. In *Notes on Literature.* New York: Columbia University Press, pp. 286–91.

Agacinski, Sylviane. 2012. *Femmes entre sexe et genre.* Paris: Editions de Seuil.

Aizura, Aren and Stryker, Susan. 2013. *The Transgender Studies Reader,* vol. 2. New York: Routledge.

Butler, Judith. 2019. Gender in Translation: Beyond Monolingualism. *philoSOPHIA,* 9(1), 1–25.

Butler, Judith and Athanasiou, Athena. 2013. *Dispossession: The Performative in the Political.* Cambridge, UK: Polity Press.

Cassin, Barbara, Apter, Emily, and Lezra, Jacques, eds. 2014. *The Dictionary of Untranslatables: A Philosophical Lexicon.* Princeton, NJ: Princeton University Press.

Clune-Taylor, Catherine. 2010. From Intersex to DSD: The Disciplining of Sex Development. *PhaenEx: Journal of Existential and Phenomenological Theory and Culture,* **5**(2), 152–78.

Derrida, Jacques. 1998. *Monolingualism of the Other.* Stanford, CA: Stanford University Press.

Dreger, Alice. 2007. Why 'Disorders of Sex Development'? (On Language and Life). alicedreger.com/dsd.

Fausto-Sterling, Anne. 2012. *Sex/Gender: Biology in a Social World.* New York: Routledge.

Gallo, Michelle. 2017. 'Gender Ideology' Is a Fiction That Could Do Real Harm. Open Society Foundation, August 29. www.opensocietyfoundations.org/voices/gender-ideology-fiction-could-do-real-harm.

Goldie, Terry. 2014. *The Man Who Invented Gender: Engaging the Ideas of John Money*. Vancouver: University of British Columbia Press.

Halberstam, Jack. 2011. *The Queer Art of Failure*. Durham, NC: Duke University Press.

Karkazis, Katrina. 2008. *Fixing Sex: Intersex, Medical Authority, and Lived Experience*. Durham, NC: Duke University Press.

Kraus, Cynthis. 2015. Classifying Intersex in DSM-5: Critical Reflections on Gender Dysphoria. *Archives of Sexual Behavior*, **44**(5), 1147–63.

Laplanche, Jean. 2008. Gender, Sex, and the Sexual. Susan Fairfield, trans. *Studies in Gender and Sexuality*, **8**(2), 201–19.

2011. *Freud and the Sexual*. John Fletcher, trans. London: International Psychoanalytic Books.

Moi, Toril. 2008. *Simone de Beauvoir: The Making of an Intellectual Woman*. Oxford: Oxford University Press.

Money, John and Ehrhart, Anke. 1972. *Man and Woman, Boy and Girl*. Baltimore, OH: Johns Hopkins University Press.

Perreau, Bruno. 2016. *Queer Theory: The French Response*. Stanford, CA: Stanford University Press.

Preciado, Paul. 2013. *Techno Junkie: Sex, Drugs, and Biopolitics in the Pharmacopornographic Era*. New York: The Feminist Press.

Reilly, Robert R. 2016. Pope Francis vs. Gender Ideology. The Catholic World Report, August 13. www.catholicworldreport.com/2016/08/13/pope-francis-vs-gender-ideology/.

Rennes, Juliette, ed. 2016. *Encyclopédie critique du genre. Corps, sexualité, rapports sociaux*. Paris: La Découverte.

Rubin, Gayle. 2011. *Deviations: A Gayle Rubin Reader*. Durham, NC: Duke University Press.

Schwarzer, Alice. 2000. *Der große Unterschied. Gegen die Spaltung von Menschen in Männer und Frauen* [*The Big Difference. Against the Splitting of Human Beings into Men and Women*]. Cologne: Kiepenheuer & Witsch.

Scott, Joan W. 2016. Gender Studies and Translation Studies: "Entre Braguettes" – Connecting the Transdisciplines. In Yves Gambier and Luc van Doorslaer, eds., *Border Crossings: Translation Studies and Other Disciplines*. Amsterdam and Philadelphia: John Benjamins, pp. 349–74.

Stoller, Robert. 1968. *Sex and Gender: On the Development of Masculinity and Femininity*. New York: Science House.

Stryker, Susan and Whittle, Stephan. 2006. *The Transgender Studies Reader*, vol. 1. New York: Routledge.

Vatican City. 2019. "Male and Female He Created Them": Towards a Path of Dialogue on the Question of Gender Theory in Education. Congregation for Catholic Education (for Educational Institutions). www.educatio.va/content/dam/cec/Documenti/19_0997_INGLESE.pdf

Wittig, Monique. 1992. *The Straight Mind and Other Essays*. Boston, MA: Beacon Press.

CHAPTER 2

Gender and the Queer/Trans* Undercommons

Jack Halberstam

GENDER IS ONE OF THE MANY METRICS BY WHICH BODies are measured in terms of the adherence to or departure from the norm. And trans* bodies have, in the past, offered a clear challenge to gender binarism on the one hand and the notion of a natural division between the two genders on the other. Careful attention to the disruption that trans* bodies sow in relation to social norms can change fundamentally the way we understand other seemingly stable oppositions such as legal and illegal, legible and illegible, known and unknowing and so on. This chapter refuses to resolve the confusion or bewilderment created by the spectacle or, as is often the case, the specter, of the trans* body. Instead, we follow disruption, disorder and bewilderment into new orientations to time, place, futurity and desire.

The form of embodiment that, in the twentieth and twenty-first centuries, we have come to call transgender is not simply a gender switching, a wrong body replaced by a right body, a shift in morphology; trans* embodiment, rather, is the argument that all bodies are uncomfortable and wrong-ish – that all bodies have been placed in relation to arbitrary forms of classification but the people who benefit from those classifications experience embodiment as "right," seamless, inevitable. Those people who feel themselves to be wrong – and trans* is only one such location – are made to feel so in relation to matrices of power and definition. If the person feels themselves to be wrong, then they are less likely to name and critique the systems of knowledge that have cast them as wrong. The coordinates of discomfort range across bodies and are swayed by other social magnets such as race and class – and so June Jordan in "Poem About My Rights" (1981) transformed an ongoing discourse in the US on rights into a raging song about wrongs. The poem begins with the poet wondering why she cannot simply clear her head by taking a walk – but to walk alone, outside, in the street, in the world, as a queer Black woman, she realizes, is to be in constant jeopardy because:

> I can't do what I want
> to do with my own body because I am the wrong
> sex the wrong age the wrong skin[1]

Extending this logic outwards, Jordan notes that just as a Black woman's violation is considered routine, so the violation of other countries by the US is barely noticed in the quotidian rhythms of racial violence. Jordan continues:

> We are the wrong people of
> the wrong skin on the wrong continent and what
> in the hell is everybody being reasonable about?

Jordan's anthemic formulation of her rights, her wrongs, offers both global formulations of geopolitical power and intimate reckonings with bodily illegibility. At one point, the poet sums up:

> I am the history of rape
> I am the history of the rejection of who I am
> I am the history of the terrorized incarceration of
> Myself

This apt phrase – "I am the history of the rejection of who I am" – speaks very particularly to the wrong body experience of Black queer women but it also reveals the dependence of systems of legibility upon the production of illegible bodies.

June Jordan used poetry as a medium to unpick the lock of normalization. And while some gay narratives imagine that naming can be an erotic mode of hailing the other or asking for

[1] Copyright © 2005 by The June M. Jordan Literary Trust. Used by permission of The June M. Jordan Literary Trust, www.junejordan.com.

recognition ("say my name"), or even blending into the other (*Call Me By Your Name*), in Jordan's poem, wrongness is the name she is given and the name she rejects. But Jordan resists the urge to claim to rightness too and instead she sings: "my name is my own, my own, my own" and ends the poem not with a plea to be heard but with a threat to the "you" who marks her as wrong: my self-determination, she insists, "may very well cost you your life."

We can use this lesson in self-determination to investigate modes of trans* life and trans* history that fall far beyond the conventional boundaries of medical knowledge and appellations. Indeed, rather than seeing in the trans* body an extension of gender norms, we might try to understand how trans* bodies undo the logic of right and wrong altogether. With this shift in focus, the wrong body, an appellation used mostly for people who have felt themselves to be out of place, out of time, comes not to claim right but to dismantle the system that metes out rightness and wrongness. Trans* bodies, in other words, function not simply as bodies that provide an image of the non-normative against which normative bodies can be discerned, but as bodies that are fragmentary and internally contradictory, bodies that remap gender and its relations to race, place, class and sexuality, bodies that are in pain or that represent a play of surfaces, bodies that sound different from they look, bodies that represent palimpsestic relations to identity. And because we do not want to replace wrong with right, we need to construct new forms of knowledge, new ways of holding bodies in place or allowing them to slip out of place, different systems for narrating life that are not about capture, fixing, stilling. In this volume, for example, Judith Butler discusses the importance of new gender vocabularies that "seek to bring about a world that is more livable for the many relations to gender that exist, the many languages for gender, and the many ways of doing or living a gendered reality."

In order to show what might be at stake in this project, I begin with a news story about a Black gender queer body that eludes all attempts to pull the body into narrative. I move then to the concept of bewilderment and a two-spirit artist who uses gender variability to mark bewilderment as a decolonial strategy. And the chapter concludes with a piece on wildness and the performance art of trans* artist boychild.

WAYWARD

An odd story appeared in the *New York Times* in several installments. Titled "Solved" in its most recent form, the story was about a gender non-conforming Black person who was shot and killed in 1970 but who could not be identified until recently. In the first version of this story, from the *New York Times* (2016) in November, Michael Wilson investigated an unsolved murder mystery involving a "woman" from Harlem who had been found murdered in Chester, New York, in 1970. The body gave evidence of an execution-style murder. The person, who, ironically, was wearing a Harlem Youth Opportunities Unlimited sweatshirt at the time of their death, had their hands bound with electrical wire and tied behind their back, had been shot in the head through a towel and had fallen backwards to the ground. By falling backwards, the journalist stresses, the hands of the victim were not exposed to the elements and so gave clean prints when the police finally found the corpse a few months later. But the prints did not match with any in the system, until suddenly, forty-five years later, they did. The story continues using only some known aliases for the murdered person and trying to fill in the details of a life lived between names, between law and disorder, and within an alternative lexicon of sexuality and gender.

The story was odd because Wilson seemed mainly focused on fixing a name to a body rather than exploring the unresolvable details of a life lived outside of the conventional logics of gender and sexuality. A focus on the waywardness of this anonymous body would have pulled into focus the straying, wandering, drifting movements of a life that flickers in and out of history, in and out of legality, in and out of recognition, and ends beyond the metrics and epistemological frames available to make sense of it. Like

Saidiya Hartman's Venus from her essay "Venus in Two Acts," this body is evidence of an "untimely story told by a failed witness" (2008: 2). While Hartman noted that the Venus in the archives, a barely knowable Black girl lost to slavery, only becomes known through evidence compiled by or "borrowed from the world of her captors and masters and applied to her," so this body enters history only through an archive of arrests – they are misremembered, misrecognized, named and unnamed, and ultimately they remain, to quote Hartman again, "entangled with and impossible to differentiate from the terrible utterances that condemned them to death" (2008: 3).

In trying to locate this gender queer body someplace other than the anonymous plot in Potter's Field where they were buried, apart from the sites where they were arrested, the locations they ran to and from, the institutions where they were held, the relations within which they were fleetingly known and seen, I want to contribute to what Saidiya Hartman has named "a counter-history of the human" (2008: 3). Bodies like this one provide evidence of the open question of violence and Blackness, a question that must remain open since to answer the questions of who, what, where and how, we risk filling in the gaps and, in Hartman's words "providing closure where there is none" (2008: 8). Nonetheless, we must enter the scene of the crime, not to change it, not to know it, not to solve it but to find a new context within which to listen to the dead. Hartman proposes that we listen to the dead not in terms of the frameworks provided by the archives created by the law, the police, the abolitionists, but in relation to what those archives leave out. This requires what she calls "narrative restraint," histories of failure and "the imperative to respect black noise" (2008: 12).

In the case of this J. Doe gender-ambiguous body, the official records tell of a life of crime, a trajectory of trouble and violence, and of intimacies that exceed the frameworks designed to explain them. Unofficially, we must not restore the body to a proper name, but instead we might think of the life lived as itinerant, wild, wayward and improvised. What happened to this person provides evidence not of a life gone bad or gone wrong, but a life that was never oriented towards good or right in the first place. For this gender queer body, rightness is unobtainable and undesirable, and murder is only the final blow dealt to a body that has been questioned, abandoned, institutionalized, arrested and finally executed even as that body lived a life attuned to alternative intimacies, pleasures and practices.

When mentioned at all in the *New York Times* story, gender variance functions only as a sensational detail; and so, the murdered person in the story was described as: "a cross-dressing, gun-toting, bisexual heroin dealer in 1960s Harlem" (Wilson, 2016). Treated mostly as a "cold case" whose mysteries finally fall away under expert journalistic scrutiny, this story of the unidentified and unidentifiable body is both the story of the permanently lost but also the story of the queer undercommons; it is what Lisa Lowe would call an "undocumented history."

The J. Doe in this story is one of many figures lost to trans* and queer history, and representative of an arc of waywardness within which Saidiya Hartman has located very specific histories of desire. In a chapter titled "A Short Entry on the Possible" in her book, *Wayward Lives, Beautiful Experiments,* Saidiya Hartman defines "waywardness" as "the practice of the social otherwise, the insurgent ground that enabled new possibilities and new vocabularies . . . it is a queer resource of black survival. It is a beautiful experiment in how to live" (2019: 227–28). *Wayward Lives* rewrites struggle in terms of errant wandering and rethinks beauty in terms of revolutionary imagination, but it also, if perhaps less obviously, offers a reimagining of queer historiography. After this book, the history of sexuality can no longer only cluster around gay, lesbian and transgender bodies and communities; it will have to be told by way of narratives of errancy and straying, revolution and free love. Queer subjects make their appearance in Hartman's book – see chapters on Mabel Hampton and Gladys Bentley – but queerness does not inhere in individual bodies; it is instead experienced as a force for change. For Hartman, queerness is a way of turning away from the good and the true; it is a desire for new and surprising arrangements of bodies and futures. Histories of the medicalization and criminalization of desire abound within queer studies, but Hartman's book reminds us that the life of desire is multifaceted. It lives in the joy of assembly, in the longing for beautiful things, in fantasies of surplus, in "moments of tenderness," in experiences of Black girls and women in "open rebellion" to systems of management, control and incarceration. In the stories that Hartman gathers here and teaches us how to read, desire spills over the categories designed to manage it and emerges as a kind of wildness within "practices of intimacy and affiliation" (2019: 221). The book is full of promiscuous scenes of sexual abandonment, flirtations expressed in song, people lost in the pleasure of purchasing the unnecessary. In other words, desire in this book is not the expression of identity but rather a term for the extravagant acts of wayward Black bodies committed to "experiments in living free" (2019: 34).

J. Doe, we might surmise by reading between the lines of the *New York Times* article, was wayward and committed to this broad experiment in "living free." They were, indeed, part of a set of such experiments that, in my own work, I have called "wild" or part of a disordered history of desire. At the conclusion of the *New York Times* story about the murdered gender queer person, the journalists who researched it are triumphant that they can fix a name to a body. The *New York Times*'s reporter, Wilson, used four arrest sheets and some census reports to track the person to a family, the Moores and to the family home in Orangeburg, South Carolina. These same public records note that the murdered person's mother and father were farm laborers who reported zero income, and that the family had four children: of J. Doe's siblings, all except one left no recorded trace and could not be found. The one surviving sibling, Jacob, is eighty-seven and has been, according to the *Times*, "mentally disabled his whole life." Neighbors did not remember the family, the family house was gone, Evelyn Moore's name was misrecorded on the birth register as Evlin, and Evelyn, when she was little, "attended the Sleighton Farm School for Girls in Philadelphia," described as "a place for chronic truants." Evelyn Moore, we also learn, used many names during their short life, including Evelyn and AC.

This story is remarkable and ordinary all at once. All the lives in the story are punctured at some point by violence, disappearance, legal entanglements and broken lines of kinship. Names are mis-recorded or changed, run-ins with the law are part of the day-to-day rhythm of life, family members lose touch with one another and people fall out of the story in parenthetical violent subplots. In an aside on Shirlene Dixon, for example, a woman with whom AC was involved romantically, the journalist offers: "In unrelated violence five years later, Ms. Dixon and her mother were murdered by the mother's boyfriend" (Wilson, 2016). We know what he means by "unrelated violence" and yet, none of this is unrelated and all of it is nonetheless part of the incoherence of Black life disassembled by what Hartman calls "the limits of emancipation."

We are forced, through stories such as AC's, to consider the status of Black life in the US as unsolved, unresolved, unresolvable within current conditions that extend the racial ideologies of slavery into the present and that subject Black life to what Hartman calls "new forms of bondage" (1997: 6). AC Moore, the forgotten, murdered, lost but also extravagant, promiscuous and defiant figure of a queer undercommons that the *New York Times* wants to locate in relation to a name, a place, a family and the law, still eludes all attempts at capture. At the end of one story that an acquaintance tells about them, AC disappears again. The acquaintance, Doug, used to be one of AC's lovers, a detail that indicates how far beyond a hetero/homo boundary this figure lives. Doug recalls sleeping with AC but also notes without any sense of contradiction that "she carried herself like a man." At the end of his story, Doug recalls that the last time he saw AC, they were being bundled into a car by two people: "As he tells it, two 'butch' females emerged from the car, grabbed A. C. and drove away. 'That was their world,' he said. 'That was the type of people she was dealing with'" (Wilson, 2016). After this, AC disappears and as

Doug puts it "life moved on," as it would in "a world of drugs, people were always coming and going." This particular disappearance is both a coming and a going – AC is not kidnapped by male drug dealers or picked up by the police. They were instead, perhaps, rescued by other butch females – people who were part of a world, "their world," as Doug put it, a world beyond what the police, the journalist, the ex-male lover might comprehend. A world where the butches fly into the face of the very thing that blows them away, a place we cannot know, can never visit, a place beyond redemption, resolution, the human, rights and recognition. Hartman offers: "The loss of stories sharpens the hunger for them. So it is tempting to fill in the gaps and to provide closure where there is none. To create a space for mourning where it is prohibited. To fabricate a witness to a death not much noticed" (2008: 8). But she also counsels against trespassing the "boundaries of the archive."

Respecting instead that stories might be permanently lost or expressed as noise, Hartman proposes that: "We begin the story again, as always, in the wake of her disappearance and with the wild hope that our efforts can return her to the world" (2008: 8). Or, I would add, with the wild hope that our efforts might return the wayward to a different world, a world that Kara Keeling calls "black futurity" (2019) and that we might name the black, queer undercommons.

BEWILDERMENT

In the long history of what Hartman and others call "the afterlife of slavery" (2008: 13), we find many instances of bewilderment, or the rupture created by a not-knowing that gathers at the edges of the known, the recognizable and the legible. Like Hartman's concept of the wayward, bewilderment offers an epistemology of movement, being, unbeing and becoming. Bewilderment shares a root, etymologically, with wildness. Bewilderment is a great concept with which to work – it holds the wild within it and refers, in a sense, to thought becoming wild. By this we seem to mean getting lost, disoriented and confused. Bewilderment probably shares in the kind of magical/delightful/scary forms of unknowing that we also associate with enchantment/bafflement/confusion. But it is more than just a synonym of these states of disorientation. Bewilderment suggests a becoming that moves in an opposite direction to colonial knowing. Since education was at the heart of so many colonial projects, as Sara Ahmed reminds us in this volume, bewilderment can function as a kind of decolonial rejection of certain forms of knowing. As she writes, "We know too that the enslaved and the colonized were positioned as children, as the ones for whom discipline was moral instruction, as the ones who were not supposed to have a will of their own, as the ones for whom obedience required giving up will." In place of obedience then, bewilderment. In its early uses, bewilderment was about navigation, the not-knowing of terrain. It reminds us that travelers three or four hundred years ago had regular experiences of being lost. States of bewilderment therefore might have been cultivated and inhabited more easily. Nowadays, we understand bewilderment as an impediment to knowledge and power. From a decolonial perspective however, and with an anti-enlightenment intent, we might find artists and thinkers who want to re-wild life, rethink nature and reintroduce bewilderment.

For example, consider the work of Kree/Irish artist Kent Monkman's "Seeing Red," from a show he did in Toronto as a kind of disruption of what was billed at Canada's 150th birthday. The show, "Shame and Prejudice: A Story of Resiliency," offers a decolonial view of history, new stories of encounter that highlight homophobia and the impact of Christianity upon First Nation peoples, and it offered capsule commentaries on Western art. Wildness, within the work of Kent Monkman, is a decolonial reshuffling of the structure of signification. In *Seeing Red* (2014), for example, a painting that first appeared, aptly enough in a show titled "Failure of Modernity," we witness the blurring of visual, political, geographical and art historical imagery. The painting offers us a startling scene bristling with symbolic systems at odds with each other and time itself. Against the backdrop of the blue of

Figure 2.1 *Seeing Red*, Kent Monkman, 2014. Image courtesy of the artist

either skies or heavens, a helicopter and an angel cast very different eyes upon the scene below. In the background of the painting, we see the familiar markers of urban riot – a burning car, masculine racialized bodies in motion, smoke, confusion, graffiti. But there are also buffaloes within this arena, creatures allied with the rioting bodies on the one hand but symbolizing the loss of space on the other. In the foreground, Monkman offers an astonishing scene of encounter between forces of transformation and forces of oppression. The painting frames the scene in very particular ways so that we do not simply see oppositions between police and bodies of color, or rioters and property, or the mob and the riot police, but we access the aftermath of a riot through an imposing matador in drag and high heels confronting the bull of Western art itself. The bull is not one of the buffaloes but wears a Picasso head and crouches before the matador holding a native blanket in one hand, posing with her other hand on her hip. In addition, the telephone pole holding up the wires that signal modern networks of communication and connection has been carved into a totemic pole, and there are multiple native characters in the scene. Some of the native bodies are arrayed behind the burning car, two others are running one way, turning to look over their shoulders – one holds a feather, the other a musical instrument. Ahead of them, a native woman kneels at the head of a white man in colonial clothing stretched out on the ground, possibly dead. This figure is lifted directly out of Edouard Manet's painting *The Dead Toreador* (1984).

Seeing Red, like many of Monkman's large-scale paintings (Figure 2.1), is extraordinary for its detail and its competing message systems. Using satire, realism, post-impressionistic style, saturated color, caricature, naturalism and many other representational strategies, Monkman wields his paintbrush in the same manner that his alter ego, Miss Chief Eagle Testickle, wields lances: with artistry and flair, he seduces the bull only to wound it, calls on it only to draw blood. Drawing blood indeed could be another name for the painting in which no blood is shed but all is lost for Western art and Western art history, and aesthetics itself hangs in the balance.

Monkman's paintings incorporate Western art, in other words, only to damage them, cut them and distribute them across a horizontal plane as one signifier among many. The details in his paintings often render them bewildering through the sheer number of bodies, the relationship between figure and ground, the clash of classical, stereotyped and native imagery, the riot of bodies, the relations between authenticity and mimicry. The paintings seek to confuse, not to sort.

Bewilderment, you will recall, in its archaic usage, meant being led into the woods and left there – be-wild-erment – both a transformation from tamed to free, from found to lost, from belonging to abandonment and from knowing to confused. The only way out is through, and the disorientation that attends to being led astray is here desirable and necessary. Being lost, disoriented, befuddled and confused are not simply part of some mysterious "postmodern condition," they are also states of being consonant with a rapidly changing and disintegrating biosphere.

Poet Fanny Howe, in a beautiful essay titled "Bewilderment" (1999) describes the term as naming both a "poetics and an ethics." For her, bewilderment ensues when characters in her novels confront impossibly contradictory situations that alert them to the complexity of life. These situations cannot be resolved, narratively or poetically, and so lead to a state of bewilderment. She writes: "In the Dictionary, to bewilder is 'to cause to lose one's sense of where one is.'" And she continues: "The wilderness as metaphor is in this case not evocative enough because causing a complete failure in the magnet, the compass, the scale, the stars and the movement of the rivers is more than getting lost in the woods. Bewilderment," she continues, "is an enchantment that follows a complete collapse of reference and reconcilability." Making bewilderment into a state of being that exceeds the simple fact of disorientation in relation to space, Howe locates bewilderment as a relation to language itself. Within a magical or "enchanted" process, language and experience simply fail to connect, creating a "complete collapse of reference." These modes of what Howe also calls "unsaying" lie within narrative itself as the unspoken or the unspeakable, the wild and the bewildering, and, every now and then, they make an eruption into representation in the form of a scream, a howl, a leap into a void. Howe describes moments of representational rupture as the basis for poetry – poetry carries the unspeakable moments out of narrative and allows them to "lead nowhere." She writes: "And ultimately I see the whole body of work as existing all but untitled and without beginning or end, an explosion of parts, the quotidian smeared."

The astonishing image of "the quotidian smeared" captures perfectly the experience of bewilderment that we might pursue rather than flee from. By taking the ordinary and just smudging its edges, it becomes unrecognizable and disorienting. This experience that can be rendered by art reminds us that, in Howe's words, the self is formed as much by what she calls "error, errancy and bewilderment" as by certainty, mastery and locatability.

If we link to this idea of a smudged quotidian and life that is only recognizable as worthwhile when we allow, in Howe's words, for "positions stunned by bewilderment" (1999), we come close to a methodology of bewilderment. For Monkman, it was the mastering of Western art only to transform its recognizable components into forms of aesthetic riot; for Howe, bewilderment allows her to not know where her characters are going. In academic pursuits, bewilderment is the opposite of what Rancière calls "stupefaction" (2009: 4); it is an opening up to not knowing and befuddlement.

WILDNESS

Wild ideas in every field both threaten the integrity and legitimacy of the narratives dear to those fields and offer alternative logics through which to rethink problems that the disciplines have been incapable of solving. And so, instead of offering students a reformed university in which to work, wild thinkers such as Fred Moten and Stefano Harney argue for fugitive knowledge that refuses policy as its end goal and teaches us not how and what to think but how to "study." Instead of using rational methods to approach an understanding of disorderly phenomenon, sociologist John Law proposes that we "find ways of living with uncertainty" (2004: 15) rather than trying to conquer and master it. Anna Tsing's (2015) work sees the world through the life of mushrooms and so on. Using concepts such as waywardness and bewilderment, and returning to the idea of a queer undercommons, I want to close with a final example of queer/wild cultural production that defies genre and gender, and returns us to the wild. The performance work and choreography of artist, boychild, captures something of the life of J. Doe from my first section. We might think about boychild's work as fugitivity in motion, as a refusal of genre, an engagement drag, and ballet and modern dance, a re-performance of the grim rigor of Butoh, a Japanese *avant-garde* movement – and the production of a new language for bodily orientations to being and unbeing, race and queerness, within which transitivity does not signify as identity but as a relation to flow (Figure 2.2).

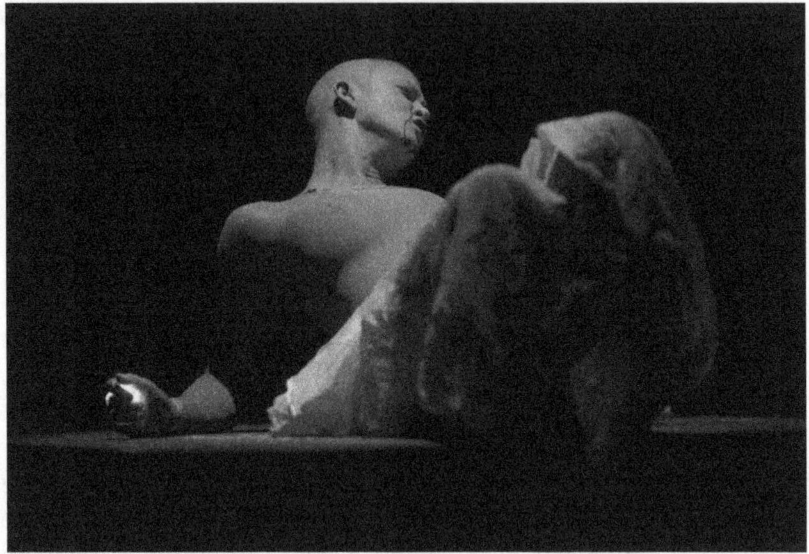

Figure 2.2 boychild. # *untitled lipsync 3* Episode 5: Hidden in Plain Sight. 26 May 2013 Tramway, Glasgow. Photo by Alex Woodward.

Not simply a version of classical dance, nor strictly a theatrical form of club drag cultures, boychild's organization of motion and flow can be linked to other great innovators of the form – certainly Martha Graham and Trisha Brown, but also nameless African American popular pioneers who made up new dances night after night in subterranean worlds of queer color dance. boychild improvises choreographies that draw on these submerged pasts and on what Sean Vogel calls "everynight performances" (2009), and shapes a future vision from forgotten histories.

In a videotaped performance for MOCATV from 2012, boychild appears to flicker under the glare of a strobe light, their twitching and kinetic disturbances miming the infrared light, and catching and holding the motion of light across flesh. The performance is literally electric – it seems as if boychild has been captured by an invisible force field and held there like clothing on barbed wire, caught, entangled and with every twitch towards freedom the body becoming more ensnared, the rhythm toward escape more insistent. The grammar of boychild's extraordinary performances can be found in those movements that arc towards freedom but find themselves captured in the process of trying to escape. We are asked to witness a *fugitivity in motion* that does not seek to arrive nor to imagine clearly a space of freedom that awaits the struggling body; rather, it is a choreography of escape that offers us the precise series of gestures needed to enter the state of fugitivity.

While boychild emerged as a performance persona in SF, in the rarefied, improvisational world of the SF drag scene, the movements she performs and the way she channels both the sacred and the profane, the grotesque and the beautiful, all at once, evokes Butoh. Many people who saw boychild perform early in her career thought maybe she had studied in Japan, and while this remains an ambition for her, the early work came out of her own body practices and perhaps expressed some similar themes as those found in Butoh without her intending for that to happen. Butoh, of course, was not just dance or a dance style: it was in the 1950s a way of thinking about the body; it was an angry protest against the literally poisoned atmosphere of post-war, post-nuclear-bomb Japan. Butoh was a furious rejection of the war generation – an intergenerational declaration of war that we can recognize today in the furious standoffs between an older generation engorged on profits, environmental ruination and political inertia.

In a manifesto from the 1960s, Tatsumi Hijikata, under the influence of Jean Genet, described his dance practice as criminal and as a "battle with nature" ([1961] 2000). This is as queer a declaration as one could hope for – a battle picked up more recently by Paul Preciado's meditations on prosthetic sexualities (2019) and my elaborations on wildness (2020). Alongside the anarchic unraveling associated with desire, we can also see the work of unmaking as part of the experience we have called trans* and that inhabits the grammars of Butoh. In this choreography we find trans* bodies such as J. Doe and the gender-ambiguous figures from Ken Monkman's archive. This choreography conjures what Hijikata, citing Genet, terms "criminal" bodies ([1961] 2000): Dance for Tatsumi was a way of moving with various bodies cast and shaped by capitalist culture as CRIMINAL and SICK: "Human remodeling is accomplished only in connection with young people who unceasingly experience the natural movements that kick the matrix of today's good sense. I dream of such a criminal dance. There will no longer be any hesitation over torching theatres" ([1961] 2000).

This is an amazing passage – it links rebellion to the "natural" choreography of young bodies that, in their movements, and through the organization and disorganization of movements, express refusal and violent resistance – "torching the theatres." Perhaps we too must dream of such "criminal dances" that unmake the world, unbuild the structures that enclose us, that kick down doors and insist upon burning the theater, the institutions that determine us, down. When a dance becomes criminal, in this sense, the theater cannot hold it – it burns the theater down.

In *I Want to Be Ready: Improvised Dance as a Practice of Freedom*, Danielle Goldman writes: "I have come to believe that improvised dance involves literally giving shape to oneself by deciding how to move in relation to an unsteady landscape" (2010: 5). In a piece boychild performed at Fire Island with artist and collaborator Wu Tsang, "Moved by the Motion," the backdrop was a literally unsteady landscape – the ocean, the wind, the sand. This performance captured precisely the terms of improvisation – an unsteady body against an unsteady landscape. Not the conventional notion of motion against stillness, but motion on motion. Fred Moten, perhaps the most important theorist of improvisation has written: "Knowledge of freedom is (in) the invention of escape, stealing away in the confines, in the form, of a break. This is held close in the open song of the ones who are supposed to be silent" (2003: 51). Freedom, in other words, resides not in the space of abstract thought, in a dialectic tension with mastery; it is rather a complete refusal of mastery per se and it is a practice, a break, a song but a song that strains at the very form that song takes – noise breaking through "the ones who are supposed to be silent" uses the body as a vessel and breaks it after emerging (2003: 51).

In an interview about the long arc of her work, Martha Graham proposed that in her early years, she was wild: "I was almost like an animal in my movements. I wanted to be a wild, beautiful creature, maybe of another world – but very, very wild" (1991). She spoke of seeing a lion padding around his cage in the Bronx Zoo and learned from the animal how to shift weight from one foot to the next. Of course, the lion was not just walking, it was pacing, measuring its cage, plotting its escape. It was performing the choreography of capture while dreaming of running and jumping. Dance captures this thin line between knowing we are caught in the social snares that surround us but offering a vision of freedom anyway. The dancer's body leaves the ground knowing it cannot fight gravity, but flings itself against the force of gravitational pull anyway.

Wildness, here, can refer to the declassification of knowledge, the undoing of logics of mastery, the embrace of failure and making our peace with the apocalypse which is already here and that we learn to inhabit. It has multiple shapes and forms, it cannot be still and moves against a backdrop of motion – transitivity as a way of life and not a crystallization of identity. The form takes shape and breaks, breaks and collapses, forms again.

While obviously a spectacularly visual performance and text, boychild also makes the surface of the body into a handmade canvas, a painting, a reflective surface that glitters and gleams, becomes a mirror and ultimately articulates to and for the viewer/spectator/other not an identity or a project, not a goal or a politics, but instead provides a multiply-fragmented mirror through which we can catch a glimpse of our own total disintegration. This fragmentation of the image is closer to the real than we will ever come – rather than miming the performances of totality that make up the arc of representation in the banality of popular media, boychild breaks the body down into incompatible fragments, pieces that do not congeal, do not form a whole, pieces of a dream scattered across the landscape of modernity. Boychild is able to make this fragmentation beautiful, compelling in its fragility, deeply moving in its ability to gesture toward other worlds and new desires, and these movements reach out to us touching our fragility and meeting us in a place of transit, a place where the coherence of gender shatters into a million pieces, never to be reassembled again.

REFERENCES

Goldman, Danielle. 2010. *I Want to Be Ready: Improvised Dance as a Practice of Freedom.* Ann Arbor, MI: University of Michigan Press.

Graham, Martha. 1991. *Blood Memory: An Autobiography.* London: Doubleday.

Halberstam, Jack. 2020. *Wild Things.* Durham, NC: Duke Press.

Hartman, Saidiya 1997. *Scenes of Subjection: Terror, Slavery, and Self-Making in Nineteenth-Century America.* Oxford: Oxford University Press.

2008. Venus in Two Acts. *Small Axe,* 26(June), 1–14.

2019. *Wayward Lives, Beautiful Experiments: Intimate Histories of Social Upheaval.* New York: Norton.

Hijikata, Tatsumi. [1961] 2000. To Prison. Nanako Kurihara, trans. *The Drama Review,* 44(1) (T165), Spring, 29–33. www.mitpressjournals.org/doi/abs/10.1162/10542040051058825.

Howe, Fanny. 1999. "Bewilderment," *How 2,* vol. 1(1) (March).

Keeling, Kara. 2019. *Queer Times, Black Futures.* New York: New York University Press.

Law, John. 2004. *After Method: Mess in Social Science Research.* London: Routledge.

Lowe, Lisa. 2015. *The Intimacies of Four Continents.* Durham, NC: Duke University Press.

Moten, Fred. 2003. *In the Break: The Aesthetics of the Black Radical Tradition.* Minneapolis, MN: University of Minnesota Press.

Moten, Fred and Harney, Stefano. 2013. *The Undercommons: Fugitive Planning and Black Study.* New York: Autonomedia.

Preciado, Paul. 2019. *Countersexual Manifesto.* New York: Columbia University Press.

Rancière, Jacques. 2009. *The Emancipated Spectator.* London: Verso.

Tsing, Anna. 2015. *The Mushroom at the End of the World: On the Possibility of Life in Capitalist Ruins.* Princeton, NJ: Princeton University Press.

Vogel, Shane. 2009.*The Scene of Harlem Cabaret: Race, Sexuality, Performance.* Chicago, IL: University of Chicago Press.

CHAPTER 3

Gender and the End of Biological Determinism

John Dupré

MY AIM IN THIS CHAPTER IS TO LOOK AT THE BIOLOGICAL and ultimately ontological foundations of the sex/gender distinction. While public debate continues as to whether gender is ultimately an expression of deep sex, or rather, as many feminists have assumed, a politically mutable feature of the organisation of society, this should no longer be an issue in light of advances in biology over the last half-century. The biological determinism of the former perspective is no longer scientifically defensible. Or so I shall argue.

ESSENTIALISM

Sex and gender, along with many other categorisations of the world, have often been understood in terms of essences. From antiquity, philosophers have supposed that the world somehow divides things up into 'natural' kinds for us, and that our words

This chapter is substantially based on Dupré (2017). Reprinted with permission.
That chapter, in turn, was based on a public lecture given as the Diane Middlebrook and Carl Djerassi Visiting Professor of Gender Studies at the University of Cambridge. I am grateful to the Centre for Gender Studies for giving me this opportunity and to Carl Djerassi for endowing the Visiting Professorship. I have also benefitted greatly from comments on an earlier draft by Juliet Mitchell and on several drafts by Regenia Gagnier. I am most grateful to Andy Greenfield for pointing out some errors in the earlier version, and for illuminating discussion. And thanks, finally, to Jude Browne and Clementine Collett for suggesting a number of significant improvements to the final text. I gratefully acknowledge the support of the European Research Council, grant SL-06034, which contributed to this work.

register these naturally given divisions (see, for example, Judith Butler in this volume). Essences are the features of things that register their place in these natural kinds. A central task for science is to identify these essences, and thereby to discover what are the real divisions determined by Nature.[1]

Classic versions of essentialism deriving from the ancients were famously criticised by John Locke. Like other contributors to the Scientific Revolution of his time, Locke thought of the natural world as ultimately composed of nothing but atoms moving in the void. If things had essences, they must be determined by the structure and relations of these atomic parts. But since we lack microscopical eyes, as he famously remarked, such essences were inescapably beyond our reach, and there was no reason to believe that the ways we divide up the world at our own gross macroscopic level correspond to any reality at the microscopic level. However, many have concluded that Locke's pessimism was premature. We may still lack microscopical eyes, but we do have electron microscopes, high throughput gene sequencers and even atomic tweezers. So, our ability to correlate the observable world with an underlying reality is very considerable and growing. Essences, it appears, are back within our grasp. Every day, the complete genome sequences of more organisms are announced. Are these perhaps contributions to a growing library of essences?

Biology, at a less rarefied level, has been a fertile breeding ground for essentialism. Anyone who enjoys the outdoors is likely to be struck by the distinct kinds of organisms that are encountered in the wild. There are foxes and rabbits, dandelions and oak trees; one rabbit is pretty much like another, very different from a fox, and there are no intermediate hard cases. Yet a wider spatial view, and, especially, reflection on evolutionary history tell us that if we look a little further in time or space there are always intermediates and always hard cases. Not so many million years ago there was a common ancestor of the fox and the rabbit. If we could go back in time observing all the ancestors of the rabbit until we

[1] For more detail on essences, see Bird & Tobin (2012); Dupré (1993), ch. 3.

reached that common ancestor, and then forwards again through the ancestors leading up to the fox, we would have a more or less smooth series of intermediates leading between these two so very different animals. With a lot more time we could do the same thing for ourselves and a mushroom.

So, to return to the main topic, our natural intuition that men and women are essentially different kinds distinguished by distinct inner natures should be treated with caution. We should at least look very carefully at what exactly the differences – and similarities – really are.

FROM ESSENCE TO PROCESS

Let me turn, then, to the broadest of the categories relevant to the present topic, male and female. It is easy to imagine that these categories denote biological universals, fundamental to the reproduction of living beings. Nothing could be further from the truth. The vast majority of organisms do not have sexes at all. This includes the single-celled organisms that constituted the living world for 80 per cent of its history and remain by far the most common organisms, but also many so-called 'higher' animals and plants. Many plants, though they may engage occasionally in sexual reproduction, generally reproduce asexually. And many organisms have more than two sexes, or mating types (Phadke & Zufall, 2009).

Even among organisms that reproduce only sexually, and that have only two sexes, sex can be fluid. Many reptiles become male or female in response to environmental conditions such as the temperature at which their eggs incubate. Some fish change their sex in midlife: as the position of dominant male becomes vacant in a group of Bluehead Wrasse (*Thalassoma bifasciatum*), the largest female turns into a male. These examples bring me to the main biological point underlying this discussion. Organisms in general, and sex in particular, must be understood developmentally.[2]

[2] Rather wonderfully, the Bluehead Wrasse just mentioned also illustrates this idea in a quite different way: young Blueheads, but not older fish, will often serve (work?) as cleaner fish.

And development, at least for complex multicellular organisms, is not something predetermined 'in the genes' but a process of interaction between the developing organism and its environment.[3]

A philosophical corollary of the above thought is the following: organisms are not things, but processes.[4] The idea of a world of process is widely associated with the Greek philosopher Heraclitus. The only constant, for Heraclitus, was change. Modern opinion has tended to embrace the alternative opinion of Democritus, that ultimately there was nothing but atoms – unchanging things – in the void. Indeed, a version of atomism was a central plank of the Scientific Revolution of the sixteenth and seventeenth centuries in the West and has tended to remain a default assumption of most thinking about science (except, perhaps, for the last hundred years, by physicists). But this view, understanding the world as ultimately composed of unchanging things, has not served biology well. A process, unlike a thing, is maintained by change. A chair can sit in the attic for decades doing nothing, but still remain the very same chair. Organisms, by contrast, maintain themselves by doing all kinds of things – metabolism, cell division, and so on. An animal that does nothing is a dead animal. The integrity of a process is maintained not by the constancy of its temporary parts, but by their causal connections. Our paradigm of a human tends to be of an average-age adult; but that is no better or worse than thinking of a child, a foetus or an old person. Biologically, what is fundamental is a life cycle: what makes parts of a life cycle stages of the same life cycle is not having the same properties at different times, but relations, of continuity, and causality between stages. The whole need not be held together by constant, still less essential, properties.

[3] Detailed defence of this assertion is well beyond the scope of this chapter. For extensive biological details of the developmental interaction between organism and environment, see Gilbert & Epel (2009). For philosophical discussion of modern understandings of genes and genomes, see Griffiths & Stotz (2013).

[4] This thought is explored from a variety of perspectives in Nicholson & Dupré (2018).

SEXUAL DIFFERENTIATION

So, let us now look at the processes through which differentiated sexes in humans develop.[5] Whereas we tend to analyse a thing into its parts, a process is naturally analysed into stages. Needless to say, perhaps, in neither case can we assume that the divisions are clear or unambiguous. However, the following provides a sufficiently clear series of stages for present purposes.

1. *Chromosomal sex.* Most women have two X chromosomes, and most men have an X and a Y chromosome; and they originated from a fertilised egg with those chromosomes. The word 'most' is very important, however. First, not all humans have either an XX or an XY genotype. There are people with XYY, XXY and XO chromosomes (or karyotypes), of which the first two are generally assigned a male gender, and the last is generally treated as female. Second, for various reasons, including now elective reassignment, later stages in gender development do not always coincide with chromosomal sex.
2. *Foetal gonadal sex.* By twelve weeks most foetuses have embryonic gonads, irreversibly committed to becoming either testes or ovaries. The development of testes appears to be triggered by a gene on the Y chromosome, the product of which binds to a gene on chromosome 17 and triggers a cascade of events involved in the production of the testes. A different sequence of genetic events pushes the as yet undifferentiated gonad in the direction of becoming an ovary. The Y chromosome gene just mentioned is known as the Sry gene, which stands for 'Sex determining region of the Y chromosome'. It is sometimes credited with the function of sex reversal, echoing the curious idea, dating from Aristotle, that being female is a default.[6] Of course,

[5] This chapter, and especially the present section, is deeply indebted to the work of biologist and gender theorist Anne Fausto-Sterling. Her *Myths of Gender* (1985) pioneered biologically informed criticism of purportedly scientific accounts of gender difference, a project developed in new directions in *Sexing the Body* (2000). The outline of the stages of sexual differentiation here closely follows her *Sex/Gender* (2012).

[6] The persistence and untenability of this idea is noted by two experts on the relevant genetics: 'The discovery that gonads develop as ovaries in the absence of the Y-chromosome (or, more specifically, the Sry gene) supported the prevailing view that the testis pathway is the active pathway in gonad development. However, as

if the Sry gene is indeed the relevant 'switch', it might equally well be described as preventing ovary development. In neither case is the ensuing genetic cascade fully understood.

3. *Foetal hormonal sex.* As the gonads develop they begin to produce their characteristic mix of hormones. The reproductive system, under the influence of these hormones, begins to differentiate towards characteristically male or female physiologies. Again, this depends not only on the production of hormones, but also on the proper functioning of receptors that recognise these hormones. So, for example, occasionally XY foetuses carry a mutation that hinders androgen recognition, and produces children born with highly feminised external genitalia. If everything follows the standard path, however, this leads us, finally, to:
4. *Genital sex.* The standard criteria that are used to distinguish the sex of babies at birth.

The process of foetal differentiation, then, is complex and multifactorial. While most babies will be born either with an XY genotype and typical male physiology, or with an XX genotype and female physiology, there are many ways in which these typical outcomes can be derailed. It is no surprise that there are a significant number of atypical outcomes, sometimes described as intersexed, now more often said to exhibit just 'Differences of Sex Development'.

The next crucial point in human development is, of course, birth. This is the point at which the wider community decides whether a baby is a boy or a girl. In the cases where this decision is difficult, standard medical practice has been to attempt to adjust the baby to one or other of the standard kinds. This often involves surgical reshaping of the external genitalia and treatment with hormones. The *exhaustive* division of people into two sexes is not a reflection of how things are in the world but of a social policy that everyone must be assigned to one or other of these categories (see Jack Halberstam, for example, in this volume). Very recently, some countries, including

Eicher and others have emphasized, the ovarian pathway must also be an active genetic pathway' (Brennan & Capel, 2004, citing Eicher & Washburn, 1986.)

Germany, Australia and New Zealand, have allowed babies to be registered at birth as of indeterminate sex, though this move is highly controversial, and has been criticised by some advocates for intersexed people as maintaining a fixed and determinate set of categories.

GENDER DIFFERENTIATION

Though techniques of foetal surveillance such as ultrasound may rapidly be changing this, to a rough approximation gender begins at birth.[7] And the countless institutions that enforce gender require that it be decided on which side of this fundamental dichotomy every individual falls. On endless forms we must say whether we are male or female – a question generally framed as a request for our sex, though more accurately it should generally ask for our gender. As noted above, however, in some places this dichotomy is being challenged, and the effects of this on the gendered organisation of social life are as yet impossible to predict.

At any rate, development moves on. For most of us this continues to follow physiologically one of two fairly well-distinguished paths of sexual differentiation, though with wide variations in detail, and with a few more along the way joining the ranks of those whose sexual development differs substantially from either norm. While the typical differences radiate out into many other parts of physiology, the further these are from the core reproductive systems, the less this difference will be sharply dichotomous, and the more it will become statistical and overlapping. The average upper body strength of men, for instance, is greater than

[7] From the point of view of development we should not, with due consideration to its significance and sometimes traumatic nature for the mother, see birth as a cataclysmic turning point. The baby is little more independent from the mother, for instance, than it was before birth, though it may derive its nutrition from a different part of her anatomy. (Though certainly being born is traumatic and a serious struggle from the baby's point of view, and the world is a very different place from the uterus. Thanks to Juliet Mitchell for reminding me of this!)

that of women, but there are many women with greater strength than many men.

Of central importance in our species, social and psychological development also takes off, with an enormous range of external factors impinging on the developmental process, many of which are relevant to the continuing bifurcation of the population into the socially condoned male and female kinds. Boys and girls are differentially hugged, given dolls or guns, pink toys or blue toys, and taught the intricacies of the gendered division of people. By three, children more or less well know that they are boys and girls, and know many of the behaviours, likes and dislikes that are expected of them as such. These systematic differences in behaviour are elaborated in distinctive ways through the life cycle. Most men and women continue to dress differently; to choose different leisure activities; and, most importantly, to do different kinds of work, both in the labour market and in the home. The nature of these differentiated pathways has certainly changed over time, though not always in the ways that feminist activists have hoped. As is often observed, increasing participation by women in the labour market has tended to be concentrated in less well-paid employment, and when on the same level of employment, pay for women is still usually lower; increased male participation in domestic work has not been commensurate (see for example Nancy Fraser in this volume).

EXPLAINING GENDER DIFFERENCE

There are certain purported explanations of gender difference that have particularly attracted scientific attention. One of these has been the exploration of differences in male and female brains, a tradition that goes back at least to the nineteenth century (Cahill, 2006; for criticism, see Fine, 2010; Fine, Dupré & Joel, 2017). Since, it is often said, brains cause behaviour, such research is often seen as a search for a fundamental cause of behavioural difference. An even more fundamental cause may then be sought in the genes if, as many also suppose, genes explain the properties of brains.

In parallel with the investigation of genetic and neurological differences between men and women has been the search for evolutionary explanations of gender difference. Here, attention has focused on realms of behaviour that are seen to be especially significant for evolutionary success, most notably mate choice and parental investment (Buss, 1999). The familiar central argument is that since women invest far more in a pregnancy than men – eggs are bigger than sperms, and gestation takes a lot longer than copulation – they will be more concerned to optimise the chances of success for any reproductive endeavour. This is taken to imply that women will have evolved to be very careful with whom they mate, looking at least for the best genes on offer, and if possible for a little help in rearing the offspring. Men on the other hand, need only make a minimal investment. The evolutionarily rational strategy is to fertilise as many women as possible and trust that some offspring will make it to maturity. As sociobiologists like to remind us, the potential reproductive success of a male is almost limitless. Approximately 8 per cent of the male inhabitants of what was once the Mongol Empire are allegedly descended directly from Genghis Khan, or approximately one man in two hundred in the entire human population (Zerjal et al., 2003).

These differences in reproductive strategy are the starting point for evolutionary speculation, but their implications are seen to ramify far more widely. It is seen as natural for women to monopolise childcare and domestic work, given their evolved concern to invest in their children; inevitably they have less time for the outside world of work. Perhaps the need to compete with other men in the labour market – and ultimately thereby for access to women – will require cognitive capacities unnecessary in the differently demanding home environment. At least, evolved cognitive capacities are likely to be different.

These stories fit together into a broader picture that understands gender difference – or here we might as well just say sex difference – in an impressively integrated way. Natural selection placed different pressures on our male and female ancestors; these resulted in the selection of different genes, which are expressed in different brain structures; different brains cause different behaviour. Let us call this the Biological Big Picture.

I think almost everything is wrong with the Biological Big Picture (see Dupré, 2003; Dupré, 2012, esp. ch. 14; Fine, Dupré & Joel, 2017). Here, however, I will concentrate on one set of pivotal players in the story, genes. Genes, in the Biological Big Picture, cause organisms to have particular properties, in this case properties of their brains that make them, for instance, keen on spreading their seed as widely as possible. Such properties make the individuals that exhibited them evolutionarily successful, and the genes that cause them are selected. But can genes really do this job?

GENES AND GENOMES

The science of genetics took off in the early twentieth century with the work of Thomas Hunt Morgan and collaborators on the fruit-fly, *Drosophila* (Kohler, 1994). This work was the study of the inheritance of difference. Some flies have red eyes, some white. When a red-eyed fly mated with a white-eyed fly, or another red-eyed fly, what proportion of the offspring had red or white eyes? Morgan and colleagues bred and counted many thousands of flies and their differentiating traits, and the results of this work were interpreted in terms of the seminal insight that an individual had two sets of genes, one from each parent who, in turn, contributed half their genes to each offspring. Entities such as genes for red or white eyes were thus inherited from parents, and these interacted in specific ways. For example, the red-eye gene is said to be dominant, as a fly with a red-eye gene from one parent and a white-eye gene from the other will have red eyes. This kind of work, describing the transmission of genes bearing specific traits, is often referred to as Mendelian genetics, honouring Gregor Mendel's pioneering work on peas fifty years earlier.

Morgan's work made fundamental contributions to the advance of genetics, and Mendelian genetics still play an important role in areas of medicine and agriculture. But Mendelian genetics is now a very small part of genetics, or as some prefer now to say genomics. This is because Mendelian genes turn out to be a very minor part of genomes (Barnes & Dupré, 2008). Most genes[8] cannot be correlated with a particular feature of the organism. Those that can, generally carry defects that make a gene nonfunctional. Consider the familiar example from human genetics, blue eyes. Blue eyes reflect the failure to make melanin in the iris. One functioning gene will suffice to produce melanin, so the brown gene is dominant. The blue-eye gene is not really a gene to make blue eyes, but a defect in the gene that makes eyes brown.[9] And of course, single gene diseases such as cystic fibrosis, or Huntington's disease, to which Mendelian models still apply, are unsurprisingly caused by dysfunctional genes.

What Mendelian genetics most crucially leaves out is *process*. While no one doubts that there is a process that leads from the zygote or embryo to the adult, talk of genes for this or that trait allows us to ignore it, and thereby allows us to ignore all the further factors that are necessary for this process to occur and all the different outcomes that interactions with these factors may make possible. This omission meshes with a related perspective on evolution.[10] Natural selection, it is sometimes said, cares only about the outcome and if a gene for outcome X is selected, then somehow or other outcome X will appear at the proper time. Development – the process – can be blackboxed. We know what goes go in and we know what comes out. We don't need to worry about what happens inside the box.

[8] I'll assume, for the sake of argument, that it is even useful to think of genomes as divided into genes. This assumption, however, is increasingly debatable (see Barnes & Dupré, 2008; Griffiths & Stotz, 2013).

[9] Eye colour, like most relations between genotype and phenotype, is really much more complicated, but the simple story will serve for present purposes.

[10] A perspective best known in the work of Richard Dawkins (1976).

One might have supposed that this lacuna would have been filled with the development of molecular genetics that followed the iconic discovery by Francis Crick and James Watson[11] of the structure of DNA, by then recognised as the genetic material. But in fact, though this did lead to the discovery of some fundamental processes, notably the way in which sequences of nucleotides, constituents of DNA molecules, could determine the production of particular proteins, the main functional molecules in living systems, processes of development were still not closely integrated into genetics.

One reason for this was that many geneticists continued to think (or anyhow speak) in terms of genes for this or that feature of the phenotype. Of course, they were well aware that when one spoke of a gene for high intelligence, or a gene for homosexuality, this did not provide the whole causal story. Many other genes – and much else besides – would be involved in the pathway from the gene to the trait it helps to cause. However, the genome as a whole was still seen as providing the complete code, recipe or blueprint for the organism. The recipe was susceptible to minor changes, no doubt, as witnessed by the variability observable in actual individuals. The variations could be understood in terms of Mendelian genes that caused molecular differences, which in turn changed the probabilities of particular outcomes. Both the standard pattern and the variations from the pattern could be seen as determined by the genes, and there was no pressing need to take the developmental processes out of their black boxes.

Within this framework, sex determination was a paradigmatic Mendelian system in which, perhaps unsurprisingly, the Y chromosome was dominant. Being female resulted from having two copies of the recessive X gene.[12] As with other Mendelian systems, the differences between individuals, the XX and XY 'phenotypes', were taken to be explained by the genetic differences.

11 And Maurice Wilkins and Rosalind Franklin.

12 An important anomaly in the system is that only XX and XY pairs are capable of mating. This curious feature underlies Fisher's (1930) famous argument for why, under most circumstances, XX and XY genotypes will be equally common.

Counterposing this model with the complexity of the process of sexual determination sketched above begins to reveal the problems with the blackboxing strategy. Though there are typical developmental trajectories for embryos with XX and XY chromosomes, there are many ways in which individual developmental histories can diverge from this. Other genes, such as the binding site for the transcript of the Sry gene, determine whether the Y chromosome has its typical effect. And, as will be explained below, the activity of genes is frequently influenced by environmental factors. A strict and exhaustive dichotomy of outcomes is enforced at birth rather than supplied by Nature.

The development of gender differences after birth may seem closely parallel to the development of sex differences: there are two standard, typical, developmental trajectories. While there is in reality a large array of different identities, as illustrated by Jack Halberstam's chapter in this volume for example, there remain two normative stereotypes, often reinforced by popular models of the evolutionary elaboration of sex roles in reproduction. In (only slight) caricature, these are heterosexual, promiscuously inclined men, competing with one another in various workplaces and marketplaces, and heterosexual, preferentially monogamous women, gossiping pleasantly with one another while taking care of the children and the home. It is admitted that many contemporary societies have relaxed the normative force of these stereotypes, opening the workplace to women and domestic labour to men, and are increasingly tolerant of those outside the stereotypical pathways of a gender binary. But this, it is often added, is always with some difficulty, requiring a battle against the tendencies laid down by Nature. We can try to get more women to be computer scientists or men to do the housework, but we are fighting against their intrinsic nature. Nature, here, is the innate tendency of the genes, as selected by millions of years of evolution.[13]

[13] In their more general theoretical statements, evolutionary psychologists are usually careful to distance themselves from genetic determinism, and note that actual outcomes depend on a range of environmental inputs. This then raises a problem in how to understand their more empirical work aimed at demonstrating that the phenotypes predicted by evolutionary speculation are indeed found in human populations. These

But Nature, or genes, do not work like this. There are no genes dedicated to heterosexuality, the love of big machines or good housekeeping that need to be diverted from their natural trajectories. There is a genome that, given a specific sequence of surrounding circumstances, and subject to a certain amount of unpredictable noise, produces an adult individual with certain characteristics and dispositions. Change the environment, and you may very well change the outcome.

So, what is a genome? We often think of genomes as sequences of letters, C, G, A and T, that form a code; and sequence can be a very useful thing to know about a genome. Technologies from molecular phylogeny, the genetic exploration of evolutionary relations, to forensic genomics, the identification of criminals by the material they leave at crime sites, depend on the comparison of genome sequences. But there is a great deal more to a genome than its sequence. Considering that the chromosomes in a human cell measure about 2 metres, and the diameter of a cell is of the order of 100 micrometres, there is an obvious question of how the genome can be made to fit. In fact, it is not just stuffed in any old how, but exquisitely coiled and folded. Moreover, the details of this folding, or condensation, are crucial to what the genome does. To put it simply, to be expressed, a gene or a section of the genome must be accessible to the transcription machinery; and condensation implies that most of it is not accessible. The shape of the genome changes constantly, and so does, partly in consequence, its activity. And these changes are brought about by other molecules in the cell responding to many features of the wider system and even environmental influences far beyond. The study of these changes is part of the science of epigenetics, the exploration of chemical and physical changes to the genes or the genome, how they occur in response to a wide range of external causes and what are their effects. Paradigmatic and detailed work here is on the development of behavioural dispositions in rodents (Champagne

phenotypes must at least be understood as typical or default developmental outcomes, even if environmental accidents sometimes derail them from this default tendency.

& Meaney, 2006; Champagne et al., 2006); but there is also a growing body of research on the way human physiology or psychology responds to developmental influences in ways that are mediated by changes to the genome.[14]

The crucial point is this. We have been encouraged to think of the genome as something static and fixed, a programme or recipe that guides or directs the development of the organism. This is quite wrong. It is important that the sequence is very stable, as the genome is indeed a repository of information about possible protein structures. But the genome does not itself say what is to be done with that information. The application of genomic information occurs as part of a process in which the genome is a dynamic participant, and which is highly sensitive to a range of external influences. Indeed, the genome itself, like the organism, is best understood as a process.

BACK TO GENDER

So, what does all this tell us about gender? Gender is a normative, bifurcated developmental process that tends to lead to two distinct suites of characteristics that are mapped onto the typical physiological states of male and female. These processes are not inscribed in the genes: nothing is; they result from an array of molecular, physiological and environmental factors coordinated reliably to produce certain typical outcomes. The fact that they are not written in the DNA does not mean that we can change them at will. Developmental processes tend to be very stable for good and obvious reasons. Indeed, life would be impossible if there were not developmental processes that fairly reliably reproduced in offspring the characteristics of parents. Parents not only provide genomes, they provide for their offspring the sequence of environments that channel development in the typical direction. This may be no more than providing exactly the right place to deposit an egg, or it may

[14] For an overview of the significance of recent advances in epigenetics, see Meloni & Testa (2014).

involve creating a complex built environment such as a bird's nest, a beaver's dam or a termite mound.[15] It will often also involve imparting behaviour through imitation or other kinds of training; and the training imparted will typically be that to which the parent, in its development, was exposed.

Humans have taken the complexity of these developmental processes far beyond that of any other organisms. The environments in which we place our children have reached a bewildering complexity, parenting is an often frighteningly difficult skill and socially provided institutions from maternity wards to universities are designed to contribute to the development of our offspring (see for example Nancy Fraser's and Cindi Katz's accounts of social reproduction in this volume). Because so much of the developmental matrix in which humans grow is constructed by us, it follows that we have unparalleled abilities to change the developmental trajectories of our children. I do not say that it is simple to change these institutions, still less that it is easy to tell what will be the consequences of changes that we make; but I do say that it is possible. Feminist scholars have for decades been pointing to the variety of gender systems found in different places and at different times, and inferred that the presence of a particular system is always contingent. Their critics, committed to a biologically grounded view of gender development, have claimed that this diversity is largely illusory. But given the view of development I have just presented, there is no reason to suppose that things are not as they so clearly seem. The institutions and norms surrounding gender development have diverged in different places and over time, and the gender system has changed too.

As all authors in this volume attest, gender is thoroughly norm-ridden. Children are taught how to be boys and girls, how men and women ought to behave, and often that they ought to behave differently from each other. The importance of norms, and

[15] For the importance to evolution of so-called niche construction, of which such environmental modifications are examples, see Odling-Smee, Laland & Feldman (2003).

many central points of the foregoing discussion, can be nicely illustrated with the issue of sexuality. Multi-sexualities are of course a huge problem for the kind of biological determinism, or at any rate biological causality, inferred from reflections on evolution. Until the technologies set out in Marcia C. Inhorn's chapter in this volume were developed, same-sex relationships seemed a poor strategy for maximising one's reproductive success. Sociobiologists and evolutionary psychologists have battled with the problem. However, there are no genes for sexuality or, perhaps better, there are so many genes for sexuality – genes that in more or less subtle ways affect the probability of becoming gay for example in specific environments – that it would be better to say there were none. It is also the worst kind of 'just so' story: beyond the fact that it might possibly explain an anomaly in a dominant system of ideas, it has no evidence going for it at all.

Sexuality is a developmental outcome.[16] Like all human developmental outcomes, it results from a complex interaction between internal, including genetic, and external causes. Crucially, the latter are partly normative. Liberal societies do not now mandate heterosexuality, though no doubt they favour it, but they do mandate a dichotomy. One is one thing or the other. When men or women after decades of heterosexual marriage take up same-sex relations, it is generally said that they have discovered that they were gay or lesbian. Their marriages are discovered to have embodied a gross failure of self-knowledge. Teenagers who feel attracted to members of their own sex agonise over whether they are gay, or whether this is some passing anomaly of desire. As with sex, this dichotomy is not an immediate problem for the many people who have no doubt on which side of the line they fall. And the suggestion that the division is a normative one is often

[16] What follows here has an obvious debt to Michel Foucault (1979 [1976]). I also continue to follow Anne Fausto-Sterling (2012). Fausto-Sterling (2019) provides pioneering reflection on the early developmental origins of sexual orientation and identity.

unwelcome to the unambiguously gay person, who understandably feels that a quasi-biological dichotomy is a more solid ground for defending their lifestyle than a normative dichotomy. However, since the pioneering studies of Alfred Kinsey over sixty years ago (Kinsey et al., 1948, 1953), it has been quite clear that in terms of the behaviour generally supposed to define these categories, people lie on a spectrum, with many engaging in sexual activities with people of different sexual identities at various stages of their lives. Nowadays we have omnigender, and while no doubt there are many strata of society in which heterosexuality remains normative, it is increasingly clear that maintaining this norm will be difficult as a growing number of people refuse to accept it as the only norm. Actual developmental histories produce mixed and diverse objects of sexual desire. Sexuality is leading the way for our interpretations of sex.

A striking perspective on the ontogeny of desire, the developmental process that leads to the preference of one object of sexual desire over another, is provided by the much-debated issue of pornography. Prominent feminists have suggested that pornography, or certain forms of pornography, may promote violence against women or normalise various demeaning treatments of women (see Catharine A. MacKinnon in this volume). Psychiatrist Norman Doidge (2007) provides a compelling and disturbing argument that pornography can, at any rate, radically reshape sexual desire. He describes patients becoming increasingly addicted to pornography and simultaneously increasingly unable to become sexually excited by their own partners. He also describes the evolution of pornography from the relatively uncomplicated depiction of sexual intercourse to the growing menu of violent, abusive or just plain bizarre genres currently available on the Internet. He even reports that consumers of Internet pornography may reach a state where they are sexually aroused not just by thinking about the activities performed in pornography, but by thinking of the computer itself. Even if the simplistic evolutionary psychological stories about universal preferences for ideally curvy female figures (Singh, 1993) proved true as statistical averages, they would be irrelevant for understanding the diversity and plasticity of desire. Desire, it appears, is almost indefinitely malleable, and can be shaped in the most unexpected ways.

CONCLUSION

The picture I have sketched is one in which both male and female sex and male and female gender point to the most common developmental trajectories, but trajectories from which many individuals diverge. At birth, or sooner as prenatal surveillance becomes more and more routine, the male/female dichotomy of sex is normatively enforced, with medical intervention common in response to atypical individuals. This dichotomy is then the basis for a more systematically normative enforcement of dichotomous gender development. While it is still commonly supposed that both stages of this process are largely determined by genes, the growing understanding of the complexity of human development, and the deep entanglement of internal and external influences that development involves, make this kind of genetic determinism wholly implausible. An essentialist perspective on sex or gender is disastrously misguided.

So, what is the importance of the sex/gender distinction for understanding the world we live in? Sex is an important biological concept and it is, of course, central to human reproduction; gender is a diverse and malleable superstructure erected socially on this biological base. Nevertheless, there are reasons, in the end, not to make too sharp a distinction between the two. The distinction between male and female sexes is important, but not wholly sharp. There are individuals who fall in the gap between these two kinds, and there is much to be said for relaxing the normative requirement of sexual dichotomy. Moreover, sexual differentiation is no more immune to external, especially epigenetic, influences than are other aspects of physiological development. These influences may well include aspects of gender, so that the system of gender differentiation may act causally on the physiological articulation of sex. Though I think that the distinction between sex and gender could continue to be pragmatically useful, most fundamentally it may be better to think of sex/gender (or gender/sex) as one seamless axis of differentiated development. But of course, this is not the pair of predetermined developmental tramlines imagined by genetic determinists; rather we should see broad and well-trodden pathways within a much wider range of more esoteric possibilities, perhaps ever widening as we increase our tolerance of difference. Those whose sex/gender development lies some way from these pathways should be welcomed, not least as reminders of the flexibility and open texture of the human developmental process. If there is a boundary between sex and gender, it is a moving and slippery one. But no problem with that. That's what biological – and social – boundaries are like.

REFERENCES

Barnes, B. and Dupré, J. 2008. *Genomes and What to Make of Them.* University of Chicago Press, 2008.

Bird, A. and Tobin, E. 2012. Natural Kinds. In *The Stanford Encyclopedia of Philosophy* (Winter Edition), Edward N. Zalta, ed. http://plato.stanford.edu/archives/win2012/entries/natural-kinds/.

Brennan, J. and Capel, B. 2004. One Tissue, Two Fates: Molecular Genetic Events that Underlie Testis versus Ovary Development. *Nature Reviews Genetics,* **5**, 509–21.

Buss, D. M. 1999. *Evolutionary Psychology: The New Science of the Mind.* Needham Heights, MA: Allyn & Bacon.

Cahill, L. 2006. Why Sex Matters for Neuroscience. *Nature Reviews Neuroscience,* **7**, 1–8.

Champagne, F. A. and Meaney, M. J. 2006. Stress during Gestation Alters Postpartum Maternal Care and the Development of the Offspring in a Rodent Model. *Biological Psychiatry,* **59**, 1227–35.

Champagne, F. A., Weaver, I. C., Diorio, J. et al. 2006. Maternal Care Associated with Methylation of the Estrogen Receptor-Alphalb Promoter and Estrogen Receptor-Alpha Expression in the Medial Preoptic Area of Female Offspring. *Endocrinology,* **147**, 2909–15.

Dawkins, R. 1976. *The Selfish Gene.* Oxford University Press.

Doidge, N. 2007. *The Brain that Changes Itself: Stories of Personal Triumph from the Frontiers of Brain Science.* London: Penguin.

Dupré, J. 1993. *The Disorder of Things: Metaphysical Foundations of the Disunity of Science.* Harvard University Press.

2003. *Human Nature and the Limits of Science.* Oxford University Press.
2012. *Processes of Life: Essays in the Philosophy of Biology*. Oxford University Press.
2017. A Postgenomic Perspective on Sex and Gender. In David Livingstone Smith, ed., *How Biology Shapes Philosophy: New Foundations for Naturalism.* Cambridge University Press, pp. 227–46.
Eicher, E. M. and Washburn, L. L. 1986. Genetic Control of Primary Sex Determination in Mice. *Annual Review of Genetics,* **20**, 327–60.
Fausto-Sterling, A. 1985. *Myths of Gender.* New York: Basic Books.
2000. *Sexing the Body: Gender Politics and the Construction of Sexuality.* New York: Basic Books.
2012. *Sex/Gender: Biology in a Social World.* New York: Routledge.
2019. Gender/Sex, Sexual Orientation, and Identity Are in the Body: How Did They Get There? *The Journal of Sex Research,* **56**(4–5), 529–55.
Fine, C. 2010. *Delusions of Gender: How Our Minds, Society, and Neurosexism Create Difference.* London: Icon Books.
Fine, C., Dupré, J. and Joel, D. 2017. Sex-Linked Behavior: Evolution, Stability, and Variability. *Trends in Cognitive Sciences,* **21**(9): 666–73.
Fisher, R. A. 1930. *The Genetical Theory of Natural Selection.* Oxford University Press.
Foucault, M. 1979 [1976]. *The History of Sexuality Volume 1: An Introduction.* Robert Hurley, trans. London: Allen Lane.
Gilbert, S. F. and Epel, D. 2009. *Ecological Developmental Biology: Integrating Epigenetics, Medicine, and Evolution.* Sunderland, MA: Sinauer.
Griffiths, P. and Stotz, K. 2013. *Genetics and Philosophy: An Introduction.* Cambridge University Press.
Kinsey, A. C., Pomeroy, W. B. and Martin, C. E. 1948. *Sexual Behavior in the Human Male.* Philadelphia, PA: W. B. Saunders.
Kinsey, A. C. et al. 1953. *Sexual Behavior in the Human Female.* Philadelphia, PA: W. B. Saunders.
Kohler, R. E. 1994. *Lords of the Fly: Drosophila Genetics and the Experimental Life.* University of Chicago Press.
Meloni, M. and Testa, G. 2014. Scrutinizing the Epigenetics Revolution. *BioSocieties.* 9, 431–56. https://doi:10.1057/biosoc.2014.22.
Nicholson, D. J. and Dupré, J. 2018. *Everything Flows: Towards a Processual Philosophy of Biology.* Oxford University Press.
Phadke, S. S. and Zufall, R. A. 2009. Rapid Diversification of Mating Systems in Ciliates. *Biological Journal of the Linnean Society of London,* **98**, 187–97.
Odling-Smee, F. J., Laland, K. N. and Feldman, M. W. 2003. *Niche Construction: The Neglected Process in Evolution.* Princeton University Press.
Singh, D. 1993. Adaptive Significance of Waist-to-Hip Ratio and Female Physical Attractiveness. *Journal of Personality and Social Psychology,* **65**, 293–307.
Zerjal, T. et al. 2003. The genetic legacy of the Mongols. *The American Journal of Human Genetics,* **72**, 717–21.

CHAPTER 4

Gender, Sexuality, Race, and Colonialism

Sandra G. Harding

TODAY, NEW HISTORIES OF SCIENCE ARE PRODUCING skeptical questions about the supposedly international philosophies of science that prevail in the North.[1] The conceptual resources of conventional Northern philosophies seem inadequate to enable them to interact effectively with how sciences and their philosophies do, could, and should function in today's economic, political, social and cultural, local and global contexts. Gender, sexuality, and race issues often are central to these queries, though not consistently recognized. In this chapter, I consider

This is an abbreviated version of Harding (2018). Earlier and later related essays are Harding (2016; 2017), and Harding & Mendoza (2020).

I am grateful to Cambridge University for The Diane Middlebrook and Carl Djerassi Visiting Professorship (Michaelmas 2017) in the Center for Gender Studies of the Department of Politics and International Studies, which gave me the time to revise and develop further this manuscript. For helpful comments on earlier drafts I thank Jane Bayes, Breny Mendoza, Tania Perez-Bustos, Luis Reyes-Galindo, Shu-Mei Shih, Margie Waller, and peer reviewers. Anjan Chakravartty's thoughtful questions greatly improved my thinking about the topic. The errors that remain here are all my own.

[1] Readers may find it confusing that I will sometimes refer to the West, at other times the North vs. the South, and at yet other times the First vs. Third World. Wouldn't it be better to use just one set of terms throughout? Alas, no! Each of these contrasts came into use in a specific era of global politics. While none have subsequently completely disappeared, their use can be misleading or irrelevant with reference to other eras. I shall tend to use the contrast most appropriate for the particular historical context at issue. Of course, use of any such contrasts can be problematic as it tends to homogenize both sides and obscure the often widespread hybrid or mixed contexts. Moreover, it can tend to distract attention from other more important issues. Yet we need to be able to refer to powerful and widespread oppressive social forces and their resistors, and without further empowering the former. We are stuck with only problematic options.

each and ask how international, or universal, are these philosophies of science in reality?

Lively debates focus on the appropriate references and meanings of such central terms as science, objectivity, progress, history of science, modernity, coloniality, diversity, pluralism, democracy, international, universal, and philosophy of science itself.[2] Such debates are beginning to succeed in negotiating intellectual and political spaces for Southern concerns in mainstream Northern epistemologies and ontologies.

One such new history of science has emerged from Latin Americans who are creating anti-colonial histories and philosophies of knowledge production. It has named itself modernity/coloniality/decolonial theory (MCD). It intends to transform typical Northern assumptions about modernity, its origins and its effects on Northern philosophies of science, as these are understood in both Latin America and around the globe.

The MCD accounts include feminist arguments about the centrality to colonialism and to modernity of the colonists' exploitations of racialized groups, and especially of their women. These often focus on the apparently indissoluble entanglement of new super-hierarchicalized and rigid racial and gender/sexual categories that the Iberians invented for the Americas, and then exported back to Europe.[3] Thus, for the MCD accounts, modernity and its new gender and racial relations in Europe are created in the Iberian colonial

[2] Some readers may find it uncomfortable that I use the term "science" here to refer to all empirical processes of producing knowledge of nature and social relations. This is not how most Northern scientists or philosophers of science use the word, nor is the term used by indigenous knowers to refer to their production of knowledge activities. Yet it is used here to shift focus to similarities between such different kinds of knowledge production, rather than emphasizing their very real differences, upon which both groups typically focus.

[3] See Lugones, 2008, 2010; Schiwy, 2010; Walsh, 2016; Mendoza, 2015. Leading MCD men have been actively participating in this project. For example, Enrique Dussel, Nelson Maldonado-Torres, and Ramon Grosfoguel, among others, co-organized and co-taught a course in Mexico City, April 10–14 2017 on *Pensamientos y Feminismos Descoloniales Latinoamericanos.* Arturo Escobar (1995, 2004, 2010) has consistently addressed feminist issues.

encounters in the Americas, and persist to this day in Europe and North America, as well as in Latin America. They continue to create distorted understandings of the worlds we live in today. What will a philosophy of science look like that can recognize and move beyond this history?

The MCD has been influenced by Marxian World Systems accounts and their *dependencia* theory, by Liberation Theology, by Paulo Freire's *conscientizacao*, or critical consciousness theory, and by tumultuous political, economic, social, and cultural processes in Latin American history.[4] Subaltern studies and continental philosophies have tried to affiliate with or even contain it.[5] The focus in this chapter is on MCD's potential contributions to more general attempts to reconfigure Northern post-positivist philosophic tendencies.

I begin by outlining some important differences between the worlds of 1492, on which the MCD accounts focus, and of the three-centuries later mostly British colonization of India and Africa that ground the more familiar postcolonial theory and set the background to the second section of the chapter. Here I illustrate some of the entangled gender/sexuality and racial issues in these Latin American histories. The concluding section identifies a valuable progressive tension for Northern philosophy of science produced in this work.[6]

[4] Important authors here include Anibal Quijano, 2007; Walter Mignolo, 2011; Boaventura de Sousa Santos, 2007, 2014; Enrique Dussel, 1995; Nelson Maldonado-Torres, 2012; Ramon Grosfoguel, Nelson Maldonado-Torres, & Jose David Saldivar, 2005; Arturo Escobar, 2010; Catherine Walsh, 2010; Marisol de la Cadena, 2010. Mignolo & Escobar 2010 includes translations of a number of the early papers, as does Morana, Dussel and Jauregui 2008. See also Mauricio Nieto Olarte 2016.

[5] See Rodriguez, 2001; Lange-Churion & Mendieta, 2001; Grosfoguel, Maldonado-Torres, & Saldivar, 2005.

[6] It deserves mention that the present author is not literate in either Spanish or Portuguese. No doubt this account would benefit from reflections on its historical claims and philosophical intentions by readers familiar with the relevant Spanish and Portuguese texts. However, these limitations are not as severe as one might imagine. That is because the huge literature in English upon which this account draws is authored mostly by first-language Spanish and Portuguese speakers.

THE DECOLONIAL BEYOND THE POSTCOLONIAL

Decolonial theory intends to counter a wide range of self-congratulatory contrasts that the North persistently invokes when focusing on the former Spanish and Portuguese colonies in the Americas.[7] That is, it will counter frequent claims by leading Northern scholars that all of the truly important and progressive advances in science and technology originated in Europe or the United States (see Judith Butler in this volume on the assumed universality of imperialist thought), and then were disseminated to Latin America. According to this view, without these disseminations, Latin Americans would remain primitive and backward, and stuck in pre-modern myths and superstitions. In contrast, decolonial theorists assert that they undertake their challenge on behalf of the most economically and politically vulnerable peoples of Latin America, and that "dissemination" does not in fact accurately identify what happened. Moreover, they point out that these peoples still suffer today from the continuing effects of the Iberian coloniality, exacerbated by the recent promotion by the United States of dictatorial regimes and of neoliberal economic and political policies, typically promoted as "development."

Thus this chapter intends to provincialize the North (Chakrabarty, 2000). Yet it does so in ways that differ from the older postcolonial theory that was focused primarily on the British colonization of India and, to a lesser extent, Africa, beginning in the mid-eighteenth century, with occasional attention also to French colonialism (Anderson, 2002; Anderson & Adams, 2008; Harding, 2011; McNeil, 2005; Seth, 2009; Tambe, 2017).

We can begin to identify the differences that motivate the decolonial theorists by asking what could be the consequences for philosophies of science of the fact that the familiar postcolonial theory, on the one hand, and the decolonial accounts of Spanish and Portuguese colonialism in the Americas, on the other hand, engage with different histories, geographies, peoples,

[7] This section expands brief and differently focused earlier accounts in Subramaniam et al., 2016: 11–14; Harding, 2016: 1066–67; and Harding, 2017.

and cultures? And that influential Western histories and philosophies of science tend to ignore both forms of anti-colonial accounts? The philosophies are supposed to be grounded in best cases of scientific practices in the past. Yet the particularities of the development of distinctive kinds of scientific and technical expertise before and during the era of colonization of the Americas virtually never figure in such thinking. Consequently, how useful, let alone universally valid, could such philosophies be?

Different Chronologies: A Different Modernity and its Scientific Revolution?

Colonial relations in the Americas began in 1492, which was more than two centuries before the British began to establish their colonies in India and the Middle East (Brotherston, 2008; Coronil, 2008; Dussel, 1995; Marques, 2014; Mignolo, 2011; Morana, Dussel, & Jauregui 2008; Mendoza, 2015).[8] Thus, philosopher Enrique Dussel (1995: 9–10, 11) insists that "Modernity appears when Europe organizes the initial world-system and places itself at the center of world history over against a periphery equally constitutive of modernity." So modernity and Iberian colonialism coproduce and co-constitute each other. From this perspective, Amerindians, too, with their own extensive scientific and technical knowledge systems, played an important role in the origins of modernity.[9]

Since the creation of modern sciences and technologies are routinely conceptualized as the most important "motors" of modernization, attention to this earlier colonial era suggests the need

[8] Though, of course, the British began to establish colonies in North America shortly after Columbus arrived in the Caribbean. Yet colonial patterns in British North America were in significant respects different from the Spanish and Portuguese colonial practices in the Americas.

[9] The typical markers of modernity for conventional historians and sociologists – such as the separation from families/households of government, economic relations, moral training, and education, the creation of public vs. private spheres, and the emergence of the nuclear family – come later. But other distinctive features of modernity are created from just about the earliest moments of the encounter between the Spanish and Portuguese and the Amerindians.

for a different history of the causes and reasons for the Scientific Revolution. "Modernity" was to be the name of the new policies and image that Europeans fashioned for themselves, as they launched what would become a global empire. It was constituted to contrast with their perception of the conditions of the supposedly backward and primitive peoples that they had encountered in the Americas. Thus, the decolonial theorists challenge the chronology favored in United States and European history, and adopted also by many intellectuals in the periphery. They challenge the typical assumptions about the origins of modernity.

A second chronological difference is that formal independence from European rule began much earlier in the Spanish, Portuguese, and French colonies in the Americas than in the British colonies (with the exception of the US). Haiti gained independence from France in 1804, and the other colonies in the Americas achieved formal independence from Spain and Portugal by 1830. Yet just what "independence" meant in the Americas had to be invented (Pratt, 2008). Did it mean giving up Roman Catholicism, disavowing loyalty to the Vatican, and expelling the clerics? To what extent did it require relinquishing the class, gender, sexual, and racial hierarchies that the Iberians had introduced? How could social order be maintained without such hierarchies? Indeed, the nineteenth century provides a history of constant social experiment in attempts to define independence.

A third chronological difference focuses on when anti-colonial thinking developed in Latin America. There are two issues here. The new histories point out that 1492 is the starting date of anti-colonial thinking. The Amerindians whom the conquistador Herman Cortes encountered, as well as Nahua intellectuals in the early sixteenth century, clearly resisted both the idea and the reality of Iberian colonization (Brotherston, 2008; Todorov, 1984). Moreover, anti-colonial arguments by Nahua intellectuals had already appeared *in Spanish* in the Americas by 1538 and continued to be produced by those intellectuals.[10] It is important to note that in making such

[10] I thank Breny Mendoza for emphasizing the point to me.

claims, the decolonial theorists are not claiming Latin America to be an *exception* to the (British) postcolonialism earlier articulated, but rather "an attempt to elaborate on what Walter Mignolo and other scholars have called *colonial difference*, understanding by that the differential time-space where a particular region becomes connected to the world-system of colonial domination" (Escobar, 2010: 36).[11]

Yet the postcolonial theory that began to appear in the British empire after the Second World War preceded the development of the Latin American decolonial theory by several decades. The decolonial theorists always assert the importance of postcolonial insights for their own thinking. Howsoever one dates Latin American anti-colonial thinking, it has a different history from the familiar British postcolonial accounts. In addition to this contrast in how to date the origins of anti-colonial thinking, the decolonial theorists see the postcolonial legacy as problematic also in that it retains implicit underlying elements of an Anglo-American Eurocentric frame that the Latin Americans identify and reject (Morana, Dussel, & Jauregui, 2008: 5).

Thus, the standard chronologies of modernity, colonialism, and postcolonialism, as well as what should count as "international" and of the history of science "in Europe," are challenged by the decolonial accounts. What effects on the philosophy of science should such challenges have?

Different Geographies, Different Sciences

Colonization of the Americas required that the voyagers interact effectively with physical worlds different from those familiar to them. Yet they lacked valuable kinds of scientific and technical knowledge to do so. They needed an astronomy of the Southern hemisphere with which to navigate back to Europe across the South Atlantic. The cartography of the South Atlantic and of their environments in the Americas had to be created. They needed climatology, oceanography, and better engineering to secure the safe travels of the

[11] This is one of the several meanings of "colonial difference" that Mignolo proposes.

voyagers and their precious cargoes. In the Americas they needed knowledge of the unfamiliar flora and fauna that they encountered.

They also needed better geology and mining to enable them to extract the gold and silver that they found in Central America and Peru. I stress that it was "better" geology, mining, and engineering that they needed. By 1492 the Amerindians had developed sophisticated technical knowledge that the Iberians lacked. Of course, the Amerindians had been mining silver and gold for centuries. The Spanish expertise depended on the appropriation of the highly advanced scientific and technical skills that the Amerindians had already developed. In 1492, the Spaniards were behind the Amerindians in these kinds of knowledge.

Moreover, in 1492 the Amerindians had already exhibited other extraordinary engineering skills. Tenochtitlan, the Aztec capital (later Mexico City), was a floating city with causeways, sewage systems, and floating gardens. It "dazzled Hernan Cortes in 1519; it was bigger than Paris, Europe's greatest metropolis. The Spaniards gawped like hayseeds at the wide streets, ornately carved buildings, and markets bright with goods from hundreds of miles away. They had never before seen a city with botanical gardens, for the excellent reason that none existed in Europe" (Mann, 2002: 49).

What was the relevance of these new voyager sciences to the developments of modern science in Europe? Steven Harris (1998) has shown how three kinds of corporations with long-distance projects played a major role in creating those particular sciences, conventionally thought of as developed "in Europe." The European empires, the European trading companies (The British and Dutch West Indian Trading Companies, the Hudson Bay Company, and others) and the Jesuits struggled to protect their ships, people, and valuable cargoes from the dangers of ocean voyages and exposure to the distinctive climate, oceanographic, and health hazards at sea and in foreign lands. They were central to the creation of *modern* European sciences in ways unacknowledged in the standard histories.[12] Without

[12] Harris also emphasizes the importance of what we can call the precursors of modern social sciences. Much of his data comes from the archived physical surveys –

diminishing the importance of Galileo, Descartes, Newton, and their disenchantment and mathematization of nature's order, the decolonial theorists argue that scholars should also recognize how Europe's colonial projects in the Americas turned a huge part of the globe into a laboratory for European sciences.[13]

Several science and technology research and teaching academies were established in both Iberia and the Americas in the sixteenth century. These were focused on training future voyagers in the new challenges of navigation, cartography, oceanography, climatology, mining, and engineering. And merchants and bureaucrats had their own interests in the success of the voyagers.

Thus, the origins of the Scientific Revolution are broader than assumed in conventional philosophies and histories of science. The new geographies of science, as well as the new histories, would seem to call for changes in standard Northern philosophies of science.

1492: Different Social Worlds of the Europeans

Both the Iberian colonizers and the colonized lived in social worlds different from those that shaped the coloniality of the British empire. The discovery of new lands across the Atlantic appeared as a solution to some of Europe's most vexing social problems. Europeans welcomed the thought of being able to leave behind the economic and political problems that they were encountering in the continual religious and political wars, as well as in

questionnaires – about conditions ship captains encountered that were requested by the funders of these voyages of the ship captains. Particularly amusing is his account of the fate of such physical survey instruments. As inspected in their archives today, it is clear that evidently they were used to light pipes, to wipe up liquor spills, and to serve as toilet paper: the perils of qualitative research! This account should be set next to Todorov's (1984) account of what we can call Cortes' "qualitative research" with the indigenes he encountered as he sought to figure out how to manage to his advantage the unfamiliar environment and peoples he would encounter in his march across Mexico to conquer the Nahua. The modern social sciences also have origins in 1492 and subsequent experiences in the Americas.

13 See Berman (1981) for an account of the centrality to the emergence of modern science of its insistence on a purely material world – a disenchanted world.

overpopulation and famines. So the thrill of discovering a new world was enhanced by the envisioned possibility of European expansion into this unexpected part of the globe. The Europeans could start over in the "Garden of Eden," as they persistently characterized it, that had been discovered across the Atlantic.

The Europeans' exerted hideous violence in dealing with the Amerindians whom they encountered (Connell, 2015; Lugones, 2008). This policy was modeled on how they had dealt with the Moors in Europe. That is, they imported to the Americas new forms of well-practiced, brutal "crusades," here against the ("infidel") indigenes instead of against Muslims. Of course all conquests are brutal and violent for the conquered.[14] Yet it is important not to forget that the discovery of America was not the beginning of a wonderful new experience for the existing residents of these lands.

1491: Who were these Amerindians that the Europeans Encountered?

It is only relatively recently that demographic, historical, and environmental research undermined long-held assumptions both that the Americas were only sparsely inhabited in 1491, and also that those inhabitants were at a much more primitive stage of social and scientific development than were Europeans (e.g., Deneven, 1992; Mann, 2002, 2005). The estimations of the number of residents in 1491 vary from 12 to 120 million: this is a contentious issue. However, there is agreement that some of the world's largest cities at the time were in the Americas, and that they were in 1491 richer and freer than most other parts of the world. They also were diverse.

What about their scientific development? Was nature in the Americas untouched by humans before 1492? No; this "pristine myth" assumed by the Europeans is no longer credible (Denevan, 1992; Mann, 2005). The Amerindians transformed their landscapes. They had extensive agriculture, and used controlled fires

[14] Think of Belgians in the Congo, the British in Africa, the English in North America, and others.

to clear the land and increase the nutrients in the soil. They established preserves of deer, bison, and elk. Indeed, some observers have referred to Amazonia as a cultural artifact. Visible still today are the residues of orchards (Mann, 2002: 50), and of the "living earth" developed by the Amerindians. This was the dark earth that could "perpetuate – and even *regenerate* itself, – thus behaving more like a living 'super'-organism than an inert material" (Mann, 2002: 52; Hecht, 2004).

In ecologists' terms, Amerindians were the keystone species of the Amazonian ecosystem. The decimation of the Indians by plagues and by the conquistadors resulted in "a population explosion in the species that the Indians had kept down by hunting . . .. [In the North B]uffalo vastly extended their range. Their numbers more than sextupled. The same occurred with elk and mule deer . . .. Passenger pigeons may be another example" (Mann, 2002: 53). Moreover forest rapidly took over the land that the Indians had farmed (Deneven, 1992: 372–73).

By 1620, more than 125 years after European contact, the Americas did appear almost empty. Over 90 percent of the Amerindian population had been eliminated thanks primarily to pandemics, but also to the persistent efforts of the colonialists to kill them and take possession of their lands, and to the superior armaments the colonists could bring to this task. Pratt (2008) argues that the causes of the high mortality produced by the pandemics have been misrepresented in the typical Eurocentric histories. The pandemics would not have created such high mortality figures if the Iberians had not systematically captured the Amerindians for forced labor, and then overworked, underfed, and refused to provide medical care for them, decimated their provisioning environments, and otherwise treated the Amerindians as disposable slaves. Nor were the Amerindians the only victims of pandemics; European animals also brought diseases that killed many species in the Americas, including those crucial to the flourishing of the Amerindians.

The Americas were a crucial source of agricultural resources for Europe. Today, more than half of the globe's agricultural crops originated in the Americas, including tomatoes, potatoes, and maize. When the colonizers brought such crops back to Europe, they created an Old World population boom. One could reasonably consider the skilled and abundant agriculture of the Americas to be among the significant enablers of the Industrial Revolution. Varieties of potatoes had been developed in the Americas that could thrive in every ecological niche of Europe except the Mediterranean. This created an inexpensive and nutritious food supply for poor Europeans who were the workers in the new factories (Weatherford, 1988).

What did the Amerindians know in 1491 in addition to their agricultural and environmental knowledge? The Nahua, Incas, and Maya had produced highly sophisticated knowledge systems (knowledge that we would refer to as scientific and technical) – systems that in 1491 were superior in many respects to those of the Europeans. For example, they had invented *quipus*, belts from which hung knotted ropes that permitted traveling tax collectors to record the populations of various regions and the particular amounts of tax that they owed the Inca empire. They effectively mined silver. They drained the swamps and then engineered the hanging gardens of the city that became Mexico City. And there was more. Yet the "invading Europeans heaped up and burned books in New Spain and *quipus* in Peru, ... whole 'libraries' of both, to use the Spaniards' own term" (Brotherston, 2008: 25). The Europeans could not understand what was in them, and saw them as a product of dangerous infidel practices. Brotherston points out that even today, "in the projection of a scarcely articulate 'other,' there has been a general reluctance to admit or recall Europe's own severe intellectual limitation (in its own terms) at the time of the first invasions" (Brotherston, 2008: 24). Anibal Quijano (2010) writes that even today conventional epistemologies of modernity deny that Latin Americans can be subjects of knowledge: they are permitted only to be objects of Northern subjectivity – that is as data for Northern theory.

Brotherston describes how Nahua scientific knowledge was superior to the Europeans' in a number of ways (2008: 24). For example, European chronology and astronomy were clearly more primitive that those of the Nahua. The Europeans had no way to project dates far into the past, that is into B.C. eras, and no precise way to measure a solar year. The Nahua could do both. Moreover, the Aztecs (one of the three Nahua groups) learned that they could locate their own calendars on the European Christian calendars; Aztec events could be celebrated through Christian events, unbeknown to the Europeans. The Europeans were also unable to detect the Aztec critical and satirical commentary embedded in the images of the combined calendars which depicted the Europeans as ignorant and comical figures.

Such a focus on the distinctive history, geography, and peoples of Spanish and Portuguese colonization of the Americas, here only briefly indicated, has produced a huge outpouring of new understandings about the intellectual and political worlds – the realities – of both the Americas and Europe in the sixteenth century and subsequently. The peoples of the Americas, their actual conditions, the ways they conceptualized their worlds and encounters with Europeans, their cultures, fears, and desires, become part of the causes of the emergence of modernity in Europe, and vice versa, in ways not otherwise visible.

What role do gender, sexuality, and race play in this new history of science?

GENDER, SEXUALITY, RACE, AND COLONIALISM: ENTANGLEMENTS

The way that the Europeans started over in the Americas was to introduce to the world extremely rigid and hierarchical classifications of the Amerindians that they encountered, the peasants who worked the land, and the Africans that they subsequently imported as slave labor for their plantations (Lugones, 2008, 2010; Mignolo, 2011, Quijano, 1992; Walsh, 2016). They did so by introducing practices that inextricably entangled racial hierarchies with similarly more rigid hierarchies of sexuality and gender than had already existed. These were subsequently exported back to Europe by the colonizers. In other words, on both sides of the Atlantic, racial, gender, and sexuality hierarchies existed before 1492 but rarely were they in as rigid and severely hierarchical forms as those initiated by the Iberians first in the Americas and then instituted back in their European homelands. Such hierarchies were strengthened through their passages back and forth across the Atlantic.[15]

Elsewhere I have identified a number of issues shared in postcolonial studies and in the feminist literature (see Harding, 2016). Yet while the postcolonial and feminist projects have shared important goals, their concerns have also diverged in significant respects.[16] First, with important exceptions (e.g., Spivak, 1988), the postcolonial authors, like the mainstream authors whom they criticize, implicitly presume that if no women are in sight, then no significant gender issues arise. Thus, they do not raise gender issues about the major figures of colonial or postcolonial history. That is, it is mostly men who have been the conquistadors, explorers, missionaries, merchants, indigenous rulers, as well as scientists, historians, anthropologists and their informants, the theorists of modernity and development, and also the leading scholars who contribute to postcolonial science and technology studies. The postcolonial authors tend implicitly to assume that men's interactions with each other are not part of gender relations. One could say that they have too limited an understanding of "the social."

15 See Harding & Mendoza (forthcoming) for an account of the illuminating arguments on this topic by today's Latin American feminists.

16 See Harding (2009) and the "Introduction" to Harding (2011).

Second, postcolonial authors tend to treat as "real science" only the narrow range of activities and thinking that have been the favored focus of Northern historians, philosophers, and social studies of science. They cannot see that many of women's conventional activities also produce valuable empirical knowledge. In this sense, they can seem co-opted by Northern concepts of what counts as science. And third, in virtue of ignoring women and their social activities, these authors cannot see women, and especially not colonized women, as agents of social change.

There is a vast and deep historical literature that has described sexuality, gender, and family forms both before and after colonization.[17] Just a few of its concerns can be noted here. One focus in this literature identifies the more fluid and transient sexualities characteristic of some of the Amerindian cultures. A person's sexuality could change over the course of one's life, and it was not constrained by the gender binaries that normatively constrain modern Western sexual practices. Another focus has been with how the control of colonized women's bodies – their sexuality and their labor – has always been crucial to the success of colonial projects (see Sara Ahmed and Jack Halberstam in this volume, who both argue this in different ways). Maria Lugones (2008), Catherine Walsh (2016), Freya Schiwy (2010), and others have explored the especially rigid, hierarchical, and entangled gender, sexuality, and racial hierarchies that the Iberians introduced to the Americas. As is characteristic of all conquests, the colonizers had to dehumanize the peoples conquered in the Americas in order to justify to themselves the violence of the colonialism they enacted. Destruction of distinctive cultural family forms of colonized groups reduces the colonized to nonhumans, to mere animals with sex differences, in the colonizers' eyes – but not in the eyes of the colonized (Lugones, 2008). Gaining control of the family relations of the colonized has always been a crucial and difficult task for colonizers.

[17] This literature is too vast and complex to review here. However, an excellent brief overview of it can be found in Terraciano and Sousa (2011: 35–37).

Medical and health histories here also focus on issues about women, gender, and race. For example, historian Nancy Stepan has produced extensive studies of the race and gender assumptions that directed eugenics in Latin America between the two World Wars.[18] And Tania Perez-Butros et al. (2014) analyze the complex caring practices of women scientists in Colombia today who are engaged in forensic genetics.

Decolonial men's studies, for example Harris (2005), points out that the Jesuits tended to reproduce their familiar European gendered domestic relations in the missions they established in the Americas. There they produced the highly profitable apothecaries that they sold around the globe. Yet it was the Amerindian male servants who in fact collected and analyzed the data about the indigenous plants, as part of the women's work – cooking, cleaning, and so on – that they were assigned in the missions. The priests were the official authors of such apothecaries, but the actual scientists were Amerindian men servants. Escobar (1995), Felski (1995), Scott (1995), and Visvanathan et al. (2011) write about the gendered, sexualized, and racialized assumptions of modernization theory and also its post-Second World War, Third World development theory, policies, and practices. Modernity itself has always meant that men should leave behind them the household and whatever is associated with it, such as support for reproduction and women's work, as they go off for more manly work in urban centers.

Harding (2004) and Park (1993) focus on the research methodology necessary to produce "science from below," that is, sciences that can produce the kinds of knowledge that exploited groups need and want. Feminist standpoint methodology emerged from post-Marxian research projects. It exemplifies a particular focus of the participatory action research that emerged in the US and around the globe after the Second World War. It argues that knowledge that is *for* women, instead

[18] See Stepan (1986, 1991). Rodriguez (2011) introduces a special issue of the *Hispanic American Historical Review* focused on her work, with a response by Stepan.

of for the dominant social institutions that exploit women, must start off its projects not from the dominant epistemic, ontological, and political frameworks, but rather from outside them – that is, from the issues important to women in their daily lives. The MCD theorists take Gloria Anzaldua's (1987) "borderlands" epistemology and ontology as articulating a similar route to anti-colonial, anti-modernity knowledge production. Mignolo names it the "colonial difference."[19] Thus standpoint methodology/epistemology is a kind of organic project. Whether or not that label is claimed, it tends to emerge whenever a new group steps on the stage of history and says "things look different from the perspective of our lives."

Moreover, several of the main MCD authors have made extensive efforts to rethink dominant Northern disciplinary assumptions from women's point of view in the context of Latin American coloniality. In addition to those mentioned above that are focused specifically on sexuality and gender/racial hierarchy, perhaps the most extensive such approach has been that of Harcourt and Escobar (2002) in *Women and the Politics of Place.*[20] Here they rethink what political economy looks like when it starts off its projects from subaltern women's needs in the particular places they occupy. This is a new form of politics, they argue, and it produces new kinds of political subjects. It also produces tensions between its commitment to place-based origins of knowledge and critics who see such approaches as re-colonizing knowledge production in terms of its geographical specificity.

Finally, it should be mentioned that there has been a huge expansion recently in global participation in conferences and workshops focused on MCD issues, and especially on feminist concerns. A conference at Penn State in May 2018, "Toward Decolonial Feminisms," brought together ninety presentations on issues stimulated by philosopher Maria Lugones' work. Moreover,

[19] Mignolo in particular develops the concept in multiple directions throughout his writings of the last decade. See, for example, the index entries for the term in his 2000 and 2011 works, and in Mignolo and Escobar (2010). See also Mignolo & Walsh (2018).

[20] See also Escobar's "Worlds and Knowledges Otherwise," in Mignolo & Escobar 2010, especially the section on "Rethinking the Economy, in the Concrete," pp. 52–54.

in recent years, a group of the Latin American MCD theorists have been producing annual, week-long workshops in several cities. Each workshop has a different topic. Feminist scholars figure prominently in many of these, including a significant number of men among the feminist faculty. One of several in 2018–2019, in Mexico City April 15–19, 2019 was completely focused on feminist issues: "Pensamientos y Feminismos Descoloniales Latinoamericanos" ["Latin American Decolonial Thoughts and Feminisms"]. Seventeen distinguished faculty were featured.[21]

CONCLUSION: ANOTHER PHILOSOPHY OF SCIENCE?

MCD intends to organize the distinctiveness of Latin American needs and desires into a non-modern philosophy of science: philosophy done "otherwise," as the issue is often phrased. Here I identify an important feature of MCD that grounds this work, and yet that generates productive tensions.[22] While this feature is indeed developed distinctively in the Latin American work, it also converges with emerging tendencies in peripheral thinking from around the globe, as well as in Northern work.

As indicated earlier, MCD calls for taking research issues not from the high theory of elite groups, but rather from the concerns

[21] Two interesting issues that cannot be pursued here are the following. What were the causes and reasons for the neglect of these histories of Latin American knowledge production? And what are the consequences today for attempts in Latin America to create post-positivist philosophies of science of the rise and fall of a distinctive Latin American positivism in the nineteenth century? (Harding, 2018.)

[22] In an earlier essay (Harding, 2016) I proposed four kinds of productive tensions that the MCD accounts produced. One focused on the fact that while these theorists proposed that their work was guided by "rear guard" theory, these theorists themselves mostly held highly privileged university positions. A second tension was that one could understand them to be "reinventing positivism" yet again in light of their commitment to systematic knowledge production focused on creating social progress. A third tension was their commitment to working outside the powerful binaries of Enlightenment modernity, and yet needing to invoke such binaries in defining their own projects. A related fourth tension was between their commitment to creating knowledge that starts off outside the conceptual frameworks of modernity, and yet their need to deal effectively with the powerful institutions and practices of modernization theory's development projects.

of the new social movements that represent the needs and desires of heretofore marginalized and exploited groups (e.g., Mignolo and Escobar, 2010; Santos, 2006, 2007, 2014). Here MCD takes up the organic standpoint methodology that had emerged from the social justice movements of the 1960s and 1970s. Can such a way of organizing research escape the "imperial eyes" that have tended to be the fate of modern Western sciences, no matter how well-intentioned the scientists and their funders (Pratt, 2008)?

Such questions focus on modern Western sciences' claim that they are "just getting the facts," and thus are free of economic, political, and social values and interests, as Pratt points out. In getting the facts, modern Western sciences rename the elements of the worlds that they observe, and organize those worlds through their own gendered, sexual, and racialized categories. If one examines who is interested in the particular facts that they produce, and what are the different interests of other groups that have not been pursued in the sciences, it becomes clear that mainstream sciences, frequently unintentionally, all too often pave the way for the forms of exploitation of nature and peoples characteristic of the activities of dominant groups.

Taking responsibility for "rear guard" research, as Santos (2006) puts the issue, will require constant reenergizing and redirecting of the progressive tendencies of such research. Much more can be said on this issue, but that must be a topic for another context.

To conclude, the complex array of resources provided by MCD writings open up valuable "lines of flight" (Marques, 2014) for possible new directions in post-positivist philosophies of science both south and north of the Rio Bravo/Rio Grande. As such, these philosophies must be anti-racist, non-heterosexist and post-androcentric.

REFERENCES

Anderson, Warwick. 2002. Postcolonial Technoscience. *Social Studies of Science*, **32** (Special issue), 643–58.

Anderson, Warwick and Adams, Vinceanne. 2008. Pramoedya's Chickens: Postcolonial Studies of Technoscience. In Edward J. Hackett et al., ed., *The Handbook of Science and Technology Studies*, 3rd ed. Cambridge, MA: MIT Press, pp. 181–207.

Anzaldua, Gloria. 1987. *Borderlands/La Frontera.* San Francisco, CA: Spinsters/Aunt Lute.

Brotherston, Gordon, 2008. America and the Colonizer Question: Two Formative Statements from Early Mexico. In Mabel Morana, Enrique Dussel, and Carlos A. Jauregui, eds., *Coloniality at Large: Latin America and the Postcolonial Debate.* Durham, NC: Duke University Press, pp. 23–42.

Chakrabarty, Dipesh. 2000. *Provincializing Europe: Postcolonial Thought and Historical Difference.* Princeton, NJ: Princeton University Press.

Connell, Raewyn. 2015. Meeting at the Edge of Fear: Theory on a World Scale. *Feminist Theory,* **16**(1), 49–66.

Coronil, Fernando. 2008. Elephants in the Americas? Latin American Postcolonial Studies and Global Decolonization. In Mabel Morana, Enrique Dussel, and Carlos A. Jauregui, eds., *Coloniality at Large.* Durham, NC: Duke University Press, pp. 396–416.

de la Cadena, Marisol. 2010. Indigenous Cosmopolitics in the Andes: Conceptual Reflections beyond "Politics." *Cultural Anthropology,* **25**(2), 334–70.

Denevan, William M. 1992. The Pristine Myth: The Landscape of the Americas in 1492. *Annals of the Association of American Geographers,* **82**(3), 369–85.

Dussel, Enrique. 1995. *The Invention of the Americas: Eclipse of "the Other" and the Myth of Modernity.* Michael D. Barber, trans. New York: Continuum.

Escobar, Arturo, 1995, *Encountering Development: The Making and Unmaking of the Third World.* Princeton, NJ: Princeton University Press.

2004. Beyond the Third World: Imperial Globality, Global Coloniality and Anti-Globalisation Social Movements. *Third World Quarterly,* **25**(1), 207–30.

2010. Worlds and Knowledges Otherwise: The Latin American Modernity/Coloniality Research Program. In Walter D. Mignolo and Arturo Escobar, eds., *Globalization and the Decolonial Option.* New York: Routledge, pp. 33–64.

Felski, Rita. 1995. *The Gender of Modernity.* Cambridge, MA: Harvard University Press.

Grosfoguel, Ramon, Maldonado-Torres, Nelson, and Saldivar, Jose David, eds., 2005. *Latino/as in the World System: Decolonization Struggles in the 21st Century U.S. Empire.* Boulder, CO: Paradigm.

Harcourt, Wendy and Escobar, Arturo. 2002. Women and the Politics of Place. *Development,* 45, 7–14. https://link.springer.com/article/10.1057/palgrave.development.1110308.

Harding, Sandra G., ed. 2004. *The Feminist Standpoint Theory Reader.* New York: Routledge.

2009. Postcolonial and Feminist Philosophies of Science and Technology: Convergences and Dissonances. *Postcolonial Studies,* **12**(4), 401–22.

ed. 2011. *The Postcolonial Science and Technology Studies Reader.* Durham, NC: Duke University Press.

2016. Latin American Decolonial Social Studies of Scientific Knowledge: Alliances and Tensions. *Science, Technology and Human Development,* **41**(6), 1063–87.

2017. Latin American Decolonial Studies: Feminist Issues. *Feminist Studies,* **43**(3), 624–36.

2018. State of the Field: Latin American Decolonial Philosophies of Science. *Studies in History and Philosophy of Science*, **78**, 48–63. https://doi.org/10.1016/j.shpsa.2018.10.001.

Harding, Sandra and Mendoza, Breny. 2020. Latin American Decolonial Feminist Philosophy of Knowledge Production. In Sharon Crasnow and Kristen Intemann, eds. *The Routledge Handbook of Feminist Philosophy of Science*, New York: Routledge.

Harris, Steven J. 1998. Long-Distance Corporations and the Geography of Natural Knowledge. *Configurations*, **6**(2).

2005. Jesuit Scientific Activity in the Overseas Missions, 1540–1773. *Isis*, **96**, 71–79.

Hecht, Susanna. 2004. Indigenous Soil Management and the Creation of Amazonian Dark Earths: Implications of Kayapo Practices. In Johannes Lehman, ed., *Amazonian Dark Earths: Origins, Properties and Management of Fertile Soils in the Humid Tropics*. Dordrecht: Kluwer, pp. 355–73.

Lange-Churion, Pedro and Mendieta, Eduardo, eds. 2001. *Latin American Postmodernity*. Amherst, NY: Humanity Books.

Lugones, Maria. 2008. The Coloniality of Gender. *Worlds and Knowledges Otherwise*, Spring, 1–17.

2010. Toward a Decolonial Feminism. *Hypatia*, **25**(4), 742–59.

Maldonado-Torres, Nelson. 2012. Epistemology, Ethics, and the Time/Space of Decolonization: Perspectives from the Caribbean and the Latina/o Americas. In Ada Maria Isasi-Diaz and Eduardo Mendieta, eds., *Decolonizing Epistemologies*. New York: Fordham University Press, pp. 193–206.

Mann, Charles C. 2002. 1491. *AtlanticMonthly*, March, 41–53.

2005. *1491: New Revelations of the Americas Before Colombus*. New York: Knopf.

Marques, Ivan da Costa. 2014. Ontological Politics and Latin American Local Knowledges. In Eden Medina, Ivan da Costa Marques, and Christina Holmes, eds., *Beyond Imported Magic*. Cambridge, MA: MIT Press, pp. 85–109.

McNeil, Maureen. 2005. Introduction: Postcolonial Technoscience. *Science as Culture*, **14**(2), 105–12.

Mendoza, Breny. 2015. Coloniality of Gender and Power: From Postcoloniality to Decoloniality. In Lisa Disch and Mary Hawkesworth, eds., *The Oxford Handbook of Feminist Theory*. Oxford: Oxford University Press.

Mignolo, Walter. 2000. Introduction: From Cross-Genealogies and Subaltern Knowledges to Nepantla. *Nepantla: Views from South*, 1(1), 1–8. https://muse.jhu.edu/article/23878/summary?casa_token=xm8mnRFTMtcAAAAA:9-zOOZnuGqH4-vTZuaL0UYlioRhxN6Q1pjEzANyNX0zNjh-kAvNj6u3SyXxNCc3-GLuLTrc5kQ.

2011. *The Darker Side of Western Modernity: Global Futures, Decolonial Options*. Durham, NC: Duke University Press.

Mignolo, Walter D. and Escobar, Arturo, eds. 2010. *Globalization and the Decolonial Option*. New York: Routledge.

Mignolo, Walter D. and Walsh, Catherine E. 2018. *On Decoloniality Concepts, Analytics, Praxis*. Durham, NC: Duke University Press. www.dukeupress.edu/on-decoloniality.

Morana, Mabel, Dussel, Enrique, and Jauregui, Carlos A., eds. 2008. *Coloniality at Large: Latin America and the Postcolonial Debate.* Durham, NC: Duke University Press.

Nieto Olarte, Mauricio. 2016. The European Comprehension of the World: Early Modern Science and Eurocentrism. In Hebe Vessuri and Michael Kuhn, ed., *The Global Social Science World: Under and Beyond European Universalism.* Stuttgart: Ibiden Verlag, pp. 97–136.

Park, Peter 1993. What is Participatory Research? A Theoretical and Methodological Perspective. In Peter Park et al., *Voices of Change: Participatory Research in the United States and Canada.* Westport, CT: Bergin and Garvey.

Perez-Butros, Tania, Olarte Sierra, Maria Fernanda, and Castillo, Adriana Diaz del. 2014. In Eden Medina, Ivan da Costa Marques, Christina Holmes, eds., *Working with Care: Narratives of Invisible Women Scientists Practicing Forensic Genetics in Colombia. Beyond Imported Magic.* Cambridge, MA: MIT Press.

Pratt, Mary Louise. 2008. *Imperial Eyes,* 2nd ed. New York: Routledge.

Quijano, Anibal. 1992/2007. Coloniality and Modernity/Rationality. *Cultural Studies,* **21**(2–3), 22–32.

2010. La crisis del horizonte de sentido colonial/moderno/eurocentrado. *Revista Casa de las Américas,* 259–60 (abril–septiembre), 32–42.

Rodriguez, Ileana, ed. 2001. *The Latin American Subaltern Studies Reader.* Durham, NC: Duke University Press.

Rodriguez, Julia. 2011. A Complex Fabric: Intersecting Histories of Race, Gender, and Science in Latin America. *Hispanic American Historical Review,* **91**(3), 409–29.

Santos, Boaventura de Sousa, 2006. *The Rise of the Global Left: The World Social Forum and Beyond.* New York: Zed Books.

ed. 2007. *Another Knowledge is Possible: Beyond Northern Epistemologies.* New York: Verso.

2014. *Epistemologies of the South: Justice Against Epistemicide.* Boulder, CO: Paradigm Publishers.

Schiwy, Freya. 2010. Decolonization and the Question of Subjectivity: Gender, Race, and Binary Thinking. In Walter D. Mignolo and Arturo Escobar, eds., *Globalization and the Decolonial Option.* New York: Routledge, pp. 271–94.

Scott, Catherine V. 1995. *Gender and Development: Rethinking Modernization and Dependency Theory.* Boulder, CO: Lynne Reinner.

Seth, Suman, ed. 2009. Special Issue: Science, Colonialism, Postcolonialism. *Postcolonial Studies,* **12**(4).

Spivak, Gayatri. 1988. Can the Subaltern Speak? In C. Nelson and L. Grossberg, eds., *Marxism and the Interpretation of Culture.* Urbana, IL: University of Illinois Press, pp. 271–313.

Stepan, Nancy Leys. 1986. Race and Gender: The Role of Analogy in Science. *Isis,* **77**(2), 261–77.

1991. *The Hour of Eugenics: Race, Gender, and Nation in Latin America.* Ithaca, NY: Cornell University Press.

Subramaniam, Banu et al. 2016. Feminism, Postcolonialism, Technoscience. In Ulrike Felt et al., eds., *Handbook of Science and Technology Studies*, 4th ed. Cambridge, MA: MIT Press, pp. 407–35.

Tambe, Ashwini, ed. 2017. Decolonial and Postcolonial Approaches: A Dialogue. *Feminist Studies*, **43**(3), 503–691.

Terraciano, Kevin and Sousa, Lisa. 2011. Historiography of New Spain. In Jose C. Moya, ed., *The Oxford Handbook of Latin American History*. Oxford: Oxford University Press, pp. 25–64.

Todorov, Tzvetan, 1984. *The Conquest of America.* Richard Howard, trans. New York: Harper and Row.

Visvanathan et al., eds. 2011. *The Women, Gender and Development Reader*. New York: Zed.

Walsh, Catherine. 2010. Development as Buen Vivir: Institutional Arrangements and (De)Colonial Entanglements. *Development*, 53(1), 15–21.

2016. On Gender and its Otherwise. In Wendy Harcourt, ed., *The Palgrave Handbook on Gender and Development: Critical Engagements in Feminist Theory and Practice.* London: Palgrave, pp. 34–47.

Weatherford, Jack MacIver. 1988. *Indian Givers: What the Native Americans Gave to the World.* New York: Crown.

CHAPTER 5

Posthuman Feminism and Gender Methodology

Rosi Braidotti

GENDER AS A CARTOGRAPHIC TOOLBOX

GENDER IS A META-METHODOLOGICAL TOOL, A NAVIGAtional instrument – gender is as gender does. In this chapter I apply gender as methodology to provide a cartography of the intersections between feminism and the posthuman predicament by arguing that feminism is not only a humanism; it needs to overcome anthropocentrism and embrace non-human life and entities.

A cartographic method aims to draw some meta-patterns in contemporary knowledge production processes, using gender as the navigational tool. In this chapter the field I want to survey is the posthuman convergence of posthumanism on the one hand and post-anthropocentrism on the other. Both these critical lines have established traditions within feminist and gender studies, but they refer to distinct genealogies and often result in different politics. Posthumanism focuses on the critique of the humanist ideal of 'Man' as the universal representative of the human, while anti-anthropocentrism criticizes species hierarchy and pleas for environmental justice. The term 'posthuman feminism' emerges at the confluence of these critical traditions and points to multiple ways out of dominant understandings of the human. The genealogical timelines of the posthuman are neither linear nor sequential, but mark the emergence of a new type of discourse that is not a synthesis or culmination of these two strands of critical thought, but a qualitative leap in new and more complex directions. The posthuman, therefore, is not a term that refers to a futuristic, let alone utopian dimension, but is rather an indicator of our present historical condition.

A cartography is a materialist method that combines the analysis of texts and theoretical representations with that of concrete factors such as capital, social structures and institutions (Braidotti, 2011b, 2013; 2019). It is therefore a situated – that is, historical and site-specific – analysis of the emergence of discursive and institutional instances that shape processes of subject formation and the social regulation of living subjects. Gender-driven critical cartographies express the experience and insights of marginalized subjects, the ways in which they both speak truth to power and document what they already know through the experience of social and symbolic exclusion. Cartographies are collective, crowd-sourced exercises in assessing both the documents (discursive production) and the monuments (material structures) that construct our present conditions. Composing and negotiating with others a gender-driven critical cartography – politically infused and theoretically framed – is a way of reaching an adequate understanding of the negative conditions of our historicity.

The task of providing an adequate account of one's locations and experiences and to explore their consequences in terms of knowledge production also constitutes the core of the feminist method of the politics of locations. It is a materially grounded empirical method that takes gender as the indicator of embodied and embedded understandings of the knowing subjects. The primary location for any gender analysis is the body, not as a biological given, nor as a mere social construction, but rather as an ontological site of becoming. Intersectionally positioned across multiple axes – sexuality, gender, age, class, race, ethnicity, able-bodiedness – the body is never one unitary entity. It is rather a field of intersecting forces, better understood in terms of carnal materialism, or embodied empiricism.

Adriene Rich coined the term politics of locations (1987, 2001) as a testimonial to the deep wisdom generated on the margins of patriarchal culture. The term received a thorough scientific reexamination as feminist epistemology entered the academic realm, resulting in 'standpoint theory' (Harding, 1986, 1991, 1993; Hartsock, 1987). This is a materialist approach that is situated and accountable, and hence immanent, intersectional in its practical application and knowledge-driven in that it grants epistemological privilege to the experiences and insights of marginal groups. It argues that there is greater objectivity on the margins than at the centre of social systems, because the marginal and oppressed have a more direct experience, and hence a more lucid perception, of how power works. Being less self-interested, the 'pedagogy of the oppressed', as Paulo Freire argues ([1970] 2005), is better placed to speak truth to power and therefore offers higher degrees of objectivity. Generated by feminist materialist and intersectional theories (Smith, 1978; Moraga & Anzaldua, 1981; Carby, 1982), the method expands to claim alternative ways of doing scientific research, notably by including the analysis of the racialized economy of science (Hill Collins, 1991; Harding, 1998). It also expresses a yearning for knowledge that cannot be contained within mainstream institutional frames (hooks, 1990).

After the poststructuralist intervention and the challenge to the unitary character of identities and the self-evidence of categories of thought such as objectivity, science and truth, the politics of locations becomes more formalized. It becomes consolidated into the epistemological practice of situated knowledges (Haraway, 1988), contingent foundations (Butler, 1991, 1993) and minor or nomadic becoming (Braidotti, 1991, 1994).

Gender cartographies are necessarily localized, situated and perspectivist because they account for specific historical and geopolitical conditions. As such, they express grounded complex singularities, not universal claims. To be situated and yet in process or transition may well sound like a contradiction, but it is one that is produced by the historical conditions of advanced, or 'cognitive' capitalism (Moulier Boutang, 2012). Thus, it is a way of locating the real-life subjects in time as well as space. A location is also an embedded and embodied memory, activated against the grain of the dominant representations of life and of living beings – the social imaginary – of capital-driven patriarchy. It is the memory of events that may not have happened to us directly, but which we forgot to forget. For gender theorists and critical feminist thinkers, it is mostly the echo of the pain of others. Something like a resonance keeps on recurring, which forces feminists to think through, again, the eternal return of the pain of exclusion, violence and the injustice of disqualification. The politics of locations and its perspectivist epistemology therefore is anything but an instance of relativism or fragmentation. It is rather a robust neo-foundational materialist epistemology that reconstructs subjectivity along alternative lines.

A cartographic account works by selecting a few significant probes that authorize alternative knowledge claims and devise alternative figurations of the kind of knowing subjects that 'we' can become. Gender cartographies are navigational tools that enable us to trace a critical path through the complexities of the present. Figurations are projective anticipations that express the virtual potential of materially embedded and embodied locations, to actualize affirmative alternatives (Braidotti, 2011a, 2011b, 2013, 2019). They are neither loose metaphors nor mere statistical data. Figurations are rather materially embedded and embodied signposts that anticipate emergent patterns of dissonant subject formations, within creative processes of collective becoming.

The function of figurations consequently is to both support and operationalize the cartographic accounts of power to reflect and respect the complexity of the differential, materially embedded subject positions. As a feminist philosopher, I see my task as providing a survey of the gender meta-patterns emerging from these cartographies. In addition, I also want to help provide the ontological grounding for the subject formation that makes it possible to say '"we" are in *this* together' with a degree of ethical credibility, because we acknowledge from the start that 'we-are-not-One-and-the-Same'. Different scales and perspectives are built into these materially embedded feminist critical cartographies.

POSTHUMAN FEMINISM AS FIGURATION

As a creative figuration, gender cartographies of the posthuman aim at constituting new communities of activist knowledge-producers. As a theoretical and ethical proposition, the posthuman is an anticipation of what we aspire to become (through *potentia*): it is both the actual and the virtual. The temporality of this process is non-linear and generative, based on collaborative efforts at enacting affirmative ethics of becoming.

In other words, posthuman feminism as both empirically grounded and speculatively orientated aims at achieving adequate understanding of ongoing processes of dealing with the human, with focus on the dehumanized others and the non-human entities caught in the posthuman convergence. As a methodological tool, it enables us to track the emergence of conflicting discourses about the posthuman predicament and its possible outcomes, that combine familiar patterns of exclusion with grandiose projects of human enhancement through technological intervention. The tension between these poles – extinction and evolutionary leap, marginalization and enhancement – frames the political economy of posthuman times.

A gender-driven cartography enables a posthuman brand of feminism, generated at the intersection of critiques of humanism and of anthropocentrism by subjects who were excluded from full humanity to begin with. The viewpoints or perspectives of marginal subjects about posthuman transformations are seldom acknowledged or taken seriously by the policy-minded experts who now dominate the field of posthuman scholarship and institutional practice. I would like to redress that balance.

But the posthuman convergence also challenges feminist practice: to what extent does the convergence of posthumanistic and post-anthropocentric perspectives complicate the issues of ethical human agency and gendered political subjectivity? To even begin to address that question, we need to explore how 'we' are in *this* posthuman convergence together, while 'we' are not-One-and-the-Same. My argument is that the posthuman turn can result in a renewal of subjectivities and practices by situating gender analyses productively in the present. I defend the posthuman feminist subject accordingly as an ongoing collective experiment with what contemporary bodies are capable of becoming.

FEMINISM IS NOT ONLY A HUMANISM

The first building block of posthuman feminism is that the notion of humanism needs to be reviewed critically. The version of humanism that plays out in the posthuman convergence is the Enlightenment-based ideal of Man as 'the measure of all things'. This European humanist ideal positions the universalizing powers of a sovereign notion of 'reason' as the basic unit of reference to define what counts as human. Just as importantly, it also defines who is excluded from this dominant category. This hegemonic idea of 'Man' as coinciding with universal reason also claims exclusive rights to self-regulating rational judgment, moral self-improvement and enlightened governance for European subjects. The human thus defined is not so much a species as a marker of European culture, society, and its scientific and technological apparatus.

The humanist idea of the 'Man of reason' (Lloyd, 1984) positions the European subject as the motor of human evolution. Deleuze calls it 'the Majority subject' or the Molar centre of being (Deleuze & Guattari, 1987). Irigaray calls it 'the Same', or the hyper-inflated, falsely universal 'He' (Irigaray, 1985a, 1985b); Hill Collins calls to account the white and Eurocentric bias of this particular subject of humanistic knowledge (1991). Sylvia Wynter calls this 'Man1', ready to unfold into the imperialist European, or 'Man2' (2015).

This dominant vision positioned hierarchically all other classes of beings as the 'others', defined as the negative counterpart of the dominant human norm. They are actually 'other than', that is to say 'different from' Man and are perceived as 'worth less than' Man. Such epistemic and symbolic violence is no abstraction: it translates into ruthless violence for the real-life people who happen to coincide with categories of negative difference. They are the women and LBGTQ+ people (sexualized others), Black and indigenous people (racialized others) and the earth-entities (naturalized others). Humanism was used as a pretext to justify the deployment of rational epistemic and social violence against these 'others', whose social and symbolic existence was denied. This violent deletion made the 'others' disposable and unprotected, raising crucial issues of power, domination and exclusion.

The power of 'Man' as a hegemonic civilizational model was instrumental to the project of Western modernity and the colonial ideology of European expansion. 'White Man's burden' as a tool of imperialist and patriarchal governance assumed that Europe is not just a geo-political location, but rather a universal attribute of human consciousness that can transfer its quality to any suitable subjects, provided they comply with the required discipline. Europe as universal consciousness posits the power of reason as its distinctive characteristic and humanistic universalism as its particularity, in a relentless pursuit of hegemony (Weheliye, 2014). The de-selected others uphold by negation the power of the master-subject that Wynter defines as 'over-represented' (2015). This makes Eurocentrism a systemic trait, rather than a matter of attitude: it is a structural element of European masculine self-representation (Plumwood, 1993, 2003; Braidotti, 1994; Rose, 2004). As such, it is also crucial to the implementation of institutional and discursive 'methodological nationalism' (Beck, 2007), an exclusionary practice quite common in scientific humanism.

There is no underestimating, however, the historical ties that bind Western feminism, in its liberal struggle for equality or the socialist revolutionary variables, to Enlightenment-based humanism. Humanism is the backbone of the feminist emancipation project carried out alternatively in the name of classical liberalism and universal human rights, or in the name of socialist humanism and universal workers' rights. The Enlightenment project of emancipation channelled the aspirations to equality of the minorities, triggering revolutionary forms of activism among women, LBGTQ+, indigenous and colonized peoples, claiming equal rights. Criticism of the idea of a common, undifferentiated humanity and the claim to humanist universalism, were raised from the eighteenth century onwards, for instance by Olympe de Gouges ([1792] 2018) on behalf of women and Toussaint Louverture ([1791] 2011) on behalf of colonized people. They both reacted against the flagrant violation of the very human rights asserted in the French Universal Declaration of 1789, by criticizing the exclusion of women from civic and political rights, and the inhumane violence of slavery and colonial dispossession. All claims to universalism lose credibility when confronted by such abuses of power.

As the chosen targets of patriarchal violence, homo- and transphobia, colonial expropriations and mass killings, sexualized and racialized others have borne a disproportionate percentage of human suffering. We are not all human in the same way, and some categories of humans are definitely more mortal than others. Therefore, it is politically impossible not to support the ongoing efforts to extend human rights across all categories, in a more equitable manner. At the same time, however, it has also become urgent to question the alleged self-evidence of the idea of the human at work in the very humanist concept of universal human rights. I think that such an idea needs to be treated with critical care.

While the philosophical poststructuralist generation developed its own brand of anti-humanism, a radical feminist wave, anti-racist critical theory, environmental activists, disability rights advocates and LBGTQ+ theorists have questioned the scope, the founding principles and the achievements of European humanism and its role in the project of Western modernity and colonialism. These social and theoretical movements questioned the idea of the human that is implicit in the humanist ideal, which skilfully combines high standards of physical, intellectual and moral perfection with civilizational standard. Michel Foucault (1970) – a master of anti-humanism – linked this ideal to a sovereign notion of 'reason' that has framed everything European culture holds dear. The humanist 'Man' claims exclusive access to self-reflexive reason for the human species, thus making it uniquely capable of self-regulating rational judgement. These qualities allegedly qualify our species for the pursuit of both individual and collective self-improvement following scientific and moral criteria of perfectibility. The boundless faith in reason as the motor of human evolution ties in with the teleological prospect of the rational progress of humanity through science and technology.

The 'death of Man', announced by Foucault (1970) formalized the epistemological and political crisis of the humanistic habit of placing 'Man' at the centre of world history. Philosophical anti-humanism de-links the human from this universalistic posture, calling the humans to task, so to speak, on their concrete actions. Different and sharper analyses of power relations become possible, once the obstacle of the dominant subject's delusions of grandeur has been removed. A more adequate self-understanding emerges, once it has become clear that no one body is actually in charge of the course of historical progress. Thanks to feminist and postcolonial analyses, we have come to regard the human standard which was posited in the universal mode of 'Man of reason' as inadequate precisely because of its parochial partiality.

In response to this normative model, feminist, anti-racist and other social movements, notably the environmental and peace movements since the 1970s, developed their own variations of activist anti-humanism or radical, reparative or methodological neo-humanism. Their criticism is focused on two inter-related ideas: the self–other dialectics on the one hand and the notion of difference as pejoration on the other. Dialectically redefined as 'other than', difference is inscribed in a hierarchical scale that spells inferiority. Such epistemic violence acquires ruthless connotations for the real-life people who happen to coincide with categories of negative difference: women, native and earth others. They are the sexualized, racialized, and naturalized 'others', whose social and symbolic existence is disposable and unprotected. Because their history in Europe and elsewhere has been one of lethal exclusions and fatal disqualifications, these 'others' raise crucial issues of power, domination and exclusion. As Donna Haraway put it (1985), some differences are playful, but others are poles of world-historical systems of domination. Feminist epistemology is about knowing the difference.

The anti-humanist feminist generation embraced the concept of difference with the explicit aim of making it function differently. Irigaray's provocative question 'Equal to whom?' (1994) is emblematic of this switch away from homologation or reduction to a masculine standard of Sameness. Feminist critiques of abstract masculinity (Hartsock, 1987), hegemonic whiteness (hooks, 1981; Ware, 1992), colonial posture (Spivak, 1999) and hegemonic able-bodiedness (Braidotti & Roets, 2012), added further criticism. The allegedly universal ideal of 'Man' is brought back to his historically contingent roots and exposed as very much a male of the species: it is a *he* (Irigaray, 1985a, 1985b; Cixous & Clement, 1986). Class, race and gender never being too far apart from each other, in the intersectional mode pioneered by feminist race theory (Crenshaw, 1995; Brah, 1996). Indigenous feminists were especially vocal in pointing out the racialization of the categories of the excluded (Moraga & Anzaldua, 1981). Black feminists criticized the whiteness of feminist theory and academic feminism (Tuana, 2008; Alcoff & Porter, 1993; Wekker, 2016). This particular vision of the human as male and white is moreover assumed to be European, a full citizen of a recognized polity, head of a heterosexual family and legally responsible for its children

(Deleuze & Guattari, 1977, 1987). And further, 'He' is also able-bodied and handsome, according to the Renaissance parameters of Vitruvian symmetry and aesthetic perfection (Braidotti, 2013), as critical disability studies point out (Shildrick, 2012; Goodley, Lawthorn & Runswick, 2014). Feminists en bloc refuse to reduce feminism to homologation or integration into this Eurocentric masculine standard of Sameness and offer more situated and hence more accurate analyses of power relations upheld by the humanist paradigm.

Another relevant strand of neo-humanist discourse emerges within environmental activism, and it combines the critique of the epistemic and physical violence of modernity with that of European colonialism. The eco-feminist and environmental 'green politics' asserts the need for both bio- and anthropo-diversity (Mies & Shiva, 1993). Other examples of this ecological and situated cosmopolitan humanism are: Avtar Brah's diasporic ethics (1996); Vandana Shiva's anti-global neo-humanism (1997); African humanism or Ubuntu is receiving more attention, from Patricia Hill Collins (1991) to Drucilla Cornell (2002). In a more nomadic vein, Edouard Glissant's poetics of relations (1997) inscribed multi-lingual hybridity and the poetics of relation at the heart of the contemporary posthuman condition.

Thus feminism is resolutely humanist in its pursuit of emancipation, or equality, but it is also proto-posthumanist in its critique of the exclusionary use made of the category of the human. Appeals to the 'human' are always discriminatory: they create structural distinctions and inequalities among different categories of humans. Humanity is a quality that is distributed according to a hierarchical scale centred on that humanistic idea of Man as the alleged measure of all things – and of all reified or thing-like entities. This subject is the Man of reason that feminists, anti-racists, Black, indigenous postcolonial and ecological activists have been criticizing for decades.

Stressing that humanity is not a neutral term but rather one that indexes access to specific powers, values and norms, rights and visibility, critics of Enlightenment humanism criticized the moral imperialism and anthropocentric exceptionalism of that tradition. After all, the categories of excluded 'others' whose humanity was denied and withheld have been arguing for the right to be human for several centuries already, in the name of their own cultural traditions and competences. Their calls for an autonomous definition of what it means to be human have met with mixed success at best and have seldom been integrated in the dominant idea of the human that informs Western human rights. Is that Western universal ideal still credible? And how does the urgency of the posthuman convergence affect their ongoing struggle?

ANTHROPOS IS OFF-CENTRE

The debate on the limitations of humanism, pioneered by feminist, postcolonial and race theorists, appears to be a simpler task than displacing anthropocentrism itself. 'Man' is now called to task as the representative of a hierarchical and violent species whose centrality is challenged by a combination of scientific advances and global economic concerns in contemporary, technologically mediated knowledge production systems. The decentring of *anthropos* challenges also the separation of *bios*, as exclusively human life, from *zoe*, the life of animals and nonhuman entities. What comes to the fore instead is a human/nonhuman continuum, which is consolidated by pervasive technological mediation. Massumi refers to this phenomenon as 'Ex-Man': 'a genetic matrix embedded in the materiality of the human' (1998: 60); an immunity system out of joint (Esposito, 2008) and as such undergoing significant mutations. This shift marks a sort of 'anthropological exodus' from the dominant configurations of the human (Hardt & Negri, 2000: 215) – a colossal hybridization of the species.

The political implications of this shift are significant. If the revisions of humanism advanced by feminist, queer, anti-racist, ecological and postcolonial critiques empowered the sexualized and racialized – but still human – 'others', the crisis of *anthropos* enlists the naturalized others. Animals, insects, plants, cells, bacteria, in fact the planet and the cosmos are turned into a political arena (Braidotti, 2013). The social constructivist habit of thought that reduces nature to the source of social inequalities is revised, in the light of methodological naturalism and neo-materialism. The case is being argued by 'matter-realist' feminist scholarship (Fraser, Kember & Lury, 2006) which emphasizes 'inventive' life and 'vibrant matter' (Bennett, 2010), while different kinds of neo-materialist feminism are in full swing (Braidotti, 1991; Dolphijn & Tuin, 2012; Alaimo & Hekman, 2008; Coole & Frost, 2010; Kirby, 2011). There is consequently a further meta-discursive level of difficulty in the post-anthropocentric turn, due to the fact that anti-humanism is essentially a philosophical, historical and cultural movement and that the bulk of feminist, queer and post-colonial theories are based in the humanities and the social sciences. The critique of anthropocentrism, on the other hand, requires a dialogue with the life sciences, genomics and information technologies.

The posthuman convergence accelerates the crisis of the humanities, exposing their constitutive anthropocentrism, which has historically entailed a conflictual relationship with science and technology. The problem is complicated by an issue of scale – both temporal and spatial: how can gender studies in the humanities and social science disciplines – history, literature, philosophy, sociology, psychology, anthropology – develop planetary and long-term perspectives in a geo-centred and not anthropocentric frame? How will the humanities react to 'destroying the artificial but time honoured distinction between natural and human histories' (Chakrabarty, 2009: 206)? Is it feasible to contemplate – in a secular ad rigorous manner – the idea of human extinction without losing sight of the aims and purposes of academic feminism?

Over the last thirty years, gender, feminist, queer studies have conducted a rigorous analysis of both dominant and marginal subject positions and their respective entitlements and knowledge production economies. They belong to a generation of critical 'studies' fields that have provided new concepts and methods, which proved inspirational for both the academic world and society. These 'studies' areas have targeted Eurocentrism, sexism, racism, methodological nationalism and species-ism implicit in the humanist ideals of reason. Acknowledging the compatibility of rationality and violence, however, does not mean that the critical 'studies' areas uniformly oppose humanism (Foucault, 1970; Said, 1978). It is rather the case that they create alternative visions of what it means to be human.

The current post-anthropocentric, or posthuman turn, cannot fail to affect the very 'studies' areas that – contrary to the field of science and technology studies – may have perfected the critique of humanism but not necessarily relinquished anthropocentrism. A widespread suspicion of the social effects of science and technology seems to pertain to the classical feminist tradition, and its Marxist roots. Shulamith Firestone's technological utopia (1970) strikes a rather lonely note in combining a passionate embrace of technology – including new reproductive technologies – with a strong environmental consciousness. The towering work of Donna Haraway in the mid-1980s – in the 'Manifesto for Cyborgs' (1985) – set an entirely new agenda and established a feminist tradition of politicized science and technology studies integrated with feminist body politics, critical race theory and transnational environmental justice. She replaced anthropocentrism with a set of relational links to human and non-human others, including technological artifacts. Challenging specifically the historical association of females/non-Europeans with nature (Haraway, 1990), Haraway stressed the need for feminist and anti-racist critiques that rest on a technologically mediated vision of the nature–culture continuum. Donna Haraway offers figurations such as the cyborg, onco-mouse, companion-species, the modest witness (1997) and other hybrids as figures of radical interspecies relationality. They blur categorical distinctions (human/non-human; nature/culture; male/female;

Oedipal/non-Oedipal; European/non-European) in attempting to redefine a programme of feminist social justice.

From there on, the collective feminist exit from *anthropos* began to gather momentum and explicit references to the posthuman appear in feminist texts from the 1990s (Braidotti, 1994; Balsamo, 1996; Halberstam & Livingston, 1995; Hayles, 1999). The post-anthropocentric turn takes off as an internally fractured converge: climate change or Sixth Extinction (Kolbert, 2014), which, as Naomi Klein claims (2014), changes everything, including the analytic strategies of feminist and postcolonial studies. The second is the fourth Industrial Revolution (Schwab, 2015) led by advanced technologies and the high degree of global mediation they entail. These challenges open up new global, eco-sophical, posthumanist and post-anthropocentric dimensions of thought. Feminist theory and gender analyses are right in the middle of this reconfiguration of knowledge production.

Displacing *anthropos* liberates a great deal of epistemological energy. The vitality is especially strong in cultural studies of science and technology (McNeil, 2007; Tsing, 2015), and media theory (Smelik & Lykke 2008; Parisi, 2004; Clarke, 2008; Fuller, 2005; Parikka, 2010). Feminist science studies goes planetary (Stengers, 1997; Franklin, Lury & Stacey, 2000; Lury, Parisi & Terranova, 2012) and displaces the centrality of the human, through sophisticated analyses of molecular biology (Margulis & Sagan, 1995; Fox Keller, 2002; Franklin, 2007) and computational systems (Lury, Parisi and Terranova, 2012). Eco-feminists (Plumwood, 1993, 2003), who always advocated geo-centred perspectives, now expand into all elements (Alaimo, 2010; Neimanis, 2017); animal studies becomes 'human-imal studies' (Hayward, 2011), as cross-species allegiances take hold (Hird & Roberts, 2011). The politics of meat (Adams, 1990, 2018) turns to radical veganism (MacCormack, 2014). Feminist theories of non- and posthuman subjectivity embrace non-anthropomorphic animal or technological others (Bryld & Lykke, 2000; Parisi, 2004; Braidotti, 2006, 2013; Alaimo,

2010), prompting a posthuman ethical turn (Braidotti, 2006; MacCormack, 2012). Even feminist interest in Darwin, which had been rare (Beer, 1983), grows (Rose & Rose, 2000; Carroll, 2004; Grosz, 2011).

It follows therefore that, both institutionally and theoretically, the gender, feminist and queer 'studies' areas, which historically have been the motor of both critique and creativity, innovative and challenging in equal measure, have an inspirational role to play also in relation to the posthuman context we inhabit. Contemporary feminist, gender, queer, postcolonial and anti-racist studies are all the more effective and creative as they have allowed themselves to be affected by the posthuman condition. This turn towards the critical posthumanities (Braidotti, 2013; Åsberg, 2018; Åsberg & Braidotti, 2018) marks the end of what Shiva (1993) called 'monocultures of the mind' and it leads feminist theory to pursue the radical politics of location and the analysis of social forms of exclusion in the current world-order of 'biopiracy' (Shiva, 1997); 'global obscenities' (Eisenstein, 1998); necro-politics (Mbembe, 2003) and world-wide dispossession (Sassen, 2014).The posthuman feminist knowing subjects are a complex assemblage of human and non-human, planetary and cosmic, given and manufactured, which requires major readjustments in our ways of thinking. But they remain committed to social justice and, while acknowledging the fatal attraction of global mediation, are not likely to forget that one-third of the world population has no access to electricity.

Posthuman bodies are co-constructed through relations with non-human agents and practices of the organic kind – *zoe* (animals, plants, other species) – but also with planetary or terrestrian forces (*geo*) and with non-organic (techno-mediated) factors through links to networks, platforms, algorithms, etc. It bears repeating that there is no foregone conclusion about what posthuman subjects constructed in *zoe*-geo-techno-mediated alliances are capable of becoming. Those patterns of transformation need to be discussed and negotiated collectively.

GENDER ANALYSIS AS META-METHODOLOGY

Taking critical distance from anthropocentrism, however, raises also a number of affective difficulties: how one reacts to the practice of disloyalty to one's species depends to a large extent on the terms of one's engagement with it, as well as one's relationship to contemporary technological developments. The practice of defamiliarization is a key gender methodological tool to support the post-anthropocentric turn. That is a sobering process of disidentification from humanistic and anthropocentric values, to evolve towards a new frame of reference, which in this case entails becoming relational in a complex and multi-directional manner. Disengagement from dominant models of subject formation has been pioneered in a critical and creative manner (Kelly, 1979) by feminist theory. It activates the sexualized (women, LBGTQ+ people), racialized (indigenous, decolonial, Black people) 'others' towards alternative patterns of becoming. The post-anthropocentric turn further challenges the anthropocentric habits of thought, by foregrounding the politics of the 'naturalized' (non-human and earth) 'others'. It thus requires a more radical break from the assumption of human uniqueness.

New materialism is the philosophy that supports the feminist intervention upon the posthuman convergence. It proposes species egalitarianism which opens up productive possibilities of cross-species relations, alliances and inter-dependence. (Braidotti, 1994; Grosz, 2001; Bennett, 2010; Colebrook, 2014; Gatens & Lloyd, 1999). Such a vitalist approach to living matter (Ansell-Pearson, 1999; Protevi, 2013; Braidotti, 2013) displaces the boundary between the portion of life – both organic and discursive – that has traditionally been reserved for *anthropos,* that is to say *bios,* and the dynamic, self-organizing structure of life as *zoe* (Braidotti, 2006, 2011b), which stands for generative vitality. As embodied and embedded entities, we are all part of something we used to call 'nature', in spite of transcendental claims made for human consciousness. *Zoe*-centred life is the transversal force that cuts across and reconnects previously segregated species, categories and domains. *Zoe*-centred egalitarianism is, for me, the core of the post-anthropocentric turn: it is a materialist, secular, grounded and unsentimental response to the opportunistic trans-species commodification of life that is the logic of advanced capitalism (Cooper, 2008).

The urgent feminist questions are: how to combine the decline of anthropocentrism with issues of social justice? Can a post-anthropocentrism come to the rescue of our species? The sense of insurgency in contemporary posthuman scholarship is palpable in the 'capitalocene' era (Moore, 2013), that Haraway recently labelled: chthulucene (2016). Does the posthuman – in its post-humanistic and post-anthropocentric inceptions – complicate the issues of human agency and feminist political subjectivity? My argument is that it actually enhances it by offering an expanded relational vision of the self, as a heterogeneous transversal assemblage (Braidotti, 1994, 2002, 2006) engendered by the cumulative effect of multiple relational bonds. The relational capacity of the posthuman subject is not confined within our species, but it includes all non-anthropomorphic elements, starting from the very air we breathe.

Living matter – including embodied human flesh – is intelligent and self-organizing, but it is so precisely because it is not disconnected from the rest of organic life and connects to the animal and the earth (Grosz, 2004). Feminist philosophy of radical immanence foregrounds embodiment and embeddedness, not disconnection from the thinking organism. We think with the entire body, or rather we have to acknowledge the embodiment of the brain and the embrainment of the body (Marks, 1998). In this respect, it is important accordingly not to work completely within the social constructivist method, but rather to emphasize process ontologies which reconceptualize the connection to the non-human, vital forces, that is, *zoe*.

There is no question that contemporary feminist theory is productively posthuman, as evidenced by the work of Barad (2007), who coined the terms 'posthumanist performativity' and 'agential realism'. Queer science studies is especially keen on a transversal alliance between humans and other species; thus Alaimo (2010) theorizes trans-corporeal porous boundaries between human and other species, while Livingston and Puar (2011) call for interspecies or 'transspeciated selves' (Hayward, 2008). Queering the posthuman is in full swing (Giffney & Hird, 2008). A techno-ecological (Hörl, 2013), posthuman turn is at work which combines organic auto-poesis (Maturana & Varela, 1972) with machinic self-organizing powers, as announced by Felix Guattari (1995, 2000) in his pioneering work on our eco-technologically mediated universe. The consensus is that there is no 'originary humanicity' (Kirby, 2011: 233) but only 'originary technicity' (MacKenzie, 2002).

To those who fear that emphasizing the posthuman aspects of our current conjuncture may result in short circuiting the process of emancipation of those who were not considered human to begin with, I reply that I share their concern, but also add that it is becoming painfully clear that those who are marked negatively as 'others', the dehumanized and marginalized others, are currently missing out on the profits and advantages of the fourth Industrial Revolution, while being excessively exposed to the ravages of the Sixth Extinction. This is the cruel imbalance that posthuman feminism wants to address, stressing that the posthuman condition is not post-power, nor post-injustice. The emphasis on 'post' in the posthuman rather implies that we move it forward, beyond traditional understandings of the human, so that the analyses of power and knowledge become an essential part of the feminist posthuman project.

As not all humans are the same to begin with, this conjuncture brings out deep structural inequalities and historically recurring forms of social and symbolic disqualification. Posthuman feminism analyses them in terms of hierarchies of sexualized, racialized and naturalized differences and the ontological disqualifications that have supported the dominant vision of the human.

The posthuman feminist position calls for a new political praxis, as a practical empirical project that aims at experimenting with what contemporary, bio-technologically mediated bodies are capable of doing in the radical immanence of their respective locations. Mindful of the structural injustices and massive power differentials at work in the globalized world, feminist theory needs to sharpen its gender navigational tools to steer a course that addresses the posthuman convergence in its complexity. Combining adequate accounts of the multiple locations of power at work in our world, feminist thought needs to actualize the virtual possibilities of becoming posthuman, starting from the position of those who were not fully human to begin with. In this respect posthuman feminism is not a new generic category but rather a navigational tool that can assist us in coming to terms with the gendered complexities of our times.

REFERENCES

Adams, Carol. 1990. *The Sexual Politics of Meat: A Feminist-Vegetarian Critical Theory.* New York: Continuum.

[1994] 2018. *Neither Beast Nor Man. Feminism and the Defense of Animals.* London and New York: Bloomsbury Academic.

Alcoff, Linda and Porter, Elizabeth, eds. 1993. *Feminist Epistemologies.* London and New York: Routledge.

Alaimo, Stacey. 2010. *Bodily Natures: Science, Environment and the Material Self.* Bloomington, IN: Indiana University Press.

Alaimo, Stacey and Hekman,Susan. 2008. *Material Feminism.* Bloomington, IN: Indiana University Press.

Ansell Pearson, Keith. 1999. *Germinal Life. The Difference and Repetition of Deleuze.* London and New York: Routledge.

Åsberg, Cecilia. 2018. Feminist Posthumanities in the Anthropocene: Forays into the Postnatural. *Journal of Posthuman Studies: Philosophy, Technology, Media,* 1 (2), 185–204.

Åsberg, Cecilia and Braidotti, Rosi. eds. 2018. *A Feminist Companion to the Posthumanities.* Cham: Springer International Publishing.

Balsamo, Anne. 1996. *Technologies of the Gendered Body: Reading Cyborg Women.* Durham, NC: Duke University Press.

Barad, Karen. 2007. *Meeting the Universe Halfway.* Durham, NC: Duke University Press.

Beer, Gillian. 1983. *Darwin's Plots: Evolutionary Narrative in Darwin, George Eliot and Nineteenth-Century Fiction.* London: Routledge & Kegan Paul.

Beck, Ulrich. 2007. The Cosmopolitan Condition. Why Methodological Nationalism Fails. *Theory, Culture & Society*, **24**(7/8), 286–90.

Bennett, Jane. 2010. *Vibrant Matter: A Political Ecology of Things.* Durham, NC: Duke University Press.

Brah, Avtar. 1996. *Cartographies of Diaspora – Contesting Identities.* New York and London: Routledge.

Braidotti, Rosi. 1991. *Patterns of Dissonance.* Cambridge, UK: Polity Press.

1994. *Nomadic Subjects,* 1st ed. Ithaca, NY: Cornell University Press.

2002. *Metamorphoses.* Cambridge, UK and Malden, USA: Polity Press/Blackwell Publishers Ltd.

2006. *Transposition.* Cambridge, UK: Polity Press.

2011a. *Nomadic Subjects,* 2nd ed. New York: Columbia University Press.

2011b. *Nomadic Theory. The Portable Rosi Braidotti.* New York: Columbia University Press.

2013. *The Posthuman.* Cambridge, UK: Polity Press.

2019. *Posthuman Knowledge.* Cambridge, UK: Polity Press.

Braidotti, Rosi and Roets, Griet. 2012. Nomadology and Subjectivity: Deleuze and Critical Disability Studies. In Dan Goodley, Bill Hughes and Lennard Davis, *Disability and Social Theory.* New York: Palgrave Macmillan, pp. 161–78.

Bryld, Mette and Lykke, Nina. 2000. *Cosmodolphins: Feminist Cultural Studies of Technology, Animals and the Sacred.* London: Zed Books.

Butler, Judith. 1991. *Gender Trouble.* London and New York: Routledge.

1993. *Bodies That Matter.* London and New York: Routledge.

Carby, Hazel. 1982. White Woman Listen! Black Feminism and the Boundaries of Sisterhood. In University of Birmingham Centre for Contemporary Cultural Studies, ed. *The Empire Strikes Back.* London: Hutchinson.

Carroll, Joseph. 2004. *Literary Darwinism. Evolution, Human Nature and Literature.* London and New York: Routledge.

Chakrabarty, Dipesh. 2009. The Climate of History: Four Theses. *Critical Enquiry,* **35**, 197–222.

Cixous, Helene and Clement, Catherine. 1986. *The Newly Born Woman.* Minneapolis, MN: University of Minnesota Press.

Clarke, Bruce. 2008. *Posthuman Metamorphosis: Narrative and Systems.* New York: Fordham University Press.

Colebrook, Claire. 2014. *Sex After Life.* Ann Arbor, MI: Open Humanities Press/ University of Michigan Press.

Coole, Diana and Frost, Samantha. 2010. *New Materialisms: Ontology, Agency, and Politics.* Durham, NC: Duke University Press.

Cooper, Melinda. 2008. *Life as Surplus. Biotechnology & Capitalism in the Neoliberal Era.* Seattle, WA: University of Washington Press.

Cornell, Drucilla. 2002. The Ubuntu Project with Stellenbosch University. www.fehe.org/index.php?id=281. Accessed on 2 January 2007.

Crenshaw, Kimberlé. 1995. Intersectionality and Identity Politics. Learning from Violence against Women of Color. In Kimberlé Crenshaw et al., *Critical Race Theory.* New York: The New Press, pp. 357–83.

Deleuze, Gilles and Guattari,Felix. 1977. *Anti-Oedipus. Capitalism and Schizophrenia.* New York: Viking Press.

1987. *A Thousand Plateaus: Capitalism and Schizophrenia.* Minneapolis, MN: University of Minnesota Press.
Eisenstein, Zillah. 1998. *Global Obscenities. Patriarchy, Capitalism and the Lure of Cyberfantasy.* New York: New York University Press.
Dolphijn, Rick and van der Tuin, Iris, eds. 2012. *New Materialism: Interviews & Cartographies.* Ann Arbor, MI: Open Humanities Press.
Esposito, Roberto. 2008. *Bios. Biopolitics and Philosophy.* Minneapolis, MN: University of Minnesota Press.
Firestone, Shulamith. 1970. *The Dialectic of Sex.* New York: Bentam Books.
Foucault, Michel. 1970. *The Order of Things: An Archaeology of Human Sciences.* New York: Pantheon Books.
Fox Keller, Evelyn. 2002. *Making Sense of Life.* Cambridge, MA: Harvard University Press.
Franklin, Sarah. 2007. *Dolly Mixtures.* Durham, NC: Duke University Press.
Franklin, Sarah, Lury, Celia and Stacey, Jackie. 2000. *Global Nature, Global Culture.* London: Sage.
Fraser, Mariam, Kember, Sarah and Lury, Celia, eds. 2006. *Inventive Life. Approaches to the New Vitalism.* London: Sage.
Freire, Paulo. [1970] 2005. *Pedagogy of the Oppressed.* London: Continuum.
Fuller, Matthew. 2005. *Media Ecologies: Materialist Energies in Art and Technoculture.* Cambridge, MA and London: MIT Press.
Gatens, Moira and Lloyd, Genevieve. 1999. *Collective Imaginings: Spinoza, Past and Present.* London and New York: Routledge.
Giffney, Noreen and Hird, Myra, eds. 2008. *Queering the Non/Human.* London: Ashgate.
Glissant, Edouard. 1997. *Poetics of Relation.* Ann Arbor, MI: University of Michigan Press.
Goodley, Dan, Lawthorn, Rebecca and Runswick, Katherine. 2014. Posthuman Disability Studies. *Subjectivity,* **7**(4), 341–61.
Guattari, Felix. 1995. *Chaosmosis. An Ethico-Aesthetic Paradigm.* Sydney: Power Publications.
2000. *The Three Ecologies.* London: The Athlone Press.
Grosz, Elizabeth. 2001. A Thousand Tiny Sexes: Feminism and Rhizomatics. In Gary Genosko, ed., *Deleuze and Guattari: Critical Assessments of Leading Philosophers.* London: Routledge, pp. 1440–63.
2004. *The Nick of Time.* Durham, NC: Duke University Press.
2011. *Becoming Undone.* Durham, NC: Duke University Press.
de Gouges, Olympe. [1792] 2018. *The Declaration of the Rights of Women.* London: Ilex Press.
Halberstam, Judith and Livingston, Ira, eds. 1995. *Posthuman Bodies.* Bloomington, IN: Indiana University Press.
Haraway, Donna. 1985. A Manifesto for Cyborgs: Science, Technology, and Socialist Feminism in the 1980s. *Socialist Review,* **5**(2), 1–42.
1988. Situated Knowledges. The Science Question in Feminism as a Site of Discourse on the Privilege of Partial Perspective. *Feminist Studies,* **14**(3), 575–99.
1990. *Simians, Cyborgs and Women.* London: Free Association Press.

1997. *Modest_Witness@Second_Millennium. FemaleMan©_Meets_ Oncomouse.* London and New York: Routledge.
2016. *Staying with the Trouble: Making Kin in the Chthulucene.* Durham, NC and London: Duke University Press.
Harding, Sandra G. 1986. *The Science Question in Feminism.* Buckingham: Open University Press.
1991. *Whose Science? Whose Knowledge?* Ithaca, NY: Cornell University Press.
1993. *The 'Racial' Economy of Science.* Bloomington, IN: Indiana University Press.
1998. *Is Science Multicultural? Postcolonialisms, Feminisms, and Epistemologies.* Bloomington, IN: Indiana University Press.
Hardt, Michael and Antonio, Negri. 2000. *Empire.* Cambridge, MA: Harvard University Press.
Hartsock, Nancy. 1987. The Feminist Standpoint: Developing the Ground for a Specifically Feminist Historical Materialism. In Sandra G. Harding, ed., *Feminism and Methodology.* London: Open University Press, pp. 157–80.
Hayles, Katherine. 1999. *How We Became Posthuman. Virtual Bodies in Cybernetics, Literature and Informatics.* Chicago, IL: The University of Chicago Press.
Hayward, Eva. 2008. More Lessons from a Starfish: Prefixial Flesh and Transspeciated Selves. *Women's Studies Quarterly,* **36**(3–4), 64–85.
2011. Sensational Jellyfish: Aquarium Affects and the Matter of Immersion. *differences,* **25**(5), 161–96.
Hill Collins, Patricia. 1991. *Black Feminist Thought. Knowledge, Consciousness and the Politics of Empowerment.* New York and London: Routledge.
Hird, Myra and Roberts, Celia, eds. 2011. Feminism Theorises the Nonhuman. *Feminist Theory,* **12**(2), 109–17.
hooks, bell. 1981. *Ain't I a Woman.* Boston, MA: South End Press.
1990. *Yearning: Race, Gender and Cultural Politics.* Toronto: Between the Lines.
Hörl, Erich. 2013. A Thousand Ecologies: The Process of Cyberneticization and General Ecology. In Diedrich Diederichsen and Anselm Franke, eds., *The Whole Earth: California And The Disappearance Of The Outside.* Berlin: Sternberg Press.
Irigaray, Luce. 1985a. *Speculum of the Other Woman.* Ithaca, NY: Cornell University Press.
1985b. *This Sex Which Is Not One.* Ithaca, NY: Cornell University Press.
1994. Equal to Whom? In Naomi Schor and Elizabeth Weed, ed., *The Essential Difference.* Robert L. Mazzola, trans. Bloomington, IN: Indiana University Press, p. 80.
Kelly, Joan. 1979. The Double-Edged Vision of Feminist Theory. *Feminist Studies,* **5** (1), 216–27.
Kirby, Vicki. 2011. *Quantum Anthropologies: Life at Large.* Durham, NC: Duke University Press.
Klein, Naomi. 2014. *This Changes Everything. Capitalism vs. the Climate.* New York: Simon & Schuster.
Kolbert, Elizabeth. 2014. *The Sixth Extinction.* New York: Henry Holt Company.
Livingston, Julie and Puar, Jasbir K. 2011. "Interspecies". *Social Text,* **29**(1), 3–13.

Lloyd, Genevieve. 1984. *The Man of Reason: Male and Female in Western Philosophy.* London: Methuen.

1994. *Part of Nature: Self-knowledge in Spinoza's* Ethics. Ithaca/London: Cornell University Press.

1996. *Spinoza and the Ethics.* London and New York: Routledge.

Louverture, Toussaint. [1791] 2011. *Lettres à la France. Idées pour la Libération du people noir d'Haiti.* Bruyères-le-Chatel: Nouvelle Cité.

Lury, Celia, Parisi, Luciana and Terranova,Tiziana. 2012. Introduction: The Becoming Topological of Culture. *Theory, Culture and Society,* **29**(4–5), 3–35.

MacCormack, Patricia. 2012. *Posthuman Ethics.* London: Ashgate.

2014. *The Animal Catalyst.* London: Bloomsbury.

MacKenzie, Adrian. 2002. *Transductions: Bodies and Machines at Speed.* New York: Continuum.

Margulis, Lynn and Sagan, Dorion. 1995. *What is Life?* Berkeley, CA: University of California Press.

Marks, John. 1998. *Gilles Deleuze. Vitalism and Multiplicity.* London: Pluto Press.

Massumi, Brian. 1998. Sensing the Virtual, Building the Insensible. *Architectural Design,* **68**(5/6), 16–24.

Maturana, Humberto and Varela, Francisco. 1972. *Autopoesis and Cognition. The Realization of the Living.* Dordrecht: Reidel Publishing Company.

Mbembe, Achille. 2003. Necropolitics. *Public Culture,* **15**(1), 11–40.

McNeil, Maureen. 2007. *Feminist Cultural Studies of Science and Technology.* London: Routledge.

Mies, Maria and Shiva,Vandana. 1993. *Ecofeminism.* London: Zed Books.

Moore, Jason. 2013. Anthropocene, Capitalocene, and the myth of industrialization. World-Ecological Imaginations: Power and Production in the Web of Life, 16 June. https://jasonwmoore.wordpress.com/2013/06/16/anthropocene-capitalocene-the-myth-of-industrialization/.

Moraga, Cherríe and Anzaldua, Gloria, eds. 1981. *This Bridge Called My Back. Writing by Radical Women on Color.* Watertown, MA: Persephone Press.

Moulier Boutang, Yann. 2012. *Cognitive Capitalism.* Cambridge: Polity Press.

Neimanis, Astrida. 2017. *Bodies of Water: Posthuman Feminist Phenomenology.* London: Bloomsbury.

Parikka, Jussi. 2010. *Insect Media. An Archaeology of Animals and Technology.* Minneapolis, MN: University of Minnesota Press.

Parisi, Luciana. 2004. *Abstract Sex. Philosophy, Bio-Technology, and the Mutation of Desire.* London: Continuum Press.

Plumwood, Val. 1993. *Feminism and the Mastery of Nature.* London and New York: Routledge.

2003. *Environmental Culture.* London: Routledge.

Protevi, John. 2009. *Political Affect.* Minneapolis, MN: University of Minnesota Press.

2013. *Life War Earth.* Minneapolis, MN: University of Minnesota Press.

Rich, Adrienne. 1987. *Blood, Bread and Poetry.* London: Virago Press.

2001. *Arts of the Possible: Essays and Conversations.* New York: W.W. Norton & Company.

Rose, Deborah Bird. 2004. *Reports From a Wild Country*. Sydney: University of New South Wales Press.
Rose, Hilary and Rose, Steven, eds. 2000. *Alas, Poor Darwin: Arguments Against Evolutionary Psychology*. London: Vintage.
Said, Edward. 1978. *Orientalism*. New York: Pantheon Books.
2004. *Humanism and Democratic Criticism*. New York: Columbia University Press.
Sassen, Saskia. 2014. *Expulsions: Brutality and Complexity in the Global Economy*. Cambridge, MA: Harvard University Press.
Schwab, Klaus. 2015. The Fourth Industrial Revolution. *Foreign Affairs*, 12 December.
Shildrick, Margrit. 2012. *Dangerous Discourses of Disability, Subjectivity and Sexuality*. Basingstoke: Palgrave Macmillan.
Shiva, Vandana. 1993. *Monocultures of the Mind: Perspectives on Biodiversity and Biotechnology*. London: Zed Books.
1997. *Biopiracy. The Plunder of Nature and Knowledge*. Boston, MA: South End Press.
Spivak, Gayatri Chakravorty. 1999. *A Critique of Postcolonial Reason*. Cambridge, MA: Harvard University Press.
Smelik, Anneke and Nina, Lykke, eds. 2008. *Bits of Life. Feminism at the Intersection of Media, Bioscience and Technology*. Seattle, WA: University of Washington Press.
Smith, Barbara. 1978. Towards a Black Feminist Criticism. *The Radical Teacher*, **7** (March), 20–27.
Stengers, Isabelle. 1997. *Power and Invention. Situating Science*. Minneapolis, MN: University of Minnesota Press.
Tsing, Anna. 2015. *The Mushroom at the End of the World*. Princeton, NJ: Princeton University Press.
Tuana, Nancy. 2008. Viscous Porosity: Witnessing Katrina. In Stacy Alaimo and Susan Hekman, eds., *Material Feminisms*. Bloomington, IN: Indiana University Press, pp. 188–213.
Ware, Vron. 1992. *Beyond the Pale. White Women, Racism and History*. London: Verso.
Weheliye, Alexander. 2014. *Habeas Viscus*. Durham, NC: Duke University Press.
Wekker, Gloria. 2016. *White Innocence*. Durham, NC: Duke University Press.
Wynter, Sylvia. 2015. *On Being Human as Praxis*. Durham NC and London. Duke University Press.

CHAPTER 6

Gender, Sperm Troubles, and Assisted Reproductive Technologies

Marcia C. Inhorn

LOUISE BROWN, THE WORLD'S FIRST TEST-TUBE BABY, was born more than forty years ago in England. For Louise Brown's infertile mother, Lesley, in vitro fertilization (IVF), developed at the University of Cambridge, was a "hope technology" (Franklin, 1997), allowing Lesley to overcome her tubal-factor infertility and nine years of heart-breaking involuntary childlessness. Lesley's story involved a complex reproductive quest, in which she traveled with her working-class husband, John, from their home in Bristol to Bourn Hall Clinic in Cambridge to undergo the IVF procedures. Then, due to intense media scrutiny and religious opposition, Lesley and John were forced to travel to yet a third location, Oldham General Hospital in the North of England, for the secret delivery of baby Louise by Cesarean section on July 25, 1978.

Four decades on, IVF has engendered reproduction among the parents of more than 8 million IVF babies now born (ESHRE, 2018). These IVF parents include people of all sexualities using a variety of assisted reproductive technologies (ARTs), including IVF, donor eggs and donor sperm, and commercial gestational surrogacy. Most recently, IVF has extended the possibility of biological reproduction to transgender men and women, who are cryopreserving their eggs and sperm for future IVF-assisted

I wish to thank both the US National Science Foundation's Cultural Anthropology Program and the US Department of Education's Fulbright-Hays Faculty Research Abroad program for providing the funding for my medical anthropological research in the United Arab Emirates.

births.[1] This development is having a profound impact on our perceptions of the gendered social order (also see Judith Butler and Jack Halberstam in this volume). Not only has IVF engendered reproduction for those who would never otherwise become parents of biogenetically related offspring, but it has also performed a profound gender intervention, by helping to overcome the tremendous social suffering of infertile women, who are often blamed and ostracized for their childlessness (Cui, 2010).

IVF has also led to a breakthrough in remediating the various "sperm troubles" found among cisgender men. These troubles may include oligozoospermia (low sperm count), asthenozoospermia (poor sperm motility, or movement), teratozoospermia (abnormal sperm morphology, or shape), and azoospermia (absence of sperm in the ejaculate). Such sperm troubles contribute to more than half of all cases of involuntary childlessness in the world today. Furthermore, as shown in a variety of recent studies from multiple nations, sperm quality appears to be decreasing globally, including in many Western countries. Scientists now view these sperm troubles as a "window on the health" of this generation, the next, and the planet as a whole (Barratt, Anderson, & De Jonge, 2019).

The problem with sperm is that very little can be done to improve its quality. Thus, sperm problems are usually refractory to treatment (Inhorn, 2012). Until the 1990s, the only known solution was donor insemination (DI), the oldest infertility technology, but one that, for some, was socially and religiously unacceptable (Becker, 2002). However, in 1991, a variant of IVF called intracytoplasmic sperm injection (ICSI) was introduced in Belgium. Through microscopic manipulation of "weak" sperm – low in number, poor in movement, or abnormally shaped – these sperm could be injected directly into human oocytes, effectively "forcing" fertilization to occur. With the invention of ICSI, otherwise "sterile" cisgender

[1] Currently, researchers are contemplating IVF pregnancies in transgender women via uterine transplantation.

men could now father biogenetic offspring. This included even azoospermic men, who produce no sperm in their ejaculate and must therefore have their testicles painfully aspirated or biopsied in the search for sperm. In short, for the first time in human history, ICSI gave seriously infertile cisgender men a chance of becoming biological fathers.

The importance of ICSI in overcoming cisgender men's sperm troubles cannot be underestimated. For such men, the inability to impregnate a partner is often highly stigmatizing, and mistakenly conflated with impotency, or erectile dysfunction (Inhorn, 2012). This "fertility–virility linkage" means that men who are infertile are assumed to be impotent, even though most are not. This sexual misattribution also means that sperm troubles are deeply hidden, with many women blamed for what, in fact, are the sperm problems of their cisgender male partners.

Given the high prevalence of sperm troubles around the world, as well as the associated stigma and secrecy, the 1990s introduction of ICSI proved to be a major breakthrough. By the mid-1990s, cisgender infertile men were flocking to IVF clinics around the globe, hoping to access this new "hope technology." Today, ICSI is the most-performed ART in the world, outstripping standard IVF cycles sixty-fold in some parts of the world. ICSI provides an interesting case study of how a problem of manhood (i.e., cisgender men's inability to impregnate) has been recast as a problem of health (i.e., a disease, like diabetes or hypertension) through a process of ICSI-related medicalization.

Over three decades as a medical anthropologist, I have been "traveling with" IVF and ICSI across the Arab world, watching how the global introduction of these two ARTs has served to reconceive Arab gender identities and relations (Inhorn, 1994, 1996, 2003, 2012, 2015, 2018). This gender reconfiguration is key to understanding the shifting burden of reproductive "blame" and responsibility away from women and toward men; the willingness among both men and women to pursue ARTs together as a sign of conjugal solidarity; and a lessening of the threat of infertility to gender identity or the achievement of adult personhood. Across the Middle East, which now has one of the top-performing IVF sectors in the world (Inhorn & Patrizio, 2015), IVF and ICSI hold out hope for millions of infertile people – making not only test-tube babies, but also fathers and mothers in the process.

In what follows, I take readers to Dubai – one of the seven United Arab Emirates (UAE) and the Middle East's only "global city" (Sassen, 2001, 2005). Dubai is now attracting medical travelers from around the world, many of whom are seeking assisted conception (Inhorn, 2015). Indeed, Dubai is fast becoming known as a transnational IVF and ICSI "reprohub," where those with fertility problems can receive expert reproductive assistance. Based on ethnographic research conducted in Conceive,[2] one of the country's first and busiest IVF clinics, this chapter explores the problem of cisgender Arab men's sperm troubles and the ICSI treatment quests of such men coming to Dubai from scores of other nations. The story of Hsain,[3] a young British Muslim man of Moroccan descent, is told in the second half of this chapter. Having been given "no hope" by British National Health Service (NHS) physicians, Hsain and his wife traveled to Conceive, where Hsain placed his "only hope" in ICSI's technological salvation.

CONCEIVE – A COSMOPOLITAN CLINIC

In 1991 – the very year that ICSI was being "birthed" in Belgium as the variant of IVF designed to overcome sperm troubles – the UAE opened its first IVF clinic in a Dubai government hospital. Since then, the UAE's assisted reproduction sector has flourished, with more than a dozen IVF clinics, most of them private facilities, opening in the country over the past three decades.

One of these private IVF centers is called Conceive, where I undertook a six-month study of "reprotravel" to Dubai.[4] At

[2] This is the clinic's real name. [3] This name is a pseudonym.

[4] The terms "reproductive tourism," "fertility tourism," "procreative tourism," and "cross-border reproductive care," which are used widely by both scholars and the

Conceive, I was able to conduct in-depth, semi-structured, ethnographic interviews with 219 ICSI- and IVF-seeking men and women coming from fifty different countries of origin.[5] They hailed from an equal number of Middle Eastern (fifteen) and European nation-states (fifteen), followed by an almost equal number of Asian (nine) and African (eight) countries. The United States, Canada, and Australia were also represented, with Latin America being the only part of the world entirely absent from this otherwise global study population. Ninety-four interviews were undertaken with infertile couples together, since marriage – as shown by a valid marriage license – is a strict requirement for assisted conception mandated by the UAE Ministry of Health. However, I also interviewed thirty-one men and women alone, either because they had traveled by themselves that day or they were waiting for their spouses to complete various medical procedures in the clinic.

Interviews ranged anywhere from one to three hours, were mostly conducted in English (the lingua franca of Dubai), although sometimes in Arabic, and focused on the often tortuous IVF and ICSI journeys of the 125 patient-couples in the study. Indeed, over the course of my research, I tracked the comings and goings of a diverse group of international medical travelers from five continents and fifty different countries.

Most of these couples had reached Conceive through circuitous global routes of referral, sometimes from friends or family members, but often through referrals from physicians in other countries. Furthermore, most of the couples in my study felt "lured" to Dubai because of its cultural cosmopolitanism – namely, they wanted to receive IVF services in a global location, where clinical

media (Gürtin & Inhorn 2011; Hudson et al., 2011), are criticized by infertile travelers themselves, who prefer the more neutral descriptor, reproductive travel. However, because reproductive travel and reproductive travelers can become cumbersome if used repeatedly, I prefer to use reprotravel and reprotravelers as convenient contractions. In this regard, I am following a long legacy of medical anthropological contractions, including, for example, biomedicine and reprogenetics.

[5] The main study was conducted from January through June 2007. However, I also made follow-up research trips to Conceive in 2009, 2010, and 2013.

care could be effectively delivered across national, ethnic, religious, linguistic, and cultural lines. In this regard, it is fair to say that Conceive had developed a global reputation for its cosmopolitanism.

With more than twenty staff members hailing from the Middle East, Africa, South and Southeast Asia, and Western Europe, Conceive could be seen as practicing a kind of "global gynecology," making infertile patients from abroad feel comfortable with its high-quality, patient-centered gynecology services, delivered multiculturally by conationals in Arabic, Hindi, Urdu, and several other regional languages. Like Dubai itself, Conceive was a place of "cosmopolitan conceptions" – a clinic where self-consciously crafted medical cosmopolitanism had worked to create a vibrant, international clientele.

Many of these reprotravelers were infertile cisgender men. According to Dr. Pankaj Shrivastav, Conceive's clinical director,[6] about 40 percent of the couples presenting to the clinic faced problems of sperm quality and quantity. This was true in my own study as well. In total, 53 of the 125 husbands, or 42 percent, were infertile. Ten of these men were azoospermic, showing no signs of sperm in their ejaculate. Of these ten men, two had banked their sperm at Conceive prior to cancer treatment, becoming azoospermic after chemotherapy and returning to Conceive for ICSI. The rest of the infertile men in my study suffered from a variety of sperm defects, including poor count, poor motility, and abnormal shape, sometimes alone but often together (e.g., low count plus poor motility). In most of these cases, men knew that they were infertile before traveling to Conceive, but in a few cases, the diagnosis was made only upon arrival.

The infertile men in my study came from twenty-one countries. As shown in Table 6.1, most were from other Middle Eastern nations or from Europe. But African and Asian men were also traveling to Conceive. This was particularly true of Indian men, who comprised the single largest group, or nearly one-third of the total sample.

[6] This is his real name and title.

TABLE 6.1 *Fifty-three cisgender men with sperm troubles: reprotravel to Conceive from twenty-one countries*

Africa	Asia	Euro-America	Middle East
Djibouti (1)	India (16)	France (1)	Bahrain (1)
Somalia (1)	Pakistan (2)	Germany (1)	Egypt (1)
South Africa (2)	Philippines (2)	Hungary (1)	Iran (2)
Sudan (3)		Netherlands (1)	Lebanon (4)
		Sweden (2)	Palestine (3)
		United Kingdom (3)	Syria (3)
		United States (1)	UAE (other emirates) 2
N = 7	*N* = 20	*N* = 10	*N* = 16

Why had these men traveled to the United Arab Emirates to obtain treatment? In most cases, they had been unable to access effective ICSI services in their home countries due to several major "arenas of constraint" (Inhorn, 2003). For men coming from Africa, resource constraints were most prominent, particularly the total absence of IVF clinics in most sub-Saharan African countries.[7] At the time of my study, infertile men from the Horn of Africa – countries such as Djibouti, Somalia, and Sudan – were heading to Conceive because ICSI services were literally unavailable to them back home.

European men faced a different arena of resource constraint. Many came from countries where IVF and ICSI cycles were available but rationed by the state. The United Kingdom and its NHS stood out in this regard (Hudson & Culley, 2011). At Conceive, I met a group of reprotravelers who I came to think of as the "NHS refugees." These NHS refugees were British couples who were seeking refuge in Dubai after being deemed ineligible for publicly funded IVF and ICSI cycles or had been put on long NHS waiting lists, sometimes for years. Some of these couples had been disqualified from IVF and ICSI altogether simply by living in the wrong postal code, where local NHS authorities refused to fund assisted

[7] Of forty-eight sub-Saharan African countries, only fifteen had at least one IVF clinic as of a 2010 international surveillance project (Jones et al., 2010). Thirty-three nations, or more than two-thirds, lacked IVF facilities.

reproduction at taxpayers' expense. Others had reached NHS clinics, only to receive ineffective, low-quality care from overextended IVF clinicians.

In addition, some of the European men in my study could be considered "reproductive outlaws," by virtue of the fact that they were attempting to evade their countries' assisted reproduction laws. These kinds of legal constraints were especially difficult for azoospermic men coming from a number of European countries where ICSI cannot be performed if sperm must be aspirated directly from the testes (because of concerns about genetic defects being passed to an ICSI child) (Pennings, 2010). Other countries forbid IVF or ICSI services if a man or woman carries an infectious disease such as hepatitis. Because Europe has the highest number of these kinds of assisted reproduction laws (Jones et al., 2010), it also has the highest number of law evaders (Pennings, 2002, 2004, 2009). Consequently, some of these European reproductive outlaws were making their way to Dubai for ICSI services. This was especially true for those needing percutaneous epididymal sperm aspiration (PESA), a form of testicular aspiration in which sperm are extracted directly from the epididymis, one of the sperm transport vessels. PESA was first invented at Conceive, making PESA a specialty service at this clinic.

Finally, quality of care was one of the main drivers of reprotravel among the men and women in my study. This was especially true for couples coming from South Asia and Eastern Europe. In many cases, reprotravelers spoke of IVF clinics in their home countries that were crowded well beyond capacity, delivering low-quality, ineffective, and even harmful treatment. Iatrogenesis, or physician-induced harm, was a major theme of many of the medical horror stories I heard at Conceive, stories filled with disenchantment and sometimes life-threatening malpractice. By the end of my study, it was clear to me that infertile couples' desires for high-quality IVF and ICSI services were a major driver of their transnational reprotravel. Indeed, the search for patient-centered care may be one of the most underappreciated aspects of global reproductive mobilities in the new millennium (Dancet et al., 2011).

ICSI – THE HOPE TECHNOLOGY FOR SPERM TROUBLES

Having said all this, for the infertile Muslim men in my study, reprotravel to Dubai was often motivated by an additional important factor. Namely, for infertile Muslim men living in home countries where ICSI is not available or accessible, they are left with few other avenues to fatherhood. This is because sperm donation – the only other solution to bypass sperm problems (Becker, 2002) – is widely prohibited across the Muslim world, from Morocco to Malaysia (Inhorn & Tremayne, 2012).[8] Sperm donation is equated with genealogical confusion, mistaken paternity, and illicit sexuality and is thus widely refused by Muslim men, who argue that a donor-sperm child "won't be my son" (Inhorn, 2006, 2012). Similarly, legal adoption as practiced in the West – where a child takes the adoptive father's surname, can legally inherit from him, and is treated as if he or she is a biological child – is also prohibited for reasons of genealogical confusion and patrilineal impurity (Inhorn, 1994, 1996, 2003, 2012).[9]

Given these Muslim prohibitions against both sperm donation and legal adoption, the introduction of ICSI – a technology that relies on a patient's own sperm – was considered a watershed event in the Muslim world. As noted earlier, ICSI solves sperm problems in a way that IVF cannot. With standard IVF, spermatozoa are retrieved through masturbatory ejaculation, and oocytes (eggs) are surgically removed from the ovaries following hormonal stimulation. Once these gametes are retrieved, they are introduced to

[8] Iran and Lebanon are the only two Muslim-majority countries in which sperm donation is practiced, because of divergent Shia Muslim *fatwas* (or non-legally binding but authoritative religious decrees) which have allowed the procedure. However, even in those countries, sperm donation is unpopular among infertile men, and is rejected by the majority of Muslim religious authorities as being *haram*, or sinful.

[9] As with sperm donation, legal adoption is practiced in very few Muslim countries – only Iran, Tunisia, and Turkey within the Middle Eastern region.

each other in a petri dish in an IVF laboratory, in the hopes of fertilization. However, "weak" sperm (i.e., low numbers, poor movement, misshapen) are poor fertilizers. Through micromanipulation of otherwise infertile sperm under a high-powered microscope, ICSI allows for the direct injection of spermatozoa into human oocytes, effectively aiding fertilization. As long as one viable spermatozoon can be extracted from an infertile man's body, it can be ICSI-injected into an oocyte, leading to the potential creation of a human embryo.

Because ICSI significantly increases the chances of producing a test-tube baby, it has acquired special meaning for infertile Muslim men as a "hope technology" (see Inhorn, 2018). Since being introduced in Egypt in 1994, ICSI has led to a virtual "coming out" of cisgender men with sperm troubles across the Muslim Middle East, as these men acknowledge their infertility and seek the ICSI solution (Inhorn, 2003, 2012).

ICSI may be a revolutionary technology for the world's infertile cisgender men. But as Franklin (1997) rightly points out, hope does not always translate into a take-home baby. Indeed, ICSI entails many challenges. For one, the precisely timed collection of semen can produce deep anxiety and even impotence, but is imperative for all ICSI procedures (Inhorn, 2012). Some men may produce no spermatozoa whatsoever, even within their testicles, eliminating ICSI as an option. Furthermore, ICSI may not succeed, leading to endless rounds of fruitless repetition among some couples. ICSI is also highly dependent on the complicated hormonal stimulation and extraction of healthy oocytes from women's bodies. Whereas the fecundity of older men can often be enhanced through ICSI, women's fertility is highly age-sensitive, with oocyte quality declining at later stages of the reproductive life cycle. In short, older women may "age out" of ICSI, causing highly gendered, life-course disruptions surrounding women's biological clocks (Inhorn, 2003, 2012). In addition, men may arrive at ICSI after years of other failed treatment options. ICSI is expensive, usually costing US$2,000–$6,000 per cycle in the Middle East, with the prices in the UAE reflecting the high end of that financial spectrum. Thus, ICSI is often deemed a last resort, especially for those without adequate financial resources. Finally, when it does succeed, ICSI may perpetuate genetic defects into future generations, through the sperm defects and other inherited disorders that may be passed by infertile men via ICSI to their sons. The ethics of passing genetic mutations to children has been a significant cause for concern (Bittles & Matson, 2000; Spar, 2006).

Despite these challenges, ICSI is the best hope – indeed, the only hope – for most infertile Muslim men, especially those with serious sperm problems. The emergence of ICSI in the Middle Eastern region has led to a boom in demand for this technology – a demand that has never waned. ICSI is by far the most common ART now undertaken in the Middle East today. IVF clinics such as Conceive are filled with ICSI-seeking men from around the globe, who are depositing their sperm for inspection, micromanipulation, and ICSI injections. To demonstrate this ICSI promise for infertile cisgender Muslim men, I highlight in the next section the reprotravel story of Hsain, a twenty-two-year-old British man of Moroccan heritage. Because of his deep frustration with visits to the British NHS, Hsain had become a reprotraveler to global Dubai, undertaking ICSI in this transnational reprohub.

A REPROTRAVEL STORY – HSAIN AND HIS HIDDEN SPERM

Hsain was the British-born eldest son of working-class Moroccan immigrants. Expected to be independent by the age of eighteen, Hsain opened a small mobile phone shop in the outskirts of London. The shop was so successful that Hsain was able to afford marriage within the first year of his store's opening. He chose Fatima as his bride. Also a Moroccan immigrant to Britain, Fatima was seventeen at the time of her marriage. Pale-skinned with an East London cockney accent, Fatima seemed more British than North African. But her long *djellaba* (a floor-length, long-sleeved dress worn in Morocco) and modest headscarf signaled that she, like Hsain, was a devout Muslim.

As teen newlyweds, Hsain and Fatima were very much in love and hoped to become young parents: "I've always said to myself that I wanted to have my children by the time I was 30," Hsain explained to me. "I want to be running with my children in the park, being close to their age. Having a child at an old, old age doesn't appeal to me. I'd rather be done when I'm young. I did want a child at an even younger age, but God didn't want it. I would have had a four-and-a-half-year-old child by now if things had gone my way." Hsain continued. "I never really took it seriously, because you come across a lot of people who are trying, trying, trying. I can certainly say that we did try! But, obviously, nothing happened. Really, over the years, nothing happened. Nothing happened at all."

Two years of marriage without any form of contraception led the couple on a trip to the local NHS IVF clinic. "I did all the blood tests, and I had ultrasounds, and a [diagnostic] laparoscopy," Fatima explained. "And they said at the end of the day that everything is fine, everything is fine." When Fatima's tests all came back normal, Hsain was asked to undergo semen analysis, which he repeated several times. The South African Muslim physician working in the NHS clinic delivered the bad news to Hsain in this way: "Look. You have no sperm. You've only got, basically, a couple of options. Either use donor sperm, or try to do ICSI. But the probability of ICSI succeeding is not very high. We would have to do an operation on you – to take out some tissue from your testicles, and see if we can find any sperm."

As devout Sunni Muslims, Hsain and Fatima were horrified by the first option of sperm donation. "Because of our religion, for us, it wasn't an option at all," Hsain told me. "But over there, they do it! The guy who recommended donor sperm to us, he is a Muslim! And he kept saying: 'Why not? You should do it! You should do it!' He was trying to convince us to do it, even though he's Muslim. I don't think he was a very religious person himself. So we spoke to my parents about this, and my father spoke to some imams in London. And, oh no! They did *not* recommend that we do that."

Having rejected sperm donation altogether, Hsain was willing to accept the second recommendation of testicular biopsy. This would determine whether Hsain was suffering from a simple blockage in sperm transport, or a more serious form of non-obstructive azoospermia, in which sperm were simply not produced in his testicles. "This is not a part of the body that you like to be operated on – not for a man!" Hsain exclaimed. "And I would not like to do this again. But really, I had no choice. In other cases with no sperm, he was telling [those men] to go to Spain, because there they have fertility units, where his clients from the NHS can get donor sperm. But for me, this was basically out of the question. So instead, they took three samples of specimens from my testicles. And they found nothing, nothing, nothing."

In early 2007, Hsain and Fatima decided to travel to Dubai, where they met with Dr. Pankaj at Conceive. As Hsain explained to me:

> When we got here, we saw this Dr. Pankaj, who consulted our files. Once he saw these results, he said, "Look, we're going to do your sperm test again." I done [*sic*] it here, and then we waited. And within half an hour, he came back to me and said, "We found sperm. We found maybe 5 percent sperm." We didn't believe him! We thought it was somebody else's. So many years in England, we were told, "Absolutely nothing. Not at all!" Here, they showed me under the microscope. Just for me – I got "special treatment." They said, "We spun it. We spun it in the machine." I'm sure they did this in the UK, or at least I reckon they did. But maybe they didn't. So Dr. Pankaj suggested to freeze it, and I didn't want to because I didn't know this clinic. And you never know what goes on inside clinics these days! Leaving your sperm and it's live sperm! But I have a bit of confidence because a) You see the pictures [of babies] here on the walls, and b) he knew our South African doctor back in London. So we froze it, and we came back three days later to give some more sperm. We left two samples. You see, the more you have, the better, because some of the sperm can die. I was, I was honestly thinking that I'd have to do another [testicular]

> biopsy. So as soon as they found sperm [i.e., in the normal ejaculate], I couldn't believe it! Because when I walked in here, the first thing I said is, "I've got no sperm." I brought my test results from England, and all the reports said zero, zero, zero. But Dr. Pankaj said, "Throw it in the bin!" He didn't want to look at the reports. He said, "I found sperm. I don't need to see that."

As it turned out, Hsain had a classic case of cryptospermia, or "hidden sperm" in his ejaculate. The Palestinian Muslim laboratory director at Conceive had taken special care to centrifuge Hsain's semen sample, creating a "pellet sample" in which even the smallest number of spermatozoa could be detected. Although Hsain was seriously infertile – with fewer than 1,000 sperm found, when a fertile man would have at least 15 million sperm per milliliter under the microscope – Hsain nonetheless produced enough viable spermatozoa to be a candidate for ICSI.

In a happy state of shock over the recovery of his hidden sperm, Hsain was eager to get on with the ICSI procedure. However, Dr. Pankaj was very honest with Hsain and Fatima that their chances of success with an ICSI cycle were no higher than 38 percent. As practicing Muslims, the couple took this in stride. "God will give me a child if he wants to," Hsain calmly told me.

Fortunately for Hsain and Fatima, Conceive was their *nasib*, or "destiny." Hsain's once-hidden sperm were effective in producing several viable ICSI embryos, three of which were transferred into Fatima's womb. On the day of the pregnancy test, I was at the clinic eagerly awaiting the news, along with the couple and several Conceive staff members. Fatima was seated on a red couch in the clinic administrator's office, while Hsain stood beside her. When the Palestinian lab director came in to deliver the news, the happy smile on her face presaged the results of a clearly positive pregnancy test. Everyone cheered and hugged, with several other staff members coming by to congratulate the young couple.

Hsain and Fatima remained in Dubai for the next six weeks, determined that Dr. Pankaj himself would undertake the initial pregnancy ultrasound. The ultrasound showed that two of the couple's three embryos had not implanted in Fatima's womb. However, Fatima was definitely pregnant with a single fetus – the product of her eggs and Hsain's hidden sperm, which, although lost in the British NHS labyrinth, had been "found" in a cosmopolitan clinic in Dubai.

CONCLUSION

As shown in the preceding reprotravel story, new global mobilities are being enacted by men such as Hsain, who are searching far and wide for technologically assisted reproduction and fatherhood. For cisgender men with sperm troubles – and especially married Muslim men – ICSI has provided a technological breakthrough for a reproductive health problem that is highly prevalent yet often hidden and exceedingly difficult to overcome. Furthermore, many men with sperm troubles live in areas of the world where access to ICSI is limited for a variety of reasons. As a result, increasing numbers are becoming reprotravelers, searching for ICSI services in sites known to be effective in this regard. Belgium, where ICSI was initially invented, was the first to achieve global ICSI fame (De Sutter, 2011), but Dubai, too, has become an ICSI reprohub, with reprotravelers from Africa, Asia, Australia, Euro-America, and many parts of the Middle East flocking there in the hopes of fulfilling their fatherhood dreams and aspirations.

As shown in this chapter, ICSI has engendered reproduction for men such as Hsain, but these men's reproductive stories are rarely told. As I and my fellow anthropologists have argued (Inhorn et al., 2009), cisgender men are relegated as the "second sex" in reproduction. We tend not to include them in our reproductive studies, or we vilify them as being inherently detrimental to women's reproductive health and child well-being (Wentzell & Inhorn, 2014). But, as I hope this chapter has shown, these omissions and derogations do not tell the whole story. As seen with

Hsain, many cisgender men do what they can to achieve their own and their partner's reproductive goals – putting their bodies, their finances, and their emotions on the line in the process.

In general, we need to generate significantly more research on men – both cis- and transgender – *as reproducers* (Almeling, 2011; Mohr, 2018; Wahlberg, 2018). When we fail to study men, we are unable to assess whether they care about reproduction, how they enact reproductive decision-making and planning, how they deal with reproductive health challenges, whether they search for reproductive technologies (including contraceptive as well as conceptive technologies), what they hope for in terms of fatherhood, how they nurture their pregnant partners, and what they do to care for their children. Men play many fundamental reproductive roles, with far-reaching implications for their own health, and the health and well-being of their families. Reproduction also fundamentally alters the gender relations between partners, and, when successful, provides an opportunity for parents to model positive gender socialization for their offspring.

Ultimately, then, we need to engage men in our reproductive studies – especially as the ARTs themselves continue to evolve in the twenty-first century. As of this writing, ART technological innovations, including uterine transplantation, mitochondrial donation, ovarian tissue freezing, and gene editing, are opening up new horizons of technological hope for *both* men and women of *all* sexual identities in a complex world of reproductive possibility.

Indeed, before his death in January 2015 at the age of ninety-one, Carl Djerassi – an emeritus Stanford chemistry professor who was widely known as the "father" of the birth control pill and who is the benefactor of the Diane Middlebrook and Carl Djerassi Professorship at the University of Cambridge – made a bold prediction (Djerassi, 2014). Namely, Djerassi opined that by the year 2050, egg freezing will be as routine among young professional women as oral contraceptive usage is today. And when the time comes to thaw and fertilize those frozen eggs, women will inevitably turn to the most guaranteed method of fertilization – which, as shown in this chapter, is ICSI.

REFERENCES

Almeling, R. 2011. *Sex Cells: The Medical Market for Eggs and Sperm.* Berkeley, CA: University of California Press.

Barratt, C. L. R., Anderson, R. A. and De Jonge,C. 2019. Male Fertility: A Window on the Health of This Generation and the Next. *Reproductive BioMedicine Online*, **39**, 721–23.

Becker, G. 2002. Deciding Whether to Tell Children about Donor Insemination: An Unresolved Question in the United States. In M. C. Inhorn and F. van Balen, eds., *Infertility around the Globe: New Thinking on Childlessness, Gender, and Reproductive Technologies.* Berkeley, CA: University of California Press, pp. 119–33.

Bittles, A. H. and Matson, P. L. 2000. Genetic Influences on Human Infertility. In R. Bentley and C. G. N. Mascie-Taylor Gillian, eds., *Infertility in the Modern World: Present and Future Prospects.* Cambridge: Cambridge University Press, pp. 46–81.

Cui, W. 2010. Mother or Nothing: The Agony of Infertility. *Bulletin of the World Health Organization*, **88**, 881–82.

Dancet, E. A. F. et al. 2011. Patient-Centred Infertility Care: A Qualitative Study to Listen to the Patient's Voice. *Human Reproduction*, **26**, 827–33.

De Sutter, P. 2011. Considerations for Clinics and Practitioners Treating Foreign Patients with Assisted Reproductive Technology: Lessons from Experiences at Ghent University Hospital. *Belgium Reproductive BioMedicine Online*, **23**, 652–56.

Djerassi, C. 2014. *In Retrospect: From the Pill to the Pen.* London: Imperial College Press.

European Society for Human Reproduction and Embryology (ESHRE). 2018. More than 8 Million Babies Born from IVF since the World's First in 1978. www.eshre.eu/ESHRE2018/Media/ESHRE-2018-Press-releases/De-Geyter.

Franklin, S. 1997. *Embodied Progress: A Cultural Account of Reproduction.* London: Routledge.

Gürtin, Z. B. and Inhorn, M. C. 2011. Introduction: Travelling for Conception and the Global Assisted Reproduction Market. *Reproductive BioMedicine Online*, **23**, 535–37.

Hudson, N. and Culley, L. 2011. Assisted Reproductive Travel: UK Patient Trajectories. *Reproductive BioMedicine Online*, **23**, 573–81.

Hudson, N. et al. 2011. Cross-Border Reproductive Care: A Review of the Literature. *Reproductive BioMedicine Online*, **22**, 673–85.

Inhorn, M. C. 1994. *Quest for Conception: Gender, Infertility, and Egyptian Medical Traditions.* Philadelphia, PA: University of Pennsylvania Press.

1996. *Infertility and Patriarchy: The Cultural Politics of Gender and Family Life in Egypt.* Philadelphia, PA: University of Pennsylvania Press.

2003. *Local Babies, Global Science: Gender, Religion, and in Vitro Fertilization in Egypt.* New York: Routledge.

2006. "He Won't Be My Son": Middle Eastern Muslim Men's Discourses of Adoption and Gamete Donation. *Medical Anthropology Quarterly,* **20**, 94–120.

2012. *The New Arab Man: Emergent Masculinities, Technologies, and Islam in the Middle East.* Princeton, NJ: Princeton University Press.

2015. *Cosmopolitan Conceptions: IVF Sojourns in Global Dubai.* Durham, NC: Duke University Press.

2018. *America's Arab Refugees: Vulnerability and Health on the Margins.* Stanford, CA: Stanford University Press.

Inhorn, M. C. and Patrizio, P. 2015. Infertility around the Globe: New Thinking on Gender, Reproductive Technologies, and Global Movements in the 21st Century. *Human Reproduction Update,* **21**, 411–26.

Inhorn, M. C. and Tremayne, S., eds. 2012. *Islam and Assisted Reproductive Technologies: Sunni and Shia Perspectives.* New York: Berghahn.

Inhorn, M. C. et al., eds. 2009. *Reconceiving the Second Sex: Men, Masculinity, and Reproduction.* New York: Berghahn.

Jones, H. W. et al. 2010. International Federation of Fertility Societies: Surveillance 2010. www.iffs-reproduction.org/documents/IFFS_Surveillance_2010.pdf (accessed January 15, 2016).

Mohr, S. 2018. *Being a Sperm Donor: Masculinity, Sexuality, and Biosociality in Denmark.* New York: Berghahn.

Pennings, G. 2002. Reproductive Tourism as Moral Pluralism in Motion. *Journal of Medical Ethics,* **28**, 337–41.

2004. Legal Harmonization and Reproductive Tourism in Europe. *Human Reproduction,* **19**, 2689–94.

2009. International Evolution of Legislation and Guidelines in Medically Assisted Reproduction. *Reproductive BioMedicine Online,* **18**(Suppl. 2), 15–18.

2010. The Rough Guide to Insemination: Cross-Border Travelling for Donor Semen due to Different Regulations. *Facts, Views and Vision in Obstetrics and Gynaecology,* 1, 55–60.

Sassen, S. 2001. *The Global City: New York, London, Tokyo.* Princeton, NJ: Princeton University Press.

2005. The Global City: Introducing a Concept. *Brown Journal of World Affairs,* **11**, 27–43.

Spar, D. L. 2006. *The Baby Business: How Money, Science, and Politics Drive the Commerce of Conception.* Boston, MA: Harvard Business School Press.

Wahlberg, A. 2018. *Good Quality: The Routinization of Sperm Banking in China.* Berkeley, CA: University of California Press, 2018.

Wentzell, E. A. and Inhorn, M.C. 2014. Reconceiving Masculinity and "Men as Partners" in ICPD Beyond 2014: Insights from a Mexican HPV Study. *Global Public Health,* **9**, 691–705.

CHAPTER 7

Gender, Capital, and Care

Nancy Fraser

WE HEAR A LOT OF TALK TODAY ABOUT "THE CRISIS OF care."[1] Often linked to such phrases as "time poverty," "family/work balance," and "social depletion,"[2] this expression refers to the pressures, coming from several directions, that are currently squeezing a key set of social capacities: the capacities available for birthing and raising children, caring for friends and family members, maintaining households and broader communities, and sustaining connections more generally. Historically, this work of "social reproduction," as I shall call it, has been cast as women's work, although men have always done some of it too. Comprising both affective and material labor, and often performed without pay, it is indispensable to society. Without it there could be no culture, no economy, no political organization. No society that systematically undermines social reproduction can endure for long. Today, however, a new form of *capitalist* society is doing just that. The result, as I shall explain, is a major crisis, not simply of care, but of social reproduction in this broader sense.

[1] An earlier version of this essay was published as "Contradictions of Capital and Care" in *New Left Review* 100 (July/August 2016): 99–117, modified here with permission. A French translation was delivered in Paris on June 14, 2016 as the 38th annual Marc Bloch Lecture of the *Ecole des hautes études en sciences sociales* and is available on the *Ecole*'s website. I gratefully thank Pierre-Cyrile Hautcoeur for the lecture invitation, Johanna Oksala for stimulating discussions, Mala Htun and Eli Zaretsky for helpful comments, and Selim Heper for research assistance.

[2] Boffey (2015); Hess (2013); Rosen (2007). For "time poverty," see Boushey (2016); Hochschild (2001). For "family/work balance," see Beck (2015); Boushey and Anderson (2013). For "social depletion," see Rai, Hoskyns & Thomas (2013).

I understand this crisis as one strand of a "general crisis," which also encompasses other strands – economic, ecological, and political, all of which intersect with and exacerbate one another. The social-reproduction strand forms an important dimension of this general crisis, but it is often neglected in current discussions, which focus chiefly on the economic or ecological strands. This "critical separatism" is problematic. The social strand is so central to the broader crisis that none of the others can be properly understood in abstraction from it. However, the converse is also true. The crisis of social reproduction is not freestanding and cannot be adequately grasped on its own.

How then should it be understood? My claim is that what some call "the crisis of care" is best interpreted as a more or less acute expression of *the social-reproductive contradictions of financialized capitalism.* This formulation suggests two ideas. First, the present strains on care are not accidental, but have deep systemic roots in the structure of our social order, which I characterize here as financialized capitalism. Nevertheless, and this is the second point, the present crisis of social reproduction indicates something rotten not only in capitalism's current, financialized form but in capitalist society per se.

These are the theses I shall elaborate here. My claim, to begin with the last point, is that *every* form of capitalist society harbors a deep-seated *social-reproductive* "crisis tendency" or "contradiction." On the one hand, social reproduction is a condition of possibility for sustained capital accumulation; on the other hand, capitalism's orientation to unlimited accumulation tends to destabilize the very processes of social reproduction on which it relies. This "social-reproductive contradiction of capitalism" lies at the root, I claim, of our so-called crisis of care. Although inherent in capitalism as such, it assumes a different and distinctive guise in every historically specific form of capitalist society – for example, in the liberal, competitive capitalism of the nineteenth century; in the state-managed capitalism of the postwar era; and in the financialized neoliberal capitalism of our time. The care deficits we experience today are the form this contradiction takes in that third, most recent phase of capitalist development.

To develop this thesis, I first propose an account of the social contradiction of capitalism *as such*, without reference to any specific historical form. Second, I shall sketch an account of the unfolding of this contradiction in the two earlier phases of capitalist development I just mentioned. Finally, I shall propose a reading of today's so-called "care deficits" as expressions of capitalism's social contradiction in its current, financialized phase.

SOCIAL CONTRADICTIONS OF CAPITALISM "AS SUCH"

Most analysts of the contemporary crisis focus on contradictions internal to the capitalist economy. At its heart, they claim, lies a built-in tendency to self-destabilization, which expresses itself periodically in economic crises. This view is right, as far as it goes; but it fails to provide a full picture of capitalism's inherent crisis tendencies. Adopting an economistic perspective, it understands capitalism too narrowly, as an economic system *simpliciter*. In contrast, I shall assume an expanded understanding of capitalism, encompassing both its official economy and the latter's "non-economic" background conditions.[3] Such a view permits us to conceptualize, and to criticize, capitalism's full range of crisis tendencies, including those centered on social reproduction.

My argument is that capitalism's economic subsystem depends on social-reproductive activities external to it, which form one of its background conditions of possibility. Other background conditions include the governance functions performed by public powers and the availability of nature as a source of "productive inputs" and a "sink" for production's waste.[4] Here, however, I will focus on the way that the capitalist economy relies on – one might

[3] For a critique of the view of capitalism as an economy and a defense of the "enlarged" view, see Fraser (2014).

[4] For an account of the necessary political background conditions for a capitalist economy, see Fraser (2015). For the necessary ecological conditions, see Moore (2015) and O'Connor (1988).

say, free rides on – activities of provisioning, caregiving, and interaction that produce and maintain social bonds, although it accords them no monetized value and treats them as if they were free. Variously called "care," "affective labor" or "subjectivation," this activity forms capitalism's human subjects, sustaining them as embodied natural beings, while also constituting them as social beings, forming their *habitus* and the cultural ethos in which they move. The work of birthing and socializing the young is central to this process, as is caring for the old, maintaining households, members; building communities and sustaining the shared meanings, affective dispositions, and horizons of value that underpin social cooperation. In capitalist societies much, though not all, of this activity goes on outside the market – in households, neighbourhoods, civil society associations, informal networks, and public institutions, such as schools; and relatively little of it takes the form of wage labor. Non-waged social-reproductive activity is necessary to the existence of waged work, the accumulation of surplus value, and the functioning of capitalism as such. None of those things could exist in the absence of housework, child-raising, schooling, affective care, and a host of other activities which serve to produce new generations of workers and replenish existing ones, as well as to maintain social bonds and shared understandings. Social reproduction is an indispensable background condition for the possibility of economic production in a capitalist society.[5]

From at least the industrial era, however, capitalist societies have separated the work of social reproduction from that of economic production. Associating the first with women and the second with men, they have remunerated "reproductive" activities in the coin of "love" and "virtue," while compensating "productive work" in that of money. In this way, capitalist societies

[5] Many feminist theorists have made versions of this argument. For Marxist-feminist formulations, see Delphy (1984); Federici (2012); and Vogel (2013). Another powerful elaboration is Folbre (2002). For "social reproduction theory," see Arruzza (2016); Bezanson & Luxton, eds. (2006); Laslett & Brenner (1989).

created an institutional basis for new, modern forms of women's subordination. Splitting off reproductive labor from the larger universe of human activities, in which women's work previously held a recognized place, they relegated it to a newly institutionalized "domestic sphere," where its social importance was obscured. And in this new world, where money became a primary medium of power, the fact of its being unpaid sealed the matter: those who do this work are structurally subordinate to those who earn cash wages, even as their work supplies a necessary precondition for wage labor – and even as it also becomes saturated with and mystified by new, domestic ideals of femininity.

In general, then, capitalist societies separate social reproduction from economic production, associating the first with women, and obscuring its importance and value. Paradoxically, however, they make their official economies dependent on the very same processes of social reproduction whose value they disavow. This peculiar relation of *separation-cum-dependence-cum-disavowal* is a built-in source of potential instability. On the one hand, capitalist economic production is not self-sustaining, but relies on social reproduction. On the other hand, its drive to unlimited accumulation threatens to destabilize the very reproductive processes and capacities that capital – and the rest of us – need. The effect over time, as we shall see, can be to jeopardize the necessary social conditions of the capitalist economy.

Here, in effect, is a "social contradiction" inherent in the deep structure of capitalist society. Like the economic contradiction(s) that Marxists have stressed, this one, too, grounds a crisis tendency. In this case, however, the contradiction is not located "inside" the capitalist economy but at the border that simultaneously separates and connects production and reproduction. Neither intra-economic nor intra-domestic, it is a contradiction *between* those two constitutive elements of capitalist society.

Often, of course, this contradiction is muted, and the associated crisis tendency remains obscured. It becomes acute, however, when capital's drive to expanded accumulation becomes unmoored from its social bases and turns against them. In that case, the logic of economic production overrides that of social reproduction, destabilizing the very social processes on which capital depends – compromising the social capacities, both domestic and public, that are needed to sustain accumulation over the long term. Destroying its own conditions of possibility, capital's accumulation dynamic effectively eats its own tail.

HISTORICAL REGIMES OF REPRODUCTION-CUM-PRODUCTION

This is the general social-crisis tendency of "capitalism as such." However, capitalist society does not exist "as such," but only in historically specific forms or regimes of accumulation. In fact, the capitalist organization of social reproduction has undergone major historical shifts – often as a result of political contestation. Especially in periods of crisis, social actors struggle over the boundaries delimiting "economy" from "society," "production" from "reproduction," and "work" from "family" – and sometimes succeed in redrawing them. Such *boundary struggles*, as I have called them, are as central to capitalist societies as are the class struggles analyzed by Marx.[6] And the shifts they produce mark epochal transformations. If we adopt a perspective that foregrounds these shifts, we can distinguish (at least) three regimes of social reproduction-cum-economic production in capitalism's history.

The first is the nineteenth-century regime of liberal competitive capitalism. Combining industrial exploitation in the European core with colonial expropriation in the periphery, this regime tended to leave workers to reproduce themselves "autonomously," outside the circuits of monetized value, as states looked on from the sidelines. But it also created a new, bourgeois imaginary of domesticity. Casting social reproduction as the province of women within the private family, this regime elaborated the ideal of "separate spheres," even as it deprived most people of the conditions needed to realize it.

[6] For boundary struggles, see Fraser (2014).

The second regime is the state-managed capitalism of the twentieth century. Premised on large-scale industrial production and domestic consumerism in the core, underpinned by ongoing colonial and postcolonial expropriation in the periphery, this regime internalized social reproduction through state and corporate provision of social welfare. Modifying the Victorian model of separate spheres, it promoted the seemingly more modern ideal of "the family wage," even though, once again, relatively few families were permitted to achieve it.

The third regime is the globalizing financialized capitalism of the present era. This regime has relocated manufacturing to low-wage regions, recruited women into the paid workforce, and promoted state and corporate disinvestment from social welfare. Externalizing carework onto families and communities, it has simultaneously diminished their capacity to perform it. The result, amid rising inequality, is a dualized organization of social reproduction, commodified for those who can pay for it, privatized for those who cannot – all glossed by the even more modern ideal of the "two-earner family."

In each regime, therefore, the social-reproductive conditions for capitalist production have assumed a different institutional form and embodied a different normative order: first "separate spheres," then "the family wage," now the "two-earner family." In each case, too, the social contradiction of capitalist society has assumed a different guise and found expression in a different set of crisis phenomena. In each regime, finally, capitalism's social contradiction has incited different forms of social struggle – class struggles, to be sure, but also boundary struggles – both of which were entwined, not only with one another, but also with other struggles, which aimed at emancipating women, slaves, and colonized peoples.

SOCIAL CONTRADICTIONS OF LIBERAL CAPITALISM

Consider, first, the liberal competitive capitalism of the nineteenth century. In this era, the imperatives of production and reproduction appeared to stand in direct contradiction to each other. Certainly, that was the case in the early manufacturing centers of the capitalist core, where industrialists dragooned women and children into factories and mines, eager for their cheap labor and reputed docility. Paid a pittance and working long hours in unhealthy conditions, these workers became icons of capital's disregard for the social relations and social capacities that underpinned its productivity[7]. The result was a crisis on at least two levels: on the one hand, a crisis of social reproduction among the poor and working classes, whose capacities for sustenance and replenishment were stretched to the breaking point; on the other hand, a moral panic among the middle classes, who were scandalized by what they understood as the "destruction of the family" and the "de-sexing" of proletarian women. So dire was this situation that even such astute critics as Marx and Engels mistook this early head-on conflict between economic production and social reproduction for the final word. Imagining that capitalism had entered its terminal crisis, they believed that, as it eviscerated the working-class family, the system was also eradicating the basis of women's oppression.[8] But what actually happened was just the reverse: over time, capitalist societies found resources for managing this contradiction – in part by creating "the family" in its modern restricted form, by inventing new, intensified meanings of gender difference, and by modernizing male domination.

The process of adjustment began, in the European core, with protective legislation. The idea was to stabilize social reproduction by limiting the exploitation of women and children in factory labor.[9] Spearheaded by middle-class reformers in alliance with nascent workers' organizations, this "solution" reflected a complex amalgam of different motives. One aim, famously characterized by Karl Polanyi, was to defend "society" against "economy."[10] Another was to allay anxiety over "gender leveling." But these motives were also entwined with something else: an insistence on masculine authority

[7] Tilly & Scott (1987). [8] Engels (1902: 90–100); Marx & Engels (1978).
[9] Woloch (2015). [10] Polanyi (2001: 87, 138–39, 213).

over women and children, especially within the family.[11] As a result, the struggle to ensure the integrity of social reproduction became entangled with the defense of male domination.

Its intended effect, however, was to soften the social contradiction in the capitalist core – even as slavery and colonialism raised it to an extreme pitch in the periphery. Creating what Maria Mies called housewifization as the flip side of colonization,[12] liberal competitive capitalism elaborated a new gender imaginary centered on "separate spheres." Figuring woman as "the angel in the home," its proponents sought to create stabilizing ballast for the volatility of the economy. The cutthroat world of production was to be flanked by a "haven in the heartless world."[13] As long as each side kept to its own designated sphere and served as the other's complement, the potential conflict between them would remain under wraps.

In reality, this "solution" proved rather shaky. Protective legislation could not ensure labor's reproduction when wages remained below the level needed to support a family, when crowded, pollution-enveloped tenements foreclosed privacy and damaged lungs, and when employment itself (when available at all) was subject to wild fluctuations due to bankruptcies, market crashes, and financial panics. Nor did such arrangements satisfy workers. Agitating for higher wages and better conditions, they formed trades unions, went out on strike, and joined labor and socialist parties. Riven by increasingly sharp, broad-based class conflict, capitalism's future seemed anything but assured.

Separate spheres proved equally problematic. Poor, racialized, and working-class women were in no position to satisfy Victorian ideals of domesticity; if protective legislation mitigated their direct exploitation, it provided no material support or compensation for lost wages. Nor were those middle-class women who *could* conform to Victorian ideals always content with their situation, which combined material comfort and moral prestige with legal minority and

[11] Baron (1981). [12] Mies (2014: 74). [13] Coontz (1988); Zaretsky (1986).

institutionalized dependency. For both groups, the separate-spheres "solution" came largely at women's expense. But it also pitted them against one another – witness nineteenth-century struggles over prostitution, which aligned the philanthropic concerns of Victorian middle-class women against the material interests of their "fallen sisters."[14]

A different dynamic unfolded in the periphery. There, as extractive colonialism ravaged subjugated populations, neither separate spheres nor social protection enjoyed any currency. Far from seeking to protect indigenous relations of social reproduction, metropolitan powers actively promoted their destruction. Peasantries were looted, their communities wrecked, to supply the cheap food, textiles, mineral ore, and energy without which the exploitation of metropolitan industrial workers would not have been profitable. In the Americas, meanwhile, enslaved women's reproductive capacities were instrumentalized to the profit calculations of planters, who routinely tore apart slave families by selling their members off separately to different owners.[15] Native children, too, were ripped from their communities, conscripted into missionary schools, and subjected to coercive disciplines of assimilation.[16] When rationalizations were needed, the "backward, patriarchal" state of pre-capitalist indigenous kinship arrangements served quite well. Here, too, among the colonialists, philanthropic women found a public platform, urging, in the words of Gayatri Spivak, "white men to save brown women from brown men."[17]

In both settings, periphery and core, feminists seeking to challenge the gender order found themselves negotiating a political minefield. (See the contributions to this volume by Judith Butler, Jack Halberstam, and Mignon Nixon, for example.) Rejecting coverture and separate spheres, while demanding the right to vote, refuse sex, own property, enter into contracts, practice professions and control their own wages, liberal feminists appeared to

[14] Hobson (1990); Walkowitz (1980). [15] Davis (1972).
[16] Adams (1995); Churchill (2004). [17] Spivak (1988: 305).

valorize the "masculine" aspiration to autonomy over "feminine" ideals of nurture. And on this point, if not on much else, their socialist feminist counterparts effectively agreed. Conceiving women's entry into wage labor as the route to emancipation, the latter, too, preferred the "male" values associated with production to those associated with reproduction. These associations were ideological, to be sure. But behind them lay a deep intuition: despite the new forms of domination it brought, capitalism's erosion of traditional kinship relations contained an emancipatory moment.

Caught in a double-bind, many feminists found scant comfort on either side of Polanyi's double movement, neither on the side of social protection with its attachment to male domination, nor on the side of marketization with its disregard of social reproduction. Able neither simply to reject nor to embrace the liberal order, they needed a third alternative, which they called *emancipation.* To the extent that feminists were able to credibly embody that term, they effectively exploded the dualistic Polanyian figure and replaced it with what we might call a *triple movement.* In this three-sided conflict scenario, proponents of protection and marketization collided, not only with one another, but also with partisans of emancipation: with feminists, to be sure, but also with socialists, abolitionists, and anti-colonialists, all of whom endeavored to play the two Polanyian forces off against each other, even while clashing among themselves.[18]

However promising in theory, such a strategy was hard to implement. As long as efforts to "protect society from economy" were identified with the defense of gender hierarchy, feminist opposition to male domination could easily be read as endorsing the economic forces that were ravaging working-class and peripheral communities. These associations would prove surprisingly durable long after liberal competitive capitalism collapsed under the weight of its (multiple) contradictions in the throes of inter-imperialist wars, economic depressions, and international financial chaos – giving

[18] For the concept of the triple movement, see Fraser (2011, 2013).

way in the mid-twentieth century to a new regime, that of state-managed capitalism.

SOCIAL CONTRADICTIONS OF STATE-MANAGED CAPITALISM

Emerging from the ashes of the Great Depression and the Second World War, this regime defused the contradiction between economic production and social reproduction in a different way – by enlisting state power on the side of reproduction. Assuming some public responsibility for "social welfare," the states of this era sought to counter the corrosive effects on social reproduction not only of exploitation, but also of mass unemployment. This aim was embraced by the democratic welfare states of the capitalist core and the newly independent developmental states of the periphery alike – despite their unequal capacities for realizing it.

Once again, the motives were mixed. A stratum of enlightened elites had come to believe that capital's short-term interest in squeezing out maximum profits needed to be subordinated to the longer-term requirements for sustaining accumulation over time. For these actors, the creation of the state-managed regime was a matter of saving the capitalist system from its own self-destabilizing propensities – as well as from the spectre of revolution in an era of mass mobilization. Productivity and profitability required the "biopolitical" cultivation of a healthy, educated workforce with a stake in the system, as opposed to a ragged revolutionary rabble.[19] Public investment in health care, schooling, childcare, old age pensions, supplemented by corporate provision, was perceived as a necessity in an era in which capitalist relations had penetrated social life to such an extent that the working classes no longer possessed the means to reproduce themselves on their own. In this situation, social reproduction had to be internalized, brought within the officially managed domain of the capitalist order.

[19] Foucault (1991, 2010: 64).

That project dovetailed with the new problematic of economic "demand." Seeking to smooth out capitalism's endemic boom/bust cycles, economic reformers sought to ensure continuous growth by enabling workers in the capitalist core to do double duty as consumers. Accepting unionization, which brought higher wages, and public-sector spending, which created jobs, these actors reinvented the household as a private space for the domestic consumption of mass-produced objects of daily use.[20] Linking the assembly line with working-class familial consumerism, on the one hand, and with state-supported reproduction, on the other, this "fordist" model forged a novel synthesis of marketization and social protection, projects Polanyi had considered antithetical.

But it was above all the working classes – both women and men – who spearheaded the struggle for public provision, acting for reasons of their own. For them, the issue was full membership in society as democratic citizens – hence, dignity, rights, respectability, and material well-being, all of which were understood to require a stable family life. In embracing social democracy, then, working classes were also valorizing social reproduction against the all-consuming dynamism of economic production. In effect, they were voting for family, country, and lifeworld against factory, system, and machine.

Unlike the protective legislation of the liberal regime, the state-capitalist settlement resulted from a class compromise and represented a democratic advance. Unlike its predecessor, too, the new arrangements served, at least for some and for a while, to stabilize social reproduction. For majority ethnicity workers in the capitalist core, they eased material pressures on family life and fostered political incorporation. But before we rush to proclaim a golden age, we should register the constitutive exclusions that made these achievements possible.

Here, as before, the defense of social reproduction in the core was entangled with (neo)imperialism. Fordist regimes financed social entitlements in part by ongoing expropriation from the

[20] Ewen (2008); Hayden (2003); Ross (1996).

periphery (including the periphery within the core), which persisted in forms old and new, even after decolonization.[21] Meanwhile, postcolonial states caught in the crosshairs of the Cold War directed the bulk of their resources, already depleted by imperial predation, to large-scale development projects, which often entailed expropriation of "their own" indigenous peoples. Social reproduction, for the vast majority in the periphery, remained external, as rural populations were left to fend for themselves. Like its predecessor, too, the state-managed regime was entangled with racial hierarchy. US social insurance excluded domestic and agricultural workers, effectively cutting off many African Americans from social entitlements.[22] And the racial division of reproductive labor, begun during slavery, assumed a new guise under Jim Crow, as women of color found low-paid waged work raising the children and cleaning the homes of "white" families at the expense of their own.[23]

Nor was gender hierarchy absent from these arrangements, as feminist voices were relatively muted throughout the process of their construction. In a period (roughly from the 1930s through the 1950s) when feminist movements did not enjoy much public visibility, hardly anyone contested the view that working-class dignity required "the family wage," male authority in the household, and a robust sense of gender difference. As a result, the broad tendency of state-managed capitalism in the countries of the core was to valorize the heteronormative male breadwinner/female homemaker model of the gendered family. Public investment in social reproduction reinforced these norms. In the US, the welfare system took a dualized form, divided into stigmatized poor relief for ("white") women and children lacking access to a male wage,

[21] In this era, state support for social reproduction was financed by tax revenues and dedicated funds to which both metropolitan workers and capital contributed, in different proportions, depending on the relations of class power within a given state. But those revenue streams were swollen with value siphoned from the periphery through profits from foreign direct investment and through trade based on unequal exchange. Baran (1957); Köhler & Tausch (2001); Pilling (1973); Prebisch (1950).

[22] Katznelson (2005); Quadagno (1994). [23] Glenn (1992, 2010); Jones (1985).

on the one hand, and respectable social insurance for those constructed as "workers," on the other.[24] By contrast, European arrangements entrenched androcentric hierarchy differently, in the division between mothers' pensions and entitlements tied to waged work – driven in many cases by pronatalist agendas born of interstate competition.[25] Both models validated, assumed, and encouraged the family wage. Institutionalizing androcentric understandings of family and work, both naturalized heteronormativity and gender hierarchy, and largely removed them from political contestation.

In all these respects, social democracy sacrificed emancipation to an alliance of social protection and marketization, even as it mitigated capitalism's social contradiction for several decades. But the state-capitalist regime began unraveling, first, politically, in the 1960s, when the global New Left erupted to challenge its imperial, gender, and racial exclusions, as well as its bureaucratic paternalism, all in the name of *emancipation*; and then, economically, in the 1970s, when stagflation, the "productivity crisis," and declining profit rates in manufacturing galvanized efforts by "neoliberals" to unshackle *marketization*. What would be sacrificed, were those two parties to join forces, would be *social protection*.

SOCIAL CONTRADICTIONS OF FINANCIALIZED CAPITALISM

Like the liberal regime before it, the state-managed capitalist order dissolved in the course of a protracted crisis. By the 1980s prescient observers could discern the emerging outlines of a new regime, which would become the financialized capitalism of the present era. Globalizing and neoliberal, this new regime is promoting state and corporate disinvestment from social welfare while recruiting women into the paid workforce. Thus, it is

[24] Brenner (1991); Fraser (1989); Nelson (1985); Pearce (1979).

[25] Holter, ed. (1984); Land (1978); Ruggie (1984); Orloff (1993, 2009); Orloff, O'Connor, & Shaver (1999); Sainsbury, ed. (2000); Siim (1990); Williams et al. (2007).

externalizing carework onto families and communities while diminishing their capacity to perform it. The result is a new, *dualized* organization of social reproduction, commodified for those who can pay for it and privatized for those who cannot, as some in the second category provide carework in return for (low) wages for those in the first. Meanwhile, the one–two punch of feminist critique and deindustrialization has definitively stripped "the family wage" of all credibility. That ideal has given way to today's more modern norm of the "two-earner family."

The major driver of these developments, and the defining feature of this regime, is the new centrality of debt. Debt is the instrument by which global financial institutions pressure states to slash social spending, enforce austerity, and generally collude with investors in extracting value from defenseless populations. It is largely through debt, too, that peasants in the Global South are dispossessed by a new round of corporate land grabs, aimed at cornering supplies of energy, water, arable land, and "carbon offsets." It is increasingly via debt as well that accumulation proceeds in the historic core. As low-waged precarious service work replaces unionized industrial labor, wages fall below the socially necessary costs of reproduction; in this "gig economy," continued consumer spending requires expanded consumer debt, which grows exponentially.[26] It is increasingly through debt, in other words, that capital now cannibalizes labor, disciplines states, transfers wealth from periphery to core, and sucks value from households, families, communities, and nature.

The effect is to intensify capitalism's inherent contradiction between economic production and social reproduction. Whereas the previous regime empowered states to subordinate the short-term interests of private firms to the long-term objective of sustained accumulation, in part by stabilizing reproduction through public provision, this one authorizes finance capital to discipline states and publics in the immediate interests of private investors, not least by requiring public disinvestment from social

[26] Roberts (2013).

reproduction. And whereas the previous regime allied marketization with social protection against emancipation, this one generates an even more perverse configuration, in which emancipation joins with marketization to undermine social protection.

The new regime emerged from the fateful intersection of two sets of struggles. One set pitted an ascending party of free-marketeers, bent on liberalizing and globalizing the capitalist economy, against declining labor movements in the countries of the core, once the most powerful base of support for social democracy, but now on the defensive, if not wholly defeated. The other set of struggles pitted progressive "new social movements," opposed to hierarchies of gender, sex, "race"-ethnicity, and religion, against populations seeking to defend established lifeworlds and privileges, now threatened by the "cosmopolitanism" of the new economy. Out of the collision of these two sets of struggles there emerged a surprising result: a "progressive" neoliberalism, which celebrates "diversity," meritocracy and "emancipation" while dismantling social protections and re-externalizing social reproduction. The result is not only to abandon defenseless populations to capital's predations, but also to redefine emancipation in market terms.[27]

Emancipatory movements participated in this process. All of them, including anti-racism, multiculturalism, LGBT liberation, and ecology, spawned market-friendly neoliberal currents. But the feminist trajectory proved especially fateful, given capitalism's longstanding entanglement of gender and social reproduction.[28] Like each of its predecessor regimes, financialized capitalism institutionalizes the production/reproduction division on a gendered basis. Unlike its predecessors, however, its dominant imaginary is liberal-individualist and gender-egalitarian – women are considered the equals of men in every sphere, deserving of equal

[27] The fruit of an unlikely alliance between free-marketeers and "new social movements," the new regime is scrambling all the usual political alignments, pitting "progressive" neoliberal feminists such as Hillary Clinton against authoritarian nationalist populists such as Donald Trump.

[28] Fraser (2009).

opportunities to realize their talents, including – perhaps especially – in the sphere of production. Reproduction, by contrast, appears as a backward residue, an obstacle to advancement that must be sloughed off, one way or another, en route to liberation.

Despite, or perhaps because of, its feminist aura, this conception epitomizes the current form of capitalism's social contradiction, which assumes a new intensity. As well as diminishing public provision and recruiting women into waged work, financialized capitalism has reduced real wages, thus raising the number of hours of paid work per household needed to support a family and prompting a desperate scramble to transfer carework to others.[29] To fill the "care gap," the regime imports migrant workers from poorer to richer countries. Typically, it is racialized and/or rural women from poor regions who take on reproductive and caring labor previously performed by more privileged women. But to do this, the migrants must transfer their own familial and community responsibilities to other, still poorer caregivers, who must in turn do the same – and on and on, in ever longer "global care chains." Far from filling the care gap, the net effect is to displace it – from richer to poorer families, from the Global North to the Global South.[30]

This scenario fits the gendered strategies of cash-strapped, indebted postcolonial states subjected to the International Monetary Fund (IMF) structural adjustment programmes. Desperate for hard currency, some of them have actively promoted women's emigration to perform paid carework abroad for the sake of remittances, while others have courted foreign direct investment by creating export processing zones, often in industries, such as textiles and electronics assembly, that prefer to employ women workers.[31] In both cases, social-reproductive capacities are further squeezed.

Neoliberalism's dualized organization of carework brings with it a dualized organization of childhood. As described in this volume by Cindi Katz, the children of professional managerial strata

[29] Warren & Warren Tyagi (2003). [30] Hochschild (2002); Young (2001).
[31] Bair (2010); Sassen (2000).

are constructed as affectively charged human capital, anxiously molded for "the imagined niche markets of the future." Meanwhile, those of the favelas, inner cities, and mega-slums are treated as "waste," expelled from any possibility of steady employment and subjected to state and para-state violence.

Two recent developments in the United States epitomize the severity of the situation. The first is the rising popularity of "egg-freezing," normally a $10,000 procedure, but now offered free by IT firms as a fringe benefit to highly qualified female employees. Eager to attract and retain these workers, firms such as Apple and Facebook provide them with a strong incentive to postpone child-bearing, saying, in effect: "Wait and have your kids in your 40s, 50s, or even 60s; devote your high-energy, productive years to us."[32]

A second US development equally symptomatizes the contradiction between reproduction and production: the proliferation of expensive, high-tech, mechanical pumps for expressing breast milk. This is the "fix" of choice in a country with a high rate of female labor force participation, no mandated paid maternity or parental leave, and a love affair with technology. This is a country, too, in which breastfeeding is *de rigeur* but has changed beyond all recognition. No longer a matter of suckling a child at one's breast, one "breastfeeds" now by expressing one's milk mechanically and storing it for feeding by bottle later by one's nanny. In a context of severe time poverty, double-cup, hands-free pumps are considered the most desirable, as they permit one to express milk from both breasts at once while driving to work on the freeway.[33]

Given pressures like these, is it any wonder that struggles over social reproduction have exploded over recent years? Northern

[32] Tran (2014). Importantly, this benefit is no longer reserved exclusively for the professional-technical-managerial class. The US Army now makes egg-freezing available gratis to enlisted women who sign up for extended tours of duty; Schmidt (2016). Here the logic of militarism overrides that of privatization. To my knowledge, no one has yet broached the looming question of what to do with the eggs of a female soldier who dies in conflict.

[33] Jung (2015: esp. 130–31). The Affordable Care Act (aka "Obamacare") now mandates that health insurers provide such pumps free to their beneficiaries. So this benefit too is no longer the exclusive prerogative of privileged women. The effect is to create

feminists often describe their focus as the "balance between family and work."[34] But struggles over social reproduction encompass much more – including grass-roots community movements for housing, health care, food security, and an unconditional basic income; struggles for the rights of migrants, domestic workers, and public employees; campaigns to unionize those who perform social service work in for-profit nursing homes, hospitals, and child care centers; struggles for public services such as day care and elder care, for a shorter work week, and for generous paid maternity and parental leave. Taken together, these claims are tantamount to the demand for a massive reorganization of the relation between production and reproduction: for social arrangements that could enable people of every class, gender, sexuality, and color to combine social-reproductive activities with safe, interesting, and well-remunerated work.

Boundary struggles over social reproduction are as central to the present conjuncture as are class struggles over economic production. They respond, above all, to a "crisis of care" that is rooted in the structural dynamics of financialized capitalism. Globalizing and propelled by debt, this capitalism is systematically expropriating the capacities available for sustaining social connections. Proclaiming the new, more modern ideal of "the two-earner family," it recuperates movements for emancipation, who join with proponents of marketization to oppose the partisans of social protection, now turned increasingly resentful and chauvinistic.

What might emerge from this crisis?

ANOTHER MUTATION?

Capitalist society has reinvented itself several times in the course of its history. Especially in moments of general crisis, when multiple contradictions – political, economic, ecological, and social

a huge new market for manufacturers, who are producing the pumps in very large batches in the factories of their Chinese subcontractors. See Kliff (2013).

[34] Belkin (2003); Miller (2013); Slaughter (2012, 2015); Shulevitz (2016); Warner (2006).

reproductive – intertwine and exacerbate one another, boundary struggles have erupted at the sites of capitalism's constitutive institutional divisions: where economy meets polity, where society meets nature, and where production meets reproduction. At those boundaries, social actors have mobilized to redraw the institutional map of capitalist society. Their efforts propelled the shift, first, from the liberal competitive capitalism of the nineteenth century to the state-managed capitalism of the twentieth, and then to the financialized capitalism of the present era. Historically, too, capitalism's social contradiction has formed an important strand of the precipitating crisis, as the boundary dividing social reproduction from economic production has emerged as a major site and central stake of social struggle. In each case, the gender order of capitalist society has been contested, and the outcome has depended on alliances forged among the principal poles of a triple movement: marketization, social protection, emancipation. Those dynamics propelled the shift, first, from separate spheres to the family wage, and then, to the two-earner family.

What follows for the current conjuncture? Are the present contradictions of financialized capitalism severe enough to qualify as a general crisis, and should we anticipate another mutation of capitalist society? Will the current crisis galvanize struggles of sufficient breadth and vision to transform the present regime? Might a new form of "socialist-feminism" succeed in breaking up the mainstream movement's love affair with marketization, while forging a new alliance between emancipation and social protection – and if so, to what end? How might the reproduction/production division be reinvented today, and what can replace the two-earner family?

Nothing I have said here serves directly to answer these questions. But in laying the groundwork that permits us to pose them, I have tried to shed some light on the current conjuncture. I have suggested, specifically, that the roots of today's "crisis of care" lie in capitalism's inherent social contradiction – or rather in the acute form that contradiction assumes today, in financialized capitalism. If that is right, then this crisis will not be resolved by tinkering with social policy. The path to its resolution can only go through deep structural transformation of this social order. What is required, above all, is to overcome financialized capitalism's rapacious subjugation of reproduction to production – but this time without sacrificing either emancipation or social protection. This in turn requires reinventing the production/reproduction distinction and reimagining the gender order. Whether the result will be compatible with capitalism at all remains to be seen.

REFERENCES

Adams, David Wallace. 1995. *Education for Extinction: American Indians and the Boarding School Experience, 1875–1928.* Lawrence, Kans.: University of Kansas Press.

Arruzza, Cinzia. 2016. Functionalist, Determinist, Reductionist: Social Reproduction Feminism and its Critics. *Science & Society,* **80**(1), 9–30.

Bair, Jennifer. 2010. On Difference and Capital: Gender and the Globalization of Production. *Signs,* **36**(1) 203–26.

Baran, Paul A. 1957. *The Political Economy of Growth.* New York: Calder.

Baron, Ava. 1981. Protective Labor Legislation and the Cult of Domesticity. *Journal of Family Issues,* **2**(1) 25–38.

Beck, Martha. 2015. Finding Work-Life Balance: How To Keep Your Job And Home Lives Separate And Healthy. *The Huffington Post,* March 10. www.huffingtonpost.com/2013/04/10/work-life-balance-job-home-strategies-for-women_n_3044764.html.

Belkin, Lisa. 2003. The Opt-Out Revolution. *New York Times,* October 26.

Bezanson, Kate and Luxton, Meg, eds. 2006. *Social Reproduction: Feminist Political Economy Challenges Neo-Liberalism.* Montreal: McGill-Queen's University Press.

Boffey, Daniel. 2015. Half of All Services Now Failing as UK Care Sector Crisis Deepens. *The Guardian,* September 26. www.theguardian.com/society/2015/sep/26/nearly-half-social-care-services-failing-uk-elderly-disabled-welfare.

Boushey, Heather. 2016. *Finding Time: The Economics of Work-Life Conflict.* Cambridge, Mass.: Harvard University Press.

Boushey, Heather and Anderson, Amy Rees. 2013. Work-Life Balance: 5 Ways To Turn It From The Ultimate Oxymoron Into A Real Plan. *Forbes,* July 26. www.forbes.com/sites/amyanderson/2013/07/26/work-life-balance-the-ultimate-oxymoron-or-5-tips-to-help-you-achieve-better-worklife-balance/?sh=22d3a2265841#7afl0a775841.

Brenner, Johanna. 1991. Gender, Social Reproduction, and Women's Self-Organization: Considering the U.S. Welfare State. *Gender & Society*, **5**(3), 311–33.

Churchill, Ward. 2004. *Kill the Indian and Save the Man: The Genocidal Impact of American Indian Residential Schools.* San Francisco, Calif.: City Lights.

Coontz, Stephanie. 1988. *The Social Origins of Private Life: A History of American Families 1600–1900.* London: Verso.

Davis, Angela Y. 1972. Reflections on the Black Woman's Role in the Community of Slaves. *The Massachusetts Review*, **13**(2), 81–100.

Delphy, C. 1984. *Close to Home: A Materialist Analysis of Women's Oppression.* D. Leonard, trans. Amherst, Mass: University of Massachusetts Press.

Engels, Frederick. 2001 [1902]. *The Origin of the Family: Private Property and the State.* Honolulu, Hawaii: University Press of the Pacific.

Ewen, Stuart. 2008. *Captains of Consciousness: Advertising and The Social Roots of the Consumer Culture.* New York: McGraw-Hill.

Federici, Silvia. 2012. *Revolution at Point Zero: Housework, Reproduction, and Feminist Struggle.* New York: Common Notions.

Folbre, Nancy. 2002. *The Invisible Heart: Economics and Family Values.* New York: New Press.

Foucault, Michel. 1991. Governmentality. In Graham Burchell, Colin Gordon, and Peter Miller, eds., *The Foucault Effect.* Chicago, Ill.: The University of Chicago Press, pp. 87–104.

2010. *The Birth of Biopolitics, Lectures at College de France 1978–1979.* Basingstoke: Palgrave Macmillan.

Fraser, Nancy. 1989. Women, Welfare, and the Politics of Need Interpretation. In *Unruly Practices: Power, Discourse, and Gender in Contemporary Social Theory.* Cambridge, UK: Polity Press, pp. 144–60.

2009. Feminism, Capitalism, and the Cunning of History. *New Left Review*, **56**, 97–117.

2011. Marketization, Social Protection, Emancipation: Toward a Neo-Polanyian Conception of Capitalist Crisis. In Craig Calhoun and Georgi Derluguian, eds., *Business as Usual: The Roots of the Global Financial Meltdown.* New York: New York University Press, pp. 137–58.

2013. A Triple Movement? Parsing the Politics of Crisis after Polanyi. *New Left Review*, **81**, 119–32.

2014. Behind Marx's "Hidden Abode": For an Expanded Conception of Capitalism. *New Left Review*, **86**, 55–72.

2015. Legitimation Crisis? On the Political Contradictions of Financialized Capitalism. *Critical Historical Studies*, **2**(2) 157–89.

Glenn, Evelyn Nakano. 1992. From Servitude to Service Work: Historical Continuities in the Racial Division of Paid Reproductive Labor. *Signs: Journal of Women in Culture and Society*, **18**(1), 1–43.

2010. *Forced to Care: Coercion and Caregiving in America.* Cambridge, Mass.: Harvard University Press.

Hayden, Dolores. 2003. *Building Suburbia: Green Fields and Urban Growth.* New York: Vintage.

Hess, Cynthia. 2013. Women and the Care Crisis. Institute for Women's Policy Research Briefing Paper, IWPR C#401, April. www.iwpr.org/publications/pubs/women-and-the-care-crisis-valuing-in-home-care-in-policy-and-practice.

Hobson, Barbara. 1990. *Uneasy Virtue: The Politics of Prostitution and the American Reform Tradition.* New York: Basic Books.

Hochschild, Arlie. 2001. *The Time Bind: When Work Becomes Home and Home Becomes Work.* New York: Metropolitan Books.

2002. Love and Gold. In Barbara Ehrenreich and Arlie Hochschild, eds., *Global Woman: Nannies, Maids and Sex Workers in the New Economy.* New York: Metropolitan/Owl Books, pp. 15–30.

Holter, Harriet, ed. 1984. *Patriarchy in a Welfare Society.* Oslo: Universitetsforlaget.

Jones, Jacqueline, 1985. *Labor of Love, Labor of Sorrow: Black Women, Work, and the Family, from Slavery to the Present.* New York: Basic Books.

Jung, Courtney, 2015. *Lactivism: How Feminists and Fundamentalists, Hippies and Yuppies, and Physicians and Politicians Made Breastfeeding Big Business and Bad Policy.* New York: Basic Books.

Katznelson, Ira, 2005. *When Affirmative Action Was White: An Untold History of Racial Inequality in Twentieth-Century America.* New York; London: W. W. Norton.

Kliff, Sarah, 2013. The Breast Pump Industry is Booming, Thanks to Obamacare. *The Washington Post,* January 4. www.washingtonpost.com/news/wonk/wp/2013/01/04/the-breast-pump-industry-is-booming-thanks-to-obamacare/.

Köhler, Gernot and Tausch, Arno. 2001. *Global Keynesianism: Unequal Exchange and Global Exploitation.* New York: Nova Science Publishers.

Land, Hilary. 1978. Who Cares for the Family? *Journal of Social Policy,* **7**(3), 257–84.

Laslett, Barbara and Brenner, Johanna. 1989. Gender and Social Reproduction: Historical Perspectives. *Annual Review of Sociology,* **15**, 381–404.

Marx, Karl and Engels, Friedrich. 1978. Manifesto of the Communist Party. In Robert C. Tucker, ed., *The Marx-Engels Reader.* New York and London: W. W. Norton, pp. 487–88.

Mies, Maria. 2014. *Patriarchy and Accumulation on a World Scale.* London: Zed Books.

Miller, Lisa. 2013. The Retro Wife. *New York Magazine,* March 17.

Moore, Jason W. 2015. *Capitalism in the Web of Life.* London: Verso.

Nelson, Barbara J. 1985. Women's Poverty and Women's Citizenship: Some Political Consequences of Economic Marginality. *Signs: Journal of Women in Culture and Society,* **10**(2), 209–31.

O'Connor, James. 1988. Capitalism, Nature, Socialism: A Theoretical Introduction. *Capitalism, Nature, Socialism,* **1**(1) 1–22.

Orloff, A. S. 1993. Gender and Social Rights of Citizenship: The Comparative Analysis of Gender Relations and Welfare States. *American Sociological Review,* **58**(3), 303–28.

2009. Gendering the Comparative Analysis of Welfare States: An Unfinished Agenda. *Sociological Theory,* **27**, 317–43.

Orloff, S., O'Connor, J. S. and Shaver, S. 1999. *States, Markets, Families: Gender, Liberalism and Social Policy in Australia, Canada, Great Britain and the United States.* Cambridge, UK: Cambridge University Press.

Pearce, Diana. 1979. Women, Work and Welfare: The Feminization of Poverty. In Karen Wolk, ed., *Working Women and Families*. Feinstein, Beverly Hills, Calif. and London: Sage Publishing, pp. 103–24.

Pilling, Geoffrey. 1973. Imperialism, Trade and "Unequal Exchange": The Work of Aghiri Emmanuel. *Economy and Society*, **2**(2), 164–85.

Polanyi, Karl. 2001. *The Great Transformation*. Boston, Mass.: Beacon Press.

Prebisch, Raúl. 1950. *The Economic Development of Latin America and its Principal Problems*. New York: United Nations Department of Economic Affairs.

Quadagno, Jill. 1994. *The Color of Welfare: How Racism Undermined the War on Poverty*, New York and Oxford: Oxford University Press.

Rai, Shirin M., Catherine Hoskyns, and Dania Thomas. 2013. Depletion: The Cost of Social Reproduction. *International Feminist Journal of Politics*, **16**(1), 1–20.

Roberts, Adrienne. 2013. Financing Social Reproduction: The Gendered Relations of Debt and Mortgage Finance in Twenty-First Century America. *New Political Economy*, **18**(1), 21–42.

Rosen, Ruth. 2007. The Care Crisis. *The Nation*, February 27. www.thenation.com/article/care-crisis/.

Ross, Kristin. 1996. *Fast Cars, Clean Bodies: Decolonization and the Reordering of French Culture*, Cambridge, Mass.: The MIT Press.

Ruggie, Mary. 1984. *The State and Working Women: A Comparative Study of Britain and Sweden*. Princeton, NJ: Princeton University Press.

Sainsbury, Diane, ed. 2000. *Gender and Welfare State Regimes*. Oxford: Oxford University Press.

Sassen, Saski. 2000. Women's Burden: Counter-Geographies of Globalization and the Feminization of Survival. *Journal of International Affairs*, **53**(2), 503–24.

Schmidt, Michael. 2016. Pentagon to Offer Plan to Store Eggs and Sperm to Retain Young Troops. *New York Times*, February 3. www.nytimes.com/2016/02/04/us/politics/pentagon-to-offer-plan-to-store-eggs-and-sperm-to-retain-young-troops.html.

Shulevitz, Judith. 2016. How to Fix Feminism. *New York Times*, June 10.

Siim, Birte. 1990. Women and the Welfare State: Between Private and Public Dependence. In Clare Ungerson, ed., *Gender and Caring*. London and New York: Harvester Wheatsheaf, pp. 93–96.

Slaughter, Anne-Marie. 2012. Why Women Still Can't Have It All. *The Atlantic*, July–August.

2015. *Unfinished Business: Women Men Work Family*. London: Oneworld Publications.

Spivak, Gayatri C. 1988. Can the Subaltern Speak? In Cary Nelson and Lawrence Grossberg, eds., *Marxism and the Interpretation of Culture*. London: Macmillan Education.

Tilly, Louise A. and Scott, Joan W. 1987. *Women, Work, and Family*. London; New York: Routledge.

Tran, Mark. 2014. Apple and Facebook offer to freeze eggs for female employees. *The Guardian*, October 15. www.theguardian.com/technology/2014/oct/15/apple-facebook-offer-freeze-eggs-female-employees.

Vogel, Lise. 2013. *Marxism and the Oppression of Women: Toward a Unitary Theory.* London: Pluto Press.

Walkowitz, Judith R. 1980. *Prostitution and Victorian Society: Women, Class, and the State.* Cambridge: Cambridge University Press.

Warner, Judith. 2006. *Perfect Madness: Motherhood in the Age of Anxiety.* London: Ebury Digital.

Warren, Elizabeth and Warren Tyagi, Amelia. 2003. *The Two-Income Trap: Why Middle-Class Parents Are (Still) Going Broke.* New York: Basic Books.

Woloch, Nancy. 2015. *A Class by Herself: Protective Laws for Women Workers, 1890s–1990s.* Princeton, NJ: Princeton University Press.

Williams, F. et al. 2007. *Gendering Citizenship in Western Europe: New Challenges for Citizenship Research in a Cross-National Context.* Bristol: Policy.

Young, Brigitte. 2001. The "Mistress" and the "Maid" in the Globalized Economy. *Socialist Register,* **37**, 315–27.

Zaretsky, Eli. 1986. *Capitalism, the Family and Personal Life.* London: Pluto Press.

CHAPTER 8

Aspiration Management: Gender, Race, Class, and the Child as Waste

Cindi Katz

IN THE EVERYDAY PLACES OF HOME, SCHOOL, AND NEIGHBORHOOD, concerns about the future are being played out in extraordinary ways – venal and beautiful. If it is here that mounting anxieties around finding a place in an increasingly global labor force are managed and negotiated, and where ontological insecurity is felt in the bones, it is also where the chance to make a livable common future resides. This chapter addresses the questions of social reproduction with a particular focus on the multiple investments – and disinvestments – in children and childhood, and the cluster of practices that reach toward and modulate possible futures for young people, defining, as they mediate, a battery of aspirations, and scrambling to manage the risks associated with them across great divides of privilege, power, and wealth. As many of the practices of social reproduction remain in the domestic sphere and the purview of women, a gendered perspective offers a crucial means of interrogating the management of insecurity in particularly insecure times. I address these contested gendered and racialized practices as a cultural politics ripe for unpacking; a structure of feeling whose drives and effects can illuminate the present as a political moment, spurring action, the outcomes of which are indeterminate. As the aftermath of the angry, anxiety-fueled 2016 US presidential election and the UK's Brexit decision made clear, it is an urgent political moment.

CHILDHOOD AND THE MANAGEMENT OF INSECURITY

Focusing largely on the US, I will look at how the lives and wellbeing of some children – middle-class and wealthier children – have been fetishized, while others – the vast majority of children – suffer the consequences of a disinvested public sphere and a radically reduced social wage (Katz, 2008; 2011). These effects seem to become more pronounced every day as the sense of precariousness stemming from the financial crises of the past decade widens and infiltrates everyday life more deeply while neoliberal ideology and its strange and punishing biopolitics are normalized in a rising tide of xenophobia. To get at these concerns I am going to look at three popular and contradictory cultural productions: the films *Race to Nowhere* and *Waiting for Superman*, and the best-selling book *Battle Hymn of the Tiger Mother* by Amy Chua.

Read through and across one another, each of these social texts – and the widespread reception of them – revolves around securing childhood and channeling anxiety; they twist and shout about futurity and offer ways to manage – if not overcome – its insecurities. This insecurity is classed, gendered, and racialized to be sure, but as these three cultural products suggest, it is experienced and expressed across these differences, haunting everyday life in myriad ways. *Race to Nowhere, Waiting for Superman*, and *Tiger Mother* are part of a broader constellation of effects that reflect, make visible, and in their own ways contribute to the altered relations of production, reproduction, and power associated with neoliberal globalism, deteriorations in the social wage, and the uneven developments of the last thirty-five years in which whole lifeworlds seem to be disappearing. These shifts have singly and in concert reconfigured social life and its expectations of the future. In the domestic realm, the middle-class family is at once a fortress – policed and policing the reproduction of its members – and a "hothouse" – cultivating perfectly commodified children for the imagined niche markets of the future. Decades of feminist theory and practice notwithstanding, women remain at the heart of these material social practices. At the same time – and constitutively – this citadel of social reproduction is built upon and tethered to the production and social reproduction of waste, wasted landscapes, scarred environments, the detritus of commodity production. As Nancy Fraser has argued in this volume, nature has become a "sink" for production's waste under capitalism. Likewise, and pointedly, children have become waste, waste that must be managed and contained (Katz, 2011; cf., Bauman, 2004; Gidwani, 2014). As whole sectors of the population risk being jettisoned from the possibility of steady employment, the material social forms and practices associated with social reproduction and the formation of new laboring subjects are altered (e.g., Heiman, 2015; Tadiar, 2013; Holloway & Pimlott-Wilson, 2012, 2016; McDowell, 2003; Dolby & Dimitriadis, 2004; Ruddick, 2003; Jeffrey & McDowell, 2004; Collard & Dempsey, 2017; Holloway et al., 2010). The racialized and gendered productions of waste and value under these circumstances may rub against each other in ways that provoke intense insecurity in varied registers that affect different parts of any particular social formation (Gidwani & Reddy, 2011; McIntyre & Nast, 2011; Goldstein, 2009; Pratt, 2005). One of the places they rub intensely is in schools and around education more generally, and it is in this realm that I offer a critique of gendered and racialized practices that render the child as accumulation strategy or commodity and the child as waste (cf., Gill-Peterson, 2015; Davidson, 2011; Gillies, 2005).

Anxiety around the political economic, geo-political, and environmental future is easy to see and understand, and my research charts the ways these concerns are channeled into various "management" strategies. People increasingly seem to be drawn to cultural forms and practices where they can assert control over something – their bodies, through diet, exercise, medicine, cosmetic surgery, and so on (e.g., Heiman et al., 2012; Guthman & DuPuis, 2006; cf., Price, 2000; McGee, 2005); their spaces, through interior design, architecture, or borders and boundaries both national and local (e.g., Atkinson & Blandy, 2007; Atkinson,

2006; Low, 2004; Colomina, 2007; Sorkin, 2008); or (my interest) securing children's futures and producing perfect childhoods in ways that resonate with the sorts of gendered domestic control identified by the architectural historian Beatriz Colomina (2007) as a means of managing Cold War anxieties in post-war United States suburbs (cf., Coontz, 1992; May, 2008; Sammond, 2015).

These anxious strivings and affective relationships can be seen in the everyday practices of social reproduction, especially around motherhood, in many US households (e.g., Coontz, 1992; Lareau, 2003; Nelson, 2012; Nelson & Garey, 2009; Warner, 2005; Katz, 2012). They include, for example, online surveillance services offered by a growing number of school districts to which millions of parents now subscribe to track the progress and problems of their child's school day in real time, Mandarin immersion programs sought by growing numbers of households in the US and UK for children as young as two years old, and various extracurricular activities intended to saturate children with a range of skills – athletic, artistic, or scholarly.

These kinds of practices smuggle with them an almost magical "investment" in the child as oneself, one's future, and *the* future (Zelizer, 1994; cf., Edelman, 2004). This "investment" requires great quantities of emotional and reproductive labor, of love, and care, as much as focused and diffuse attention to sharing knowledge of all kinds. In her illuminating study of childrearing across class, sociologist Annette Lareau (2003) coined the term "concerted cultivation" to describe middle-class childrearing practices, wherein the domestic environment within and beyond the home is constructed as a continuous context for learning, offering opportunities for cultural enrichment in every direction. Children's talents are cultivated; learning and development are consciously woven into the activities of everyday life; and chances for exposure to novelty, potential new interests, and rewarding experiences are sought and seized upon. Each an investment in what Peter Demerath and his colleagues (2008; Demerath, 2009) frame as children's "psychological capital."

The social reproductive practices associated with the concerted cultivation of children are labors of love, but they are also a means of disciplining parents – especially mothers – in a Foucauldian sense. These cultural forms and practices of class formation make a space of conformity and competition, a realm of gendered social life that parents often feel compelled to participate in so their children "stay in the game." All the more so when the game is unclear (Liechty, 2003; cf., Rouse, 1995). These concerns were on display in the responses to Amy Chua's *Battle Hymn of the Tiger Mother*, published in 2011, and the 2010 documentary film *Race to Nowhere*, which I will discuss below. Such classed normative practices were pointedly criticized by Valerie Walkerdine and Helen Lucey (1989) who saw in these insistent practices of middle-class "domestic pedagogy" a means of reproducing inequality while diminishing and misrecognizing the efforts and interests of working-class parents (cf., Gillies, 2005).

When every mundane practice becomes a learning situation, parents – particularly mothers – are expected to be ever alert for the always-latent teachable moment. Walkerdine's and Lucey's research exposes the often-corrosive nature of the affective labor of bringing up children with the cognitive and communicative capacities associated with middle-class ideals (cf., Clough et al., 2007). They point to its iterative tyranny – first in regulating middle-class parents and children, and second in its imposition upon working-class and poor households as the way to produce "normal" children ready for the imagined future (Walkerdine & Lucey, 1989; cf., Donzelot, 1979; Lareau, 2003; Gillies, 2005; McDowell, 2007; Hays, 1996; Holloway & Pimlott-Wilson, 2016). I will return to these concerns in my discussion of *Waiting for Superman,* which concludes this piece.

If middle-class households tend to imbue their children with resources and capacities to enhance their life chances in an uncertain future, it is likely that these practices will be ratcheted up as the future comes to feel more insecure. Under these circumstances, gendered middle-class childrearing practices such as

Lareau's "concerted cultivation" or sociologist Sharon Hays's "intensive mothering" tend to be intensified, as so much of the popular literature on parenting laments (Lareau, 2003; Hays, 1996; cf., e.g., Holloway & Pimlott-Wilson, 2016; Druckerman, 2012; MacVean, 2011; Warner 2005; Douglas & Michaels, 2004). Drawing a parallel with Clifford Geertz's (1969) compelling notion of "agricultural involution," I think of these practices as "parental involution." Observing land and resource pressures in the wet rice cultivation areas of Indonesia, Geertz argued that farmers concentrated on fewer rice plants with increasingly elaborate care practices, and called this intensification of labor and attention, agricultural involution. While these practices increased production per plant or hectare, increasing numbers were drawn into the process with no growth in production per cultivator. Parental involution describes the embellishment of contemporary middle-class parenting practices and the ways they can preoccupy parents, albeit sometimes grudgingly. The all-consuming nature of these practices can also distract parents, rerouting their potential attention from the sources of their insecurities to attend to their symptoms as they simultaneously commodify their children as ideal class subjects of the imagined future embodying evermore elaborate attributes, and regard their successful upbringing as a zero-sum game (cf., Sammond, 2005: 370). Social childhood – that is, other people's children – is a casualty here, as witnessed in the underfunded childcare centers, ill-equipped playgrounds, and poor schools in which so many children come of age.

TIGER MOTHERING

These practices reach their apogee in Amy Chua's (2011) narcissistic romp of a memoir, *Battle Hymn of the Tiger Mother,* which received a frenzy of attention. Chua's now legendary "Chinese" parenting practices (the stereotypes fly off the pages unencumbered by subtleties of any kind) include extremely long hours of music practice every day no matter what. The younger daughter's violin is a companion on every holiday, and Chua frantically arranges rooms in every hotel for her elder daughter to practice piano. Chua's parenting precludes television, sleepover dates, actually a complete – almost hysterical – avoidance of playdates period, computer games, and laxity of any kind. She records her lacerating punishments for failures in accomplishment, sloth, resistance to her "Chinese" methods in which "mother not only knows best," but child knows nothing of what is good, desirable, worthy of time. She describes fights that go on for hours because she will not give up no matter how willful or hysterical her daughter's response is. Chua's parenting practices are highly gendered in that she locates them solely in the mother's remit and demands that her daughters submit. As Sara Ahmed tells us in the volume, "girls who refuse to submit their wills are threatened with a life of unhappiness."

Chua's parenting ideals are also racialized. She is scathing about what she casts as Western practices of overpraise and indulgence of children. Her tough love is *tough* she insists, but it is also love, and will lift her children to their highest heights, as premature praise or encouragement will not. She is proudly confident that her methods will produce not simply marvels of children but extraordinary adults, which for her means Ivy League-educated, near virtuosic piano or violin playing (no other instrument was acceptable), athletic, and high performing in every way. She is sure that her children will not only be grateful to their pushy tiger mother, but revere her as they embody and exude the highest standards of filial piety and personal success. Indeed, in 2019 one daughter became a clerk for US Supreme Court Justice Kavanaugh, whose praises were sung by Chua during his contentious confirmation hearings.

Even when she is self-conscious about it, Chua renders a sort of "clash of civilizations" comes home, and this framing is part of the book's provocation. She oozes elitism. A named professor at Yale Law School, Chua mentions her Harvard degrees and those of her family members many times throughout the book, and without any apparent basis or whit of consciousness claims that kids who teased her during her own childhood for being "different" ended up as janitors. She was also the author of two other best-selling books, *Day of Empire: How Hyperpowers Rise to Global Dominance – and Why They Fail* (2009) and *World on Fire: How Exporting Free Market Democracy Breeds Ethnic Hatred and Global Instability* (2002), and with her husband co-author of *The Triple Package: How Three Unlikely Traits Explain the Rise and Fall of Cultural Groups in America* (Chua & Rubenfeld, 2014). Chua does not go for shades of grey, and her preoccupations – global and intimate – are of a piece.

What is significant about *Battle Hymn*, though, is the swirl of attention it received. The book is sensationalist and cynical. The professed recognition of the error of her ways when her younger daughter rebels and scales down her commitment to the violin (she does not quit) does not really happen; it is performed. Parents across the US blogged their horror. Even as Chua made the rounds of talk shows insisting over and over that it was a memoir not a manual, she was pummeled with questions about her harsh parenting tactics, and reviled as abusive. Chua's book might have been a flash in the mommy pan, but for the ways it haunts the heart of contemporary ontological insecurity and how it is projected onto children's performance. Its sales might have been boosted by the publication a month earlier of statistics showing US students scoring way behind Chinese students in math and science. The only area where US students scored higher than Chinese was self-esteem. Chua's book launched like a mini-Sputnik, exposing the angst-ridden terrain of contemporary middle-class parenting, and provoking its (often defensive) interrogation.[1] At the same time, and not insignificantly, it revealed how these concerns are sutured to racialized anxieties about the future of the nation within and without, and to simmering

[1] Sputnik was the first human-made satellite to orbit the earth. Its launch by the Soviet Union in 1957 caused panic in the US about falling behind, leading to enhanced attention to science and math education, and the "space race" to the moon.

gendered and heteronormative concerns about what it means to be a "good mother."

Battle Hymn rattled people precisely around how children are commodified and construed as accumulation strategies. Without diminishing the deep gratification and unparalleled pleasure of seeing one's children grow and succeed at what draws them, I want to look at what else animates contemporary parenthood and its involution. Alongside the parental investment in the child as an accumulation strategy is also the pleasure and sense of accomplishment in helping to create a valuable commodity, and – as made disturbingly clear in Chua's book – the narcissistic pleasure of realizing their investments in a successful child. But we know from Marx that commodities conceal the social relations of their production. Whether through the determined labors of "concerted cultivation" or its elaboration in "parental involution," privileged parents strive to pass on their assets, including class position, to their children, while others struggle to secure their children's future chances (cf., Brantlinger, 2003; Devine, 2004). As accumulation strategies, children are offered resources that their parents think, and hope, will enable them to succeed in the market – cultural and political economic – in which they come of age (Allatt, 1993).

My research suggests that such projects of intergenerational capital accumulation are not only irresistible for many middle-class and more privileged parents in the US, but intensified under more precarious conditions. As poor and working-class parents attempt to better position their children in this same future market, the child as waste looms larger across the board; haunting all classes and figurations of the child. Naming it as such is a means to signal the dialectic between waste and value, but also to indicate the emotional, social, and economic costs of children lost to violence, addiction, suicide, incarceration, the military; the physical and psychological toll of growing up in disinvested and dangerous environments in and outside the home; or the "softer" effects of unemployment or long-term underemployment (e.g.,

Nolan & Anyon, 2004; Tilton, 2010; Saltman & Gabbard, 2011). The idea of the child as waste also carries with it the disquiet of wasted resources, wasted time, and wasted opportunities at all scales.

RACING, WAITING, SCHOOLING

The production of, distribution of, and response to the 2010 films *Race to Nowhere* and *Waiting for Superman* illustrate these concerns and contradictions well. *Race to Nowhere* is a compelling documentary produced and codirected by Vicki Abeles, a San Francisco Bay Area mother of three and former Wall Street lawyer. The film is a powerful response to the pressured conditions of young people's lives and the overheated educational and domestic environments associated with them. It was designed to galvanize action against these conditions among parents, students, and educators. Indeed, Abeles was drawn to filmmaking as she realized that her children's panic attacks and stress-related illnesses were not isolated, but rather symptomatic of the achievement culture in which they were steeped. The film examines many of the issues noted here, as well as cheating, excessive homework, high stakes testing, teenage suicide, substance abuse, anxiety disorders, the despair and frustration of many teachers, and overwhelmed parents as crises of contemporary social life sutured to competitive advantage in unsure times.

The film makes a strong case that childhood, family life, and education are compromised and eroded by these stressful practices and concerns. Its core argument is that education has been degraded by the ascendance of standardized testing, which brings along the tedium of "teaching to the test" and the often-disabling benchmarks of "achievement" for both students and teachers. *Race to Nowhere* makes the case that "the dark side of America's achievement culture" affects all groups no matter what class or color, but it concentrates on middle-class and privileged households struggling with and reproducing this culture.

Race to Nowhere is a call to action, intended to spark community-based responses across multiple localities, with national change its ambition. Despite its skilled production values and aspiration to produce a national conversation, the film did not secure a national distributor. Undaunted, Abeles focused on community-sponsored screenings and discussions of the film nationwide. Jumping scale and connecting diverse schools and sites, Abeles and her collaborators did in fact spark a national discussion, and seem to have found deep wells of anxiety that gush with anger and frustration. The film's website provides research documents and guidance for concerned parents, educators, and others to counter the problems it portrays. It also urges some reflection on the self-inflicted aspects of "achievement culture" and its lures. "Unplugging" is encouraged in the film and the talk-back sessions that swirl around it.

I attended my first screening of *Race to Nowhere* on a freezing January night in Charlottesville, Virginia, and witnessed all of the issues the film raises and their panicky hold on people's imaginations. The auditorium was packed with people who had paid $10 to attend the screening, and I found a seat in the back just as the film was starting. When the lights came up, I was not surprised that the middle-class audience was nearly all white – even though about 25 percent of Charlottesville is non-white, the school and the town are quite segregated along racialized class lines – but I was surprised to see so many high school students there. During the talk-back session, students voiced concerns about too much homework, too little down time, but as one of them put it, they did not want "to be at a school that doesn't push" them, making clear that "pushing" was all they had ever known. The raw nerve touched by the film was exposed quickly. When the economic future feels so precarious and questions of waste hover in every direction, the pressured practices examined by Abeles may feel like the only option to young people groomed – and self-managed – as accumulation strategies. The carefully curated entrepreneurial self appeared to be alive and well at the screening.

The talk-back discussion was led by the high school principal, an admissions officer at the University of Virginia, and a psychologist/counselor from a local private school. The audience seemed quite moved by the film's painful arguments. From all over the theater parents, teachers, and students asked questions and spoke out about things that underscored the film's message. A student complained, "there's so much testing," while adults made comments such as, "most of us are average," "we need to change the culture," "we need to change household practices," "most successful people in this country didn't go to prestigious schools," and so on. But the "dark side of America's achievement culture," as the film puts it, is half of an intense dialectic with its light side, and *Race to Nowhere* draws and moves people who travel their insecure edges. The tension of this relationship was quickly exposed. One mother asked, "If we deemphasize Advanced Placement classes,[2] how can we change the attitudes of kids so they are not such high achievers?" Given this phrasing we might conclude that the pursuit of high achievement was a natural instinct. While the panelists urged parents, teachers, and counselors to encourage students to ease up on their drive to achieve at the highest levels, they failed to mention that most of the middle-class white students had been "tracked" since elementary school in the direction of advanced and honors classes. Also not mentioned was the extensive scaffolding that the adults in their lives provide to prop them up in and outside of school (cf., Gillies, 2005). The figure of the child as waste troubles that of the child as accumulation strategy, just as the more common educational tracks haunt the advanced ones. "Peer pressure" not to be a "loser" is rampant in high school, and for many young people (and their parents) the prize is getting into a good university, which is seen as the fulcrum to everything else. They know without knowing that of the 1.6 million students who take the SATs[3] in a year, just

[2] AP or "Advanced Placement" classes are honors-type classes in selected disciplines. Many colleges and universities will grant college credit for AP classes completed successfully.

[3] SAT originally stood for Scholastic Aptitude Test, suggesting more of an Intelligence Quotient orientation. The designation was changed in the early 1990s to Scholastic

2 percent get into the top twenty schools in the US. In the course of the discussion the abyss of waste seemed to open; in a flash making clear that "the race" is not to nowhere. Many in the auditorium seemed to feel that in their bones.

These issues are brought to the fore in Davis Guggenheim's 2010 film, *Waiting for Superman*. This film had no trouble finding a distributor or massive public relations campaign upon its release. Indeed, it was bankrolled by a combination of hedge fund and high-tech billionaires, among others with deep interests in privatizing what is perhaps the last great commons – public education. The film follows five hardworking students and their families as they try to get out of their failing and limited public schools – and the fate it is projected to seal for them – as they strive to get into beautiful, wonderful, high-performing, attentive charter schools. The film is essentially a well-crafted extended "infomercial" for charter schools. It presents public schools – "the system" – as a big unfixable machine that fails students, particularly poor brown and black ones who need "us" the most. While liberal critics commonly praised the film's even-handed approach, it was anything but.

Waiting for Superman utterly demonizes teachers' unions – while extolling the life-changing wonders of particular great teachers – and strategically ignores decades of structural disinvestment in public education and its hideous and not at all surprising gendered, racialized, and classed geography. The film relentlessly points out that schools are awash in money that is misspent on overpaid and fatly pensioned teachers who cannot be fired. There is no talk of the costs – psychic or financial – of standardized testing, which has all but "consumed" contemporary education in the US. The film is similarly silent on the "soft dispossessions" of the testing industry, which makes huge profits from public education money in producing, administering, and scoring

Assessment Test, the term's redundancy suggesting a lack of intelligence on the designators' part, and finally has become an empty signifier – a trademark of the College Board. The name notwithstanding, SAT scores are considered as part of the college admissions process, and remain a crucial and often stressful hurdle for high school students vying for a place in selective universities and colleges.

standardized examinations, to say nothing of the ancillary industries that prepare children whose parents can afford for them to take tests (Fine & Ruglis, 2009; Fabricant & Fine, 2013). Neither does the film refer to the drain on public funds for "securing" public schools with private security guards, metal detectors, RFID-enhanced identity cards, or the online parental surveillance systems mentioned earlier (cf., Saltman & Gabbard, 2011; Nguyen, 2016). Additionally, schools in the US are now being offered free facial recognition software in an attempt to improve security, but which also serves to regulate students by race and gender from infancy (Browne, 2015; Buolamwini & Gebru, 2018; Hamidi et al., 2018). Structural issues such as racism, gendered social ordering, or poverty are avoided entirely in the film. Instead, the focus is trained on bloated teachers' unions and the ways they are the "dam" holding back good education. Among the policy documents produced by some of the film's backers (Democrats for Education Reform!) are those that call for "bursting" the dam. Perhaps this combination's most cynical and revealing sentiments were expressed in a conference session disgracefully entitled, "Does Education Need a Katrina?"

Geoffrey Canada and the Harlem Children's Zone (HCZ) are the heroes of this film. As Michelle Fine (2010), Stan Karp (2010), Barbara Miner (2010), and Ira Shor (2010), among others, have written in a great collection of papers from *Rethinking Schools*, there is no mention that HCZ received $50 million in private funding that year alone (and according to the most recent annual report, received almost $52 million in private funds for fiscal year 2018), or that it wildly outstrips public school spending per student (and that is without counting the significant resources expended through its aegis for students outside of school) (cf., Ravitch, 2010). Neither does *Waiting for Superman* acknowledge the ways public education and "strategic public investment" matter and *have* worked in many school districts. It takes as a given that charter schools are better, even though there is ample empirical evidence demonstrating that they do not outperform public schools in any systematic way. Yet desire and justification for these schools are amped up by the film as it portrays several children's desperate attempts to attend one through a truly barbaric public lottery system. Such lotteries are federally mandated whenever demand outstrips the number of places in a given charter school. The film depicts these brutal events as the chance for "everything" versus being churned into waste. While this abhorrent process mirrors the concerns that drive my project, it is a distortion mirror offering a perspective that naturalizes the distinctions and the processes that produce them rather than casting them in a larger frame of racialized and gendered structural inequality. Making the lotteries public events instantiates and makes visible the constitutive role played by waste in children's education and social reproduction more broadly. The lottery performs dispossession and makes it seem fair.

Waiting for Superman presents as a given what was once a radical critique of education. That critique, from political economists Sam Bowles and Herb Gintis (1977) or sociologists Pierre Bourdieu and Jean-Claude Passeron (1977), was that tracking *is* the system – sorting the population roughly into 20 percent professional managerial class, 20 percent mid-level professional management, and 60 percent manual workers with gender and racial segregation throughout.[4]

Waiting for Superman then skips over the core of their critique, which argues that the intentionality of this system is masked by the material social practices associated with "achievement," testing, behavior, and the like so that failure is individualized while the chance for success makes the whole apparatus turn on seemingly meritocratic (and thus fair) grounds. *Waiting for Superman* contends that this sorting mechanism worked beautifully when factory or farm work was widely available, but now when those conditions no longer obtain (or more accurately their geographies are stretched globally), the grounds of education are changed.

4 See the USA Bureau of Labor Statistics (2019) data.

The film perpetuates the myth that everyone can be, should be, and wants to be university educated. Of course, if everyone's aspiration and capacity for employment were ratcheted upward – even into the second 20 percent – the whole system of capital accumulation as we know it would collapse even further. The questions at hand are structural. The system works as it was intended to work, but with production and social reproduction increasingly global, capital can more easily draw on cheap labor, suppress wages, and undermine if not destroy unions. In a different register, many manual labor jobs have been eliminated by technology – again with labor market gender segregation at its core.

With these new geographies of production and reproduction, the US has little call for as many manual workers as its education system produces. Waste is more than an occasional byproduct now. By waste I mean "unusable or unwanted," but also an "excess that is unruly and improper," to use terms Gidwani and Reddy (2011) draw from the *OED*. This waste is managed and contained through a variety of means. Neoliberal strategies of self-management, charter schools, and community colleges might be considered relatively benign means of waste management. More pernicious is the so-called "school to prison to pipeline," which in effect criminalizes *so as to waste* young people who are, not surprisingly, disproportionately poor, male, and non-white through school security, policing, and detention practices (e.g., Monahan & Torres, 2010; Nolan & Anyon, 2004; Fabricant & Fine, 2013). There is also the larger juvenile justice and prison system, the military, and self-eating violence among disenfranchised and disaffected youthful populations when other means of absorbing and managing waste fail. The current heroin and opioid addiction crisis among white, often rural, working-class young people in the US is a case in point, as are the soaring teen suicide rates of the past decade, which cross class, race, and gender.

Waiting for Superman is a call to arms. It ends with the exhortation, which I paraphrase here: "Our system is broken, and it seems impossible to fix. It is possible to fix, but it can't wait. Great schools won't come from lotteries, they won't come from Superman, they'll come from YOU!" Perhaps this exhortation is not so surprising. Davis Guggenheim also directed Al Gore's *An Inconvenient Truth*, which while making an important point about climate change, occluded the truly inconvenient truth that it is not enough to resist or change individually if big coal, the automotive industry, or petrochemical producers keep on with business as usual. I am all for individual action and responsibility, but it is a shameful fallacy to argue that the solution to poor education will come from bright young inexperienced people "teaching for America," (a bit of youth management strategy of its own),[5] or the individual saturation points known as charter schools, which, when not "superfunded" sites, only marginally outperform traditional public schools when they do at all (Fabricant & Fine, 2013). Indeed, it is crucial to recall the combination of new and old big money, powerful Democrats, and conservative Republicans who backed the film and managed its extravagant publicity – none of which was forthcoming for any number of laudable recent documentaries about education, among them, *Race to Nowhere, America's Broken Education System* (2016) and *Teach Us All* (2017). This formidable combination of forces has deep and varied interests in undermining – to the point of undoing – public education in the US. Flawed as our public education system is and has been historically, it is predicated on a truly democratic notion of free education as a right under various forms of public control, not as a sort of privately managed boutique or "disposable franchise" that rises

[5] Teach for America started in 1989 with a mission to bring high-achieving college graduates to teach in schools in low-income areas across the United States. The recently graduated students are required to commit to teaching for two years, and are paid by the school districts where they work. TFA, a non-profit organization, became a charter member of the federal government's AmeriCorps, a sort of domestic Peace Corps, established in 1993. While initially the "corps members" served as student teachers, by the mid-1990s they were leading their own classes, albeit with little training beyond their college degrees.

and falls "as the market 'churns'" (Karp, 2010), and treats children as commodities whose value is assessed by test scores.

WASTE, VALUE, AND DISPOSABLE TIME

The lottery displays the fault line between the child as waste and the child as value, at once naturalizing the sort and pretending the problem is bad public schools rather than disinvestment in the social wage, local inequalities in school funding, structural racism, and obdurate systemic poverty. What can we make of an historical geography of social reproduction where such productions of waste or the threat of being wasted rub against Amy Chua's almost parodic performance of fashioning a "hyperpowered" child for the new century, or the children in *Race to Nowhere* so saturated with resources and the pressure to make use of them that they are suicidal? In a talk-back session at Google headquarters in the heart of Silicon Valley featuring Abeles and a couple of the young people in the film, an audience member suggested that kids should "take it easy," maybe cut a class here and there or slack off on their homework once in a while. "But," one of the girls responded, "we have to get our assignments from our teachers," completely missing the point of what cutting school means. Abeles then sort of crazily added that parents should encourage these laxities. If young people need a parent to encourage them to skip class or slack off, they are really in trouble. And if we have lost the art of "doing nothing," so are we.

"Doing nothing" is an unabashed pleasure of a "good" childhood – perhaps its most endangered aspect and not to be underestimated. It is in essence "disposable time," which Marx recognized as a time of both invention and consumption, and thus the basis of social wealth. Disposable time is a resource and reservoir of much creativity for adults as well as children (Goldstein, 2009). It is something that we might have in abundance if it were recognized as a social resource and more equitably shared (along with incomes). What might we take away from *this* notion of disposability? From this perspective it is possible to reimagine all that gets cast as a waste of time. Disposable time is another instance of how things seemingly outside the realm of value are at once its constitutive edge and potential source. So too, children as waste. Under the hideous metric of contemporary capitalism, it is the production, containment, and management of this waste that abets capital accumulation (cf., Ruth Wilson Gilmore's [2007] work on the "prison industrial complex" or Melissa Wright's [2006] work on disposable women). Productions of the child as waste are entangled with concerted productions of other children as accumulation strategies – hothouse gems – who often suffer in the process. This situation, which sustains longstanding structural inequalities and is self-reinforcing in their face, is as untenable as it is unjust. The need to answer feels visceral. The problem exceeds social reproduction, but the resonance of the social texts I've traced here suggests its importance to the critical questions we face collectively concerning an increasingly unequal future. It need not be this way, and lots of great work is being done to rework and resist these metrics and logics of social life and labor – the Black Lives Matter and Prison Abolition movements in the US are two of the most notable at present. Connecting to and advancing these and similar struggles are the redress of geography and feminist praxis.

The questions of waste, value, subjectivity, and structure rattle around one another in the gendered, classed, and racialized material social practices of children's everyday lives and upbringing. Reimagining the time-spaces of childhood, children, and education can begin to remake the contours and horizons of social reproduction. In one way I mean this quite concretely – extending truly public education across the life course to reach much younger children, for example, and also across the day and year with creative programming enhances children's and others' everyday lives and life chances, has been shown to reduce economic inequality over the long term, and would also produce meaningful jobs in the public interest. In a more capacious way, we can take Marx's ideas around disposable time as a guide and begin to think about a politics of disposable time. The US educational calendar remains structured around agricultural time, while the workweek adheres stubbornly to the timetables of Fordist industrialism. Neither makes sense anymore. With a shorter (but fully compensated) workweek more people could be employed as disposable time was expanded and socialized. With extended school times, particularly for the sorts of enrichment programs and oases of creative or active time that have been privatized and thus privileged in recent years, we might begin to retreat from the anxious provocations that schedule some children to death as others are passed by. Challenging the uneven gendered, classed, and racialized practices of social reproduction; remaking disposable time; and restoring desecrated spaces will help level the playing field in actual grounds of play, reworking the alchemy between value and waste, and opening a terrain of practice in which anything is possible.

REFERENCES

Advexon Science Network (2016). Documentary: *America's Broken Education System.* www.youtube.com/watch?v=iiNts6rVfQY.

Allatt, Patricia. 1993. Becoming Privileged: The Role of Family Processes. In I. Bates and G. Riseborough, eds., *Youth and Inequality.* Buckingham: Open University Press, pp. 139–59.

Atkinson, Rowland. 2006. Padding the Bunker: Strategies of Middle-Class Disaffiliation and Colonisation in the City. *Urban Studies,* **43**(4), 819–32.

Atkinson, Rowland and Blandy, Sarah. 2007. Panic Rooms: The Rise of Defensive Homeownership. *Housing Studies,* **22**(4), 443–58.

Bauman, Zygmunt. 2004. *Wasted Lives: Modernity and its Outcasts.* Cambridge: Polity Press.

Bourdieu, Pierre and Passeron, Jean-Claude. 1977. *Reproduction in Education, Society and Culture.* London: Sage Publications.

Bowles, Samuel and Gintis, Herbert. 1977. *Schooling in Capitalist America: Educational Reform and the Contradictions of Economic Life.* Boston, MA: Beacon Press.

Brantlinger, Ellen. 2003. *Dividing Classes: How the Middle Class Negotiates and Rationalizes School Advantage.* New York and London: RoutledgeFalmer.

Browne, S. (2015). *Dark Matters: On the Surveillance of Blackness.* Durham, NC: Duke University Press.

Buolamwini, J. and Gebru, T. 2018. Gender Shades: Intersectional Accuracy Disparities in Commercial Gender Classification. Proceedings of the 1st

Conference on Fairness, Accountability and Transparency, PMLR 81: pp. 77–91.

CBS This Morning. 2017. Documentary: *Teach Us All.* www.youtube.com/watch?v=4n6iVk_wsa4.

Chua, Amy. 2002. *World on Fire: How Exporting Free Market Democracy Breeds Ethnic Hatred and Global Instability.* New York: Doubleday.

2009. *Day of Empire: How Hyperpowers Rise to Global Dominance – and Why They Fail.* New York: Doubleday.

2011. *Battle Hymn of the Tiger Mother.* New York: Penguin.

Chua, Amy and Rubenfeld, Jed. 2014. *The Triple Package: How Three Unlikely Traits Explain the Rise and Fall of Cultural Groups in America.* New York: Penguin Press.

Clough, Patricia T. et al. 2007. Notes Towards a Theory of Affect-Itself. *Ephemera: Theory and Politics in Organization,* **7**(1), 60–77.

Collard, Rosemary-Claire and Dempsey,Jessica. 2017. Capitalist Natures in Five Orientations. *Capitalism Nature Socialism,* **28**(1), 78–97.

Colomina, Beatriz. 2007. *Domesticity at War.* Cambridge, MA and London: The MIT Press.

Coontz, Stephanie. 1992. *The Way We Never Were: American Families and the Nostalgia Trap.* New York: Basic Books.

Davidson, Elsa. 2011. *The Burdens of Aspiration: Schools, Youth, and Success in the Divided Social Worlds of Silicon Valley.* New York: New York University Press.

Demerath, Peter. 2009. *Producing Success: The Culture of Personal Advancement in an American High School.* Chicago, IL: University of Chicago Press.

Demerath, Peter, Lynch, Jill, and Davidson, Mario. 2008. Dimensions of Psychological Capital in a US Suburb and High School: Identities for Neoliberal Times. *Anthropology & Education Quarterly,* **39** (3), 270–92.

Devine, Fiona. 2004. *Class Practices: How Parents Help their Children Get Good Jobs.* Cambridge: Cambridge University Press.

Dolby, Nadine and Dimitriadis, Greg with Paul Willis, eds. 2004. *Learning to Labor in New Times.* New York and London: RoutledgeFalmer.

Donzelot, Jacques. 1979. *The Policing of Families.* New York: Pantheon.

Douglas, Susan J. and Michaels, Meredith W. 2004. *The Mommy Myth: The Idealization of Motherhood and How It Has Undermined All Women.* New York: Free Press.

Druckerman, Pamela. 2012. *Bringing Up Bébé: One American Mother Discovers the Wisdom of French Parenting.* New York: The Penguin Press.

Edelman, Lee. 2004. *No Future: Queer Theory and the Death Drive.* Durham, NC and London: Duke University Press.

Fabricant, Michael and Fine, Michelle. 2013. *The Changing Politics of Education: Privatization and the Dispossessed Lives Left Behind.* Boulder, CO and London: Paradigm Publishers.

Fine, Michelle. 2010. Memo from Lois Lane. *Not Waiting for Superman.* www.notwaitingforsuperman.org/Articles/20101101-FineLoisLaneMemo.

Fine, Michelle and Ruglis, Jessica. 2009. Circuits and Consequences of Dispossession: The Racialized Realignment of the Public Sphere for Youth. *Transforming Anthropology,* **17**(1), 20–33.

Geertz, Clifford. 1969. *Agricultural Involution: The Processes of Ecological Change in Indonesia.* Berkeley and Los Angeles, CA: University of California Press.

Gidwani, Vinay. 2014. Waste Makers: Informal Economies and Commodity Detritus in Delhi, India. *Asia Colloquia Papers,* 4(2). Toronto: York Centre for Asian Research. www.yorku.ca/ycar.

Gidwani, Vinay and Reddy, Rajyashree N. 2011. The Afterlives of "Waste": Notes from India for a Minor History of Capitalist Surplus. *Antipode,* **43**(5), 1625–58.

Gillies, Val. 2005. Raising the "Meritocracy": Parenting and the Individualization of Social Class. *Sociology,* **39**(5), 835–53.

Gill-Peterson, Julian. 2015. The Value of the Future: The Child as Human Capital and the Neoliberal Labor of Race. *Women's Studies Quarterly,* **43**(1 & 2), 181–96.

Goldstein, Jesse. 2009. Human Waste Management and the Survival of Capitalism. Paper presented at the Marxist Literary Group's Summer Institute. Portland, Oregon.

Guthman, Julie and DuPuis, Melanie. 2006. Embodying Neoliberalism: Economy, Culture, and the Politics of Fat. *Environment and Planning D: Society and Space,* **24**, 427–48.

Hamidi, F. et al. 2018. Gender Recognitions of Gender Reductionism? The Social Implication of Automatic Gender Recognition Systems. In *Proceedings of the 2018 CHI Conference on Human Factors in Computing Systems, Paper No. 8.* Montreal: AML, pp. 1–13.

Hays, Sharon. 1996. *The Cultural Contradictions of Motherhood.* New Haven, CT: Yale University Press.

Heiman, Rachel. 2015. *Driving After Class: Anxious Times in an American Suburb.* Oakland, CA: University of California Press.

Holloway, Sarah L. et al. 2010. Geographies of Education and the Significance of Children. *Youth and Families, Progress in Human Geography,* **34**(5), 583–600.

Holloway, Sarah L. and Pimlott-Wilson, Helena. 2012. Neoliberalism, Policy Localisation and Idealised Subjects: A Case Study on Educational Restructuring in England. *Transactions of the Institute of British Geographers,* **37**(4), 639–54.

2016. New Economy, Neoliberal State and Professionalised Parenting: Mothers' Labour Market Engagement and State Support for Social Reproduction in Class-Differentiated Britain. *Transactions of the Institute of British Geographers,* **41**(4), 376–88.

Jeffrey, Craig and McDowell, Linda. 2004. Youth in a Comparative Perspective. *Youth & Society,* **36**(2), 132–41.

Karp, Stan. 2010. Superhero School Reform Heading Your Way: Now Playing in Newark, NJ. *Not Waiting for Superman.* www.notwaitingforsuperman.org/Articles/20101129-karpnj.

Katz, Cindi. 2008. Childhood as Spectacle: Relays of Anxiety and the Reconfiguration of the Child. *Cultural Geographies,* **15**(1), 5–17.

2011. Accumulation, Excess, Childhood: Toward a Countertopography of Risk and Waste. *Documents d'Anàlisi Geogràfica,* **57**(1), 47–60.

2012. Just Managing: American Middle-Class Parenthood in Insecure Times. In R. Heiman, C. Freeman, and M. Liechty, eds., *The Global Middle Classes: Theorizing Through Ethnography*. Santa Fe, NM: SAR Press, pp. 169–88.

Lareau, Annette. 2003. *Unequal Childhoods: Class, Race, and Family Life.* Berkeley and Los Angeles, CA: University of California Press.

Liechty, Mark. 2003. *Suitably Modern: Making Middle-Class Culture in a New Consumer Society.* Princeton, NJ: Princeton University Press.

Low, Setha. 2004. *Behind the Gates: Life, Security, and the Pursuit of Happiness in Fortress America.* New York: Routledge.

MacVean, Mary. 2011. Parents Take a Deep Breath. *Los Angeles Times,* March 12. http://articles.latimes.com/2011/mar/12/home/la-hm-parent-anxiety-20110312, accessed April 2011.

May, Elaine T. 2008. *Homeward Bound: American Families in the Cold War Era,* 2nd ed. New York: Basic Books.

McDowell, Linda. 2003. *Redundant Masculinities? Employment Change and White Working Class Youth.* Oxford: Blackwell.

2007. Spaces of the Home: Absence, Presence, New Connections and New Anxieties. *Home Cultures,* 4(2), 129–46.

McGee, Micki. 2005. *Self-Help, Inc.: Makeover Culture in American Life.* New York: Oxford University Press.

McIntyre, Michael and Nast, Heidi. 2011. Bio(Necro)Polis: Marx, Surplus Populations, and the Spatial Dialectics of Reproduction and "Race." *Antipode,* **43**(5), 1465–88.

Miner, Barbara. 2010. Ultimate $uperpower: Supersized Dollars Drive "Waiting for Superman" Agenda. *Not Waiting for Superman.* www.notwaitingforsuperman.org/Articles/20101020-MinerUltimateSuperpower.

Monahan, Torin and Torres, Rodolfo D. 2010. *Schools Under Surveillance: Cultures of Control in Public Education.* New Brunswick, NJ: Rutgers University Press.

Nelson, Margaret K. 2012. *Parenting Out of Control: Anxious Parents in Uncertain Times.* New York: New York University Press.

Nelson, Margaret K. and Garey, Anita Ilta, eds. 2009. *Who's Watching? Daily Practices of Surveillance Among Contemporary Families.* Nashville, TN: Vanderbilt University Press.

Nolan, Kathleen and Anyon, Jean. 2004. Learning to Do Time: Willis's Model of Cultural Reproduction in an Era of Postindustrialism, Globalization, and Mass Incarceration. In N. Dolby and D. Dimitriasis, eds., *Learning to Labor in New Times.* New York and London: RoutledgeFalmer, pp. 133–49.

Nguyen, Nicole. 2016. *A Curriculum of Fear: Homeland Security in U.S. Public Schools.* Minneapolis, MN: University of Minnesota Press.

Pratt, Geraldine. 2005. Abandoned Women and Spaces of the Exception. *Antipode,* **37**, 1052–78.

Price, Patricia L. 2000. No Pain, No Gain: Bordering the Hungry New World Order. *Environment and Planning D: Society and Space,* **18**: 91–110.

Ravitch, Diane. 2010. The Myth of Charter Schools. *The New York Review of Books,* November.

Rouse, Roger. 1995. Thinking Through Transnationalism: Notes on the Cultural Politics of Class Relations in the Contemporary United States. *Public Culture*, **7**(2), 353–402.

Ruddick, Sue. 2003. The Politics of Aging: Globalization and the Restructuring of Youth and Childhood. *Antipode*, **35**(2), 334–62.

Saltman, Kenneth A. and Gabbard, David A., eds. 2011. *Education as Enforcement: The Militarization and Corporatization of Schools*, 2nd ed. New York and London: Routledge.

Sammond, Nicholas. 2005. *Babes in Tomorrowland: Walt Disney and the Making of the American Child, 1930–1960*. Durham, NC and London: Duke University Press.

2015. Touched by Le Roy: Teens, Tourette's, and YouTube in the Twilight of Neoliberalism. *Women's Studies Quarterly*, **43**(1 & 2): 29–50.

Shor, Ira. 2010. Ira Shor is Not "Waiting for . . . ". *Not Waiting for Superman*. www.notwaitingforsuperman.org/Articles/20101004-IraShor.

Sorkin, Michael, ed. 2008. *Indefensible Space: The Architecture of the National Insecurity State*. New York and London: Routledge.

Tadiar, Neferti X.M. 2013. Life-Times of Disposability within Global Neoliberalism. *Social Text*, **31**(2 (115)), 19–48.

Tilton, Jennifer. 2010. *Dangerous or Endangered? Race and the Politics of Youth in Urban America*. New York: New York University Press.

The USA Bureau of Labor Statistics. 2019. Employed Persons by Detailed Industry, Sex, Race, and Hispanic or Latino Ethnicity. www.bls.gov/cps/cpsaat18.htm.

Walkerdine, Valerie and Lucey, Helen. 1989. *Democracy in the Kitchen: Regulating Mothers and Socializing Daughters*. London: Virago.

Warner, Judith. 2005. *Perfect Madness: Motherhood in the Age of Anxiety*. New York: Riverhead Books.

Wilson Gilmore, Ruth. 2007. *Golden Gulag: Prisons, Surplus, Crisis, and Opposition in Globalizing California*. University of California Press.

Wright, Melissa W. 2006. *Disposable Women and Other Myths of Global Capitalism*. New York: Routledge.

Zelizer, Viviana A. 1994. *Pricing the Priceless Child: The Changing Social Value of Children*. Princeton, NJ: Princeton University Press.

CHAPTER 9

Gender, Race and American National Identity: The First Black First Family

Patricia Hill Collins

BARACK OBAMA'S ELECTION AS THE FIRST AFRICAN American President seemed to be a validation of the American Dream as well as a model of what others could achieve.[1] Obama's success suggests that an individual who holds fast to the values associated with the American Dream – hard work, commitment to family and fairness – can achieve an adequate standard of living and societal respect. Yet the centrality of family narratives in Barack Obama's campaign and subsequent presidency also signaled the significance of gender and race within American national identity. While racial and gender inequalities have not disappeared, the interpretive climate of our alleged post-racial and post-feminist era has rendered public discussions of racial equality and gender equity risky. This context mandates a search for a new language to discuss social inequalities generally, and gendered and racial inequalities in particular. Here family rhetoric is the symbolic carrier of multiple, often contradictory stories about race, gender, class, sexuality and citizenship.

1 Here I capitalize and use the terms "Black people" and "African Americans" interchangeably to refer to the historically constituted, ethnic group originating in American slavery that has incorporated earlier waves of immigrants of African descent.. I distinguish African Americans/Black Americans from contemporary immigrants of African descent from the Caribbean and continental Africa. Although this chapter speaks to broader racial politics that affect these groups, incorporating a more comprehensive analysis of the contentious terminology of "blackness" is beyond the scope of this chapter. I use lower-case "black" and "white" as descriptions for systems of ideas, ideologies or any construct that does not refer to African Americans as a historically constituted collectivity, e.g., "black masculinity" or "white culture."

Moreover, family structures are vital institutional carriers for economic transformations of the new global economy and public policies can be made comprehensible via the rhetoric of family. In this sense, the symbolic and structural dimensions of family have been an important part of the American national story.

FAMILY, COLORBLINDNESS, AND THE AMERICAN DREAM

The traditional gendered construct of family rhetoric navigates two significant social phenomena of early twenty-first century American society; namely, (1) economic transformations associated with the new global economy that have challenged the economic security long promised to those who believe in the American Dream; and (2) the emergence of a rhetoric of colorblindness where talking openly of race ostensibly fosters racism. Traditional gendered ideas about family not only operate within both dimensions but also link them together.

First, the erosion of economic opportunity associated with the new global economy has catalyzed ongoing, dramatic shifts in the contours of work, marriage and family. Deindustrialization, job export, population migration, entrenched unemployment and the reliance on consumerism (and related phenomena of credit and debt) as the engine of economic growth have dramatically altered the contours of work, marriage and family. One outcome has been a heightened concern within the United States about the economic security of families. On a macroeconomic level, family serves as a core social institution for organizing economic relations, regardless of the values of individual family members. Some families achieve intergenerational economic security without any of their members ever having to take paid employment. In contrast, other families find that even if *all* of their members work (including children), they have little hope that they will ever achieve economic security. Thus, families can be seen alternately as sites of intergenerational hoarding of wealth or as being at intergenerational risk for poverty.

The strong connections between families and intergenerational economic security and vulnerability become increasingly significant in weathering the economic transformations of the new global economy. Social policies drafted with certain family forms in mind, for example, homeowner tax credits for married-couple families, access to health care benefits through employer-sponsored policies, the structure of school calendars and schedules that penalize working mothers, and social welfare policies that benefit widows over unmarried mothers seem less effective in ensuring economic security for the middle class. In this context, the idealized gendered family form of the two-parent, married heterosexual couple living with their own biological children in a privately owned house financially supported by a high-income male partner and a stay-at-home mother remains difficult to achieve in the face of shrinking union jobs, the mortgage crisis and the skyrocketing cost of higher education. Despite the fact that American families have *never* reflected this idealized structure – there has been far more family diversity than is routinely attributed to "the American family" – this ideal is the mainstay of the American Dream (Coontz, 1992). In the face of these new economic realities coupled with changing family structures and dynamics, people turn to their families for help in times of economic hardship. Getting men to pay child support directly to their families (and not the government), housing relatives who may have lost their jobs and/or homes, sending remittances to relatives in other countries, and fostering children whose parents are unable to care for them are all important ways that families serve important economic functions in times of stress.

Narratives about desirable and undesirable families take on added significance in this context. Currently, many people have grown up in "families beyond the stereotypes," namely, families maintained by divorced and single mothers and fathers, as well as same-sex couples, families where both parents work, and extended families (Gerson, 2010: 15–45). Despite this diversity, the structures and assumed dynamics of those families who appear to be more economically secure than others, primarily middle-class, become idealized and associated with the American Dream. In contrast, families who live in poverty and/or who experience chronic economic vulnerability can be stigmatized for *causing* their own disadvantage by ostensibly rejecting dominant norms. Moreover, because the discourse on the idealized family is fundamentally a moral discourse, it misrecognizes the interdependence of macroeconomic and macro-political forces and family outcomes. In the US context, class politics concerning the distribution of property and political rights intersect with racial policies in ways that advance ideas about strong families as a powerful explanatory text for economic security. In this setting, distinctive patterns of family organization of indigenous peoples, African Americans, Mexican Americans, Puerto Ricans, undocumented Latinx immigrants, and poor and/or working-class families of color have long served as benchmarks of what *not* to be. For example, many Americans believe that African American families living in poverty remain economically disadvantaged because African American men have largely abandoned their duties as husbands and fathers, leaving mother-headed families in their wake; and that Latinx families are a threat to the nation because high rates of childbearing among young Latinas, stereotyped as disproportionately illegal, take unfair advantage of the social welfare state. Conversely, Asian American achievement as a so-called "model minority" uses family rhetoric to mask the actual costs paid by poor and working-class families for their children's achievement, as well as the ways in which class privilege enhances the achievement outcomes for wealthy Asian American youth. Racial politics have been refracted through a lens of work and social welfare policies that privilege married heterosexual couples with their own biological children. In this fashion, class and race both rely on ideas about the idealized gendered family.

The second significant dimension of early twenty-first century American society, namely, the emergence of a colorblind racial formation within American racial politics, has occurred concurrently with challenges to economic security spawned by the new global economy (Bonilla-Silva, 2010). Colorblind ideology contends that *not* seeing color should enable American society to overcome historical color-conscious practices that produced racial discrimination and encourages people to practice a willful blindness toward racial practices. Armed with the components of colorblindness, well-intentioned anti-racist projects stemming from the Civil Rights Movement aspired to build a colorblind society by attacking the constellation of racial practices that *excluded* people of color from the best neighborhoods, housing, jobs and social services based on their race. Recognizing that such exclusionary racism was hard-wired into social institutions such that certain populations disproportionately bore the negative effects and risks of society overall, anti-racist strategies aimed to achieve *inclusion* for African Americans and similarly raced groups in existing social institutions. Yet such inclusion required a willful blindness to the ongoing significance of systemic racism.

Developments in the post-Obama era clarify how colorblind social policies, on their own, have failed to address historically entrenched, deep-seated systemic racism. Yet the belief in colorblindness as a worthwhile social goal persists, despite a growing body of literature that identifies its limitations. Societies can have public policies of not seeing race (being "blind" to it) yet reproduce racial inequalities: structural racial inequalities persist, despite claims that they have been eliminated (Bonilla-Silva, 2010; Collins, 2004; Brown et al., 2003). Critical race theory has advanced sophisticated analyses of how the rhetoric of colorblindness can produce structural inequalities through legal frameworks, social institutions and state policies (Guinier & Torres, 2002; Goldberg, 2002). Colorblindness catalyzes a form of racial muteness, where people see speaking of race as stirring up old patterns of color-conscious, racialized language associated with Jim Crow racism. Racial discourse was crucial to color-conscious racism, yet the shift to a seemingly more polite colorblind racism continues to reproduce racial disparities while not talking directly about race at all.[2]

[2] The racial muteness of a colorblind society must be manufactured. The sociological subdiscipline of whiteness studies has investigated everyday strategies that whites use to

How does a society grapple with race and racism in a context of colorblindness that makes it difficult to talk about race? In a context of racial muteness, family rhetoric can serve as a malleable and ambiguous placeholder for a range of racial meanings that in turn are refracted though ideas about gender, class and national identity. As a social construct, race relies on ideas about family lineage (kinship models of biological families extended to broader imagined racial and/or ethnic communities) as a justifiable marker of unequal distribution of social goods (class and/or status) (Banton, 1998). Conversely, family has been a major social institution for the regulation of racial practices, with the state taking an active interest in producing and policing racial categories (Collins, 2001). In short, the rhetoric and practices of family and race have been recursive and mutually constructing whereby family can be fraught with racial meaning.

Further, family may serve as a touchstone in shaping connections between concerns about the seemingly discrete issues of economic security and the racial muteness of colorblind racism. When combined, these interdependent social phenomena present substantial challenges to the rhetoric and practices associated with the American Dream. Can American national identity still be conceptualized as a national family composed of numerous strong families patterned after the idealized American family? If the idealized American family is a dinosaur, and if this family form has been so closely tied to understandings of the American Dream, what are the implications of the uncoupling of these ideas?

In this context, Barack Obama's use of family rhetoric signaled a three-fold mechanism that enabled him to (1) discuss race in a context of colorblindness by invoking the traditionally gendered construct of family; (2) explain economic transformation by using

avoid seeing race and that maintain their own and others racialized identities (Bonilla-Silva, 2010). Several studies have analyzed allegedly non-racial documents for how they function in producing racial hierarchy. Texts as diverse as public policy documents (Van Dijk, 1993) and mass media representations of black popular culture (Collins, 2009: 135–74) have been analyzed as sites that ostensibly uphold universalistic criteria of colorblindness yet help reproduce race.

family rhetoric to knit together cultural arguments (e.g., family values) and structural arguments (e.g., the economy and the state); and (3) recast American national identity in ways that aimed to incorporate diverse populations and experiences (e.g., the multicultural American national family). Barack Obama's ideas about family in general and his personal family stories in particular suggested paths to economic security that tied the significance of family to questions of American national identity and the American Dream. Yet, when Obama highlighted personal family stories, he walked a fine line in positioning himself in relation to common perceptions, on the one hand, of African American families as culturally inferior in ways that foster poverty and economic vulnerability and, on the other, of the idealized traditional American family as the route to economic security.

AFRICAN AMERICAN FAMILIES AND SYSTEMIC RACISM

The unique position that African American families have occupied within broader relations of marriage, family and systemic racism in the US provides an important structural backdrop for assessing Barack Obama's use of personal family stories as well the class, race and gendered meanings suggested by them. Black families have been historically disadvantaged by racially discriminatory public policies concerning work, marriage and family, with correspondingly negative effects on their economic security. Any changes to assumptions about marriage and family, especially those that emanate from the White House, thus have potentially far-reaching implications for African Americans as well as American families overall.

All social groups within US society are affected by the ways in which work, marriage and family privilege some groups and disadvantage others. Yet African Americans as a collectivity constitute a particularly visible and deeply entrenched version of these more general relations as well as a hyper-visible moral text for society overall. My intent here is not to present African Americans as a special case, an exception to the rule of normal marriage/family/economic security relations, but rather as an especially visible site where these broader relations can be observed. Families are central to the intergenerational transfer of wealth and/or debt and are not, as commonly assumed, private spheres that are far removed from public sphere processes of capitalist development and state policy. US social class inequality persists across generations because it is reproduced via family placement in the economy as well as citizenship rights afforded varying family formations. Rather than viewing African American families solely as sites for the intergenerational transmission of *cultural* capital, such families become intergenerational locales for the transmission of *actual* capital.

Idealized gender norms among white men and white women allegedly constitute normal and ideal gender practices against which African Americans have been evaluated and stigmatized as deviant. African American progress, or lack thereof, in achieving white gender norms, has long been used as a marker of racial progress, and often used to explain and justify racial inequality itself (Collins, 2004: 181–212). For African American women, marital status remains linked to both family status and the property rights that flow from being single without children, married, separated, divorced and a never-married mother. Because African American men have been discriminated against in schooling and the labor market, and have high rates of incarceration that render many unemployable, poor and working-class African American women also have found it difficult to find African American male partners who earn an adequate income. Families supported by working-class Black women are at a decided disadvantage. Historical patterns of wealth and debt that characterized the color-conscious, institutionalized racism of the past are unlikely to yield quickly to contemporary exhortations to rely on families in hard times. For example, encouraging African American women to find and marry men with property, regardless of race (color) is unlikely to solve institutionalized social problems such as the ghettoization of poor, young African Americans in inner city schools, neighborhoods and prisons, or stubbornly persistent racial achievement gaps in educational attainment. At the same time, urging African American men to become financially responsible for their wives and children requires access to quality education and good jobs.

It is important to point out that not all Black families are poor. The late-twentieth-century expansion of the African American middle class suggests that a significant segment of the African American population has been able to accumulate sufficient income (if not property) to acquire education, attain good jobs and buy homes (Patillo-McCoy, 1999). These changes demonstrate, in part, how public policies that created educational, housing and employment opportunities for all Americans was effective during times of economic growth when coupled with Civil Rights legislation that ensured fair access to opportunities. When viewed against the historical backdrop of intergenerational poverty among African Americans as a collectivity, the work, marriage and family patterns of middle-class African Americans, such as the Obama family, could be held up to their poorer counterparts as a path out of poverty. This expansion of the African American middle class seemingly signaled a new chapter in US race relations, one where racial assimilation in an ostensibly colorblind society provided a pathway to economic success.

Within this structural context, the Obama family also faced an interpretive context that long placed in the public eye cultural frames to evaluate African American families as dysfunctional, culturally inferior and justifiably poor, while rejecting structural analyses that identify factors such as wealth, work and public policies as equally if not more significant in accounting for their economic insecurity. The emergence of the African American middle class ostensibly refutes this thesis of African American family deviancy, mainly by presenting African American, middle-class families as culturally indistinguishable from their white counterparts and attributing their economic success to shared values. Racial difference is only allowed when it defines black culture as a positive, optional ethnicity that middle-class families can enjoy (*The Cosby Show* provided a template for this depiction) (Jhally & Lewis, 1992). As a result, deviant (and ostensibly authentic) black culture becomes increasingly assigned to poor, urban African Americans who seemingly hold fast to the anti-authoritarian values of hip hop culture. In essence, cultural values become the cause of African American, middle-class economic success, veiling the ongoing significance of structural factors to economic outcomes.

The visibility of the First Black First Family in the public eye highlighted how ideas about family invoke connections among race, gender, economic security and American national identity. Three themes stand out: (1) countering the stigmatized gender ideology attributed to African American families by depicting Barack Obama as a strong family man; (2) using responsible fatherhood initiatives to support an agenda concerning race, masculinity and public policy; and (3) supporting public policies of work–family balance via Michelle Obama's media visibility as First Lady.

COUNTERING BLACK GENDER IDEOLOGY: BARACK OBAMA AS A STRONG FAMILY MAN

Barack Obama's presentation of himself as a strong family man illustrates an unresolved tension concerning the connections between idealized gendered families, economic security and racial politics. By sharing his own personal story of how his *past* upbringing was central to his current economic prosperity and political success, Barack Obama intentionally valorized non-traditional family structures, namely, blended families with stepfathers and half-siblings, families maintained by single mothers, extended families that include grandparents as primary caretakers, and families formed across racial, ethnic and national boundaries.

The family values he learned within these diverse family forms signal a new politics of race that more closely resembles the multiracial, multi-ethnic and multicultural fabric of American society. If strong families are the foundation of American society, then Obama's showcasing of his family diversity expanded notions of a multicultural American national identity within an ostensibly colorblind society.

Michelle Obama's family story contains different details but reinforces the significance of strong families. In telling her *past* family story, Michelle Obama focused on growing up in her intact, working-class African American family in Chicago. Her opening speech at the 2008 Democratic National convention focused on the intact African American family of her childhood, highlighting the significance of family values to economic security: "I come here as a daughter – raised on the South Side of Chicago by a father who was a blue-collar city worker and a mother who stayed at home with my brother and me" (M. Obama, 2008). Moreover, she drew connections between family support and upward mobility: "thanks to their faith and hard work, we both were able to go on to college. So I know firsthand from their lives – and mine – that the American dream endures" (M. Obama, 2008).

As President, Barack Obama's family experiences within the first-ever Black First Family, namely, as a devoted husband and father in a racially homogeneous, married heterosexual nuclear family with legitimate children, signaled more traditional conceptions of the links between family and economic success. Barack and Michelle Obama may have followed different paths to their middle-class family status, but their shared values enabled them to create a traditional American family. The family values that are associated with the Obama family's nuclear structure, such as teaching their children the importance of education, hard work, exercise, healthy food consumption and service to the less fortunate, upheld traditional ideas about the family that ostensibly fostered the American Dream.

Barack Obama's relationship to his wife and children enabled him to present himself as a strong family man and thereby avoid the stigma of African American male irresponsibility that has been part of the gendered analysis of African American family deviancy. This perception of African American male irresponsibility reflects the thesis that African American women are "too strong" and African American men are "too weak," an ideological outcome of deviant sex role behavior attributed to African American families. "This strong-black-woman/weak-black-man thesis has taken an especially pernicious form in the post-Civil Rights era, the same period of the growth of changing marriage and family patterns for everyone as well as the emergence of colorblind racism. Increasingly, gender relationships among African American men and women are often depicted as one of perpetrator and victim" (Collins, 2004: 181–212).

Within the strong-black-woman/weak-black-man thesis, two specific dimensions are allegedly responsible. One dimension is the putatively flawed relationship between African American mothers and their children; strong African American mothers allegedly baby their sons yet raise their daughters in their own, "too strong" image. As a result of flawed gender socialization, African American men never fully grow up to become men, and succumb to irrational, childish acts of unrestrained violence or sexual irresponsibility. The second dimension centers on one alleged outcome of this flawed gender socialization, namely, the seeming absence of commitment to marriage among African Americans. As indicated by high rates of mother-headed families, African Americans seemingly have difficulty committing to each other via marriage and maintaining healthy families.

The First Black First Family's unique and highly visible media presence required protection from this negative black gender ideology, especially its depiction of African American men as immature as a result of flawed gender socialization, and therefore unwilling to form healthy, adult relationships. Barack Obama's 1995 autobiography, *Dreams from My Father: A Story of Race and*

Inheritance, refutes these stereotypes by detailing his family experiences in Hawaii, Indonesia and Kenya. During the campaign, he repeatedly referred to the family that raised him, specifically, his mother, his grandparents, his Indonesian stepfather, and his reactions to not having his biological Kenyan father as part of his upbringing. Working against the trope that blames African American mothers for producing weak African American sons, Barack Obama extracted himself from this negative stereotype by drawing upon his past family story to acknowledge and praise the (white) women who raised him. In this way, he shared his progressive views on women, especially working women; yet avoided suspicion that an African American mother emasculated him. Combining these multiple narratives of Michelle Obama's family story of working-class intact African American family life, Barack Obama's family of origin that lacked an African American mother, and his current family where he is successfully partnered with a strong but not "too-strong" African American woman, enabled Barack Obama to valorize female strength within families by retaining ambiguity about which exact women he means. Combining the (white) women of his family of origin with the (black) woman who is most significant within his current nuclear family creates space to *celebrate* female strength.

This family story of Barack Obama's childhood is especially significant in sidestepping the weak-black-son/strong-black-mother dimension of black gender ideology by showing that the trope simply did not apply to him. Yet sustaining a commitment to family, motherhood and women without alienating African American women, one of his most faithful groups of supporters, meant that African American women could not be excluded from the Obama family story. During the 2008 presidential campaign, Barack Obama took pains to acknowledge his love for his wife. Quite simply, Barack Obama publicly stated that he is a man married to a woman he loves, raising two children that they clearly adore. However, in the context of mass media spectacles where the African American single mother has been demonized, Michelle Obama stands out. She did not fit media representations of African American female beauty, namely, light-skinned, longhaired, and/or biracial black and ethnic women. Moreover, her visibility as a professional woman contradicted the strong-black-woman/weak-black-man thesis. Barack Obama could present himself as a strong family man because he chose to marry a strong African American woman and build a strong family with her. For the public at large, theirs was an idealized, ordinary marriage, but when placed in the context of black gender ideology, their successful marriage was extraordinary.

The Obama campaign routinely drew upon multiple depictions of family, with the connections between family and economic security implied but not explicitly expressed. When combined as one Obama family story, with Barack Obama as the protagonist, the multiple narratives suggested a temporal pathway to economic security where *past* actions shape *contemporary* economic realities. For example, one story, that of the single mother whose biracial child is cared for within families maintained by his stepfather and by his grandparents, emphasized the significance of caring for children to ensure their upward social mobility. Michelle Obama's family story of upward social mobility from the working class to the middle class offered another script of how past parental actions fostered contemporary economic success. When shorn of the stigma of slavery, her story suggests that, for working-class African American families, intact, married-couple families constitute a viable path to economic security. Both stories suggest that values learned in the past can foster economic security, regardless of the past – for Barack Obama, the past of his racial/ethnic otherness within his non-traditional families, and for Michelle Obama, the past of urban working-class life a few generations removed from slavery. In both stories, the values of education and hard work learned from families were essential to their economic success.

The Obama family narratives that identified their family structures and dynamics as critical to their success is a morality story about adhering to the values of the American Dream. Going to the best schools, working in the best jobs, and living in a heterosexual, married-couple family with one's own biological children is central to achieving the American Dream. Because people who are fortunate enough to be born into intact, middle-class nuclear traditionally gendered families, regardless of racial heritage, are more likely to enjoy economic security, they have the responsibility for modeling their family values for others. The racial subtext of the Obama family story heightened the significance of this values argument. The Obama family stood for itself, but also provided evidence for African American, middle-class achievement. Those not currently in married-couple, nuclear families could look to the Obama family for hope and inspiration. In this sense, the First Black First Family became a model for emulation and a symbol of national leadership.

BARACK OBAMA: RESPONSIBLE FATHERHOOD REDEFINED MASCULINITY AND PUBLIC POLICY

For Father's Day 2008, President Obama presented his views on responsible fatherhood at a White House event to a handpicked gathering of exemplary father figures:

> Let's be clear: Just because your own father wasn't there for you, that's not an excuse for you to be absent also – it's all the more reason for you to be present. There's no rule that says that you have to repeat your father's mistakes. Just the opposite – you have an obligation to break the cycle and to learn from those mistakes, and to rise up where your own fathers fell short and to do better than they did with your own children .... That's what I've tried to do in my life. When my daughters were born, I made a pledge to them, and to myself, that I would do everything I could to give them some things I didn't have. *And I decided that if I could be one thing in life, it would be to be a good father.* (B. Obama, 2008a) [emphasis added]

Barack Obama's personal and national focus on fatherhood enabled him to couch economic and social policy within the rhetoric of responsible fatherhood. This commitment to fatherhood delivered messages to overlapping constituencies: (1) African American men who sought new leadership in redefining black masculinity; (2) American men from varying socioeconomic, racial and ethnic backgrounds about the challenges that confront fathers in times of economic adversity and how those challenges signal the changing nature of American masculinity; and (3) the general public (men and women) about how Barack Obama's support for strong and compassionate father figures granted him legitimacy to be a strong leader.

Making fatherhood central to family discourse enabled Barack Obama to speak to African American men about responsible fatherhood as part of a redefined black masculinity. Several elements of his argument about fatherhood and black masculinity are especially noteworthy. For one, Barack Obama revealed the pain caused by father-absence. Because father-absence has been so visible within African American communities, directly confronting this issue in ways that do not excuse this practice broke new ground. For example, Barack Obama's letter, published in a widely distributed newspaper supplement, discussed the pain of father-absence:

> In many ways, I came to understand the importance of fatherhood through its absence – both in my life and in the lives of others. I came to understand that the hole a man leaves when he abandons his responsibility to his children is one that no government can fill. We can do everything possible to provide good jobs and good schools and safe streets for our kids, but it will never be enough to fully make up the difference . . .. That is why we need fathers to step up, to realize that their job does not end at conception; that what makes you a man is not the ability to have a child but the courage to raise one. (B. Obama, 2008b)

Here, Barack Obama's emphasized *responsible* fatherhood, not biological fatherhood. This statement also points to the boundary distinguishing family and governmental responsibilities and the balance between them; each have their place and neither can fully replace the other. Barack Obama also refuted the cultural norm that children from so-called "broken homes" (father absent, households maintained by women) are irreparably damaged. By skillfully using his own family narratives to hammer home this point, he proclaimed that he was especially committed to being a good father to his children because he realized the pain of father-absence. The absent biological father of his childhood became an object lesson of what not to be, whereas his image as a strong caring father spoke to a path of potential redemption for all those fathers who take responsibility.

In a Father's Day speech delivered at an African American church, Barack Obama sent a clear message to African American fathers. Claiming that responsible fatherhood is *especially* needed in African American communities because so many fathers have abandoned their duties, Barack Obama explained why fathers are integral to families: "Of all the rocks upon which we build our lives, we are reminded today that family is the most important. And we are called to recognize and honor how critical every father is to that foundation" (B. Obama, 2008a: 238). Barack Obama identified two significant ways that fathers should be central within families. For one, fathers should help set high expectations for children by being role models to their children and setting examples of excellence in their own lives. Second, fathers should set good moral and emotional examples for children: Obama encouraged men to "pass along the value of empathy to our children ... we forget about our obligations to one another. There's a culture in our society that says remembering these obligations is somehow soft – that we can't show weakness, and so therefore we can't show kindness" (B. Obama, 2008a: 238). Resisting the pressures to embrace dominant gender ideology that advances views of black masculinity that requires female subordination, Barack Obama reclaimed empathy and emotions as part of a redefined masculinity. Instead, he redefined a strong father (and by implication a strong man) as one who willingly chose to commit to others, who did not see commitment as a sign of weakness, but of humanity.

Responsible fatherhood initiatives spoke to a second dimension of the centrality of fatherhood within Barack Obama's family narratives, namely, how responsible fatherhood initiatives enabled him to address men as a collectivity concerning the challenges they faced in times of economic adversity. Focusing on fatherhood enabled Barack Obama to examine shifting patterns of masculinity in a changing US economy where men had lost their place in the traditional nuclear family as breadwinners and as so-called natural authority figures. Whereas these trends have disproportionately affected African American and/or working-class men, all men have been increasingly vulnerable to broader macroeconomic forces. When Barack Obama stated, "what makes you a man is not the ability to have a child but the courage to raise one" (B. Obama, 2008b), he may have been addressing an African American audience, yet he counseled all men to develop new conceptions of masculinity that incorporate, to the degree possible, both financial support for children and non-financial contributions. In this sense, responsible father initiatives provided important clues concerning what kinds of men would be needed to meet the challenges of contemporary society.

Finally, Barack Obama's responsible fatherhood initiatives enabled him to sketch out his work and family policy to the general public. In essence, by couching social policy through the rhetoric of family generally and fatherhood in particular, Barack Obama presented a "family values" argument from the liberal left that refused to cede the language of family as being hopelessly embedded in the right-wing rhetoric of the idealized nuclear family. In place of a feminist discourse on motherhood that argued for many of the same policies as the Obama administration, Barack Obama's fatherhood initiatives aimed to reclaim the language of fatherhood and change its meaning. Groups as diverse as African Americans, women and conservative "family values" groups could all claim a space within responsible fatherhood initiatives. Barack Obama expressed support for working parents, long a demand of women's groups, but sidestepped the claim that his administration pandered to feminist groups by couching his policies within the language of fatherhood and family.

Barack Obama's use of responsible fatherhood rhetoric to address multiple publics suggested that the same family narratives that helped him win the election also enabled him to position himself as a strong leader. Ideas about fatherhood within idealized nuclear families have long served as the template for ideas about strong leadership within American politics. Female and/or non-white candidates face the dilemma of presenting themselves as viable leaders within this traditional understanding of family and of political leadership. Because he was African American, biracial, and had a "funny name," Barack Obama faced the challenge of convincing citizens that he could be a strong leader who could command the reins of power. Barack Obama also faced the specific challenge of refuting claims that his background of father-absence (by his African biological father) made him less fit for leadership than his political counterparts who grew up in white, intact married-couple families. Thus, ideas about responsible fatherhood reach out in many directions to negotiate the politics of race and gender in a seemingly colorblind setting where race and masculinity are especially visible.

MICHELLE OBAMA: FIRST LADY, MOM-IN-CHIEF AND WORKING MOTHER

Just as Barack Obama had to walk a fine line regarding black masculinity and its discourse about fatherhood, Michelle Obama encountered similar issues concerning her appropriateness as a wife to such a powerful husband. Because of her gender and race, she was the antithesis of what the First Lady traditionally represented (Williams, 2009: 839–40). Moreover, just as Barack Obama deployed family narratives as a way of explaining economic and social policies, Michelle Obama used family narratives to redefine black femininity. Her media visibility and "celebrity" status enabled the Obama administration to package arguments regarding the connections between economic security, race, gender and national identity within publicly accessible family rhetoric. In *Becoming Michelle Obama*, for example, the then First Lady explained "Rather than doing interviews with big newspapers or cable news outlets, I began sitting down with influential 'mommy bloggers' who reached an enormous and dialed-in audience of women .... With my soft power, I was finding I could be strong" (M. Obama, 2018: 372–73).

Here I focus on three elements of Michelle Obama's media representations where family rhetoric was designed to shape social meanings of gender, race, class and/or nation: (1) her reinterpretation of the role of First Lady to move beyond traditional functions of being a homemaker and hostess for the White House to being a public figure that advanced the agendas of the White House; (2) her reinterpretation of motherhood from a stay-at-home endeavor to a "Mom-in-Chief" enterprise; and (3) her efforts to highlight the needs of working mothers primarily by blurring work/family boundaries. Via these three themes, Michelle Obama expanded women's issues in ways that encapsulated seemingly contradictory views of traditionalists and feminists.

Michelle Obama's interpretation of her status as First Lady refracted the politics of gender and race through family rhetoric. As an unelected position lacking any constitutionally defined job description, the role of First Lady historically constituted an exemplar of traditional femininity and therefore carried great social meaning. As the nation's hostess and housekeeper, the traditional social and ceremonial duties of the First Lady are essential not only because they are symbols of the First Lady, but also because they directly reflect upon the President, and in turn, the nation (Williams, 2009). While staff and budgetary support had grown for the increasingly professionalized position of the First Lady, the First Family remains a social script for women concerning the benefits and responsibilities of marrying wealthy and powerful men. This script carries a powerful racial subtext, one suggesting that a white nation should have a white, heterosexual family at its helm, and that the "Lady" of the house is responsible for modeling the morals and values of the American family. Because Michelle Obama could never become white, how could she ever become a true Lady?

As First Lady, Michelle Obama had to demonstrate not only that she could perform the traditional duties of this visible social position, but also that she could negotiate a racialized gender ideology. Moreover, she needed to do so in a context where she remained on public display, yet also needed to find ways to make her highly visible race invisible in the context of a colorblind racism. In response, Michelle Obama's shaping of the role of First Lady drew upon the image of the "Black Lady," a trope that many African American women have long used to reject their stereotypical treatment. Working-class and middle-class African American women alike have responded to the derogated image of the strong and emasculating black woman by embracing a politics of respectability modeled on the traditional femininity symbolized by the First Lady position. Middle-class African American women have drawn upon this Black Lady standard in their professional positions – the case of Condoleezza Rice as Secretary of State during the George W. Bush administration comes to mind – but the cost of respectability has often been remaining unmarried and childless. Traditionally, Black Ladies did not have out-of-wedlock children, nor did they publicly flaunt their unmarried sexual experiences (Collins, 2004: 138–46).

Michelle Obama engaged in a sophisticated fusion of three social scripts, those attached to the First Lady, the Black Lady and the strong Black woman. She fulfilled traditional ideals about domesticity associated with the position of First Lady by positioning herself as a Black Lady. In essence, whiteness was no longer a requirement for being a Lady. She also drew upon the Black Lady standard in that she depicted a person of high morals with her professional career and path of upward social mobility demonstrating her commitment to hard work. She also drew upon and redefined yet another dimension of black gender ideology, the strong black women representation. Here Michelle Obama softened the negative impact of black female strength by placing her strength in service to her husband's ambition to run for President. Her "softness" bolstered Barack Obama's public persona as a responsible father and husband. Michelle Obama seemed to "have it all" – she was attractive, married to a strong African American man, had two beautiful children, and a new profession (albeit unpaid) of managing the White House.

To have it all, however, Michelle Obama had to simultaneously show that her career harmed neither her marriage nor her family life. Barack and Michelle Obama's private life has been extensively covered in their autobiographies as well as in magazines and in the popular press. Interestingly, the Obamas used the media to refute the notion of the traditional idealized family, even though their own family seemed to fit the mold, bringing a candid and non-idealized view of what it takes to make a marriage work, with special attention to the challenges facing working mothers (Kantor, 2009). In *The Audacity of Hope*, Barack Obama acknowledges the difficulty Michelle faced, despite the gender egalitarianism of their marriage, in balancing "the desire to be the woman her mother had been, solid, dependable, making a home and always there for her kids; and the desire to excel in her profession, to make her mark on the world" (B. Obama, 2006: 340–41). This portrayal humanized Michelle Obama, pulling her back from the place of black superwoman to show, instead, how difficult it was to hold a professional position and be a good mother.

Michelle Obama's reinterpretation of motherhood from a stay-at-home endeavor to a "Mom-in-Chief" enterprise constituted a second site where family rhetoric concerning Michelle Obama shaped social meanings of race, gender, class and/or nation. First Ladies must be good wives, and if they are mothers, they must be good mothers. In contrast to the First Lady image, one that is often devoid of children or where servants care for children, or the professional "Black Lady" who is married to her job and remains single, "Moms" are actively involved in their children's lives. Being a Mom-in-Chief meant showing concern for children, both one's own children and the children of the nation. Having children of her own certainly helped facilitate Michelle Obama's Mom-in-Chief image. More importantly, her fusion of being both a loving mother and a Mom-in-Chief enabled her to use her position as mother to exert leadership for the nation.

As Mom-in-Chief, Michelle Obama recast traditional views of motherhood as a privatized affair within the confines of one's nuclear family to a broader social role of tremendous significance. Her commitment to "healthy eating" illustrated this redefined and revalorized motherhood as important to families and to the national family. Mothers routinely do chores such as meal planning, food shopping and meal preparation for their families, with the goal of wanting their children to live healthy lives. Yet these activities have historically been treated as privatized chores that women naturally do. Michelle Obama's public campaign concerning healthy eating told all those individual mothers that childrearing was not just a solitary activity but was also important for the nation. Speaking out against childhood obesity catalyzed visibility for a major public health issue in the United States and helped to shed light on the politics of food. First Ladies have gardeners – they do not food shop, cook or garden. In contrast, Moms and Michelle Obama's public persona as Mom-in-Chief were intimately concerned in all aspects of the welfare of their children.

Collectively, Michelle Obama's (1) reinterpretation of the role of First Lady, especially her status as the first Black First Lady; (2) her reinterpretation of motherhood from a stay-at-home endeavor to a "Mom-in-Chief" enterprise; and (3) her efforts to highlight the needs of working mothers via attention to work–family balance, enabled her to advance specific policy initiatives of concerns of diverse women's groups in ways that eschew being labeled either traditional or radical.

CONCLUSION: JUST ANOTHER AMERICAN STORY?

The arrival of the First Black First Family in the White House served as a symbolic touchstone for several issues that are directly tied to family concerning connections between gender, race, economic security and American national identity. As I have tried to demonstrate here, three themes stand out: (1) depicting Barack Obama as a strong, family man to counter a stigmatized black gender ideology by (2) highlighting responsible fatherhood initiatives to support an agenda concerning gender, race, masculinity and public policy; and (3) publicizing family policies that benefitted women by using Michelle Obama's media visibility as First Lady. Collectively, these three issues illustrate how ideas about family operate in an interpretive colorblind racial formation that has rendered public discussions of racial equality and gender equity risky. Moreover, they illustrate how public policies concerning the economic transformations of the new global economy can be made comprehensible via the rhetoric of family, and how the gendered family frames understandings of American national identity.

REFERENCES

Banton, M. 1998. *Racial Theories.* London: Cambridge University Press.

Bonilla-Silva, E. 2010. *Racism without Racists: Color-Blind Racism and the Persistence of Racial Inequality in the United States,* 3rd ed. Lantham, MD:Rowman & Littlefield.

Brown, M. I. et al. 2003. *Whitewashing Race: The Myth of a Color-Blind Society.* Berkeley, CA: University of California Press.

Collins, P. H. 2001. Like One of the Family: Race, Ethnicity, and the Paradox of US National Identity. *Ethnic and Racial Studies,* **24**(1), 3–28.

2004. *Black Sexual Politics: African Americans, Gender, and the New Racism.* New York: Routledge.

2009. *Another Kind of Public Education: Race, Schools, the Media, and Democratic Possibilities.* Boston: Beacon Press

Coontz, S. 1992. *The Way We Never Were: American Families and the Nostalgia Trap.* New York: Basic Books.

Gerson, K. 2010. *The Unfinished Revolution: How a New Generation is Reshaping Family, Work, and Gender in America.* New York : Oxford University Press.

Goldberg, D. T. 2002. *The Racial State.* Malden, MA: Blackwell.

Guinier, L. and Torres, G. 2002. *The Miner's Canary: Enlisting Race, Resisting Power, Transforming Democracy.* Cambridge, MA: Harvard University Press.

Jhally, S. and Lewis, J. 1992. *Enlightened Racism.* Boulder, CO: Westview Press.
Kantor, J. 2009. The First Marriage: It's Modern, It's a Formidable International Brand, and It's an Ongoing Negotiation. *New York Times Magazine,* 44.
Obama, B. 2006. *The Audacity of Hope: Thoughts on Reclaiming the American Dream.* New York: Crown Publishers.
2008a. Father's Day 2008. In *Change We Can Believe In: Barack Obama's Plan to Renew America's Promise.* New York: Three Rivers Press, pp. 233–43.
2008b. A More Perfect Union. In *Change We Can Believe In: Barack Obama's Plan to Renew America's Promise.* New York: Three Rivers Press. pp. 215–33.
Obama, M. 2008. Transcript: Michelle Obama's Convention Speech. NPR, April 18. www.npr.org/templates/story/story.php?storyId=93963863.
2018. *Becoming Michelle Obama.* London: Penguin/Viking Books.
Patillo-McCoy, M. 1999. *Black Picket Fences: Privilege and Peril among the Black Middle Class.* Chicago, IL: University of Chicago Press.
Van Dijk, T. A. 1993. *Elite Discourse and Racism.* Newbury Park, CA: Sage.
Williams, V. L. 2009. The First (Black) Lady. *Denver University Law Review,* **86**(SI), 833–50.

CHAPTER 10

Gender and the Collective

Bina Agarwal

GENDER INEQUALITY IS PERHAPS THE DEEPEST FORM OF persisting inequality we face today, especially as it intersects with inequalities of class, caste and race. It adversely affects not just a country's economy but also its social and political fabric. Indeed, gender inequality is embedded in all our major institutions – the family, the market, the community and the State. Not surprisingly, a gender lens gives us insights into the world we live in which are rarely obtainable otherwise. Many aspects of gender inequality are visible, but many others remain hidden within gendered social norms and biased perceptions, as several other authors of this volume have also noted (for example, Nancy Fraser, Judith Butler, Jack Halberstam and Sara Ahmed). These norms and perceptions, in turn, lead to unequal outcomes for women in multiple arenas.

Practitioners and policy-makers have sought to address persisting gender inequalities in different ways, but especially using the power of collectives, which bring women together to achieve shared goals. Yet women's relationship with collectives in general is complex. On the one hand, historically, women have largely

This chapter is based on my Diane Middlebrook and Carl Djerassi Visiting Professorship lecture, delivered at the University of Cambridge on 10 October 2018. It also draws on my Balzan Prize acceptance speech, my book on environmental governance (Agarwal, 2010), and recent papers on women's farm collectives (Agarwal 2018, 2019a, 2019b). I warmly thank Jude Browne, Lauren Wilcox, Joanna Bush and the Managing Committee of the Cambridge University Centre for Gender Studies for the wonderful opportunity provided by this Professorship.

been excluded from ostensibly mixed-gender collectives – parliaments, village councils and community institutions of governance – and recent inclusions are often due to gender quotas. On the other hand, women have frequently been at the forefront of social movements, and all-women collectives are widely promoted as mechanisms for social empowerment. Both types of collectives, however, raise further questions. In mixed-gender collectives, what proportion of women would be effective? Is there a measurable critical mass? In all-women groups, should homogeneity by class/caste/ethnicity be promoted for better cooperation, or heterogeneity for the benefits of diversity? And is there power simply in numbers – 'women-*in*-themselves' – or is a gendered consciousness – 'women-*for*-themselves' – essential for impact? More particularly, while women's presence in collectives is intrinsically important for social justice, does it also affect economic outcomes?

This chapter addresses these questions both conceptually and through empirical insights based on primary surveys of two types of collectives in South Asia: one constituted of community members managing local forests (a common pool resource) and the other constituted of women farming in groups on agricultural land (a private property resource). Eschewing the much-beaten narrative of women's exclusion, I focus on the little-examined economic impact of their inclusion. Can such inclusion, for example, enhance forest conservation in the one case, and farm productivity in the other?

WHAT IS A COLLECTIVE?

We can think of a collective as a group of people united by a common purpose. Familiar examples would include parliaments, municipalities, village councils, political parties, trades unions, clubs and cooperatives. These can all be seen as collectives, as can protest groups and social movements. Hence although we may think of ourselves as individuals, in fact we are constantly interacting with collectives and are often even embedded in them.

But collectives can be of many types. They can be constituted for diverse purposes. Their modes of interaction can differ, as can their social composition and motivation. All these factors have gender implications. To begin with, consider purpose. Some collectives are mainly political in nature, such as political parties or parliaments. Others are mainly social in scope, such as clubs or reform groups. Yet others are focused on economic gain, such as trades unions or producer cooperatives. A few may cover several functions. Parliaments, for instance, also legislate on economic and social policy.

Second, collectives differ in their degree of formality: formal groups are clearly delineated and have authority to make and enforce rules, derived either from the State or some other body. Informal groups typically lack delineation and such authority (Stewart, 1996).

Third, the nature of collective functioning can differ. Here, it is useful to distinguish between agitational collective action and cooperative collective action (Agarwal, 2000). Agitational collective action, such as a protest demonstration, is sporadic, situation-specific and typically mobilized to demand action from the State. This would include anti-war movements such as described by Mignon Nixon in this volume. 'Cooperative' collective action is continuous and requires regular monitoring and decision-making, such as by community members protecting common resources or farming in groups.

Fourth, some collectives, such as political parties, tend to have well-defined ideologies. Others may be formed around implicitly shared interests centered, say on gender, race or caste.

Fifth, collectives can vary in the diversity of their social composition. Some may be largely homogenous by gender, class, race or caste; others can be heterogeneous across these categories. Those forming the collectives may proactively decide whether they want to be relatively homogenous or heterogeneous, and of what size.

Sixth, motivations for forming or participating in a collective can range from narrow self-interest to altruism, but these motivations can also change with time, say with self-interest transforming into other-regarding interest.

The noted differences can apply generically across the genders, but in practice tend to be gendered. For instance, in South Asia and possibly elsewhere, women tend to be located more in informal than in formal collectives (unless there are quotas). And they are more likely to be a part of groups organized around social and political issues than around economic issues. They are most often in all-women collectives, such as women's wings of political parties, self-help groups, or autonomous women's groups, than in mixed-gender collectives. Within mixed-gender collectives, women tend to be more present in agitational collective action than in cooperative collective action or everyday decision-making. We have many examples, for instance, of Indian women leading protests, such as against forest logging in the Chipko movement in the 1970s (Jain, 1984), or in tenant farmers' movements for land rights, as in Telangana and Tehbhaga in the 1940s (Lalita et al., 1989; Custers, 1987), but they were rarely part of the decision-making forums of these movements.

Most research on the gender gap in collectives, especially in developing countries, has focused on women's low numbers in formal institutions of State governance, such as parliaments or village councils, and the factors underlying their absence. This absence is typically decried on grounds of justice and equality rather than on grounds of effectiveness and efficiency. In particular, inadequate attention has been paid to the likely impact of their presence on outcomes. For example, in many countries women's groups have lobbied for gender quotas in parliament, with varying degrees of success. But if we were to ask: what difference has that made to the policies formulated or the bills passed, research is rather sparse and limited to developed countries (Bergqvist, 2004; Thomas, 1994). In particular, there is relatively little work on the impact of women's presence in collectives formed to manage economic resources, with rare exceptions such as micro-credit institutions, and to lesser degree village councils (Chattopadhyay & Duflo, 2004).

Focusing on this neglected area, I examine two types of economic collectives in South Asia, one relating to community management of common property resources, in particular forests, and the other relating to private property resources, namely farm land. In both cases, I move past the standard question of why women are largely absent from formal collectives, and ask – what impact do women have when present?

In this context, I also seek to identify what proportion of women can make a difference. Is there a critical mass? And is there power simply in numbers, which we can term 'gender-*in*-itself', or do women also need to develop a conscious sense of solidarity, which we can term 'gender-*for*-itself'? This distinction parallels the Marxist one between class-in-itself and class-for-itself (Lukacs, 1971), but without implying that women suffer from false consciousness. In the Marxist literature, for example, a move to 'class-for-itself' requires the proletariat to overcome false consciousness and overtly express its common class interests. However, as I argue elsewhere (Agarwal, 1994), even when women recognize their common gender interests, they may express that understanding covertly and individually rather than overtly and collectively, not because of false consciousness but due to social and economic vulnerabilities.[1] But let us first examine the power of numbers with empirical examples.

FOREST COLLECTIVES

Background

Historically, in South Asia, women played little role in village affairs. They were usually excluded from village councils, even in disputes that directly affected them. This changed dramatically in the 1990s with one-third reservation of seats for women in village councils, but it did not spill over to community forestry.[2]

[1] See also Scott (1985), for an ungendered perspective on this.

[2] For a detailed discussion see Agarwal (2010, chapter 3).

Community forestry itself was not widespread. In India, 96 per cent of forest land and a similarly high proportion in Nepal is government-owned. However, in the late 1970s, satellite images showed high levels of forest degradation, highlighting the enormity of State failure in protecting forests. Parallel to this was the emergence of successful protection by village communities. Hence, by the late 1980s, there was a growing consensus among governments globally in favour of co-managing forests with communities, and over fifty countries launched co-management programmes in the 1990s (Agarwal & Gibson, 2001). India was among the first to launch a Joint Forest Management Programme (JFM) in 1990. Nepal followed suit in 1993. Under these programmes, villagers were given tracts of degraded local forests to manage and, as an incentive, allowed to reap specified benefits from regeneration. In fact, under JFM, communities had a considerable say in deciding what could be extracted from the forest and how frequently, as well as the mode of distribution among the village households. Protection was via a community guard jointly paid for by the villagers, or a voluntarily organized village patrol. In addition, villagers kept an informal lookout for intruders, as they went about their daily tasks.

By the early 2000s, India had an estimated 84,000 such groups, involving 8.4 million families protecting 22.4 per cent of recorded forest area. Nepal had nearly 10,000 groups covering one million households and covering 11 per cent of its forest land. These community forestry groups (CFGs) usually had few or no women. Most Indian states prescribed having 'at least two women' on the understanding, shared by many village institutions, that one woman would feel lonely! Some states later raised the prescription to one-third women. In practice most CFGs did not follow these prescriptions.

And where women *were* allowed membership, their effective participation in decision-making was restricted by social norms which frowned upon women attending gatherings where mostly men were present, or speaking in front of village elders. Given their housework and childcare responsibilities (again due to social norms), the inconvenient timing of meetings was also a constraint. Additional barriers included social perceptions that women could contribute little since many of them were illiterate (although this was not considered a barrier for illiterate men!), or that men had already established prior rights over the protected area and therefore should have the most say in determining the rules of forest use (Agarwal, 2001).

Women's exclusion created situations of gender conflict within communities, since millions of rural women in South Asia depend on forests for collecting items of daily needs such as firewood, fodder, supplementary food items and other non-timber products, while rural men depend on forests largely for timber for house building and repairs which are occasional needs (Agarwal, 2010).

But what would women's inclusion in community forestry mean? Basically, CFGs have a two-tier structure: a general body with members drawn from the whole village and an executive committee (EC) of between nine and fifteen people. Both bodies interactively define the rules of forest use, forms of protection, benefit distribution and conflict resolution. But the core decision-making unit is the EC. Hence who has voice in the EC bears critically on how the group functions, and who gains or loses from the collective. For instance, forest protection involves restricting the entry of people and animals, and regulating extraction of forest produce. Hence if, say, the EC bans firewood collection, it can cause poor women intense hardship, since firewood is still a major cooking fuel largely collected by women. In the early 2000s, for example, 94 per cent of rural domestic energy in India came from traditional biofuels such as firewood, cropwaste and cattle dung (NCAER, 2001–02), and dependence on these fuels was even higher in Nepal, firewood being the most important (GoN, 2004). Even in 2011–12, 67 per cent of India's rural households were found to depend on firewood and chips for cooking (GoI, 2011–12), and much of this was gathered. Hence, having a voice in the EC was of key importance to the women.

But having a voice means going beyond token membership. Consider the typology in Table 10.1. Participation can range from nominal to empowered. Effective or empowered participation requires people to attend meetings, speak up at them and be able to influence at least some decisions, at least some of the time. In fact, this typology can be applied to any collective, even university committees.

Typically, women were not even nominal members of the ECs within these groups: some ECs had no women and most others had one or two women, too few a number to be able to exercise influence. Moreover, due to restrictive social norms and perceptions mentioned above, many did not attend meetings. Those who attended rarely spoke up, and if they spoke their opinions tended to carry little weight. These 'participatory exclusions', as I term them, were widespread (Agarwal, 2001). Yet there were some exceptions. Some mixed-gender groups had 30–40 per cent women and there were also some all-women ECs. These deviations from the common pattern of exclusion could be traced to historical factors (such as a prior history of women being formed into groups for health or other issues), or progressive local leaders or non-governmental organizations (NGOs), or (occasionally) to women acting on their own out of necessity.

TABLE 10.1 *Typology of participation*

Form/level of participation	Characteristic features
Nominal participation	Membership in the group
Passive participation	Being informed of decisions *ex post facto*; or attending meetings and listening in on decision-making, without speaking up
Consultative participation	Being asked an opinion in specific matters without guarantee of influencing decisions
Activity-specific participation	Being asked to (or volunteering to) undertake specific tasks
Active participation	Expressing opinions, whether or not solicited, or taking initiatives of other sorts
Interactive (empowering) participation	Having voice and influence in the group's decisions

Source: Agarwal (2016, 3: 184)

For me, this pattern raised several questions: Would women's inclusion affect decisions on forest use? Would it lead to better conserved forests? Would women's class matter? And how many women were needed to make an impact? These questions – which are foundational for effective environmental governance – were the central concern of my book *Gender and Green Governance* (Agarwal, 2010). Based on a primary survey and many years of fieldwork, I tested what impact the gender composition of the EC has on women's effective participation, rule-making, rule violations, forest condition, and firewood and fodder shortages. Here I summarize the results relating especially to the impact on participation and conservation.

Data and Results

My data relates to 135 CFGs, of which 65 are drawn from three districts in Gujarat in West India and 70 from three districts in the middle-hills of Nepal. Since the EC is the main decision-maker, the sample was based on the EC's gender composition, through stratified random sampling. In Gujarat, CFGs were stratified into two categories – ECs with 2 women or less and ECs with >2 women – since the guidelines suggested including at least 2 women. In percentage terms, two women in an eleven-member EC comes to 18 per cent. Gujarat had very few all-women groups, so none were selected. In Nepal three categories of CFGs were selected: those with ≤2 in their ECs, those with >2 women and those with only women.

I first tested for a threshold point, the *critical mass* needed for women to participate effectively in mixed-gender groups. The underlying idea is that the presence of other women will help individual women overcome social restrictions and personal reticence. Globally, a range of studies (mostly from the Global North, and mostly on political institutions) have suggested percentages between 15 and 40 as being the critical mass,[3] but these are

[3] See, among others, Kanter (1977), (1989); Dahlerup (1988); Lovenduski (1997); Bratton (2005).

typically based on broad observations and guesstimates rather than actual measurement.[4] I tested the threshold point empirically for CFGs and found that the likelihood of women attending meetings, speaking up, and holding office was significantly higher in ECs with 25–33 per cent women. This could be seen as the critical mass.

Table 10.2 provides some illustrative results for meeting attendance in mixed-gender CFGs. We note that women's attendance improves with more women in the EC. For instance, in Gujarat's ECs with <2 women, only 59 per cent of the meetings had some women attending (41 per cent had none), while in ECs with >2 women there were women attendees in 87 per cent of the meetings. In Nepal, again, women were present in 94 per cent of the meetings where the EC had >2 women members, but were present in only 64 per cent of the meetings where the EC had <2 women.

But for identifying the critical mass, we need the attendance rate given in Table 10.3. In both states, the female attendance rate was much higher among ECs with more than two women relative to those with less women, being the highest with 25–33 per cent

TABLE 10.2 *Percentage of EC meetings with women attending mixed-gender CFGs in Gujarat (India) and Nepal*

Percentage attendees who are women	Gujarat			Nepal		
	<2 EC women (136)	>2 EC women (167)	All CFGs (303)	<2 EC women (139)	>2 EC women (196)	All CFGs (335)
	% EC Meetings					
0	41.2	13.2	25.7	36.0	6.1	18.5
>0 - <15	25.7	16.2	20.5	38.1	17.3	26.0
>15 - < 25	16.9	21.6	19.5	15.1	14.3	14.6
>25 - <33	8.1	27.5	18.8	9.4	17.9	14.3
>33	8.1	21.6	15.5	1.4	44.4	26.6

Note: Figures in brackets give the number of meetings.
Source: Agarwal (2010: 190)

[4] Bratton and Ray (2002), who examine Norwegian municipalities over 1975–1991, are one of the rare exceptions.

women but falling subsequently in Gujarat and levelling off in Nepal (Table 10.3). Thus for a typical EC of 11–13 members, the highest female attendance rate occurred with 3–4 women.

Similarly, women were found more likely to speak up at meetings when they were present in larger numbers. Also, contrary to theorizing by some feminist philosophers that prior social equality is necessary for participatory parity (e.g., Fraser, 1990), I found that poor women, if present in sufficient numbers, tended to be more outspoken than well-off women, since they were less constrained by social norms and had much to gain if they could influence the framing of forest use rules to allow greater extraction, especially of firewood.

The second key question examined was whether forest improvement was greater where ECs had more women. An increase in canopy cover overall and regeneration of degraded patches were used as the main markers of improved forest condition. Assessments of changes were based on several sources: an index created by the research team based on forest visits, the villagers' perception of changes, the forest departments' written assessment of forest condition at the time of my survey versus their assessment when community protection began, and satellite data of forest cover calibrated to village forests. To demarcate the effect of

TABLE 10.3 *Female attendance rate (mixed-gender CFGs: means) in Gujarat (India) and Nepal*

	Gujarat (32)	Nepal (38)
CFGs with given number of women in the EC		
≤2 women	0.43	0.45
>2 women	0.54	0.58
CFGs with given % of women in the EC		
<25% women	0.39	0.43
≥25-< 33% women	0.74	0.56
≥33% women	0.42	0.59
All CFGs	0.50	0.53

Note: Figures in brackets give the number of CFGs.
Source: Agarwal (2010: 190)

gender, I controlled for other factors, such as the caste, age and education of members; the method of protection; the size and initial condition of the forest; and village characteristics, including landlessness.

Overall, the vast majority of forests showed improvement simply with community protection. Indeed, in the first decade of JFM (1991–2001), the forest canopy, which was earlier depleting rapidly, increased notably, both in India as a whole (by 3.6 metres per hectare), and on my research sites. But this improvement was markedly greater where the CFGs had a larger percentage of women on their ECs, after controlling for other factors.

In Nepal, for example, there was a 51 per cent higher probability of improvement in forest canopy with all-women ECs relative to groups with men, despite all-women groups receiving more degraded and smaller forests. Similarly, in Gujarat (India), mixed-gender groups with >2 women had better outcomes by three out of four assessment measures than groups with 2 women or fewer. And one district in Gujarat – Panchmahals – did strikingly well. Here, the probability of forest canopy being thicker was 75 per cent greater and the probability of forest regeneration was 57 per cent higher where ECs had >2 women than in ECs with ≤ 2 women.

What made Panchmahals different? A key factor was the high percentage of landless women on its EC. Normally they would have been most hostile to forest closure, but when included in the EC they complied with the rules themselves and persuaded other landless women to do so too. They also had more incentive to comply, since they were able persuade the EC to allow greater extraction of essential forest products without harming conservation (the rules framed were more lenient).

Why did groups with more women (landless or other) perform better? First, women's inclusion substantially improved protection. As noted, women who earlier broke the rules were found more likely to follow the rules when they were themselves on the EC and had participated in rule-making. Some EC women in

Nepal put it clearly: 'We feel the forest is ours . . .. I used to steal grass from the forest, but after becoming an EC member I have stopped stealing.'

Second, EC women shared information about rules with other women and persuaded them to comply, even motivating them to be vigilant and stop intruders. As some women EC members said: 'Having women in the CFG helps. Often village women would cut firewood from the protected forest in times of need. We held a meeting and they stopped cutting.' EC women also inducted other village women into informal patrolling and sometimes their alertness helped spot forest fires before they could cause much damage. Basically, including women vastly increased the numbers of committed villagers protecting the forest.

Third, women had a greater stake in keeping out intruders and promoting forest regeneration because of their greater dependence on the forests than men, given their lesser access to earnings and to private property resources such as land. And such dependence is highest among the poor and landless, who lose the most when forests decline, degrade or are enclosed.

Fourth, a more women-inclusive EC enlarged the knowledge pool on forest ecology, and skills on how to extract products without harming the trees, which species to plant, and so on. Since men and women use forests for different products, they also differ in their knowledge of ecosystems. Women tend to know more about the plants and tree species from which they collect, and men more about what *they collect.* Pooling women's and men's knowledge thus benefits conservation and biodiversity. Women on the EC often made suggestions which the men had not thought of, such as about what and where to replant (see also, Westerman et al., 2005).[5]

Conservation apart, CFGs with more women reported fewer firewood shortages. In other words, by including women and especially poor women on the EC, there was a win–win – better conservation and more equal benefit-sharing by gender and class.

[5] Some studies also find that conflict resolution is better in groups with women (Eckel, 2008; Sell, 1997).

What my results also suggest is that at the local level where the women have implicitly common interests, the power of numbers, 'women-*in*-themselves', can be effective, even without an explicit recognition of solidarity.

FARM COLLECTIVES

Now consider farm collectives. Unlike forests which involve cooperation around common property resources, that is, resources owned by communities or the State, joint farming involves cooperation around private property resources, namely agricultural land.

Background

While there are many examples and a considerable global literature on farmers cooperating for joint marketing, especially in the dairy industry (India's Amul milk cooperative is a case in point), group farming goes much beyond marketing. It involves joint production and cooperation on a daily basis – what I term fully integrated cooperation. Given that 84 per cent of farmers across 111 countries cultivate under 2 hectares of land each (FAO, 2014), which is usually too small to be economically profitable, such integration could provide an alternative, more viable model of farming. The collectives I focus on are all-women groups leasing in land, and pooling labour and capital to farm together.

Conceptually, joint cultivation can help production by increasing farm size, providing scale economics, saving on hired labour, bringing in a larger pool of funds and skills, and raising farmers' bargaining power in markets and with government agencies (Agarwal, 2010). For women, it can also provide autonomy in production decisions, control over output and an independent identity as a farmer. This is seldom possible within male-managed family farms, where women's contributions often go unrecognized. Also, through the group even women who own little land themselves can take up farming. And, as we saw with forest collectives, being part of a group can help individual women overcome social restrictions on their mobility and public interactions.

To examine if this promise of group farming is fulfilled in practice, I posed these question: Are women's farm collectives more economically productive and profitable than individual, typically male-managed, family farms? Does farming in groups also empower women socially and politically? The group farms in Kerala differed notably from previous farmers' collectives, both in India and globally. Earlier examples include five types of farm collectives historically (Agarwal, 2019a). The best known (or most infamous) are the socialist collectives formed through forced collectivization of peasant farms under communism, in the USSR and elsewhere. These had seriously negative effects on farmers' welfare and output. In the 1960s, however, farm cooperatives were promoted in the post-colonial countries of Asia, Africa and Latin America as part of agrarian reform (Ghose, 1983). These were also implemented largely top-down, with inadequate attention to institutional design or understanding of how cooperation works, and most failed. Independent of these, however, dating from the 1960s we find in some European countries, especially France, relatively successful, largely male-managed group farms (Agarwal & Dorin, 2018). In the 1990s, group farms also emerged in many post-socialist countries, such as in Romania, Kyrgyzstan and East Germany: here farming families pooled resources to overcome land and machine scarcity.[6] They did well in production, but were mostly male-managed, women typically remaining unpaid workers within family farms.

The 2000s farm collectives (the most recent examples) which I have studied in India are quite different from all of the above: they are voluntarily constituted by a few, egalitarian in functioning, and based largely on an adaptation of the self-help group (SHG) model.[7] Also they are managed entirely by women, outside

[6] See, for example, Sabates-Wheeler (2002) and Sabates-Wheeler and Childress (2004), and the detailed review of these and other studies in Agarwal (2010).

[7] SHGs are voluntarily constituted thrift-and-credit groups of between ten and twenty people of similar socio-economic backgrounds, who pool their savings to create

the framework of family farms. These group farms were promoted in two states of India – Kerala and Telangana – to empower women economically and socially. The models used and catalyzing agencies, however, were quite different in the two cases leading to divergent effects. I will focus on Kerala, in the southernmost tip of India, for its special insights. This is the first study on the economic effects of these farm collectives relative to individual farms (Agarwal, 2018; 2019b).

The initial idea of group farming came from a few village women in Kerala who had experimented with leasing land in groups. But the State-wide programme was crafted by senior government officials and intellectuals in the 1990s, using the tool of 'participatory planning' which opened up the planning space for ideas to emerge both from the grassroots and from experts (for details see Agarwal (2019a)). Village-level neighbourhood groups were constituted as savings-cum-credit groups, located within a multi-level structure of governance with three pillars: the State Poverty Eradication Mission (the Kudumbashree Mission or K. Mission); the Kudumbashree community network (K. Network), an autonomous registered body with office bearers elected from the members; and the village council (*panchayat*), the lowest elected arm of the State government. The group farms were constituted of women who were prior members of neighbourhood groups. There are over 64,000 such farms across Kerala today.

Data and Results

I selected two districts for my study: Alappuzha, which is dominated by the food crop, paddy, and Thrissur, which is dominated by the commercial cultivation of banana. Both districts also grow vegetables and small amounts of other crops. My sample consists of 69 all-women groups and 181 individual family farms (95 per cent of which are male-managed). Over 2012–13, weekly

a common fund from which group members can borrow with mutual agreement. The majority of these groups in India are constituted by poor women (Tanka, 2012).

data were collected for every input and output for each crop and plot used by these 250 farms. In addition, information on farm and farmer characteristics was collected via focus group discussions.

The groups were heterogenous and included women across caste and religious lines and from both poor and less-poor homes. This heterogeneity went against the common assumption by NGOs and early collective action theory that homogeneity was essential for successful cooperation. Group heterogeneity was encouraged in the Kerala experiment to root the groups in neighbourhoods which are themselves heterogenous; and to ensure leadership. The K. Mission's logic was that local women's leadership comes not from the poorest but from those just above the poverty line. To reduce social divides (especially of caste), weekly meetings where tea was served were rotated among the member households, and those who refused to accept tea from the lowest caste women were asked to either overcome their prejudices or leave the group. None left. Heterogeneity also provided a wider arena of social capital for accessing land.

The groups accessed subsidised credit from the National Bank for Agriculture and Rural Development (NABARD), and received State support in terms of technical information and training. This reduced endemic gender gaps on these counts. The group farms on average had six women. Almost all came from small landowning farming families. All the groups leased in land, mostly from outside the group, but occasionally from other group members who received a rent in return. Individual male farmers, by contrast, owned all or most of the land they cultivated.

The women's group farms faced five initial disadvantages compared to the largely male-run family farms:

1. Dependence on leased land: this leads to high transaction costs in finding suitable land in a single plot. The leases are mostly oral and informal.
2. Oral leases: these create insecurity of tenure, and also mean that women lack proof of being farmers and so cannot access government subsidies.

3. Structurally embedded gender biases in access to land, inputs, extension services, machine and markets.
4. Social restrictions on their mobility and public interactions.
5. Limited prior experience in *managing* farms on an independent basis: most tend to be workers on family farms or housewives.

Some of these disadvantages could be overcome with State support and by forming groups. The group farms were also larger than individual farms. And they dealt with collective action problems, such as someone not turning up for work, by insisting on replacement labour or fines. But women still lacked a level playing field vis-à-vis male-managed family farms.

Despite their challenges, women's collectives performed strikingly better than individual family farms in terms of productivity and profits. As seen from Table 10.4, taking both districts together, the annual average farm output per hectare of group farms was 1.8 times that of individual farms. Also, their yield of banana, the major commercial crop, was on average 1.6

TABLE 10.4 *Annual average value of output per hectare (Rs./ha), and annual average net return per farm, Kerala (India)*

Group farms	Individual farms	Pair wise t-tests
		t-values: differences in means (group minus individual farms)
Annual average value of all crop output per hectare of gross cropped area		
179,183.7	101,156.2	78,027.5
(69)	(181)	3.189***
Average value of paddy, Alappuzha (Rs./ha)		
69,548.15	80,741.02	-11,198.9
(7)	(23)	0.962
Average value of banana, Thrissur (Rs./ha)		
413734.2	258064.1	155,669.9
(14)	(17)	1.717*
Annual average net returns per farm[1]		
1,21,048.5	23,578.3	4.20***
(69)	(181)	

Note: t-values, significance: *** at 1%, * at 10%.
Figures in brackets are the N values.
[1] Net returns = value of total output minus value of all purchased inputs.
Source: Agarwal (2018)

times that of individual farms. The women fine-tuned their banana sales to market demand, taking advantage of high prices during festival seasons. Some negotiated contracts with local temples to supply special varieties. As groups, they were able to deliver better on contracts than small individual farmers. Only in paddy cultivation did the women's groups perform less well, largely due to their inability to lease in good quality paddy land, since the owners preferred to cultivate such land themselves. These results were also supported by my regression analysis which controlled for farm size, fertilizer and manure use, labour inputs and other factors. The regressions showed that a shift from individual farms to women's group farms could increase annual output by 30 per cent.

Women's collectives did even better in their net returns. These were calculated by deducting all paid out costs from the total value of output, but without imputing values to owned land or family labour. For group farms the average net returns per farm were Rs. 121,048, namely five times higher than those of individual farms (Table 10.4), and three times that year's average of Rs. 45,000 per farm for the State of Kerala as a whole. Groups of medium size benefited especially by saving on hired labour, which is quite expensive in Kerala due to high wage rates. The results also demonstrate that despite difficulties in leasing good-quality land, women's group farms can notably outperform individual male farmers in small-scale commercial farming.

Beyond production, women reported that group farming has helped them enhance their capabilities. For instance, they have developed strong identities as farmers in their own right with management skills, moving way beyond their earlier identities as farm labourers or farm wives: 'Group farming has enriched my farming experience. Through the group, I realized that I have good leadership qualities and could also manage the technical aspects of farming. Other group members now listen to me carefully' (Dhanashree, Thrissur).

Group farming has also acquainted these women with the wide range of public institutions and services that they need to draw upon in the course of farming: 'Before joining the group . . . we had no contacts with bank officials, agricultural officers and government officials. After registering as a group, we could start a bank account, attend training classes, and develop a good rapport with these officers' (Sreedurga Thrissur).

In addition, group members have learnt to judge land quality and negotiate lease terms in land markets, and to assess prices of other inputs in input markets. Most importantly, women have learnt to make production decisions and manage the farms independently. And they report being more respected by their families and communities.

Notably, too, an increasing number of Kudumbashree women (including those doing group farming) have begun to stand for and successfully win village council elections.

CONCLUDING REFLECTIONS

What have we learnt about women's relationships with collectives from these forest and farm groups, that helps us better understand the world we live in – the question with which we began?

First, both types of collectives have empowered disadvantaged rural women. Effective inclusion in a forest collective gave poor women a voice and more access to essential forest produce. The farm collectives provided women with an identify as a farmer, supplementary income and more bargaining power across all arenas – families, communities, markets and the State.

Second, the women report being more respected by the village community. Among farm collectives, they are even sought after by male farmers for their knowledge of new farming practices and crops. In fact, some male farmers have formed their own farm collectives by emulating those constituted by women. I found nine all-male groups in Allapuzha, Kerala.

Third, for better economic results, somewhat heterogeneous collectives are found to have an advantage since this enlarges the potential leadership and social capital base, compared with collectives which are homogenous.

Fourth, while gender balance in mixed groups gives positive results, all-women groups appear to have a special dynamism in terms of cooperation and outcomes. We noted this both in forest collectives and farm collectives. SHG and micro-credit experience also point in this direction. SHGs in India and the Grameen Banks in Bangladesh began with both male and female groups, but ended up with over 90 per cent all-female groups with excellent repayment records. Moreover, many grassroots activists argue from their field experience that women's groups work better than mixed-gender ones. They also maintain that women are more willing to work in collectives than are men. For example, as P. Prasanthi and J. Kameshwari, the catalysts for women's farm collectives in Telangana, told me: 'We do think that women are more willing to work in collectives. Their lives are so difficult, and their experience has shown that if they are together they can deal better with the issues that affect them.'

It is likely that several factors contribute to better cooperation among all-women rural groups, such as greater dependence on each other in everyday life due to their resource scarcity, and the benefits of working in groups for overcoming restrictive social norms. This is especially important in a gender-segregated society.

But should all-women groups be especially promoted? Some activists argue that first interacting in separate groups enhances women's ability to participate more effectively in mixed-gender groups. Maya Devi Khanal, a senior Nepalese grassroots worker, had this to say (author's interview in 1999):

> In mixed groups when women speak men make fun of them .... When women join a [separate] group they gradually lose their fear of making fools of themselves when speaking up .... Women need their own small groups. This is what I know from my 22 years of experience working with the government and NGOs.

At the same time, political power and economic resources are largely concentrated in men's groups. Hence dependence solely on all-women's groups is likely to prove restrictive and women's equal presence in men's groups and mixed groups is also clearly needed.

Fifth, women's numbers matter *in themselves.* In forest collectives, simply having one-third women membership changed the group dynamics, given women's common interest in forest products, even if they did not strategize to speak in one voice. What they had in common was the same individual interest in accessing forest resources, especially firewood and fodder, and hence a shared stake in protecting the forest and negotiating for rules which would allow greater extraction.

However, beyond numbers, it is likely that conscious solidarity among women would improve their effectiveness in achieving common goals. This solidarity could be either strategic or empathetic. Strategic solidarities are no doubt easier to forge and can be based on enlightened self-interest. But even they may not emerge spontaneously and may need to be promoted by civil society. A number of feminist political theorists have argued that forums for deliberation can help women get to know each other, share information, sort out their differences and resolve conflicts (Young, 1997, 2000; Mansbridge, 1990). Young (1997: 52) argues that such sharing across difference can generate 'understanding across difference'.

There are also concrete examples of CFGs in some Indian states using deliberation as a tool, as in Malwadi village, Karnataka (author's interview 1999):

> We discussed how benefits should be shared, whether we should differentiate between rich, poor, and middle-income households .... The poor often have no employment, so they need ... forest products for making leaf plates and pickle. They also extract gum. We have enough firewood and agricultural wage employment for now, but what about later? We have to discuss all this, and seek to resolve our differences.

Deliberation prior to EC meetings between women members could also help them arrive at *group* priorities about what forest products to extract, when and for how long the forest should be opened for extraction, which species to plant, etc. Speaking in one voice would prove more effective in mixed-gender CFGs, than speaking as individuals without prior consultation.

Similarly, in farm collectives, alliances between individual groups could help them bargain more effectively for leasing in land in consolidated plots at lower rents, or save on input costs by purchasing in bulk, and get better prices for output by collaborating on sales. Such cooperation would enhance productivity and profits beyond those reaped by each group on its own. Solidarity could also help loss-making groups tide over to the next season. In fact, groups could link horizontally and vertically to form a federation – an association of organizations. In India, SHG federations are common and the K. Network serves as a kind of federation for women's group farms in Kerala. But there could also be benefits from creating interlinked federations of CFGs and women's group farms, since both are rural-based and would have overlapping membership.

Empathetic solidarity is likely to prove more difficult, although it may well develop over time among those practising strategic solidarity. For example, many SHGs have become advocacy groups, reaching out to help non-members and the poor (Nair & Shah, 2007; NCAER, 2008). But some NGOs in India have also been working to help women forge a group identity to create trust and empathy. The NGO, MYRADA, for example, is the catalyst for 'self-help *affinity* groups', building trust among women by evoking commonalities, such as their belonging to the same ancestral village, or having the same livelihood source, or sharing social and economic connections.

In general, forging a 'web of alliances' between groups (whether out of strategic or empathetic motivations) and formalizing them into federations could help scale up village-level collectives, for both forests and farms. Nature itself has many examples of such cooperation, such as the wood wide web connecting trees as described by Merlin Sheldrake (Macfarlane, 2016), or the image of the spider weaving silken threads across trees, as evoked by the poet Coral Bracho:

> . . . pools of silver shimmer
> from one leaf to another, from one path trodden to another . . .

To conclude, in the economic sphere, collectives offer an alternative system for overcoming State and market failures and embedded gender inequalities. Involving women in resource management can also help fulfil national and global goals. For instance, improved forest conservation is a key element of climate change mitigation. And raising farm productivity is key to enhancing national food security.

While collectives can be built on narrow self-interest, or enlightened self-interest for strategic benefits, as we think ahead about the many problems facing our societies and economies, moving from self-interest to other-regarding interest and from individual to collective responsibility appears deeply necessary.

REFERENCES

Agarwal, B. 1994. *A Field of One's Own: Gender and Land Rights in South Asia.* Cambridge, UK: Cambridge University Press.

2000. Conceptualising Environmental Collective Action: Why Gender Matters. *Cambridge Journal of Economics,* **24**(3), 283–310.

2001. Participatory Exclusions, Community Forestry and Gender: An Analysis for South Asia and a Conceptual Framework. *World Development,* **29**(10), 1623–48.

2010. *Gender and Green Governance: The Political Economy of Women's Presence Within and Beyond Community Forestry.* Oxford: Oxford University Press.

2016. *Gender Challenges: Environmental Change and Collective Action,* vol. 3. Delhi and Oxford: Oxford University Press.

2018. Can Group Farms Outperform Individual Family Farms? Empirical Insights from India. *World Development,* **108**: 57–73.

2019a. How Ideas Shape and Are Shaped by Institutions and Organisational Innovations: The Case of Group Farming in India. *ESID working paper No 116,* University of Manchester.

2019b. Does Group Farming Empower Rural Women? Lessons from India's Experiments. *Journal of Peasant Studies,* **47**(4), 841–72. https://doi.org/10.1080/03066150.2019.1628020.

Agarwal, B. and Dorin, B. 2018. Group Farming in France: Why Do Some Regions Have More Cooperative Ventures than Others? *Environment and Planning A.* https://doi.org/10.1177/0308518X18802311.

Agarwal, A and Gibson, C. 2001. *Communities and the Environment.* New Brunswick, NJ: Rutgers University Press.

Bergqvist, C. 2004. On the Road to Equal Democracy? Women and Parliamentary Representation in the NORDIC countries. In M. Tremblay, ed., *Women and Parliamentary Representation Around the World.* Montreal: Remue-Menge.

Bracho, C. 1998. Hilo en una tela de arania. In *La voluntad del ambar.* Mexico: Ediciones Era, p. 16. A recorded translation is available at: www.poetrytranslation.org/poems/thread-in-a-spiders-web#audioBox.

Bratton, K. A. 2005. Critical Mass Theory Revisited: The Behaviour and Success of Token Women in State Legislatures. *Politics & Gender,* **1**(1), 97–125.

Bratton, Kathleen and Ray, Leonard. 2002. Descriptive Representation, Policy Outcomes, and Municipal Day-Care Coverage in Norway. *American Journal of Political Science,* **46**(2), 428–37.

Chattopadhyay, R. and Duflo, E. 2004. Women as Policy Makers: Evidence from an India-Wide Randomized Policy Experiment. *Econometrica,* **72**(5), 1409–43.

Custers, P. 1987. *Women in the Tebhaga Uprising: Rural Poor Women and Revolutionary Leadership: 1946–47.* Calcutta: Naya Prokash.

Dahlerup, D. 1988. From a Small to a Large Majority: Women in Scandinavian Politics. *Scandinavian Political Studies,* **11**(4), 275–98.

Eckel, C. 2008. Gender Differences (Experimental Evidence). In S. Durlauf and L. Blume, eds., *The New Palgrave Dictionary of Economics,* 2nd ed. Basingstoke: Palgrave Macmillan, 3, pp. 578–81.

FAO. 2014. The State of Food and Agriculture Report: Innovation in Family Farming. Rome: UN FAO.

Fraser, N. 1990. Rethinking the Public Sphere: A Contribution to the Critique of Actually Existing Democracy. *Social Text,* **25/26**, 56–80.

Ghose, A. K., ed. 1983. *Agrarian Reform in Contemporary Developing Countries.* London and Canberra: Croom Helm.

GoI. 2011–12. Energy Sources of Indian Households for Cooking and Lighting. National Sample Survey 20011–12. National Sample Survey Organisation, Report 567. Delhi: Dept. of Statistics, Government of India.

GoN. 2004. Nepal Living Standards Survey 2003–04, Statistical Report. Kathmandu: CBS, Government of Nepal.

Jain, S. 1984. Women and People's Ecological Movement: A Case Study of Women's Role in the Chipko Movement in Uttar Pradesh. *Economic and Political Weekly,* **19**(41), 1788–94.

Kanter, R. M. 1977. Some Effects of Proportions on Group Life: Skewed Sex Ratios and Responses to Token Women. *The American Journal of Sociology,* **82**(5), 965–90.

1989. The New Managerial Work. *Harvard Business Review*, Nov/Dec. https://hbr.org/1989/11/the-new-managerial-work.
Lalita, K. et al. 1989. *We Were Making History: Life Stories of Women in the Telangana People's Struggle.* Delhi: Kali for Women.
Lovenduski, J. 1997. Gender Politics: A Breakthrough for Women? *Parliamentary Affairs*, **50**, 708–19.
Lukacs, G. 1971. *History and Class Consciousness: Studies in Marxist Dialectics.* Rodney Livingstone, trans. Cambridge, MA: MIT Press.
Macfarlane, R. 2016. The Secrets of the Wood Wide Web. *The New Yorker*, August 7.
Mansbridge, J. 1990. Feminism and Democracy. *American Prospect*, **1** (Spring).
Nair, A. and Shah, P. 2007. Self-Help Works. *Times of India*, 27 December.
NCAER. 2001–02. Evaluation Survey of the National Programme on Improved Chulha. New Delhi: National Council of Applied Economic Research.
2008. Impact and Sustainability of SHG Bank Linkage Programme. New Delhi: National Council of Applied Economic Research.
Sabates-Wheeler, R. 2002. Farm Strategy, Self-Selection and Productivity: Can Small Farming Groups Offer Production Benefits in Post-Socialist Romania? *World Development*, **30**(10), 1737–53.
Sabates-Wheeler, R. and Childress, M. D. 2004. Asset-Pooling in Uncertain Times: Implications of Small-Group Farming for Agricultural Restructuring in the Kyrgyz Republic. *IDS Working Paper No. 239.* Institute of Development Studies at Sussex.
Scott, J. 1985. *Weapons of the Weak.* New Haven, CT: Yale University Press.
Sell, J. 1997. Gender, Strategies and Contributions to Public Goods. *Social Psychology Quarterly*, **60**(3), 252–65.
Stewart, F. 1996. Groups for Good or Ill. *Oxford Development Studies*, **24**(1), 9–25.
Tanka, A. 2012. *Banking on Self-Help Groups.* Delhi: Sage.
Thomas, S. 1994. *How Women Legislate.* Oxford: Oxford University Press.
Westerman, O., Ashby, J. and Pretty, J. 2005. Gender and Social Capital: The Importance of Gender Differences for the Maturity and Effectiveness of Natural Resource Management Groups. *World Development*, **33**(11), 1783–99.
Young, I. M. 1997. *Intersecting Voices: Dilemmas of Gender, Political Philosophy, and Policy.* Princeton, NJ: Princeton University Press.

CHAPTER 11

Willfulness, Feminism, and the Gendering of Will

Sara Ahmed

WHY IS GENDER IMPORTANT FOR UNDERSTANDING the world in which we live? In this chapter I show how understanding gender offers an important way of understanding the world. I do not begin by assuming what gender is in order to establish its importance. Rather we can explore gendering as a dynamic and social process, which requires the development of new tools of analysis. Making sense of how gender works allows us to show how gender matters even where it does not appear to matter; gender is a technique for building worlds as well as bodies.

The research that informs this chapter is a genealogical investigation of "willfulness."[1] I begin, in a way, with a word, willful, but also a judgment, to be judged as willful is to be made into a problem. The word willfulness caught my attention because I had, as a girl, been called willful. We learn from an assignment when we receive an assignment. It might seem that to start with a word is not to say something about worlds. But as Judith Butler's chapter in this volume shows, words bring worlds with them; words can teach us about worlds. The word willful is of course a will word – to be willful is to be full of will, to be too willing, or to be willing too much. This is a typical definition of willfulness, from the Oxford English Dictionary: "asserting or disposed to assert one's own will against persuasion, instruction, or command;

[1] The research was published as a monograph, *Willful Subjects* (2014). I also returned to the research in the third chapter, "Willfulness and Feminist Subjectivity" in *Living a Feminist Life* (2017).

governed by will without regard to reason; determined to take one's own way; obstinately self-willed or perverse." There is a family of words around willfulness (stubborn, obstinate, defiant, rude, reckless), which creates a structure of resemblance (we feel we know what she is like). It is useful to note that the meaning of willfulness in "the positive sense of strong willed" is described by the Oxford English Dictionary as both obsolete and rare. The negative senses of willfulness have become deeply entrenched.

To offer a history of willfulness is to make sense of these negative senses. I will show how the distinction between willfulness and will, as well as between good will and an ill will, functions as a gendered distinction. If we understand the gendering of will, we are learning the importance of gender to the organization of worlds. That judgment of willfulness, simply put, does things. Stories about the miserable fate of willful girls are used as warnings about the costs of not being willing. They also function as promises of happiness; in other words, they promise that if you become willing, if you give up a will of your own, you will become happier (see also Ahmed, 2010). In this chapter, I first explore the figure of the willful girl before reflecting on how feminism has been and can be judged as willfulness, as a product of not willing in the right way. I then consider how willfulness has been, and can be, taken up by feminists in doing our work, with specific reference to complaint as willful work.

WILLFUL GIRLS

The figure of the willful child is exercised across a range of materials – from philosophy (in particular the philosophy of education) to fairy tales and folklore. My project is to follow this figure, to learn from where and how she turns up. Let me begin with a story, "The Willful Child."

Once upon a time there was a child who was willful, and would not do as her mother wished. For this reason God had no pleasure in her, and let her become ill, and no doctor could do her any good, and in a short time she lay on her deathbed. When she had been lowered into her grave, and the earth was spread over her, all at once her arm came out again, and stretched upwards, and when they had put it in and spread fresh earth over it, it was all to no purpose, for the arm always came out again. Then the mother herself was obliged to go to the grave, and strike the arm with a rod, and when she had done that, it was drawn in, and then at last the child had rest beneath the ground (Grimm & Grimm, 1884: 125).

In this Grimm story, which is certainly grim, the willful child is the one who is disobedient, who will not do as her mother wishes.[2] If authority assumes the right to turn a wish into a command, then willfulness is a diagnosis of the failure to comply with those whose authority is given. The costs of such a diagnosis are high: through a chain of command (the mother, God, the doctors) the child's fate is sealed. It is ill will that responds to willfulness; the child is allowed to become ill in such a way that no one can "do her any good." Willfulness is thus compromising; it compromises the capacity of a subject to survive, let alone flourish. The punishment for willfulness is a passive willing of death, an allowing of death. Note that willfulness is also that which persists even after death: displaced onto an arm, from a body onto a body part. The arm inherits the willfulness of the child insofar as it will not be kept down, insofar as it keeps coming up, acquiring a life of its own, even after the death of the body of which it is a part. Willfulness involves persistence in the face of having been brought down, where simply to "keep going" or to "keep coming up" is to be stubborn and obstinate. Mere persistence can be an act of disobedience.

In the story, it seems that will and willfulness are externalized; they acquire life by not being or at least staying within subjects. They are not proper to subjects insofar as they become property, that can be alienated into a part or thing. The different acts of willing are reduced to a battle between an arm and a rod. If the

[2] We might think here of Cindy Katz's description of the struggle between the Tiger Mother and her child in this volume.

arm inherits the child's willfulness, then what can we say about the rod? The rod is an externalization of the mother's wish, but also of God's command, which transforms a wish into fiat, a "let it be done," thus determining what happens to the child. The rod could be thought of as an embodiment of will, of a will that is made into a command. And yet, the rod does not appear under the sign of willfulness; it becomes instead an instrument for its elimination. One form of will seems to involve the rendering of other wills as willful; one form of will assumes the right to eliminate the others.

How can we account for the violence of this story? How is this violence at once an account of willfulness? The story belongs to a tradition of educational discourse that Alice Miller in *For Your Own Good* (1983) describes as a "poisonous pedagogy," a tradition which assumes the child as stained by original sin, and which insists on violence as moral correction, as being for the child. The Grimm story is pedagogic in another sense: it teaches us to read the distinction between will and willfulness as a grammar, a way of ordering human experience, as a way of distributing moral worth.

The story could be thought of not only as a representation of a child but also an address to a child. A willing girl, a girl who is willing to obey, who does not appear in the story, might be the one who is addressed by the story: the story is a warning to her of the consequences of not being willing to obey.

There is another story about Jane, a willful girl, which teaches us how willfulness is used to describe some kinds of girls and not others. We begin with Jane herself: "Jane was a willful girl. She did not submit cheerfully to those whom it was her duty to obey, but was always contriving to how she could have her own way, as much and as often as possible" (Trowbridge, 1855: 16). Note here how obedience is associated with good cheer: to be willing is to be happy to obey. She is happily willing or willing happily. The girl who does not cheerfully submit is the girl who insists on getting her own way.

What happens to Jane? The girls from the school are told by the teacher not to go to the orchard. The teacher makes this command because the apples in the orchard are ripe and she knows the girls will be tempted to eat them. Jane disobeys: she eats the apples. She wants them; she has them. This story of the willful girl borrows from old lexicons; we learn from the familiarity of the story. Eating the forbidden fruit, the story of Jane, becomes a thread in the weave of the stories of willful women: returning us to Genesis, to the story of a beginning, to Eve's willful wantonness as behind the fall from Grace. The willfulness of women relates here not only to disobedience but to desire: the strength of her desire becoming a weakness of her will. In this history of willfulness, women are found wanting.

From this story we get another sense of the kind of girls who are diagnosed as willful. When Jane is "determined" to go to the orchard and eat the apples, she declares her intent by exercising the language of injustice: "She declared that it was very unjust in their teacher not to permit them to play there" (Trowbridge, 1855: 17). The declaration of injustice, we might note, becomes, in the story, yet another piece of evidence of the child's willfulness. In the end, Jane's friend Lucy tries to dissuade Jane from her course of action, but Jane's "obstinate will" carries her in this direction, as if her will has acquired its own will. Willfulness becomes here a will weakness: your will is not strong enough to stop you from doing the wrong thing. So what happens to Jane? The teacher, when realizing Jane has disobeyed, addresses not her as the guilty party but a class of children as if they are all guilty parties. She gives them a lesson on the right of some to govern: "Whose will should govern in this classroom?" And then, "I see from the looks on your faces that you do not wish to be governed by the will of any one of the pupils who attend it" (Trowbridge, 1855: 19). Only then does the teacher speak of the willful disobedience of one child. The children identify with the teacher by making Jane's willfulness into an obstacle to their general will. Willfulness becomes how, in going astray, an individual gets in the way of the happiness of others. And the moral lesson is assumed by Jane as a willingness to become willing: "She also resolved that she will try never to be willful again"

(Trowbridge, 1855: 20). Jane assumes in the firmness of a resolution a will to eliminate willfulness from her own character.

I can hear something in Jane's forgotten but familiar story. I can hear how girls who are not willing to obey an order, who are not compliant, are judged as imposing their will upon others. Her will becomes a willful will insofar as it is defined against a collective will. Her own will gets in the way of what a collective wills. She is deemed as willing to govern the others (her willfulness, in other words, is interpreted as a will to power). And then when she speaks the language of injustice, that speech is heard as just another way she imposes her own will on others. The language of injustice is treated as a screen behind which a will lurks: a will that is wanting.

Perhaps boys are more likely to be described as strong-willed and girls as willful because boys are encouraged to acquire a will of their own. Another willful girl who might help us to make sense of the gendered nature of the assignment is Maggie Tulliver. Maggie appears in George Eliot's ([1860] 1965) *The Mill on the Floss.* As I noted in my introduction to *Willful Subjects* (Ahmed, 2014), I first embarked on my research into willfulness because I was so struck by how Maggie's will was used to explain what was behind her troubles. We might put this in another way: Maggie seems willingly to get into trouble, which is not the same thing as saying she has any choice in the matter.

The novel contrasts Maggie and her brother Tom, not by suggesting Maggie is willful and Tom is not, but by showing how although they both act in ways that might ordinarily be designated as willful, Tom escapes the consequences of being judged in these terms: "Tom never did the same sort of foolish things as Maggie, having a wonderful distinctive discernment of what would turn to his advantage or disadvantage; and so it happened, that although he was much more willful and inflexible than Maggie, his mother hardly ever called him naughty" ([1860] 1965: 59). The narrator here describes Tom as even more willful or inflexible than Maggie but as not suffering the judgment. Tom is allowed to get away with it, Maggie not. When willfulness sticks, you become the trouble you cause: "It was Mrs. Tulliver's way, if she blamed Tom, to refer his misdemeanour, somehow or other, to Maggie" ([1860] 1965: 114).

Gender matters here at the level of consequence: the same actions have different consequences for boys and girls. Another way of saying this: gendering here gives boys more room, more room to err, to stray, to be. Perhaps in becoming the reference point for other people's misdemeanours you become not only aware of injustice but willing to speak out about injustice. And indeed, when Maggie speaks out about the injustice of her extended family's lack of compassion in response to her father's loss of the mill; she is described as bold and thankless ([1860] 1965: 229). Speaking out against injustice becomes yet another symptom of willfulness; and being heard as such is dismissed as such. Perhaps we are learning what it takes to speak out against injustices; perhaps if willfulness is how you are judged, willfulness becomes what you require to survive that judgment.

But of course, the consequences of being perceived as difficult can be difficult. A key moment in the text is when Maggie reads Thomas á Kempis's *An Imitation of Christ* and has an epiphany. The answer to her troubles is to give up her will, as an act of giving up desire and inclination: "it flashed through her like the suddenly apprehended solution of a problem, that all the miseries of her young life had come from fixing her heart on her own pleasure as if that were the central necessity of the universe" ([1860] 1965: 306). From the point of view of the parents, their daughter has become good because she has submitted to their will: "Her mother felt the change in her with a sort of puzzled wonder that Maggie should be 'growing up so good'; it was amazing that this once 'contrary' child was becoming so submissive, so backward to assert her own will" ([1860] 1965: 309). The mother can thus love the daughter, who can support the family by staying in the background: "The mother was getting fond of her tall, brown girl, the only bit of furniture now in which she could bestow her anxiety and pride" ([1860] 1965: 309). When you treat someone like furniture you put them into the background. To recede into the background requires giving up a will other than the will of others.

The novel does not present Maggie's emptying herself of will as a wrongful submission. If anything, giving up a will of one's own is presented as an ethical ideal that Maggie fails because she is willful, as Sally Shuttleworth has suggested (1984: 104). We can hear this judgment of willfulness in the very description of Maggie's reading of Kempis: "that renunciation means sorry, though a sorrow born willingly. Maggie was still panting for happiness, and was in ecstasy because she had found the key for it" ([1860]1965: 307). Although Maggie thinks she has found the key in renunciation, her finding is represented as born out of inclination, and thus contradicts in form the content of what is found. The narrative gives us a profile of Maggie's character as willful from which we conjure a behind: "from what you know of her, you will not be surprised that she threw some exaggeration and willfulness, some pride and impetuosity, even into her self-renunciation; her own life was still a drama for her in which she demanded of herself that her part should be played with intensity" ([1860] 1965: 308). Of course, as readers we can come to different views of Maggie's action: if we bring willfulness to the front, we have a different view of the behind.

Maggie is, of course, a fictional character. It is worth noting how many feminists have found a promise in her story, a promise that is not disconnected from Maggie's failure to give up her will. Maggie Tulliver has in fact been the object of considerable feminist desire and identification over time. Simone de Beauvoir identified with Maggie so strongly that she was reported to have "cried for hours" upon her death (Moi, 2008: 265). Lyndie Brimstone in her personal reflections on literature and women's studies similarly relates her own experience to Maggie's: "Maggie with her willful hair" who "made one dash for passion then went back to rue it for the rest of her truncated life" (2001: 73). We might share affection for Maggie as feminist readers, as we might share affection for the many willful girls that haunt literature.

Even though Maggie's fate was the same fate that awaited other willful girls in fables – unhappiness and death – her character, with all its flaws, becomes a kind of feminist inheritance. Perhaps from stories of willful girls we learn how we need, how much we need, the qualities that have been deemed pathological if we are to resist the demands of a gendered social order; we might need to be willful, creative, bold, daring, and imaginative. We also learn about how gender works; to be willful is to refuse to align your will with the will of the family, but also the collective will; the general will. When a particular will is aligned with a general will, a part can recede, becoming part of the background. A willful part stands out. Willfulness then might not only be how some are judged; willfulness might bring into view what ordinarily recedes. I will return to the implications of this argument for the "worldliness" of willfulness in due course.

RECLAIMING WILLFULNESS

Who is judged as having a will that is wanting? It is not just that girls and women are more likely to receive that judgment. Girls and women who are unwilling to accept femininity as a renunciation of will receive that judgment. It is for this reason alone that we can claim willfulness as a feminist history. This history seems to condense in a series of figures of female disobedience: from Eve to Antigone, a history of women who pulse with life before law.

Not surprisingly, then, feminist histories are full of self-declared willful women. Take the Heterodoxy Club that operated in Greenwich Village in the early twentieth century, a club for unorthodox women. They described themselves as "this little band of willful women" (Schwarz, 1986: 103). Heterodoxy refers to what is "not in agreement with accepted beliefs." To be willful is, here, to be willing to announce your disagreement, and to put yourself behind it. To enact a disagreement might even mean to become disagreeable. Feminism we might say is the creation of some rather disagreeable women. (See, for example, Mignon

Nixon's account in this volume of Webb's and Firestone's anti-war protest.)

We can listen to what, to whom, is behind us. Alice Walker describes a "womanist" in the following way: "A black feminist or feminist of color . . .. Usually referring to outrageous, audacious, courageous or *willful* behavior. Wanting to know more and in greater depth than is considered 'good' for one . . .. Responsible. In charge. Serious." (2005: xi, emphases in original). Julia Penelope describes lesbianism as willfulness: "The lesbian stands against the world created by the male imagination. What willfulness we possess when we claim our lives!" (1992: 42). Marilyn Frye's radical feminism uses the adjective willful: "The willful creation of new meaning, new loci of meaning, and new ways of being, together, in the world, seems to me in these mortally dangerous times the best hope we have" (1992: 9). Gloria Anzaldúa describes her book *Borderlands, La Frontera: The New Mestiza* as a willful entity: "The whole thing has had a mind of its own, escaping me and insisting on putting together the pieces of its own puzzle with minimal direction from my will. It is a rebellious, willful entity, a precocious girl-child forced to grow up too quickly" ([1987] 1999: 88). Together, these statements can be heard as claims to willfulness: willfulness as audacity; willfulness as standing against; willfulness as creativity; willfulness as rebelliousness. Feminist, queer, and antiracist histories can be thought of as histories of those who are willing to be willful, those who are willing to turn a diagnosis into an act of self-description.

I want to pick up on Alice Walker's descriptions of willful womanism. Alice Walker suggests here that the word willful conveys what being a black feminist or feminist of color is all about. To claim willfulness as womanist provides an alternative commentary on the grim history of will. Walker makes clear that womanism derives specifically from black culture, language, and history. Womanist is from "the black folk expression of mothers to female children, 'You acting womanish, i.e., like a woman'" (Walker, 2005: xi). To be woman is not to be girl or girlish, "i.e., frivolous, irresponsible, not serious" (2005: xi). Black folk expression might offer an alternative to the Grimm story. In the Grimm story, the daughter is deemed willful because she disobeys the mother. The daughter is likely to be understood as irresponsible and silly. In black folk expression, the daughter's willfulness is womanist, not girlish: responsible and serious. In affirming the girl as womanist, the mother is not on the side of the rod; the mother is on her daughter's side.

Willful womanism thus offers us another handle on the story of the willful girl. In the Grimm story, the girl who is deemed willful (from the point of view offered by the fable) is going out on her own limb; she separates herself from her family, an act of separation that is sustained by the transfer of willfulness to her arm, which appears as a limb on its own. The drama of willfulness might appear to be restricted to the drama of the family. But other sources of authority are evoked: the doctor, God; medicine, religion. The police are not in the story perhaps because the police are the rods.

It is by thinking of these other sources that we can open up what it might mean to reclaim willfulness. Willfulness might not simply be affirmed as what a daughter needs to disobey her parents, or to challenge their authority over her life; willfulness might be what is needed to disobey the power of a sovereign, of those who assume a right to be right. After all, Alice Walker's description of womanism suggests willfulness can be a connecting tissue between African American mothers and daughters. Perhaps then willfulness is what is required in order for women to sustain family relations given that the past of slavery is, as Christina Sharpe describes, "not yet past" (2010: 26). Sharpe also notes, "We know that in North American slavery Black women were regularly separated from their children who were sold away or sent to other women in the plantation to be taken care of" (2010: 18). The forced separation of mothers from children is part of what has to be survived. When histories demand a separation (mothers from daughters, people from people), then willfulness enables the act of not severing: willfulness as persevering.

If we think of willful womanism as rewriting the Grimm story of the willful girl, we are showing how that story became a weapon in different ways in different worlds; how the story does things in different hands. We might show how poisonous pedagogy has its roots in the ruling of people as well as the domination of children. We might also describe the domination of children as a primary technique for the domination of people. As Eli Clare describes: "What better way to maintain a power structure – white supremacy, patriarchy, capitalism, a binary and rigid gender system – than to drill the lessons of who is dominant and who is subordinate into the bodies of children" ([1999] 2015: 150). We know too that the enslaved and the colonized were positioned as children, as the ones for whom discipline was moral instruction, as the ones who were not supposed to have a will of their own, as the ones for whom obedience required giving up will. (See Sandra G. Harding in this volume, for example.)

Education was of course a crucial technology of colonial rule. The Grimm story of the willful child could also then be understood as circulating throughout empire. The willful child is also the story of the subaltern: she is addressed as a member of the subordinate class. She is insubordinate when she refuses to be a member of that class. The demand to be willing is here not articulated as the demand to obey the colonizer (who takes the mother's place): the rod comes to embody his sovereign will. The willful child would function as an early warning system for subalterns at large: she is a warning of the consequences of insubordination.

If she persists, she is willful. Her arm: it keeps comes coming up. When this history is not over, the arm comes up. The arm testifies to the survival of willfulness after the death of the body of which it is a part. This is why willfulness acquires different valences when understood as a black feminist and feminist of color inheritance. Because of what we inherit, willfulness points to the worlds in which we reside and which we have to survive. Histories of slavery, of colonization, positioned the enslaved and the colonized as children, as those who must give up their will, who must let go of kin, culture, memories, language, land. We might have to reclaim willfulness in refusing to let go of these histories, to refuse to forget the severances that have been performed and narrated as the spread of light to the dark corners of earth; to persevere embodies that refusal.

One history of will is a history of the attempt to eliminate willfulness from people; those deemed a different class, a different race. Given this, willfulness might be required to recover from the attempt at its elimination. Willfulness then becomes a charge in Alice Walker's sense: being in charge. If we are charged with willfulness, we accept and mobilize this charge. To accept a charge is thus not simply to agree with it. Acceptance can mean being willing to receive. We can distinguish between willfulness as a character diagnosis (as what is behind an action) and willfulness as the effect of a diagnosis (as what is required to complete an action). Sometimes you can stand up only by standing firm. Sometimes you can hold on only by becoming stubborn.

We all know the experience of "going the wrong way" in a crowd. Everyone seems to be going the opposite way than the way you are going. No one person has to push or shove for you to feel the collective momentum of the crowd as a pushing and shoving. For you to keep going you have to push harder than any of those who are going the right way. The body who is "going the wrong way" is the one that is experienced as "in the way" of the will that is acquired as momentum. (See Jack Halberstam's interpretation of this point for trans* bodies in this volume.) For some bodies, mere persistence, "to continue steadfastly," requires great effort, an effort that might appear to others as stubbornness or obstinacy, as an insistence on going against the flow. You have to become insistent to go against the flow and you are judged to be going against the flow because you are insistent. A life paradox: you have to become what you are judged as being.

Political histories of striking, of demonstrations, are indeed histories of those willing to put their bodies in the way, to turn their bodies into blockage points that stop the flow of human traffic, as well as the wider flow of an economy. We might think of the suffragettes chaining their bodies to gateposts; we might think of hunger strikes – the obstruction of the passage into the body can be a feminist obstruction. Think too of Reclaim the Night marches: the willed and willful act of populating the streets by and for women, a claiming back of a time as well as a space that the reality of sexual violence has taken from us. To reclaim the streets as a reclaiming of night is to enact what we will: a world in which those who travel under the sign of women can travel safely, in numbers: feminist feet as angry feet. When willfulness becomes a style of politics, it means not only being willing not to go with the flow, but to cause its obstruction. A history of willfulness is a history of those who are willing to put their bodies in the way, or to bend their bodies in the way of the will.

If you are not going the way things are flowing, you might need to become willful to keep going. A flow is also an effect of bodies that are going the same way. To go is to gather. A flow can be an effect of gatherings of all kinds: gatherings of tables, for instance, as kinship objects that support human gatherings. Conversations too are flows; they are saturated. We hear this saturation as atmosphere. The willful subject shares an affective horizon with the feminist killjoy as the ones who "ruin the atmosphere." A colleague says to me she just has to open her mouth in meetings to witness eyes rolling as if to say "Oh, here she goes." My experience of being a feminist daughter in a conventional family taught me much about rolling eyes. I have an equation: rolling eyes = feminist pedagogy. Say, we are seated at the dinner table. Around this table, the family gathers, having polite conversations, where only certain things can be brought up. Someone says something you consider problematic. You respond, carefully, perhaps. You might be speaking quietly; or you might be getting "wound up," recognizing with frustration that you are being wound up by someone who is winding you up. However she speaks, it is the one who speaks as a feminist who is usually heard as the cause of the trouble, as disturbing the peace.

A feminist killjoy can also kill feminist joy because of what we bring up. As Audre Lorde describes so well, "When women of Color speak out of the anger that laces so many of our contacts with white women, we are often told that we are 'creating a mood of helplessness,' 'preventing white women from getting past guilt,' or 'standing in the way of trusting communication and action'" (1984: 131). To speak out of anger about racism is to be heard as the one who is stopping or blocking the flow of communication, preventing the forward progression sometimes described as reconciliation. We learn the way things are going by who (and what) is deemed to get in the way. This is why killjoys have so much to teach us about worlds.

We become willful when we are willing not to go with the flow. When we are not willing to adjust, we are maladjusted. Perhaps willfulness turns the diagnosis into a call: don't adjust to an unjust world! As with other political acts of reclaiming negative terms, reclaiming willfulness is not necessarily premised on an affective conversion, that is, on converting a negative into a positive term. On the contrary, to reclaim willfulness might involve not only hearing the negativity of the charge but insisting on retaining that negativity: the charge, after all, is what keeps us proximate to scenes of violence. In willingly receiving the charge of willfulness, we stay close to those scenes of violence; as we must.

WILLFULNESS AND COMPLAINT

From willfulness we learn how gender matters for understanding the world we live in. We learn who is given room, including room to err, to stray; we learn who is given space and time to do their own thing; be their own thing. We learn who is not. Willfulness also teaches us about violence; how so much violence disappears from view, domestic violence, violence that happens in house; violence against those who are not willing to submit to an authority that is assumed by others. That violence disappears, even violence that seems so hard to miss, like the violence in the Grimm story by becoming right or a right. The one who is judged willful is certainly, as we have learned, at the receiving end of violence.

I want in this concluding section to think more about how willfulness can teach us about worlds. Those who receive this judgment are often those who are trying to transform the world; we come to know about worlds when we try to transform them. Since completing my research into willfulness, I have begun a new empirical project on complaint.[3] I have been interviewing people who have made formal complaints about harassment and bullying within universities. A complaint can be an expression of grief, pain, or dissatisfaction; something that is a cause of a protest or outcry, a bodily ailment, or a formal allegation. My aim is to show how the latter sense of complaint as a formal allegation brings up other more affective and embodied senses.

The impetus for the project was my own experience of supporting students through a series of enquiries into sexual harassment at my former university. Although my original research into willfulness was a humanities project, which brought together a diverse range of materials in which the figure of the willful subject came up, that research gave me a handle to make sense of many of the testimonies I have gathered. In other words, willfulness has provided a useful lens with which to think about what is required in doing the work of complaint. The work of complaint is willful work.

I noted earlier that it can take willfulness not to go with the flow or to cause an obstruction. It can also take willfulness to challenge what has acquired momentum. An institution is the acquisition of momentum, a way of directing human traffic. To make a complaint is to refuse to go along with something; making a complaint can feel like going against the flow; a complaint as counter-momentum. A complaint is a way of saying "no," and the

[3] I have completed forty interviews for this project as well as collected a number of written testimonies. I have begun writing a new book, *Complaint!* which will present my findings. Please see my blog for posts and discussion of this research, www.feministkilljoys.com.

"no" of complaint has to be repeated, often again and again, to get a complaint through the system. It is because of the difficulty of getting through that complaints often end up being about the system. One administrator describes: "It takes a really tenacious complaining student to say, no, I am being blocked." It takes tenacity; it takes willfulness. The harder it is to get through, the more work you have to do.

Complaints are often blocked. Why? Complaints are data rich. In making a complaint you have to collect evidence of wrongdoing; a complaint often creates a stuffed file. And that data is often judged to be dangerous to the organization: one person described her complaint as "sensitive information." Complaints are treated as potentially damaging of an organization's reputation as being progressive and inclusive; equal and diverse. The efforts to stop a complaint are about trying to contain information. One way of doing that is to contain the complainer. If the complainer reveals a problem, she is often treated as the problem. I have been struck by how often those who complain are treated as spoilt children. One postgraduate student who made a complaint about harassment describes: "I always felt they were treating us like siblings who were having an argument." Those who complain are often treated as naughty willful children who need to be disciplined or straightened out. We learn from how universities can operate rather like nuclear families. Harassment and bullying in universities is often explained in similar ways to how violence in the family is explained either by being projected onto strangers or by being made familiar and forgivable. One lecturer describes an incident:

> It was really weird, it was in the school office, and he started talking about one of my classes and he said the external examiner said something, and I said, I don't actually agree with the external examiner ... and he said "well fuck you, you don't fucking know anything, the external examiner is a major professor, fuck off, who the fuck do you think you are talking about him like that" in front of other people .... I later found out that the external examiner was one of his closest friends. So I went to the head of

> school and I said this happened, she said: "You know [he] is like the naughty uncle of the school that's just how he is, you just have to let it go.

The naughty uncle appears here as a figure, he is familiar, but also as an instruction to her: to let it go, not to complain, to accept the shouting and abusing behavior; this is how he is, how we are; what will be. A complaint can be stopped because of what is shared, who is shared; loyalties, personal, professional; affection becoming binding; you are being told who will be protected. It is out of loyalty (to the family, or to some we or another) that you are supposed to accept the violence; the family as fate, as fatalism, as a fatal bond. Perhaps it takes willfulness to snap the bond.

By listening to those who have made complaints I have been learning about the different methods through which complaints are stopped. Those who indicate they might make a complaint are often warned that by complaining they would damage themselves; they would damage their careers, reputations, and relationships. Warnings can often work as threats: that you will lose the connections you need to progress. One student describes:

> I was repeatedly told that "rocking the boat" or "making waves" would affect my career in the future and that I would ruin the department for everyone else. I was told if I did put in a complaint I would never be able to work in the university and that it was likely I wouldn't get a job elsewhere.

Here, complaining becomes a form of self-damage as well as damage to others, ruining a department, no less. This student goes onto to describe how the pressure not to complain is exerted: "In just one day I was subjected to eight hours of gruelling meetings and questioning, almost designed to break me and stop me from taking the complaint any further." A wall can be what comes up, or a wall can be what comes down, a ton of bricks. This is how power often works: you don't have to stop people from doing something, just make it harder for them to do something.

I have been hearing about the work you have to do to keep a complaint going; to keep a complaint alive; to keep complaining. One student who made a complaint about bullying from a professor in her department described: "I feel like my complaint has gone into the complaint graveyard." When complaints are filed away, filing cabinets become graves. If many complaints are indeed buried it does not mean they have gone away. We can think back to the story of the willful arm; we can remember how it came up after the burial of the child. The arm is life after death. Perhaps the arm can be, despite the morbid nature of this story, a signifier of political hope. Even after the willful child has been brought down, something, some spark, some kind of energy, persists. The arm gives flesh to this persistence. The arm has to disturb the ground, to reach up, to reach out of the grave, that tomb, that burial.

It can take willfulness to keep a complaint going; or just to keep going. One student who talked to me about three different complaints she made about harassment and bullying, none of which got anywhere, evoked the hope of complaint:

> You know the process is broken, but still you know you must do it, because if you don't, more falls to the wayside. So, it's like a painful repetitive cycle where you do what you know is right, knowing it may not make a difference at that time, but you always hope, you always have that hope, that maybe because I did this, it paves the way for something else. I think that is why I keep doing it: because I have hope. I have hope that justice maybe confronted at some point. But it is hard to say, hard to say what will happen.

To pave the way is to make something possible, even though it might be hard to say, hard to know what will happen. Perhaps that paving can become pavement; you try to create a different ground in the present by insisting that the present is not enough. This is not a bright hope, agentic, forward, and thrusting. This is a hope that is close to the ground; slow, below.

Perhaps the hope of complaint, rather like willfulness, comes up from below the ground. We are back to the scene of a burial. I shared with one person the image of a complaint graveyard that had been shared with me by another. A dialogue is possible by connecting stories; tales; trails. She said:

> You have to think about the impact of doing this. Because having yet another complaint, it means that you give more credibility to the one who comes after you. When you talk about haunting you are talking about the size of the graveyard. And I think this is important. Because when you have one tombstone, one lonely little ghost, it doesn't actually have any effect; you can have a nice cute little cemetery outside your window, but when you start having a massive one, common graveyards and so on, it becomes something else; it becomes much harder to manage.

A complaint can be a willful collective. We become harder to manage. Such collectives are not simply those who are in the same place and the same time. A collective can be created by what follows, who follows. The ghosts can gather; the more we complain, the louder we become; it can be explosive. We might not be able to hear it now; it might not have happened yet. We might feel like a lonely little ghost. But there are more to come. Willfulness as a feminist history is a story of a gathering momentum. Each complaint gathers momentum, more and more; we do not know what a complaint can become. The complaints in the graveyard can come back to haunt institutions. We can come back to haunt institutions. It is a promise.

A complaint, then, could be thought of as an arm that is still rising. We might try to catch the arm in that moment of suspension. This grim story is of course not the story of feminist complaint. The story is told from the rod's point of view. It offers a warning: be willing or you will be beaten. It offers an invitation: identify with the rod and you will be spared. So much violence is abbreviated here: so much silence about violence is explained here, as if by not bringing up violence up, not noticing it, not mentioning it, you might be spared. Even if the Grimm story is not the story of feminist complaint, those who are doing the work of complaint can hear something about their own experiences in that story. One of the women I interviewed, who made a complaint about bullying, told me how reading about the Grimm story helped her to understand what happened to her. She said: "Reading of it was upsetting but at the same time it makes sense.

They are hurting me because I am raising my arm." If you raise your arm in order to lodge a complaint about violence, that violence is redirected back at you.

A judgment can follow an action; you are judged as willful not only because of what you know but what you show. No wonder: whenever someone brings violence up, the willful child quickly comes after her. She is a way of coming after her: as if to say, speak up and her fate will be yours. The figure of the willful child is a container; making her refusal, her "no," appear to be lonely and unsupported: her protest becoming babble; her voice scrambled, a stray, faint, so faint, becoming fainter, until she disappears. It will take willfulness to prevent her disappearance.

Willfulness as a feminist history: we assemble, we gather; we protest. And in that work – the work of saying no to an existing social order – we learn about the order and how it works, for whom it works. Gender is an order in many senses, a way of creating order, ordering as a social pattern; but also, an order in the sense of an instruction: do this; be this; accept this. To refuse an instruction is to know the instruction.

REFERENCES

Ahmed, Sara. 2010. *The Promise of Happiness.* Durham, NC: Duke University Press.

2014. *Willful Subjects.* Durham, NC: Duke University Press.

2017. *Living a Feminist Life.* Durham, NC: Duke University Press.

Anzaldúa, Gloria. 1999 [1987]. *Borderlands, La Fontera: The New Mestiza.* San Francisco, CA: Aunt Lute Books.

Brimstone, Lyndie. 2001. Refusing to Close the Curtains Before Putting on the Light: Literature and Women's Studies. In Elizabeth L. MacNabb et al., eds., *Transforming the Disciplines: A Women's Studies Primer.* Binghamton, NY: The Howarth Press, pp. 71–78.

Clare, Eli. [1999] 2015. *Exile and Pride: Disability, Queerness and Liberation.* Durham, NC: Duke University Press.

Eliot, George. 1965 [1860]. *The Mill on the Floss.* New York: The New American Library.

Frye, Marilyn. 1992. *Willful Virgin: Essays in Feminism, 1976–1972.* New York: Crossing Press.

Grimm, Jacob and Grimm, Wilhelm. 1884. *Household Tales,* vol. 2. Margaret Hunt, trans. London: George Bell.

Lorde, Audre. 1984. *Sister Outsider: Essays and Speeches.* New York: The Crossing Press.

Miller, Alice. 1983. *For Your Own Good: The Roots of Violence in Child-Rearing.* London: Virago Press.

Moi, Toril. 2008. *Simone de Beauvoir: The Making of an Intellectual Woman.* Oxford, Oxford University Press.

Penelope, Julia. 1992. *Call Me Lesbian: Lesbian Lives, Lesbian Theory.* New York: Crossing Press.

Schwarz, Judith. 1986. *Radical Feminists of Heterodoxy.* Hereford, AZ: New Victoria Publishers.

Sharpe, Christina. 2010. *Monstrous Intimacies: Making Post-slavery Subjects.* Durham, NC: Duke University Press.

Shuttleworth, Sally. 1984. *George Eliot and Nineteenth-Century Science: The Make-Believe of a Beginning.* Cambridge: Cambridge University Press.

Towbridge, Katherine M. 1855. Jane Munson: Or the Girl Who Wished to Have her Own Way. In Norman Allison Calkins, ed., *Student and Family Miscellany.* New York: N. A. Calkins, pp. 16–20.

Walker, Alice. 2005. *In Search of Our Mothers Gardens.* Phoenix, New Edition.

CHAPTER 12

Gender and Emigré Political Thought: Hannah Arendt and Judith Shklar

Seyla Benhabib

GENDER AND WOMEN POLITICAL THEORISTS

IS GENDER A USEFUL CATEGORY OF HISTORICAL ANALYSIS, even when the women thinkers involved neither show an interest in it nor use it as a category when they invoke related dimensions, such as sexuality and the family, in their works? This is the formidable challenge posed to feminist scholars by Hannah Arendt[1] and Judith Shklar. In the case of Arendt, her distinctions

Parts of this discussion have previously appeared in Benhabib (2018: 125–45). It has been revised for inclusion in this volume. Chapters of that book were completed during my stay at Cambridge University's Center for Gender Studies as Diane Middlebrook and Carl Djerassi Visiting Professor, in Spring 2017. Many thanks to Jude Browne for this invitation and her hospitality during my stay.

1 Arendt was aware of early women's movements and efforts at organizing for women's rights among German left parties. But she was skeptical that "women" as such could form the subject of a political movement. In *The Emancipation of Women* ([1933] 1994: 68), she writes:

> whenever the women's movement crosses a political front it does so as a unified, undifferentiated whole, which never succeeds in articulating concrete goals (other than humanitarian ones). The vain attempt to found a women's political party reveals the problem of the movement very sharply. The problem is like that of the youth movement, which is a movement only for the sake of youth. A women's movement only for the sake of women is equally abstract.

But insofar as Arendt believed that one must always defend oneself politically when one is attacked because of who one is, she believed that womens' equal citizens' rights needed to be defended and fought for not merely formally but also substantively. (([1933] 1994: 67).

between the public and the private, the political and the social have proven useful and controversial for feminist theorizing.[2] As Jacqueline Rose argues in this volume, "Arendt is not, to put it mildly, most famous for her contribution to feminism." A similar prodding of Shklar's work has not yet taken place. Nevertheless, there is much to be gained from reading Arendt and Shklar in conversation. Their lives are like parables of women of formidable intellect in the past century as they made their way across continental divides geographically and intellectually. Not only the biographical parallels in their stories of exile and displacement, but also the academic mores governing the relationship between the older (Arendt) and the younger scholar (Shklar) are striking. Following Harold Bloom's famous phrase, I name Shklar's lifelong engagement with, and eventual distantiation from, Arendt's work a case of "the anxiety of influence" ([1973] 1997).

SHKLAR'S PATH OUT OF EUROPE

During the controversy that erupted around Hannah Arendt's *Eichmann in Jerusalem* (1963),[3] a little-known lecturer in the Government Department at Harvard University by the name of Judith Nisse Shklar published *Legalism. An Essay on Law, Morals and Politics* (1964). Written in the direct and acerbic style that would become her mark, Shklar states: "This is, then, a polemical and opinionated book. It is, however, not meant to be destructive ....

[2] See Bonnie Honig (1995). Jacqueline Rose gives a powerful feminist reading of the relationship between violence and the household in Arendt's work in her chapter, 'Feminism and the Abomination of Violence' in this volume.

[3] The controversy centered around three major issues: (1) Arendt's strong, and at times, caustic and sardonic remarks on the conduct of the Israeli Court, and its Chief Prosecutor, Gideon Hausner, as well as her critique of the final judgment of the court; (2) her reconstruction of the history of the "final solution," and in particular her remarks about the behavior of the *Judenraete*, the Jewish Councils entrusted by the Nazis with administering the occupied territories of Poland and Lithuania; (3) the phrase, "the banality of evil," which she used to describe Eichmann's personality – although the provenance of the phrase appears to have been her teacher, mentor and friend, Karl Jaspers. For a more detailed account, see Benhabib (2000).

The object here is to stir up controversy by a clear confrontation of incompatible positions, not just to upset the genteel academic applecart" (1964: viii). Shklar's wish to stir up controversy was not fulfilled. At the time the book was largely ignored by legal theorists[4] as well as political philosophers, but it did signal the emergence of the singular voice of one younger than German-Jewish luminaries such as Hannah Arendt and Leo Strauss who dominated American academia in political theory during those years.

Shklar (1928–1992) belonged to the generation of European Jewish emigrés whose world was shattered, and as she expressed it in one of her most poignant and, to my knowledge, only piece of autobiographical writing, whose childhood had been brought to an end by Hitler (1996).[5] Born in the north-eastern city of Riga, in Latvia, subject over the years to German as well as Russian influences, Shklar, her sister, and her parents, both doctors, fled in

4 See Samuel Moyn (2013: 500): he observes that very few reviews had appeared in legal journals and contrasts this with increasing references to her work in recent years. Early reviews of Shklar's book include: Bedau (1967); Brown (1967); Aumann (1965).

5 This lecture was originally delivered as the Charles Homer Haskins Lecture, American Council of Learned Societies, Washington DC, April 1989 and published as ACLS Occasional Paper No 9. Shklar writes: "By 1939, I already understood that books, even scary ones, would be my best refuge from a world that was far more terrible than anything they might reveal. And that is how I became a bookworm. It was also the end of my childhood" (1996: 264). For further discussion of Shklar's life, see Andreas Hess (2014: 23–39).

Hess draws upon the remarkable autobiographical conversation which Judith Shklar conducted with Judith B. Walzer in 1981, and which is housed in The Murray Research Archive of Harvard University, located in Radcliffe College. See Walzer (1988). I had a chance to visit these archives and listen to this conversation which, if it could be published, would be invaluable not only for understanding Shklar better but for illuminating the development of political theory in the 1950s in the US and women's place in it as well. Judith Walzer asks many questions concerning gender discrimination and Shklar's answers are impressively forthright – particularly around her non-tenuring. Convinced that she would not receive tenure, Shklar then made a deal with the faculty of the Government Department to remain as lecturer and raise her family of three children. She was given tenure by Harvard University President Bok in 1971 and was named the John Cowles Professor of Government. Of particular importance is the role of Carl Friedrich, Shklar's teacher, in bringing certain Weimar problems and concerns to American academe. In addition to Shklar, Zbigniev Brezinski, Henry Kissinger and Stanley Hoffman were among Friedrich's students.

1939 via Sweden to Siberia, then to Japan and finally settled in Montréal, Canada, after a brief but disappointing stint in New York. Judith Shklar's older sister, who was admitted to study in Columbia, died unexpectedly, and the family's hopes of using this as an entrée to settle in New York were henceforth dashed. Judith, the older of the remaining sisters, would eventually come to study political theory at Harvard with another emigré intellectual from Weimar Germany – Carl J. Friedrich. She would meet Hannah Arendt for the first time in one of the symposia organized by Friedrich on totalitarianism.

What Shklar called her "bare bones liberalism" (1964: 5) carried the indelible marks of disbelief in the face of a world gone insane. Yet what is distinctive about her voice as an emigré political theorist, and what sets her apart from Strauss and Arendt, both half a generation older than she, is the lack of pathos with which she registered the destruction of her familial world and the end of her childhood. Although brought up in a German-speaking Jewish household, Judith Shklar was not a German-Jewish philosopher. Her skeptical and restrained temperament put her rather in the company of East-European ironists such as Franz Kafka, Milan Kundera or György Konrad.[6]

Shklar carried out a complex and little-noted dialogue with Arendt over the years. Calling this a dialogue may not be quite right because Arendt did not appear to have been listening at the other end. Still, between 1963 and 1984, Judith Shklar wrote about Arendt on five occasions.[7] First is a "Review Essay" of *Between Past and Future* in *History and Theory* (1963). Second is an elegiac and deeply appreciative article published in *The New Republic,* on December 27, 1975, shortly after Arendt's death on December 4 of that year, and called "Hannah Arendt's Triumph" (1975). Third is an essay named "Rethinking the Past" (1977), which considers quite sensitively the peculiarities of Arendt's approach to political philosophy. Fourth is the magisterial and bitter article, "Hannah

[6] Parts of this discussion have previously appeared in Benhabib (1994).
[7] Shklar, 1963; 1975; [1977] 1998; [1983] 1998; 1982.

Arendt as Pariah" (1983), written after the publication of Elisabeth Young-Bruehl's biography of Hannah Arendt, *Hannah Arendt: For Love of the World* (1982). Fifth, and finally, is a rather terse commentary on Arendt's *Lectures on Kant's Political Philosophy* (1984). What accounts for the shift in Shklar's appreciation of Arendt between 1977 and 1983? We don't quite know. I will conjecture that it was Arendt's affair with Martin Heidegger,[8] the details of which came to light in Young-Bruehl's biography, that caused Shklar to erupt in bitterness. Nonetheless, shortly before her death, Shklar started lecturing and writing on exiles, refugees and migrants, finding herself one more time treading on familiar ground which Hannah Arendt had traveled before her through her well-known reflections on "the right to have rights" in *The Origins of Totalitarianism* (1979).[9]

I begin with a brief excursion into Shklar's early book, *Legalism. An Essay on Law, Morals and Politics* (1964). Shklar's critique of criminal international law is being revived today in the name of a certain skepticism toward these institutions, but this critique needs to be balanced against her full-throated defense of the legitimacy of the Nuremberg Trials. Her discussion of the Nuremberg Trials will then be discussed along with Hannah Arendt's *Eichmann in Jerusalem* (1963).

[8] Martin Heidegger (1889–1976) was one of the most influential and original German philosophers of the twentieth century. Arendt had come to the University of Freiburg in 1925 to study with him. They had an affair and Arendt left Freiburg to study with Karl Jaspers in Heidelberg. Heidegger was elected rector of the University of Freiburg on April 21, 1933 and on May 1 of that year, he joined the Nazi Party. While some in the Nazi establishment ridiculed him and never considered him as one of their own, Heidegger followed the orders of the Nazi Party and even banned his own former mentor and friend, Edmund Husserl, from using the University Library. Although Arendt was outraged by Heidegger's behavior and wrote critically about him on more than one occasion, she forgave him and resumed their friendship after the war. More than her youthful dalliance, it is Arendt's subsequent forgiving of Heidegger (who, by the way, never apologized for his actions) that confounded friend and foe alike. See Young-Bruehl (1982) and Benhabib ([1996] 2003: chapter 4). See also Howe (2013).

[9] This was originally published in the UK in 1951 as *The Burden of Our Times* (London: Secker and Warburg).

LEGALISM: AN ESSAY ON MENTALITÉ

With the memory of the Nuremberg Trials and the McCarthy hearings in the United States still very much alive, Shklar positioned herself in *Legalism* against too much self-congratulation on the part of liberal democracies. Drawing a sharp line between ideologies of free market capitalism and the political essence of liberalism, she wrote of her contribution:

> It is, at its simplest, a defense of social diversity, inspired by that bare bones liberalism which, having abandoned the theory of progress and every specific scheme of economics, is committed only to the belief that tolerance is a primary virtue and that a diversity of opinions and habits is not only to be endured but to be cherished and encouraged. The assumption throughout is that social diversity is the prevailing condition of modern nation-states and that it ought to be promoted. (Shklar, 1964)

But what is legalism? "It is the ethical attitude that holds moral conduct to be a matter of rule following, and moral relationships to consist of duties and rights determined by rules" (1964: 1). This suggests at first that Shklar's concern is with moral philosophy of a certain kind. Shklar, who was to write a book (1976) on Hegel's *Phenomenology of Spirit*, could have been thinking of Hegel's critique of the legalism and abstract rigor of Kant's moral philosophy. In a famous discussion of the *Phenomenology of Spirit*, called *gesetz-prüfende* (law-testing) and *gesetz-gebende Vernunft* (law-giving reason), Hegel dissected the antinomies of Kantian moral theory (1977: chapter 6). If moral reason was to test the maxims of human action, would the operation of non-contradiction alone be sufficient to distinguish among them? But if practical reason was to legislate such maxims, how could it derive more concrete maxims out of the pure form of the categorical imperative alone? Kantian moral reason was either empty or, if it generated content, it did so because it smuggled in presuppositions about human beings or society into the content of the Categorical Imperative.

Although she devotes a few pages to a critique of Kantian morality (1964: 47–49; 57), Shklar was not really concerned with moral theory but rather with legalism as a way of thinking that tries to insulate law from morals as well as from politics. The first part of the book deals with a critique of analytical positivism – including the views of Hans Kelsen and H. L. A. Hart – as well as of natural law theories.

Legalism is said to be the "ideology" of its practitioners, in that they believe that the legal system consists of the rule of law, and that the law rests on formally correct rationality in the sense specified by Max Weber (1964: 21). Shklar calls this an "ideology" (before going on to call legalism also a "creative policy" and "the ethos of the law") because the coercive power as well as the fact that it is obeyed by those it addresses are far from evident in legal systems (1964: 35); rather, these aspects of the law accomplish their goals because the legal system is "part of a social continuum" (1964: 3). This critique of legal formalism and her insistence that law must be seen in a social context have led some to call Shklar a "postmodernist" (Steven White), or more plausibly, to classify her as a precursor of the "critical legal studies movement" (Samuel Moyn). Neither classification can do justice to Shklar's own conflictual account of the relation of legalism to liberalism. Shklar herself tried to capture this relationship in a paradoxical formula:

> The great paradox revealed here is that legalism as an *ideology* is too inflexible to recognize the enormous potential of legalism as a *creative policy* but exhausts itself in intoning traditional pieties and principles which are incapable of realization. This is, of course, the perennial character of ideologies. It should not, however, in this case, lead one to forget the greatness of legalism as an *ethos* when it expresses itself in the characteristic institutions of the law. (1964: 112; emphasis added)

Shklar may have been a bit too optimistic in thinking that once legalism is viewed to be an ideology, it would also be respected as creative policy as well as impartial exercise of the law. Here we must turn to her considerations of the Nuremberg Trials in order to understand her critique of the legal professional mentality.

THE SIGNIFICANCE AND PUZZLES OF THE NUREMBERG TRIALS

From 1962 to 1963, the young Judith Shklar sat in the Harvard University Library reading the transcript of the Nuremberg Trials, just as Hannah Arendt, who had traveled to Jerusalem to attend the opening sessions of the Eichmann Trial, would pore over the thousands of pages of trial transcripts she had brought with her. Shklar is one of the first to address the philosophical puzzles of international criminal law in the post-Second World War period. "There was and is no system of international criminal law," she wrote, "just as there are no international community and international political institutions to formulate or regularly enforce criminal laws" (1964: 157). Shklar's observations about the conceptual absurdities of the Tokyo Trials, and her sardonic comments on the work of the Chief Prosecutor, Joseph Keenan, anticipate many postcolonial critiques of international law in our times (1964: 181 ff.).[10] Commenting on Mr. Keenan's claim that the "Christian-Judaic absolutes of good and evil," had universal validity, Shklar exclaims: "What on earth could the Judeo-Christian ethic mean to the Japanese?" (1964: 183). With this outburst, was Shklar objecting to the obtuseness of the American prosecutor alone, or did she have in mind a more radical objection, questioning the legitimacy of holding a trial for war criminals across such vast cultural divides at all? Why couldn't one see the Tokyo Trials as a form of "creative policy" much the same way as she did Nuremberg? After all, Japan was not as removed from and as uninformed about Western conceptions of legality as Shklar may have assumed.[11]

[10] For a postcolonial critique of international law, cf. Anthony Anghie (2007).

[11] For a recent judicious account of the controversies concerning the legitimacy of the Tokyo War Crimes Trial in the light of new historical evidence, see Totani (2008).

Despite her almost militant dismissal of international criminal law, Shklar reaches the surprising conclusion that, "What makes the Nuremberg Trial so remarkable is that, in the absence of strict legal justification, it was a great legalistic act, the most legalistic of all possible policies, and, as such, a powerful inspiration to legalistic ethos" (1964: 170). While the trial was a political one in that it aimed to punish a political enemy and its ideology, "it need have given offense neither to legalistic nor to liberal values." And it was "[o]nly because the crimes against humanity were the moral center of the case that all this was possible" (1964: 170).

It is surprising that of the three charges considered in the trial – crimes against the peace or waging aggressive war; war crimes; and crimes against humanity – Shklar should focus insistently on crimes against humanity. Her reasons were as follows: she thought that the first charge against the Nazis was justifiably subject to the argument *tu quoque* (1964: 161), that is, that the leaders of states judging the Nazis had committed no less criminal acts against the peace than the Nazis had.

Regarding the charge that the Nazis had committed war crimes, Shklar's riposte is that, of course they had, but they had also engaged in acts that went far beyond the Hague Convention of 1907, which the French representative on the Tribunal wanted to consider as the binding document. Shklar, like Arendt, is convinced that what justifies the charge of crimes against humanity is the *novelty* of the acts in which the Nazis had engaged: "To say that the charge of crimes against humanity was unknown is therefore no argument against it" (1964: 163).

In *Eichmann in Jerusalem* Arendt had argued that the Jerusalem Court erred in condemning Eichmann for "crimes against the Jewish people" in the first instance and by naming "crimes against humanity" only as the third and separate charge ([1963] 1994: 244–45). In the dramatic Epilogue to *Eichmann* ([1958] 1973: 277), speaking in the voice of the Judges of Jerusalem, Arendt explained what the term crimes against humanity meant for her. Genocide, the highest of the crimes against humanity, is an attack upon the human status and human plurality, which is the condition "under which life on earth has been given to man." For Arendt, nothing less than a full-fledged ontological defense of human plurality could justify the significance of crimes against humanity and its pinnacle, genocide.[12]

Shklar says nothing about the justification of crimes against humanity. Undoubtedly, she would dismiss Arendt's ontological anchoring of this concept in the human condition of plurality as a variant of natural law thinking. Can we rest satisfied though with the simple positing of a new criminal statute to deal with new and unprecedented acts? As is well known, the German defense lawyers, both in Nuremberg and during the Eichmann Trial, kept raising the objection of "*nulla crimen, nulla poene sine lege*" ("no crime, no punishment without the law"), although none went so far as to claim that the mass slaughter of innocent civilians, women and children was a justifiable act of war. Rather, they maintained that the overall criminality of the regime left no choice but to consider the will of the Führer as the law of the land. In that sense, legality in the Third Reich, meant criminality.

This form of perverted legalistic consciousness, exercised by the likes of Eichmann, clearly was what Shklar herself also had in mind by "legalism," that is, blind obedience to orders and the law of the land, no matter how perverse and criminal. Yet by leaving the concept of crimes against humanity so unelaborated and philosophically unjustified, she left her own argument open to the charge of *Siegerjustiz* (victor's justice), meaning that the law was imposed on the loser by the winner and thus was an act of might rather than of justice. "As for the Eichmann case it, too, does not really create new problems for legal theory," she writes. "Eichmann, alas, was always a Jewish problem" (1964: 155). According to her, from the non-legal point of view, the trial had to be judged in terms of its political value for the various Jewish communities involved, but from a theoretical point of view, the

[12] For a detailed discussion of Hannah Arendt on plurality, see Benhabib (2018: chapter 5).

problems being the same in Nuremberg and in the Eichmann Trial, there was no need to consider them separately (1964: 155). This is not so, however. Without the evidence concerning the Nazi genocide of the Jews, which was not all that central to the Nuremberg Trials, the category of crimes against humanity hangs in mid-air. In this sense, the Eichmann Trial contributed far more to the project of international criminal law than Shklar may have been willing to admit. Was this a case of the possible anxiety of influence on her part vis-à-vis Arendt's towering contribution, or was it indicative of deeper differences among the two thinkers? Or possibly of both?

THE ANXIETY OF INFLUENCE? SHKLAR ON ARENDT

Shklar's first essay on Arendt, written in 1963, is a review of Arendt's *Between Past and Future,* and is appreciative and non-polemical in tone. This tone begins to change however, after Arendt's death in 1975, from reverent appreciation to impatience to a certain ironic dismissiveness by 1983.

In "Hannah Arendt's Triumph", Shklar eulogizes her as "the very last and finest voices" of a shattered culture. "Now there is no one left who can speak about and out of the depth of the experience of German Jewry. She was one of the last survivors of a spiritual republic whose social history was as terrible and brief as it was intellectually radiant and enduring" (1975: 8).

Only eight years later in 1983, in "Hannah Arendt as Pariah," Shklar abandons this attitude of respectful admiration and chides Arendt for her use of the distinction between "pariah" and "parvenu" to reflect on the Jewish condition, arguing that to condemn Jewish assimilation "not as false and foolish, but as vulgar," is sign of ultimate snobbery (1983: 363). Arendt is said to have clung "to a bizarre notion" that being Jewish was "an act of personal defiance and not a matter of actively maintaining a cultural and religious tradition with its own rites and patterns of speech" (1983: 364). Arendt did not even know Yiddish or Hebrew (Shklar knew both), but she did receive superb German *Bildung*, including Greek, Latin and philosophy. Perhaps the most intemperate words are Shklar's concluding observations that "American Jewry is a flourishing community, while German-Jewish culture died with Hannah Arendt" (1983: 375).

The Eichmann Trial occupies a large place in Shklar's "Hannah Arendt as Pariah" piece but it was barely mentioned in earlier articles.[13] It is as if, twenty years after the Eichmann controversy (1963), there was still some settling of accounts that Shklar had to engage in as well. After asserting that Arendt had nothing very new to say about how one should assign responsibility for acts committed by public agents in their capacity as government functionaries or those who should try them, she concludes that in *Eichmann in Jerusalem*, "they are discussed in a derivative and amateurish way. Legal theory was not her forté" (1983: 372). Shklar then goes on to marvel at the arrogance and "extraordinary ignorance" with which Arendt "generalized wildly about the infinitely complex and diverse communities of Eastern Europe, about whose history and structure she knew exactly nothing" (1983: 372, 373).

"Extraordinary ignorance" is not a charge that is often leveled against Arendt's work. Arendt's heavy reliance on Raoul Hilberg's *The Destruction of European Jews* in her reconstruction of the Holocaust in the pages of *Eichmann in Jerusalem* is well documented.[14] This may have been inadequate, but it was hardly extraordinarily ignorant.

Shklar then goes on to maintain that "more than ignorance and dissociation" which Arendt had displayed in *Eichmann in Jerusalem*, she had also "caused pain and justified rage. She meant to inflict

[13] Shklar's review of Arendt's *Between Past and Future* (1963) does not deal with the Eichmann book; there is also no mention of the controversy in her last review of Arendt's *Lectures on Kant's Political Philosophy* in 1984. Most interestingly, Shklar does not even refer to Eichmann in her 1975 encomium to Arendt, "Hannah Arendt's Triumph", restricting herself to a discussion of *The Origins of Totalitarianism*, *The Human Condition* and *On Revolution*. Nor is *Eichmann in Jerusalem* discussed in "Rethinking the Past" ([1977] 1998).

[14] I discuss these issues extensively in Benhabib (2000).

the first and need not have been astonished at the latter" (1983: 373). To inflict pain willingly and with intent is cruelty, and for Shklar cruelty is a principal moral vice. A year later in *Ordinary Vices* (1984: 2), Shklar would ask: "How can we be expected to endure the humiliations inflicted by an uncontained snobbery? Our only consolation may well be that without moral aspirations there would be no moral hypocrisy, and that without trust there would be no betrayals. But there is nothing to redeem cruelty and humiliation." By accusing Arendt of harbouring at least two of four cardinal vices, namely hypocrisy and snobbery – the others being betrayal and misanthropy – Shklar delivered her own version of Scholem's famous judgment on Arendt that she lacked "Ahabath Israel," that is, love of the Jewish people in that she would go so far as to willingly inflict cruelty upon them.[15]

This certainly is not right. Shklar was unable to assess sympathetically the degree of pain and self-implication that Arendt's *Eichmann in Jerusalem* also evinced. We can only speculate about what caused Shklar's outburst twenty years after the Eichmann controversy, and what prompted the change of heart between the elegiac and respectful tone of affection displayed in "Hannah Arendt's Triumph" and the strange glee with which the end of German Jewry is announced in "Hannah Arendt as Pariah" only eight years later.

As is well known, the Eichmann controversy roiled the American Jewish community, and in particular, the New York Jewish intellectuals, for years to come. The trauma of the Holocaust of European Jewry is so deep that like a wound that is scratched before it is healed, it will keep bleeding. Arendt's *Eichmann in Jerusalem* scratched where it had not healed and probably never will. That is why Irving Howe's wise words (2013), that the controversy will "die down, simmer," but "erupt" again and again are quite appropriate.

[15] A good account of this controversy is given by Kohn & Feldman (2007: Introduction).

My personal suspicion is that it was not just the Eichmann controversy that led Shklar to erupt in bitterness in 1983. Shklar, like most of us, first found out about the Arendt-Heidegger affair through Young-Bruehl's account and may have been quite shocked by it and unwilling to indulge Arendt's weakness vis-à-vis Heidegger, for whom Shklar expressed the deepest contempt. "Eventually she found it easy to forgive Heidegger," writes Shklar of Arendt. "She had always seen through the cult that surrounded him, knowing perfectly well that none of his admirers had a clue about what he was saying. That, in fact, is still the condition of the thriving Heidegger industry. Arendt, however, not only understood him, she was and remained under his philosophical spell" (1983: 365).[16]

Though Shklar had little admiration for Heidegger's philosophy, as this quote amply makes clear, the puzzle as to why one of the most important thinkers of the twentieth-century would be seduced by National Socialism, continues to consternate many. Was there an "elective affinity" between Heidegger's philosophy and Nazism or was this merely a mistake in judgment, to which Heidegger was led by the narcissism of his own personality? Arendt thought it was the latter; though she also believed right after the Second World War ended that there were elements in Heidegger's philosophy that made it congenial to authoritarian politics.[17]

The younger scholar from Latvia finally lost patience with the revered senior German-Jewish scholar and was willing to indulge neither Arendt's weaknesses as a woman vis-à-vis her teacher and lover, Martin Heidegger, nor her snobbery vis-à-vis the dilemmas of Jewishness and assimilation. Shklar did not ask why private life

[16] If I may be permitted a personal recollection here: I was Judith Shklar's junior colleague in political theory at Harvard from 1987 to 1989. Shklar was greatly dismayed by the growing influence of Heidegger (as well as of Carl Schmitt) in the American academy and Arendt's essay, "Martin Heidegger at Eighty" (1969 [1971]), in which Arendt seemed to forgive Heidegger his political mistake in becoming rector of the University of Freiburg under the Nazis, loomed large in Shklar's mind as all the details of their personal relationship began to come to light.

[17] For an account of the Heidegger controversy which includes original texts by his former students and colleagues, see Wolin, ed. (1993).

and a woman's amorous choices should colour one's judgment of her work. Weren't there gender inequities in disrespecting Arendt for her weakness vis-à-vis Heidegger? But let us admit that Arendt was no ordinary person whose life could have been easily shielded from scrutiny: she was an outstanding political thinker, thus her judgment mattered. And she was a Jewish intellectual who spoke out forcefully on Jewish questions. Thus, her willingness to forgive Heidegger seemed like a double insult: both to her as a woman and as a Jew. The struggle that broke out among the New York intellectuals about *Eichmann in Jerusalem* and Arendt's persona, and that eventually evolved into a shouting match between the "Ost Juden" and "the Jeckes" (the German Jews) appears to have affected Shklar's views of Arendt as well. Toward the end of her life, Shklar returns to the themes of exile, statelessness and migration, and once more finds Arendt's work inspirational.

OBLIGATION, LOYALTY AND EXILE

In the final years of her life, Shklar was preparing a course on obligation and exile to be offered under the rubric of "Moral Reasoning" in Harvard's core curriculum. She had given lectures on this topic at various American universities and was gearing up for a series of lectures to be offered in Cambridge, England in Fall 1992 before her wholly unexpected death on September 17 of that year. It is, of course, fascinating that at this point in her life Shklar would return to themes that had such autobiographical resonance for her.

In "Obligation, Loyalty and Exile," Shklar defines obligation as "rule-governed conduct" referring to laws and law-like demands made by public authorities (1998: 40). Moral and political quandaries do not arise at this level: it is only when one's "chosen obligations," that is one's commitments, begin to come into conflict with other *unchosen attachments* that significant moral conflicts emerge. Loyalty is understood as "attachment to a social group," in which membership may or may not be chosen. "And when it comes to race, ethnicity, caste, and class, choice is not obvious. The emotional character of loyalty sets it apart from obligation" (1998: 41). Not only are there conflicts between these various types of human attachments, but there may be contradictions embedded within each of them, such as when family and friends to whom one is loyal may have their own conflicts and one is caught in between.

Conflict between loyalty and obligation is most characteristic of the age of nationalism, when state and nationality do not coincide, as they rarely do (1998: 44). Despite the ideologies of nationalism, modern states are not homogeneous ethnically, linguistically or in terms of religion or ideology; hence, such conflicts of attachments are bound to increase in the age of nation-states. By examining the fate of exiles, Shklar thought, one may gain some understanding of the conflicts inherent in such multiple loyalties. Admitting that she despairs ever of "completing her list" of what makes an exile, she nonetheless ventures to define an exile as "someone who involuntarily leaves the country of which he or she is citizen. Usually it is thanks to political force, but extreme poverty may be regarded as a form of coercive expulsion" (1998: 45).

Shklar's analysis of the exile is principally modeled after the political dissident, the prisoner of conscience, and the resistance fighter. Clearly, the vast majority of German Jews and Japanese Americans, who were persecuted on the basis of *ascriptive* grounds rather than consciously chosen allegiances or political opposition, would not fit this model; yet, the line between exile and refugee is often porous. Acknowledging this, Shklar writes of refugees, "[t]he dreadful reality of our world is that no one wants to accept this huge exiled population. What they need is a place to go, and these are increasingly hard to find" (1998: 51). Noting that the "pieds noirs" from North Africa can return home, much like the Jews the world over who may go to Israel if they so choose, Shklar observes that this is not the case for the vast majority of the world's exiled populations (1998: 52). Shklar's words lack the right tonality: "The dwellers in refugee camps can best be compared to America's

African slaves. And as we look on helplessly at the *ever-growing number of human refuse heaps,* we might perhaps listen to the voice of conscience" (1998: 52, emphasis added).

Shklar was too astute a student of history not to recognize that this analogy between African American slaves and contemporary refugees was wrong. Slaves had a place in society while refugees had been forced to lose theirs, but she, like Arendt, whom she invokes once more in these last pages, believed that refusing human beings membership in a polity because they speak a different language, practice a different religion or belong to a different race or ethnicity perpetrates gross injustice. "Offering citizenship to exiles may prove the most significant means of taming political loyalty," (1998: 54) she observes. And while it is hard to believe that the world can ever reach a modus vivendi such that many will not have to seek refuge in other lands, "[n]evertheless, the less injustice there is, the less likely it is that refugees will populate the world and bring with them their *terrible misery and mischief*" (1998: 55, emphasis added). Shklar's language about exiles and refugees vacillates between moral compassion for their lot and hard-headed realism about the sheer vulnerability of their condition in a world of recalcitrant and selfish politics of states.

CONCLUSION

Having arrived at Harvard at the age of twenty-one and staying there until her death, Shklar enjoyed great stability and academic eminence; yet it is as if that long and perilous journey from Riga to Sweden, then across Siberia to Japan, unto New York and finally to Montréal left its traces in her writings as she continued to ponder the human conditions of fear and cruelty, exile and marginalization.

Compared with Hannah Arendt's analysis in *The Origins of Totalitarianism* of the "Decline of the Nation-State and the Perplexities of the Rights of Man," summarized in that famous phrase of "the right to have rights" and its enduring paradoxes

(1979: 296–97), Shklar's statements, while they express moral sympathy and outrage, are incapable of clarifying the significance of the condition of refugees and exiles for our times.

There is no deep analysis of the paradoxes of the state system with its dual commitments to human rights and to the rule of law, on the one hand, and national sovereignty on the other. Shklar's brilliant method of moral psychology forces her to return repeatedly to the level of individual experience and sensibility rather than focusing on institutional structures. As important as personal conflicts of loyalty and obligation may be, they miss something essential both about exile and the refugee condition when there is no analysis of the loss of world or membership of political communities. In fact, it is fascinating that Shklar draws many examples from the ancient world in which the practice of exile by those such as Alicibiades was a personal choice.

Nonetheless, what makes rereading Shklar today fascinating is her enduring sense of the fragility of liberal institutions and her sharp understanding of moral psychology. In her famous essay on "The Liberalism of Fear" (1996), Shklar put preventing cruelty even ahead of justice in a liberal society. Whereas for Arendt, politics at its best makes us come close to our ontological capacity to create a new world of freedom and weave new narratives, Shklar was a skeptic but not a cynic: she thought that there was a lot of pious self-congratulation on the part of liberal democracies but she still believed that the task of government was to prevent cruelty and to achieve justice. In her later years, she grew increasingly close to John Rawls's vision of social-democratic liberalism and never accepted the pieties of the free market liberals. Her last books, *The Faces of Injustice* (1990) and *American Citizenship* (1991) evidence this more robust expectation of what a social-democratically regulated liberal society should achieve.

Arendt's work is shot through with the tragedy of the political and the sadness as well as outrage that absurd historical contingencies generate. In Shklar's work there is a less heroic and more down-to-earth contemplation of the cruelty and humiliation that political failure can cause. For us as their readers and students today, both the tragedy of the political and the cruelty and humiliation it has given rise to are all too present.

To return to the question posed at the beginning of this essay: In what ways then is gender a useful category in analyzing the work of such distinguished women political theorists? It is clear that in the case of Shklar, she suffered significant gender discrimination in that for many years she was not promoted to the post of professor in government which she richly deserved and instead accepted the status of a part-time lecturer. As the interview with Judith Walzer (1988) makes clear, Shklar very well knew that her not being promoted to lecturer position upon the completion of her dissertation had very much to do with the fact that she was a young woman and was expected to have children. Her formidable intellect and her commitment to her work enabled her eventually to sail past all that. But the category of gender discrimination did not find theoretical articulation in her work as one of the many "faces of injustice," to echo the title of one of her books. Obviously, "gender" becomes a critical analytical tool for a thinker, not through personal experience primarily but through intellectual and political conviction. Shklar's liberalism did not make room for gender but neither is it wholly incompatible with it. There is no reason why gender discrimination could not be one of the "faces of injustice" in Shklar's own terms, since injustice occurs when we have the power to prevent something from happening but choose not to do so.

With Hannah Arendt, matters are more complicated and not only because a younger generation of feminist scholars have begun prodding her work along lines significant for feminist scholarship but also because, as the most important political thinker about totalitarianism as a form of political rule, she held unto a normative conception of the private sphere as the counterpart to her conception of the public one.[18] It is interesting that

[18] See my early essays: 1992, 1993.

Shklar was hardly interested in this aspect of Arendt's thought, except of course, when blaming Arendt for her youthful love affair with Heidegger, she showed that the private "sticks" to public women in a fashion it hardly does to men – though in the age of the #MeToo movement, we see a younger generation of women criticizing this bastion of male privilege as well.

The challenge to us as feminist scholars is to find the subtle ways in which the public and the private, the political and the personal are interwoven with one another in the work of these formidable women thinkers, without reducing their delicate balance to stereotypes.

REFERENCES

Anghie, Anthony. 2007. *Imperialism, Sovereignty and the Making of International Law.* Cambridge: Cambridge University Press.

Arendt, Hannah. [1969] 1971. Martin Heidegger at Eighty. *The New York Review of Books.* www.nybooks.com/articles/1971/10/21/martin-heidegger-at-eighty/.

[1958] 1973. *The Human Condition.* 8th ed. Chicago, IL: University of Chicago Press.

1979. *The Origins of Totalitarianism.* New York: Harcourt, Brace Jovanovich.

[1933] 1994. The Emancipation of Women. In Jerome Kohn, ed., *Essays of Understanding: Formation, Exile and Totalitarianism 1930–1954.* New York: Schocken Press.

[1963] 1994. *Eichmann in Jerusalem. A Report on the Banality of Evil.* New York: Penguin Books.

Aumann, Francis R. 1965. Review. *Journal of Politics,* **27**, 703–05.

Bedau, H. A. 1967. Review. *Philosophical Review,* **76**, 129–30.

Benhabib, Seyla. 1992. Models of Public Space. Hannah Arendt: The Liberal Tradition and Jurgen Habermas. In Craig Calhoun, ed., *Habermas And the Public Sphere.* Cambridge, MA: MIT Press, pp. 73–99.

1993. Feminist Theory and Hannah Arendt's Concept of the Public Sphere. In *History Of The Human Sciences,* **6**(2), 97–115.

1994. Judith Shklar's Dystopic Liberalism. *Social Research. An International Quarterly,* **61**(2), 477–88.

2000. Arendt's Eichmann In Jerusalem. In Dana Villa, ed., *The Cambridge Companion To Hannah Arendt.* Cambridge: Cambridge University Press, pp. 65–86.

[1996] 2003. *The Reluctant Modernism of Hannah Arendt.* New Jersey: Rowman and Littlefield.

2018. *Exile, Statelessness, and Migration. Playing Chess with History from Hannah Arendt to Isaiah Berlin.* Princeton, NJ: Princeton University Press.

Bloom, Harold. [1973] 1997. *The Anxiety of Influence. A Theory of Poetry*. Oxford: Oxford University Press.

Brown, Brendan F. 1967. Review. *University of Toronto Law Journal*, **17**, 218–25.

Hegel, G. W. F. 1977. Hegel's Phenomenology of Spirit. A. V. Miller, trans. Foreword by John Findlay. Oxford: Clarendon Press.

Hess, Andreas. 2014. *The Political Theory of Judith N. Shklar*. New York: Palgrave Macmillan.

Honig, Bonnie. 1995. *Feminist Interpretations of Hannah Arendt*. University Park, PA: The Pennsylvania State University Press.

Howe, Irving. 2013. Banality and Brilliance: Irving Howe on Hannah Arendt. Reprinted in *Dissent Magazine*, June 5, from the archives. wwwdissentmagazine .org/online_articles/banality-and-brilliance-irving-howe-on-hannah-arendt.

Moyn, Samuel. 2013. Judith Shklar versus the International Criminal Court. *Humanity*, **Winter**, 473–500.

Kohn, Jerome and Feldman, Ron H. 2007. *Hannah Arendt. The Jewish Writings*. New York: Schocken Books.

Shklar, Judith N. 1963. "Review Essay" of Between Past and Future by Hannah Arendt. *History and Theory*, **2**(3), 286–92.

1964. *Legalism. An Essay on Law, Morals and Politics*. Cambridge, MA: Harvard University Press.

1975. Hannah Arendt's Triumph. *The New Republic*, **173**, 26.

1976. *Freedom and Independence: A Study of the Political Ideas of Hegel's Phenomenology of Mind*. Cambridge: Cambridge University Press.

1982. Review of Hannah Arendt. In Ronald Beiner, ed. *Lectures on Kant's Political Philosophy*. Brighton: Harvester Press. Also in: 1984. *Hegel Bulletin*, **5** (1: 9), 42–44.

1984. *Ordinary Vices*. Cambridge, MA: Belknap Press of Harvard University Press.

1990. *The Faces of Injustice. The Storrs Lectures*. New Haven, CT: Yale University Press.

1991. *American Citizenship. The Quest for Inclusion. The Tanner Lectures on Human Values*. Cambridge, MA: Harvard University Press.

1996. A Life of Learning. In Bernard Yack, ed., *Liberalism Without Illuisons. Essays on Liberal Theory and the Political Vision of Judith N. Shklar*. Chicago, IL: University of Chicago Press, pp. 263–81.

1996. The Liberalism of Fear. In Nancy Rosenblum, ed., *Liberalism and the Moral Life*. Cambridge, MA: Harvard University Press.

[1977] 1998. Rethinking the Past. In Stanley Hoffmann, ed., *Shklar, Political Thought and Political Thinkers*. Chicago, IL: University of Chicago Press, pp. 352–61. Originally published in *Social Research*, **44**(1), 80–90.

[1983] 1998. Hannah Arendt as Pariah. In Stanley Hoffmann, ed., *Shklar, Political Thought and Political Thinkers*. Chicago, IL: University of Chicago Press, pp. 362–75. Originally published in *Partisan Review*, **50**(1), 64–77.

[1993] 1998. Obligation, Loyalty, and Exile. In Stanley Hoffmann, ed., *Political Thought and Political Thinkers*. Chicago, IL: University of Chicago Press.

Totani, Yuma. 2008. *The Tokyo War Crimes Trial. The Pursuit of Justice in the Wake of WW II. Harvard East Asian Monograph 299.* Cambridge, MA and London: Harvard University Press.

Walzer, Judith B. 1988. Oral History of Tenured Women in the Faculty of Arts and Sciences at Harvard University. Hadl. 1902.1/00709 Murray Research Archive.

Wolin, Richard, ed. 1993. *The Heidegger Controversy.* Cambridge, MA: MIT Press.

Young-Bruehl, Elisabeth. 1982. *Hannah Arendt: For Love of the World.* New Haven, CT and London: Yale University Press.

CHAPTER 13

Feminism and the Abomination of Violence: Gender Thought and Unthought

Jacqueline Rose

We live at a moment when violence against women has never been so visible, when, despite the various achievements of gender equality, cruelty against women – whether in the form of rape as a war crime, domestic abuse, sexual harassment, so-called 'honour-based' violence, female genital surgery – has never been so prominently in the public eye. There was a time when such violence against women was almost exclusively addressed by radical feminists. Today it is something which no feminist, whatever their orientation, cannot *not* talk about. For feminists, like myself, who have always stressed the precarious psychic nature of the category of 'woman' – the endless tension between the complexity of human sexuality and the crude gendered division of the world, one thing seems clear: violence against women is not an aberration, an outlier in relation to the conventional arrangements. Rather it is one of the chief means of forcing these arrangements, with increasing desperation, into their allotted place (see Akbar Ahmed in this volume for one such example).

I do not, however, want to document all the forms of global violence against women as it is one feminist tactic to do. Feminism is not served by turning violence into a litany. When we look at the

This chapter, originally delivered as the Michaelmas 2014, Diane Middlebrook/Carl Djerassi lecture, was published in the 30th anniversary issue of *Cultural Critique*, Fall, 94, 2016. A fuller version of this chapter, as originally delivered as the Michaelmas 2014 Diane Middlebrook/Carl Djerassi lecture is published in Rose (2020). My thanks to Juliet Mitchell, founding Director and to Jude Browne and Lauren Wilcox, Director and Deputy Director of the Cambridge Centre for Gender Studies.

picture of a woman who died on 9/11, the first and only feminist question should not, to my mind, be – to cite legal feminist scholar Catharine A. Mackinnon – 'Who hurt her before?'; nor, when we look at the bones of a woman from an ancient civilisation, do I want us to see her, and them, as, inevitably, broken (2007: 28). 'What I most want to know about women in the past' is not, as MacKinnon puts it, 'how did she die?' but rather: 'how did she live?' (2007: 28). And I also want that question to be able to gather on its journey whatever it may find, however messy and unexpected. Central to this chapter is the proposition that feminism has nothing to gain by seeing women solely or predominantly as the victims of their histories. Such a strategy does not help us to think.

It is a central argument of this chapter that violence against women is a crime of the deepest thoughtlessness. It is a sign that the mind has brutally blocked itself. The best way, I will argue, for feminism to counter violence against women is to speak of, to stay and reckon with, the extraordinary, often painful, and mostly overlooked, range of what the human mind is capable of. Violence for me is part of the psyche. A crime to be detested and cast off, but also something which one feminism, in the very force of that gesture – however necessary, however right at one level – then itself repudiates, renders unthinkable, shuns beyond the remit of the human (precisely abominates). At that moment, feminism finds itself replicating that part of the mind which cannot tolerate its own complexity. It thereby becomes complicit with the psychic processes which lead to the enactment of violence itself. For me it then becomes crushing – or to put it more crassly, cuts off its nose to spite its face.

I take my idea of thoughtlessness from Hannah Arendt, to whom – along with Melanie Klein – I appeal here as offering a new way of thinking about violence against women in our time. Both Arendt and Klein suggest that there is something about the process of human thought that is often insufferable, not least because thinking acts as a break on the fantasy that the world is there to be mastered, and thereby prevents that dangerous fantasy from doing untold damage by running amuck or away with itself. For Arendt, violence is a form of radical self-deceit – or 'the impotence of bigness' to use her phrase – which punishes the world, punishes women we can say, for the limitations of human power (the gender implications of her phrase 'impotence of bigness' are surely glaring even if she does not fully draw them out herself) (1972: 34). 'What I propose, therefore, is very simple', she writes at the beginning of *The Human Condition*, 'it is nothing more than to think about what we are doing' (1958: 5). As often with Arendt, such simplicity is deceptive. Thinking as process has to be fought for. It is threatened from all sides, by modern pseudo-knowledge which leaves us at the mercy of every gadget which is technically possible 'however murderous it is'; and by the muteness of sheer violence: 'Only sheer violence', she writes, 'is mute' (1958: 5). For Arendt, therefore, the mind is under siege, and thinking is the only restraint against murderous know-how and the cruel silence of sheer violence which mutes both itself and its victims.

Arendt wrote *The Human Condition* in the 1950s (it was published in 1958), when the power of death-dealing technology had reached new heights: from industrial genocide to the atom bomb. 'The technical development of the implements of violence', she writes in her later 1970 study *On Violence*, 'has now reached a point where no political goal could conceivably correspond to their destructive potential or justify their actual use in armed conflict' (1970: 3). The 'suicidal' development of modern weapons involves 'a massive intrusion of criminal violence into politics' (1970: 14). Behind this analysis is her indictment of the myth of Progress which the United States, where she arrived as a refugee from Nazism in the 1930s, believed itself to embody beyond any other nation. For Arendt, 'Progress' is a ruthless illusion, a self-fulfilling prophecy, which leaves itself no escape clause other than the increasingly violent enactment of itself. Or to put it another way, so-called Progress leads directly to the burnt bodies of Vietnam.

Arendt is not, to put it mildly, most famous for her contribution to feminism, any more indeed than Melanie Klein, on which more later, although the case for Arendt's contribution to feminism has been made strongly by scholars such as Seyla Benhabib (1993) and Mary Dietz (1994) whose readings are the starting points for mine. But there is an important gender dimension to her work (and, I will be arguing, to Klein's). It is there in that 'impotent bigness' – a phrase to which I will return. But, almost despite herself, Arendt can be seen as the forerunner of one feminist analysis which traces women's subordination, and the violence which is so often its consequence, first and foremost to the division of labour in – or rather consignment of women *to* – the home. Arendt's political ideal is the Greek city space of the polis. Indeed, so invested is she in the Athenian model of democracy, that she has often been accused of overlooking, or worse reinforcing, the status of women and slaves on whose bodies and backs it built itself. But Arendt makes it clear that if the home and family life are pre-political, it is because, she writes, they are the place 'where the household head ruled with uncontested despotic powers' (1958: 27). It is because the paterfamilias rules with such absolute power in the household that it remains outside the domain of politics: 'Even the power of the tyrant was less great, less "perfect" than the power with which the *paterfamilias*, the *dominus*, ruled over the household of slaves and family' (1958: 27).

The consequence is violence in the home. Freedom belonged exclusively in the political realm, whereas the household was the place of necessity – read the base environment of creaturely life (or housework as we call it today) – which must be mastered for man to be free. Out of this forced discrimination, violence surely follows. Because, in Greek thought, 'all human beings are subject to necessity', Arendt explains, 'they are entitled to violence towards others' (1958: 31). Violence then becomes the 'pre-political act of liberating oneself from the necessity of life for the freedom of the world' (1958: 31). That is why to be a slave means not just loss of freedom, but being subject to man-made violence.

And this is also why there is no real sexual division of labour – nothing one could even grace with the epithet of 'separate spheres' – since such a notion relies on an at least formal assumption of equality between men and women whereas no such assumption existed. Women and slaves – Arendt is surely hardly condoning the equation – stand in, and for, the place where the necessity of the world is subject to brute mastery. While the ancient household head might of course exert a milder or harsher rule, he knows 'neither law nor justice' (1958: 34). Or to put it another way, it is because women and slaves are called upon to redeem the frailty of human, bodily, life – what Judith Butler would call 'precarious life' – that they are the objects, in fact they *must be* the objects, of violence (2004).

The key word is 'mastery'. It is for Arendt, in the world and in the heart, a delusion. Thus when she goes on to make her famous distinction between violence and power which is at the centre of *On Violence*, what matters is that a government will have recourse to violence in direct proportion to a decline in its authority and power, a decline which violence is desperate to redress (violence is always desperate). 'Rule by sheer violence', she writes, 'comes about when power is being lost' (Arendt, 1970). State violence, we could say, is the last resort of the criminal (as we saw so cruelly in the crackdown on the streets of Egypt, post the Tahrir Square uprising of 2011, and throughout the world). When a state 'starts to devour its own children', Arendt observes, 'power has disappeared completely' (think Syria). 'We know or should know', she insists, 'that every decrease in power is an open invitation to violence – if only because those who hold power and feel it slipping from their hands ... have always found it difficult to resist the temptation to substitute violence for it' (1970: 87). And she observes: 'Impotence breeds violence and psychologically this is quite true' (1970: 54).

Arendt's distinction between violence and power is important in relation to a feminism that wishes to align violence with male power of which it then becomes the inevitable expression (which makes female power, as Catharine A. MacKinnon once famously put it, 'a contradiction in terms' (1987: 53)). Instead, Arendt allows us to see such an equation as the lie that violence *perpetuates about itself,* since it will do anything – destroy women and the world – rather than admit that its power is uncertain. Women then become the scapegoats for man's unconscious knowledge of his own human, which means shared – that is, *shared with women* – frailty ('The Frailty of Human Affairs' is the title of one section of *The Human Condition*). Such frailty takes us to the darkest corridors of life and of the mind, to 'the realm of birth and death' which must be excluded from the public realm because 'it harbors the things hidden from human eyes and impenetrable to human knowledge. Impenetrable because man does not know where he comes from when he is born and where he goes when he dies' (Arendt, 1958: 62–63). Or to put it another way, violence is man's response to the fraudulence of his power and the limits of his knowledge. 'Impotent bigness' indeed, as we might say.

In her constant return to what cannot be mastered or fully known by the mind, Arendt, as I read her, is – perilously or brilliantly depending on your viewpoint – skirting the domain of psychoanalysis for which her stated antipathy is well known. But it is very hard not to read her account of things impenetrable to the human mind as having much in common with the Freudian concept of the unconscious which signals – over and above the sexual debris of its contents – the limits of man's cognizance of the world and of himself. In Arendt's account such limits strike the body politic as much as they do the human heart. This is her vocabulary for both these realms: 'boundlessnesss', 'unpredictability', and 'the darkness of the human heart' (1958: 191, 244). We live, she states, in an 'ocean of uncertainty', against which there is no redress (1958: 244). It is the human condition. Men are fundamentally unreliable since they 'can never guarantee who they will be tomorrow' (1958: 244). And how, she asks, can you see or foretell the consequences of an act 'within a community of equals where everybody has the same capacity to act?' (1958: 244). To be part of the body politic means relinquishing your control over the future – yours and that of the other who is your equal, *because* they are your equal. Man's 'inability to rely upon himself or have complete faith in himself', which, she insists, 'is the same thing', is 'the price human beings pay for freedom', while 'the impossibility of remaining unique master of what they do' – read subordinating another to your power – 'is the price they pay for plurality and reality' (1958: 244). If Arendt describes such open, equal, participation in the unpredictable reality of the world as a 'joy' (her word), she has also laid out with stunning clarity the unwelcome nature of her own insight and, hence, the lengths men will go to deny that insight and subordinate the world, in which I include women, to their purpose.

In *The Life of the Mind*, which was Arendt's last work, she takes this further. Now thinking appears even more clearly as the other side of false mastery and knowledge. This is why, for example, Arendt insists that the correct translation of Kant's *Verstand* is not 'understanding' but 'intellect' or 'cognition' because it represents the 'desire to know', as distinct from *Vernunft* which arises from the 'urgent need to think' (1978: 57). 'To expect truth to come from thinking signifies that we mistake the need to think with the urge to know', a need 'that can never be assuaged' (1971: 61, 55). Both are anguished but one in the service of hammering the world into place, the other by its own interminable process, which has no end on which it can brand its name. Only intellect or cognition believes it can answer the unanswerable questions; that it can seize the world in its mental coil. Philosophers of this persuasion, she tells us, are 'like children trying to catch smoke by closing their hands' (1971: 122).

Against this false and futile knowing, Arendt places, even more strikingly in this last meditation, a thinking ego which moves among 'invisible' essences, that is strictly speaking 'nowhere', 'homeless in an emphatic sense', which led, she suggests, to the early rise of 'cosmopolitanism' among philosophers (1971: 199). Way ahead of her time, Arendt calls up her answer to the violence of the times in the terms – homeless, nowhere, cosmopolitan –

which will be so central to the literary and cultural theory that will follow, although rarely acknowledge, her. And in doing so, she shows these terms seized from the history of the refugee and the exile – homeless, nowhere – the stateless, as we might say, whose predicament had been her own and which she did so much to articulate and dignify. In her chapter in this volume, Benhabib points to the state of exile which Arendt and philosopher Judith Shklar had in common.

True thought, then, is a form of memory which exerts no dominion, ousts no one from their own space, because it remembers that it is or once was radically homeless. We could not be further from the despotic ruler of the Athenian household who dispenses violence to his women and slaves because it is in the remit of his own power, or rather because it is the only way he can struggle to exert control over the debasing, corporal, necessities of life. Nor from the modern-day state that turns to violence in order to shore up a power that has lost all legitimacy. Arendt's life of the mind does not, then, point to some realm of abstract contemplation – her plea for thought is the child of its time.

Perhaps, then, we should not be surprised, although I admit that I was, to find Arendt slowly inching her way to the world of the dream – the 'royal road to the unconscious' as Freud called it (till the end of his life, he saw *The Interpretation of Dreams* as his most important book). Whatever the achievements of the thinking ego, it will, Arendt writes, never be able to 'convince itself that anything actually exists and that life, human life, is more than a dream' (1971: 198). To illustrate this suspicion – among the most characteristic of Asian philosophy – she then selects the Taoist story of Chuang Tzu who dreamt he was a butterfly only to wake, not to the unerring sureness of who he really was, but to the realisation that perhaps he was a butterfly dreaming he was Chuang Tzu (1971: 198) (the same example evoked by Jacques Lacan by the way to evoke the vanishing of the human subject in relation to the unconscious ([1973] 2004: 76). But Arendt being Arendt does not of course leave it there. The dream returns – in the conclusion to *The*

Life of the Mind – as the great equaliser in the shape of the king who dreams he is an artisan (since his quotient of life in that moment is no different from the poor artisan who dreams he is king) (1971: 150). Moreover, she writes, since 'one frequently dreams that he is dreaming' (she is citing Pascal's critique of Descartes), nothing can guarantee that what we call our life is not wholly a dream from which we shall awaken in death (1971: 150). The personal resonance of such moments in this, her last, uncompleted, book are surely striking. Arendt is exploring and relinquishing her own powers.

Something is creeping back into Arendt's writing. Remember the Greek citizen who mingled freely in the polis on condition of ruling with a rod of iron in his home. Remember too that, if women had to be subdued, it was because women were required to subdue in turn, and on his behalf, the messy, bodily frailties of life, the realm of birth and death that 'harbors the things hidden from human eyes and impenetrable to human knowledge'. What seems, therefore, to be happening here is that this banished domain of the Graeco-Roman dispensation is, in this final work, taking vengeance on the murderous technocratic know-how of the modern world, as slowly but surely it beats a path back into modernity as its only hope. I think we are talking about the return of the repressed. The options are stark. Violence or the dark, shadowy, innermost recesses of the hearth and heart where all knowing comes to grief. Violence or the world of the dream.

Cue Melanie Klein. But before leaving Arendt for Klein, there is a crucial link to be made to Rosa Luxemburg for whom Arendt's enthusiasm knew no limits. There is the deepest and fully acknowledged debt. In all the works by Arendt I have been discussing so far, spontaneity – Luxemburg's central concept and another humble reminder of the unpredictable reality of the world – is a repeated refrain.[1] But there is one moment when Arendt evokes Luxemburg which is of particular value for what I am trying to

[1] See also Arendt's essay on Luxemburg (1968) and my discussion of Luxemburg (2014).

evoke here. She is talking about love. In its highest manifestation, Arendt writes, when the willing ego pronounces '*Amo: Volo ut sis*', what it means is 'I love you; I want you to be'. Not, she goes on, 'I want to have you', or 'I want to rule you' (1971: 150). Love without tyranny. Compare this free-wheeling, uncontrolling version of love with Rosa Luxemburg. 'Blessed are those without passion', she wrote to her last lover, Hans Diefenbach – a relationship conducted by correspondence from prison – 'if that means they would never claw like a panther at the happiness and freedom of others.' Then she qualifies: 'That has nothing to do with passion .... I possess enough of it to set a prairie on fire, and still hold sacred the freedom and the simple wishes of other people.'[2] True passion stakes no claim. Like democracy, it does not own, control or master the other. It lets the other be. With Luxemburg, you barely have to scratch the surface. We are talking about sexual politics.

***

In the middle of the Second World War, the pioneering psychoanalyst Melanie Klein finds herself with an unexpected opportunity – to analyse a ten-year-old-boy over what they both know in advance will be the restricted timeframe of four months. She will take notes after every session – several verbatim – and then collect them into one of the first full-length accounts of what her editor Elliott Jacques describes in his Foreword to the published volume as a 'total analysis' (1984). The fact that this is only made possible by the conditions of the war – evacuation from London – a war which will colour the analysis at every turn, is seen not as obstacle but as the core of the process. Richard's distress is multi-layered and over-determined. This in itself demonstrates the futility of trying to locate childhood anxiety either inside the mind or outside in the world (as if one precluded the other). He is an avid follower of the war – reads three newspapers a day, listens to all the news on the wireless, and threatens suicide at the fall of Crete if

[2] Luxemburg to Hans Diefenbach, 1917 (complete date not given), cited in Ettinger (1988: 213).

Britain should be defeated. But his fear of Hitler is overlaid – driven, perhaps, we do not have to decide – certainly matched, by his fear of his father. The two are inseparable. And what he fears most from his father is what he is doing, or capable of doing, to his mother.

'Just now he had spoken of the terrible things the Austrian Hitler did to the Austrians. By this he meant that Hitler was in a way ill-treating his own people, including Mrs K., just as the bad Daddy would ill-treat Mummy' (1984: 22). Or again: 'Mrs K. interpreted R's desire for peace and order in the family, his giving way to Daddy's and Paul's authority, as a means of restraining his jealousy and hatred. This meant there would be no Hitler-Daddy, and Mummy would not be turned into the "pig-sty" Mummy, for she would not be injured and bombed by the bad father' (1984: 194). Hitler-Daddy. Klein's interpretations are famously blunt, some would say coercive. But this very bluntness, I would like to suggest, has served to obscure something that is also staring us in the face. 'Ill-treat', 'injure' 'bomb'; Mummy as a 'pig-sty' for the garbage of the world and of the heart. Like Arendt, Klein is not best renowned as a feminist thinker. Nonetheless, when she looks into Richard's fantasy world, what she sees there – what she urges him to see – is a scene of domestic violence. At one point Richard asks obsessively and solicitously about the number of Klein's other, especially child, patients. Interpreting this as the rivalry and fear of displacement it clearly is, she then also suggests that perhaps he wishes Mrs Klein to have child patients in the same way as he wanted Mummy to have babies, because, I quote, '*they were less dangerous than men*' (1984: 347).[3]

It is central to one radical feminist argument that the world of war and peace are no different. For MacKinnon, the 1990s assault on Bosnian women and their resistance to it challenges 'the lines between genocide and war and, ultimately, between war and peace' (2007: 2). The significance of 9/11, which she describes as an 'exemplary day of male violence', is that the number of people killed in the Twin Towers on that day was almost identical

[3] Emphasis added.

to the number of women murdered by men, mostly their male partners, in the US over the average year (2007: 260–61). MacKinnon is rightly challenging the indifference of national and international law towards violence against women compared with the military response to the attacks of 9/11, although when she asks 'Do these women not count as casualties in some war? Will the Marines not land for them?' (2007: 272) I take my leave. To my mind the last thing feminists should be calling for is the US Marines landing anywhere in the world any more than they do, mostly disastrously, already.

But what is never discussed in this argument, which assumes a perfect fit or continuity between manhood and a violence of which it becomes the supreme and deadly fulfilment, is the terrain in which men, and before them boys, do psychic battle. Crucially, in Klein's account, that terrain is not free of violence. It is drenched in it. She is the arch theorist of psychic violence, more specifically of matricide, as Julia Kristeva points out in her study of Klein (2001). In the case of Richard, the line between war and peace is indeed thin to the point of breaking. To differentiate them is his most urgent task. It is the work to be done. Richard's challenge we might say is to resist the pull of the most deadly masculine identifications the world has on offer. Were that not an available option for him, indeed for men more generally, then feminism would surely be on a hiding to nothing; it would be on a losing battle – for ever. If the child is father to the man, then, Melanie Klein's life's work suggests, what that means is always, urgently and painfully, up for grabs. There is always still everything to play for.

If there is a profound link here for me to the ideas of Hannah Arendt, it comes through the category of thought. Richard is a boy who 'knows his blows' (a slip of the tongue as fateful as it is wondrous) (1984). Goebbels and Ribbentrop become especially intense objects of hatred when they dare to say that Britain was the aggressor in the war. In this flagrant act of projection, they are way behind Richard himself since the whole of his analysis is an inner negotiation with the violence which he feels himself capable of. He knows his blows. Remember that lying was the target of some of Arendt's fiercest political critique ('Lying in Politics', which gave rise to her idea of impotent bigness, was the title of her 1972 critique of the Vietnam war). Lying is, as we know, the collateral damage of warfare whose first casualty is truth. Klein is providing the psychic backdrop to Arendt's protest against the corruption and deceptions of political life, which are if anything more flagrant today. In Richard's narrative, lying is a form of self-harm, an act of blinding which then becomes the trigger for increasing violence against the other. When Klein suggests that Richard's moral outrage at Ribbentrop's lies might be due to the fact that he too is capable of aggression, I read her as saying that the one who deceives himself on such matters becomes his own – although by no means only his own – worst enemy. Lying drives aggression in deeper, leaving it no outlet finally other than the destruction of everything that litters its path (Hitler-Daddy assaulting pig-sty Mummy). When Klein offers this interpretation, Richard remains silent, 'obviously thinking over the interpretation and then smiled'. When she asks him why he smiled, 'he answered that it was because he liked thinking' (1984: 25). This does not mean that he mentally submits to her or lacks his own psychic freedom: 'How', he insists at one moment, 'can you really know what I think?' (1984: 111).

For psychoanalysis, thinking is not of course exactly thinking as it is most commonly understood. Returning to Arendt's insistence on the Kantian difference between the 'urge to know' and the 'need to think', we could say that psychoanalysis pitches its tent firmly on the side of the latter. Unconscious thinking does not know its own ends. Epistemophilia, as the strongest impulse of the infant, was a term introduced by Klein into the psychoanalytic lexicon. We yearn to know (*Sehnsucht* or yearning was Rosa Luxemburg's favourite word). Driven by sexual curiosity, the infant is pitched into a dark, shadowy world where she or he will struggle to find a place and which she or he cannot fully control, an 'ocean of uncertainty' as Arendt might say. Such control would be as murderous as it is phoney. It is the violent solution of the bad father who lashes out at the mother as a way of getting rid of what he cannot bear to countenance in himself.

In this sense, Klein can be seen as the silent psychoanalytic partner of Arendt. Klein, we might say, is giving flesh and blood to the 'passions of the hearth' outlawed from the polis by the Greek city state. And for Klein, as for Arendt, what is at issue is once again what we might call 'impotent bigness'. 'Richard's love was genuine,' she comments, 'when his predominant attitude was to protect me against the bad father, or when he himself felt persecuted by the internal father and expected protection from me' – that is, when Richard refuses the invitation to identify with the violent father in his head (1984: 426). 'He became artificial and insincere', she continues, '*when he felt he possessed the powerful penis with which he could ally himself in a hostile and dangerous way against me*' (1984: 426). Only a boy who relinquishes the fantasy of the powerful penis will stop himself from attacking the mother. Ceding his omnipotence at the very moment he is most compelled by it is the only path to a viable masculinity – calling the bluff on impotent bigness as we might say. Certainly it is the only way that this young boy, on the verge of puberty, can behave towards his woman analyst like a gentleman. Or to put it another way, violence against women is the boy's deepest wish and worst fantasy. But if he knows this, can give it thought, then it becomes a fantasy he is less likely to act upon.

If Klein is key to this discussion, it is because she is sentient of just how high the stakes are, how treacherous the ground on which she moves. She is dealing with psychotic anxiety in which she believes all human subjects have their share. The greatest anxiety that afflicts the infant is that she or he has destroyed the object; a fear which Klein distinguishes crucially from the anxiety that she or he might do so (which at least leaves open the possibility that you and the world might survive). On such finally graded psychic distinctions, the health of her patients relies. Hitler-Daddy goes on killing because he has nothing left to lose. For Klein, to skirt this perilous domain in the analytic encounter is, therefore, a sop to a world in denial (Ribbentrop's claim that Britain was the aggressor in the war). The implications for her practice – what made her and still I think makes her so controversial – resides in this. It was also at the heart of her famous dispute with Anna Freud.[4] In an extended footnote to the twenty-first session with Richard, she explains why she goes so far and why she believes it makes her patients better.

It is in fact striking that very painful interpretations – and I am particularly thinking of the interpretations referring to death and to dead internalised objects, which is a psychotic anxiety – could have the effect of reviving hope and making the patient feel more alive. My explanation for this would be that bringing a very deep anxiety nearer to consciousness, in itself produces relief. But I also believe that the very fact that the analysis gets into contact with deep-lying unconscious anxieties gives the patient a feeling of being understood and therefore revives hope. I have often met in adult patients the strong desire to have been analysed as a child. This was not only because of the obvious advantages of child analysis, but in retrospect the deep longing for having one's unconscious understood had come to the fore. Very understanding and sympathetic parents – and that can also apply to other people – are in contact with the child's unconscious, but there is still a difference between this and the understanding of the unconscious implied in psychoanalysis (1993: 100n). In such moments, Klein is making a plea – one I would wish to endorse – for a more psychoanalytically attuned world.

So, in what, then, might the renewal of hope consist (which must be the only question)? At the end of a treatment whose long-term effects Klein is not in a position to predict, Richard begins to feel compassion for his enemies. We are on the last page: 'He no longer felt impelled to turn away from destroyed objects but could experience compassion for them .... Richard, who so strongly hated the enemies threatening Britain's existence became capable

[4] See Rose (1993).

of feeling compassion for a destroyed enemy' (1993: 466). This too is a political as much as a psychic point. Before we dismiss it as unrealistic or sentimental (or both), we might remember that had the Allies felt sympathy for, and been less punitive towards, a defeated Germany after the First World War, we might not have witnessed the Second.

In her important essay on brotherhood and the law of war, Juliet Mitchell suggests there is an irreconcilable contradiction in how women are viewed in war (2013). They are both the defeated and protected – in double jeopardy as we might say. Rape as a war crime would then belong at the opposite psychic pole to what Richard arrives at here. No compassion. Probably no recognition of what you have done. Certainly, no place for your own dead objects inside your head. Instead the enemy you have defeated has to be destroyed and degraded over and over again. On this, for me, Klein's bombed, damaged, pig-sty Mummy and Arendt's thoughtlessness belong together. Klein was no social commentator, but she has described a world which repeatedly condemns itself to violence, and where women pay the price for men's self-blinding repudiation of the life of the mind.

Understanding the inner complexity of the psyche, the havoc it can play with the expected gendered arrangements, is crucial for our understanding of violence against women, and how to counter it. The fightback is in what a mind – the life of a mind no less – can do with its own history. Along with the necessary fight for public and legal recognition of violence against women today, this struggle continues to be, as I see it, one of women's best weapons against cruelty and injustice. As feminists, we do not have to – should not be asked to – choose between the two, at least, not in the world I want to live in.

REFERENCES

Arendt, Hannah. 1958. *The Human Condition*. Chicago, IL: University of Chicago Press.

1968. Rosa Luxemburg: 1871–1919. In *Men in Dark Times*. London: Jonathan Cape, pp. 33–56.

1970. *On Violence*. New York: Harcourt, Brace, Jovanovich.

1978. *The Life of the Mind*, one volume ed. New York: Harcourt, Brace, Jovanovich.

1972. Lying in Politics. In *Crises of the Republic*. New York: Harcourt, Brace, Jovanovich, pp. 1–48.

Benhabib, Seyla. 1993. Feminist Theory and Hannah Arendt's Concept of Public Space. *History of Human Sciences*, **6**(2), 97–114.

Butler, Judith. 2004. *Precarious Life – The Powers of Mourning and Violence*. London: Verso.

Dietz, Mary. 1994. Hannah Arendt and Feminist Politics. In *Hannah Arendt – Critical Essays*. Albany, NY: Suny University Press, pp. 231–60.

Ettinger, Elzbieta. 1988. *Rosa Luxemburg: A Life*. London: Harrap.

Jacques, Elliott. 1984. Foreword. In *Melanie Klein, Narrative of a Child Analysis – The Conduct of the Psycho-Analysis of Children as seen in the Treatment of a Ten-Year-Old Boy*. London: Hogarth, p. 1.

Kristeva, Julia. 2001. *Melanie Klein*. Ross Guberman, trans. New York: Columbia University Press.

Lacan, Jacques. 1973. *The Four Fundamental Concepts of Psychoanalysis*. Alan Sheridan, trans. London: Penguin.

MacKinnon, Catharine A. 1987. *Feminism Unmodified: Discourse on Life and Law*. Cambridge, MA: Harvard University Press.

2007. *Are Women Human? And Other International Dialogues*. Cambridge, MA: Harvard University Press.

Mitchell, Juliet, 2013. The Law of the Mother – Sibling Trauma and the Brotherhood of War. *Canadian Journal of Psychoanalysis*, **21**(1).

Rose, Jacqueline. 1993. War in the Nursery. In *Why War? Psychoanalysis, Politics and the Return to Melanie Klein*. Oxford: Blackwell.

2014. Woman on the Verge of Revolution: Rosa Luxemburg. In *Women in Dark Times*. London: Bloomsbury, pp. 29–66.

2020. *On Violence and on Violence Against Women*. London: Faber; New York: Farrar, Straus, Giroux.

CHAPTER 14

Trafficking, Prostitution, and Inequality: The Centrality of Gender

Catharine A. MacKinnon*

NO ONE DEFENDS TRAFFICKING; FEW DEFEND INEQUALity. Prostitution is not like this. Some support it. Many believe it politically correct to tolerate it and oppose doing anything effective about it. Most assume that, even if not desirable, prostitution is necessary, harmless, and inevitable. On my analysis, views about prostitution structure the debate on trafficking, whether prostitution is distinguished from trafficking or seen as a form of it, whether seen as a human right or a denial of human rights, and whether seen as a form of sexual freedom or its ultimate violation.

Worldwide, discussion of prostitution tracks five moral distinctions that divide what is considered the really, really bad from the not so bad. Adult prostitution is distinguished from child prostitution, indoor from outdoor, legal from illegal, voluntary from forced, and prostitution from trafficking. In the moralist view, child prostitution is always bad. Adult prostitution is not always so bad. Outdoor or street prostitution can be pretty rough. Indoor prostitution, house or brothel, less so, and maybe even can be sort of good. Illegal prostitution has problems that legal prostitution is imagined to solve. Forced prostitution is very bad. Voluntary prostitution can be not so bad. Trafficking is really, really bad.

Full citations for this shortened version of my work can be found in earlier publications (2011 (its original publication); 2017). Max Waltman is thanked for his assistance and translation of the Swedish materials.

Prostitution, if voluntary, indoor, legal, and adult, can be a tolerable life for some people.

Measured against the known facts, these distinctions occupy points on a continuum, overlap substantially, and despite being largely illusory, have very real consequences.

Within and across nations, the two fundamental positions in this debate are the sex work model and the sexual exploitation approach. When termed "sex work," prostitution is usually understood as the oldest profession, a cultural universal, consensual because paid, stigmatized because illegal, a job like any other denied that recognition, sometimes a form of liberation. Sex workers are expressing what its academic advocates term "agency." This piece of jargon variously means freely choosing, actively empowering, deciding among life chances, asserting oneself in a feisty fashion, fighting back against the forces of femininity, and resisting moralistic stereotypes, maybe a model of sex equality. The agentic actors called "sex workers" – most of them women – control the sexual interaction, are compensated for what is usually expected from women for free, and have independent lives and anonymous and autonomous sex with many partners – all behaviors usually monopolized by men. Hence liberating for women.

The sexual exploitation approach sees prostitution as the oldest oppression, as widespread as the institution of sex inequality to which it is foundational. The noun "prostitute" is seen as misleading as well as denigrating, equating who people are with what is being done to them. "Prostituted" is used instead, to highlight the people and social forces acting upon them. Not an *a priori* attribution of victim status, this term is based on considerable information on the sex trade from the women themselves,[1] when they have left prostitution termed "exited" women, who often help design and conduct the research. In this view, people are empirically found prostituted through choices precluded, options restricted, and possibilities denied.

[1] The best ever analysis of prostitution is by Rachel Moran (2015).

Prostitution in the sexual exploitation approach is observed to be overwhelmingly a product of lack of choice, the resort of people with the fewest choices or none. The coercion behind it, physical and not, produces an economic sector of sexual abuse in which the majority of the profits go to other people. The money in these transactions coerces the sex, it does not constitute consent to it, making prostitution a practice of serial rape. There can be nothing equal about it. Prostituted people pay for paid sex. People in prostitution, in this view, are wrongly saddled with a stigma that belongs to their exploiters.

Each account has its legal approach. The sex work approach favors across-the-board decriminalization with various forms of legalization, usually with state regulation, sometimes with unionization as a first step. The goal is to remove criminal sanctions from all actors in the sex industry so that prostitution becomes as legitimate as any other livelihood – as in the Netherlands, Germany, New Zealand, some Australian states, and ten counties in Nevada, although some of these, including the Netherlands and Germany, citing harms they never intended and few of the benefits they did intend, are beginning to retreat from it.

The sexual exploitation approach seeks to abolish prostitution. The best way is debated. Criminalizing the buyers – the demand for prostitution – as well as the sellers, the pimps, and traffickers, while eliminating sanctions for prostituted people, "the sold," and providing them with services and job training they say they want – is the concept pioneered in Sweden. The Swedish model, also termed the Nordic or Equality Model, has been passed in Iceland (2009), Norway (2009), Canada (2014), Northern Ireland (2014), France (2016), Ireland (2017), and Israel (2019), and is being considered in many other places.

For the Swedish model to work, at least as crucial as criminalizing the buyers and enforcing it is decriminalizing prostituted people, removing all penalties against them and providing support for exit, a strong point of the French law. This model, having shown real and well-documented promise, is increasingly favored by abolitionists at the principled and practical forefront of this movement.

Each position can be measured against a body of evidence on the sex industry, much of it uncontested, most of it provided by survivors, on the conditions of entrance, realities of treatment, and the possibilities for exit.

Everywhere, prostituted people, with few exceptions, are poor, normally destitute. Urgent financial need is the most frequent reason mentioned for being in the sex trade. Almost no one gets out of poverty through prostitution. It is not unusual to get further into poverty and deeper in debt. And the women are lucky to get out with their lives, given the mortality figures.

Disproportionately, people in prostitution are members of socially disadvantaged racial or ethnic groups or lower castes. In Vancouver, Canada, and elsewhere prostituted people are indigenous women in numbers that far exceed their proportion of the population.[2] In India, although caste is illegal, some prostitution is intergenerationally caste-based. Men heads of households in the Nat caste in some parts of India are empowered to select which young woman will support the family by prostitution; higher caste men expect Nat men to pimp women in their families and may punish them for resisting.[3] No one (*pace* Gandhi) chooses poverty. No one chooses the racial or ethnic group or caste they are born into. Based on who is in prostitution, these circumstances – that powerfully determine who is used in this industry – are not chosen by any of them.

Another global commonality is that people typically enter prostitution in childhood, well below adult age, often previously sexually abused in their intimate circle. This is not a time when you are empowered to make a choice about the rest of your life, or when you have much power to stop adults from doing things to you. In

[2] See, e.g., Christine Stark (2019).

[3] The information on the Nat caste is based on my extensive direct work, including legal, over decades with people from this caste. For further information largely from survivors, see APNE APP Women Worldwide (2015); Ghosh (2011); and the film *Love Sonia* (Noorani, 2018).

India, Nat women reported their first sexual abuse, actually their first sexual experience, in prostitution at age ten. Resistance then or later produced gang rape and torture. Extreme abuse by pimps and traffickers – in this case he could be your father – typically occurs at the beginning. Caste and sexual abuse in childhood function similarly here: they tell you who you are, what your life is for. In Kolkata, girls around age thirteen line the streets of the red light area. Once, down a narrow alley, I saw a naked girl with her legs being spread wide, tiny crotch toward the street. So when exactly did she choose?

Given the terms on which prostitution is defended, it dawned on me that this might be a good time to define sex. How about: sex is chosen and wanted and uncoerced. Presumably this is the reason prostitution's supporters defend prostitution in sexual terms. When you are having sex with someone you want to be having sex with, I would hazard that you aren't generally paying each other. Being one of those things that money cannot buy, the real thing is neither bought nor sold. In this light, if sex is for survival – the term "survival sex"[4] is sometimes used as a synonym for prostitution – *the sex is coerced by the need to survive.* Where women have sex equality rights, the law of sexual harassment recognizes this transaction as a human rights violation. The point is: what you get out of sex as such is that you are doing it. Illuminatingly, the law of Namibia crisply defines prostitution as sexual acts for consideration that is non-sexual (Henriques, 1962: 17). The consideration for sex is sex. This is what sex as a human right could look like: the right to have sex that is mutual, so equal that it is its own reward. When sex is not its own reward, women and girls, sometimes men or boys, are bought for sexual use, for proceeds that largely line the pockets of other men.

Women in prostitution in Kolkata – in numbers not that different in the United States – told me they service twenty to thirty men a day on average, with no choice over the sex or the men.

[4] "Survival sex" denotes "sex ... in exchange for food, water, shelter, protection" (UNAIDS, 2008).

Assuming two days a week off, a mercy few are shown, each woman services as many as 8,000 men a year, a few less for repeat customers.

I speak here of the demand: those who demand the sex industry exist. Some are aggressive, some contagiously ill. All are invisible in the sense that they can go anywhere in the privacy of anonymity and not stand out as buyers of women. In most languages, they have the dignity of an identity shared with non-purchaser-users of women: client, buyer, guest, passenger. In the United States, he has a real man's name: "john." Johns, often violent, make prostituted women's lives unhealthy and dangerous.

Beyond the paid sexual transactions, many prostituted women are raped by johns, meaning here *not* paid.[5] Or beaten by criminal gangs or by pimps and landlords if they show resistance or express a desire to leave, or when such abuse is the sex that the buyers want to buy.[6] Far from having police protection, in most places police sweep in to arrest the women for whatever reasons are invented: guilty of the crime of being victimized. Even prostituted children are still widely regarded not as victims but as criminals, although this is changing. In many places, she is not even old enough to have sex, it's statutory rape, but when found being sold for sex, she is booked as a criminal.

Prostituted women of color in racist cultures may be disproportionately likely to be arrested.[7] When arrested, the women typically fall even further into debt to the pimp who bails them out or pays their fine. From a legal perspective, the state contributes to her bondage by this official sex discrimination, making it even harder to leave, because now she has a criminal record. And he doesn't.

[5] Following years of intensive investigation, Dr. Mimi Silbert concluded that prostituted women were "the most raped class of women in history" (Hunter, 1993).

[6] The vast majority of prostituted people report being physically assaulted in prostitution, most often by johns. See Parriott (1994) (50 percent by john, 90 percent by someone other than john, over half of this 90 percent being beaten once per month or more); Vanwesenbeeck (1994: 91) (60 percent).

[7] See, e.g., the 2018 Federal Bureau of Investigation ("FBI") statistics, which show that 45 percent of arrests made on account of "prostitution and commercialised vice" were made of people of color (Federal Bureau of Investigation, 2018: Table 43). Presumably this includes pimps.

Proponents of sex work often insist that indoor prostitution gives one more control. Inconsistently, they sometimes also contend, with no factual support, that criminalizing the buyers makes prostitution more dangerous because it drives it indoors, hence underground. In reality, any protection or power from being indoors is a delusion (Waltman, 2014a). Street women are at the bottom of the sex industry's transnational hierarchy, the call girl, escort, and courtesan at the top for men who pay more for the upscale packaging. If this class structure of prostitution has some reality, the distinction between indoor and outdoor is a poor proxy for it. Although street women do not have much choice over johns, they can decide not to get in that car if he seems creepy or they were warned. Women in brothels usually have no choice at all. They are lined up for selection; the men pick them. The video surveillance in the brothels – pimps do watch this live pornography – and the panic buttons in the rooms often fail to get her help soon enough. Indoor prostitution, the dominant form of legalized prostitution, tends to mean more pimp control and even less accountability.

The indoor–outdoor distinction also feeds the illusion that the women in prostitution who appear classy really do have upper-class options: that they are exercising free choice – perhaps a bad one – are being well paid, enjoying themselves (some women being "like that"), could leave anytime they want, are relatively safe if careful, and are not being compelled or hurt, at least not much. All this is belied by the empirical studies and reported survivor experience.

Not long ago, sex work proponents denied any harm in prostitution. Overwhelmed by the reality survivors have revealed, these days some harm is at times recognized, usually attributed to prostitution's illegal status, in the "harm minimization," "harm reduction" (prominent in New Zealand) approach. These terms concede some harm will remain. The imperative is to clean up some harms so prostitution itself can stay, as if the two can be separated.

Groups dedicated to this notion suck up vast amounts of international funds devoted to addressing HIV/AIDS. The sex work cabal discovered this lucrative profit center, supporting the pernicious brothel system in India, for example, so that condoms could be distributed there. When prostitution is seen as commercial sexual exploitation, resulting cases of AIDS are understood as a symptom, the cause of which is prostitution itself – sex with thousands of men a year under conditions that you cannot realistically control. The sex work perspective protects the buyers from the women, so they can keep using them without getting sick, rather than protecting the women from the buyers, who are making them lethally ill. Everyone supports less harm to the women. But harm elimination is not part of the sex work agenda because it is inconsistent with sex for sale.

Whether on the street or in a brothel, legal or illegal, the majority of prostituted women's measured level of post traumatic stress (PTSD) is equivalent to that of combat veterans, victims of torture, or rape (Farley et al., 2004). PTSD results from living through atrocities you cannot mentally sustain. Understandably, it often produces dissociation: you put the violation away, leave mentally because you cannot leave physically, later forget or repress or deny it or act like it is not there inside you, although it is. You disappear the self who knows about this, the one who goes out and does it, to get through the day, or the night. Often drugs or alcohol are used for similar reason – partly numbing the pain of the constantly reinflicted trauma, distancing the body and mind from what is being done – while making her dependent on the pimp for the next fix.

The abuse that is constant in prostitution, endemic to it, requires dissociation from oneself and the world to survive. You may create another self, give her another name. "She" does this, and may defend doing it. If you cannot live inside your own head and be who you are – is that what freedom looks like? Being subjected to constant rape, beaten to stay, prevented from looking into other options, sustaining the trauma of a torture chamber, needing drugs to get through it – is this what you mean by employment? Do you want this job?

Across cultures and at all levels of economic development, street or house, legal or illegal, union or not, when asked what do you need most, the spontaneous answer of an average of 89 per cent of people in prostitution is to leave prostitution but I don't know how (Farley et al., 2004: 51). Whether you are in your own country or another, however you entered the sex industry, being in a situation of prostitution that you cannot get out of when you want to has been aptly defined by Kathleen Barry as "sexual slavery" (1984: 39–40).

Many women are prostituting in their country of origin, but many in richer destination countries are from destitute, poverty-stricken families from poorer countries. Someone said they could get her a good job and she woke up locked in a brothel. Someone sold her to someone else who bought her. She is then owned by someone who rents her out to others who use her sexually. These events and dynamics are not limited to exotic far-away places; they are paralleled and reproduced inside nations all over the world.

Slavery is internationally defined as the exercise of powers of ownership over a person (UN OHCHR, 1926). When pimps sell you for sex to johns who buy you and you want to leave but cannot, you are a sex slave by international legal definition, whether you have ever been beaten or crossed a border.

So far, I have been analyzing prostitution as an institution of class, race, caste, and age inequality. Men and women both are poor, young, and members of disadvantaged classes, racial groups, and lower castes. Yet men are not found selling sex in anything like the numbers that women, including trans women are, although sometimes they do. So: why are prostituted people so often women? The answer – with little disagreement in an otherwise contentious debate – is gender inequality. Some women rank higher than other women on the basis of race, ethnicity, religion, caste, or class, as well as in the terms of their sexual use. Women try to work their way up within the female sex to avoid or deny the existence of a denigrating sexual definition, or its application to them. Those who fail and fall to its floor are in prostitution, where those who are defined as being for sex reside. No one fights to become a prostitute against all the odds. She is in prostitution when the odds beat her.

If prostitution were a choice, one would think that more men would be found exercising it.[8] But boys, even sexually abused or prostituted boys, grow into men, with the options masculinity provides men, which are better than most women's, even when they are not good. Nobody chooses the single attribute that most prostituted people share, the single most powerful determinant for being sold for sex: the sex they were born with, thus the gender society assigns them. Or, if transgender, the sex or gender they affirm or transition to, combined with gender-discriminatory exclusion from gainful employment as who they are.

Worldwide sex inequality gives most members of the male sex the privilege to have being bought and sold for sex defined as not your true destiny, character, and worth. Something went wrong for you. Men also have masculinity's privilege of choosing to sell and buy women, men, trans people, and children of both sexes. This is a real choice. The sex industry exists because millions of men, whom no one is forcing, exercise this free, if conditioned, choice.

So, what exactly is bought and sold in prostitution? Mainly, some men are selling women to other men for intimate access and power. The buyers are buying "you do what I say" sex: the sex of no backtalk, of not having to relate to her as a person, of being served and serviced, of being with a switched-off, dissociated person who is not really there. This gaze of prostituted women is the look of women in pornography: the blank, gone, what men call "sexy" look, counting the cracks in the ceiling, watching the clock, thinking of England. This is the sex of not doing anything for the

[8] "Seldom do we see proposals that poor men should make their way out of poverty by welcoming the insertion of penises and other objects into them on a regular basis" (Ekberg, 2002).

woman sexually, as he kids himself that all she wants is to be there doing exactly this for big, sexy, irresistible him.

To be fair, most johns know the women don't enjoy the sex. They know the women are there out of economic necessity for the most part. But "consenting" is what he thinks she is doing, even though he knows she doesn't want to do this and has no viable alternative.[9] This is an ideological position. Consent in liberal philosophy is used to legitimize the rule of the rulers over the ruled, specifically to legitimize the state, although women, for instance, had no say in it whatever. The ruled are deemed to perform this "consent" just by not rebelling and by keeping silent and not leaving, whether dissent or exit are possible or not. In law, one also "consents" to something that may be necessary but would be harmful without agreement, or is inherently dangerous, like having your body cut into. Sex does not have to be like this, but men apparently think that, for women, it is. Get real. "We consented" is not how anyone describes an exciting, intimate, sexual encounter. Consent is a pathetic standard for sex between free people. What it is doing in the debate over prostitution is making men feel better about sex they know the women did not sexually want, which makes it good for business (as well as for male dominance, i.e., rule). For her, she is having the sex of the sexually abused child, that is, sex that you would never be having except that he has more power than you do.

Consent is an intrinsically sex-stereotyped unequal concept: an actor and acted-upon with no guarantee of any kind of equality between them, of circumstance or condition or interaction, or typically even any interest in inquiring into whether such equality is present or meaningful.[10] A lot of sex, such as in marriage, it is said, is unequal, although the old rule of deeming consent to sex via consent to marriage is not respected in many places anymore. There is an exit ramp built into marriage, despite its uneven

9 See, e.g., Macleod et al. (2008); Malarek (2009: 103).

10 For further discussion, see MacKinnon (2016: 431).

availability, called divorce, for which no parallel exists in prostitution.

Sex that is unequal by physical force, we have decided we can do something about. It's called rape. Sex that is unequal by third-party constraint, we have decided we can do something about that, too. It's called trafficking and pimping. Sex that is unequal by economic survival in the paid labor force – sexual harassment – we do something about that; it's called sex discrimination. Sex for survival pure and simple – the coercion of prostitution – we can do something about that too.

Prostitution is not just like any other job. Setting limits on the intimacy and intrusiveness of the demands that can be made on a person is the whole purpose of human rights and labor law. Yet the notion that prostitution is work generates the same illuminating parallels everywhere. What's the matter with prostitution that isn't also wrong with cleaning toilets? Disposing of hazardous waste? Losing your hand in a factory? Dying building a bridge abutment? The progressive people who proffer these comparisons have never defended these jobs or conditions or accidents as examples of human rights before or since. I suspect those who see prostitution as a sad but kind option for some poor and unfortunate women – an option they are so enlightened, tolerant, and considerate as to defend as a matter of policy – would be among the first to identify the human rights violations involved if everyone who was doing these things was of one disadvantaged race, or all were undocumented immigrants, far less if 89 percent wanted to leave but were kept from doing so and someone else was pocketing most of their earnings. And if this was not women and sex. None of these jobs is prepared for by sexual abuse in childhood. None produces prostitution's PTSD rates. The operative shared underlying assumption is "someone has to do it." Without passing on the need for clean toilets or factories or bridges, no one has to do what is done in prostitution. No one ever died from lack of sex.

If the line between sex and labor can seem indistinct at times, it is not because being sexually violated is a job, even if money is thrown at the violated person. And it is not only because a lot of women's work is sexualized to our disadvantage. It is because, as many of the authors in this book show, a lot of labor is gendered unequal. This includes sexual exploitation, and many people who are trafficked for labor end up in the sex industry.

The work analogy also overlooks the relations involved, which, this being sex, overlooks everything. Slavery doesn't make the work not work, but the relations don't make it just a job either, and what is mainly done in slavery *is* work, no longer defended as such. Nor does unionization change who is used in prostitution and how, or make it easier to leave. If prostitution is work, a human right, so is debt bondage. Debt bondage involves actual work; choices are made every step of the way. There are often contracts. Does that mean it is just a job, an alternative to the welfare state, not a human rights violation? Are decisions forced by desperation and precluded alternatives what human rights means by choice?

Finally, in the analogy department, with respect to my academic colleagues who contend that prostituting is not all that different from the thinking and writing they do[11] – we all sell ourselves, they say – prostitution in the real world is not a metaphor for their luxurious appropriation. Apart from the differing assault and mortality rates, and that no one has ever put a gun to anyone's head to make them be a law professor, some of us do not do "you do what I say" scholarship. Our thinking and writing is not for sale.

Proponents of the sex work model sometimes suggest that anyone who is against prostitution is against sex. The sex they are talking about is the abuse described here. It is like saying that being against rape is being against sex. Indeed, it actually *is* saying that. The same group sometimes also insists that the abuse, rape, and beatings are invented or exaggerated by us ideologically motivated, repressed, sex-panicked Victorian prudes and whiners who just don't have what it takes to make it as whores. The pimps

[11] See, e.g., "Professors, factory workers, lawyers, opera singers, prostitutes, doctors, legislators – we all do things with parts of our bodies for which we receive a wage in return" (Nussbaum, 1998: 693).

are invented too, apparently. Prostituted women, in their view, are independent entrepreneurs; well, maybe some have managers.

The first fault line in the denial of prostitution's harm came when it was conceded that children should not be prostituted. No one ever says precisely why. If prostitution is freedom, equality, liberation, and empowerment, if it makes a woman's life more autonomous and independent, if it is a chosen career, and its harms are occasional or negligible and can be minimized and contained, do tell what on earth is wrong with children doing it or seeing it being done? Nobody says. They also don't say what precisely changes when she's 17 years and 366 days old. If no one could enter commercial sex as a child, the sex industry would be depopulated overnight (making attractive a look-back legal provision for adults who were abused as children). Few try to deny that most women enter the sex industry as children with previously violated childhoods. What is denied is that defending the prostitution of adults supports their continuous violation on the rationale that they are no longer little girls.

Adults and children in the sex trade are not two separate groups of people. They are the same group at two points in time. One consequence of childhood sexual abuse, fought by its survivors in or outside prostitution, is feeling valued and approved when you are being sexually violated, while also feeling ashamed, humiliated, and worthless. Sexual abuse in childhood makes it seem that prostitution is where you belong, while law, policy, and popular culture just wait for you to live long enough to be written off as a consenting adult. Recognizing the harm of prostitution to children only is a strategic retreat to allow its intrinsic harms to continue.

The second concession by the sex work defenders has been to criticize sex trafficking while defending prostitution. But what is trafficking? Internationally, the Palermo Protocol definition (UN OHCHR, 2000), which is sweeping the world, includes being sexually exploited through force, fraud, or coercion for commercial sex. That definition and the industry's reality also include terms often elided by sex work's avatars: sexual exploitation through "abuse of power or of a position of vulnerability."[12] Caste, race, or age can be conditions of vulnerability, as, actually, can poverty, sex, and gender.[13] Sex trafficking is transportation, transfer, harboring, or receipt of a human being for purposes of sexual exploitation, so defined. This is simply what pimps do. Movement across jurisdictional lines is not, and has not been, an element of the international definition of trafficking since at least 1949 (United Nations OHCHR, 1949: 33). The *sine qua non* of trafficking is thus neither border crossing nor severe violence. It is *third-party involvement.* Most prostituted people are pimped, meaning trafficked.[14] You cannot traffic yourself, which distinguishes trafficking, in theory, from some prostitution. Sexual exploitation can also be slavery: internationally, exercising rights of ownership over a person.[15] You cannot enslave yourself either. Johns, of course, exploit prostituted people as well.

While most places make prostituted people criminals because they are being victimized, those who victimize them are typically let off the hook in law or fact. What Sweden has done since 1999, seeing that prostitution is violence against women,[16] is penalize

[12] One use of the Palermo definition that elides these elements; *see* ECOSOC (2002).

[13] South Africa's trafficking law defines "abuse of vulnerability" as

> any abuse that leads a person to believe that he or she has no reasonable alternative but to submit to exploitation, and includes, but is not limited to, taking advantage of the vulnerabilities of that person resulting from – (a) the person having entered or remained in the Republic illegally or without proper documentation; (b) pregnancy; (c) any disability of the person; (d) addiction to the use of any dependence-producing substance; (e) being a child; (f) social circumstances; or (g) economic circumstances

unless context indicates otherwise. Prevention and Combating of Trafficking in Persons Act, 2013, Act 7-2013 (No. 36715) (S. Afr.).

[14] Farley et al. (2014: 1042), calculating internationally an average of 84 percent of prostituted people are under third-party control, pimped, or trafficked.

[15] See, e.g., UN OHCHR (2000), incorporating "slavery or practices similar to slavery" into its definition of trafficking.

[16] The bill criminalizing purchase of sex in Sweden in 1998 stated: "Men's violence against women is not consonant with the aspirations toward a gender equal society, and has to be fought against by all means. In such a society it is also unworthy and

the driver of the industry, the buyer, making purchasing sex a crime and enforcing it.[17] It has extended support to those who want to leave, although more is needed, which France provides (National Assembly, 2016). Eliminating her criminality raises her status; criminalizing him lowers his privilege, usually higher to begin with. That makes Sweden's a substantive sex equality law in inspiration and effect (Waltman, 2014b: 277–86, 294–98). There, the law cut street prostitution by about two-thirds from 1998 to 2014 (Mujaj & Netscher, 2015: 9–10, 18–19). The notion that "the Nordic countries are special," some egalitarian paradise, as the reason the Swedish model has worked by gravity outside the law itself, is belied by the experiences of her Scandinavian neighbors. In Denmark, and Norway, where buying sex was legal at the time, prostitution, indoors and outdoors, increased dramatically during the same period (Kotsadam & Jakobsson, 2014). Sweden has reported the lowest trafficking rate in Europe, likely due to pimps' and johns' fears of detection.[18] Prostitution happens when nothing is in its way. Demand for prostitution, in other words, is soft demand. No substantial amount of prostitution can go undetected, since prostituted people need to be sufficiently visible, online or otherwise, to attract potential johns.[19] The Swedish law creates no underground. If the johns can find their desired targets, the police can find the johns, and the researchers can find them all.

unacceptable that men obtain temporary sex with women for remuneration." Prop. 1997/98:55 Kvinnofrid 22 (Swed.).

[17] See *Lag om förbud mot köp av sexuella tjänster (Svensk författningssamling [SFS] 1998:408)* (Sweden); *Lag om ändring i brottsbalken* (SFS, 2005:90) (parliamentary amendment of *Brottsbalken [BrB] [Penal Code]* 6:11 (Swed.); *Lag om ändring i brottsbalken* (SFS, 2011: 517); *see also* Proposition [Prop.] 2010/11:77 *Skärpt straff för köp av sexuell tjänst.*

[18] National Criminal Investigation Department [*Rikspolisstyrelsen*] (2009: 10; 2003: 34). "[T]he ban on the purchase of sexual services acts as a barrier to human traffickers and procurers considering establishing themselves in Sweden" (2003: 37).

[19] See, e.g., National Criminal Investigation Department [*Rikspolisstyrelsen*] (2003: 120). Note the police receive information on prostitution "through Internet surveillance, physical surveillance, tip-offs from the public at large and other sources" (2003: 35).

No woman has been murdered in prostitution in Sweden since 1999. In Germany, at least eighty-four completed and forty-eight attempted murders of prostituted persons were committed by johns or others in the prostitution milieu between legalization in 2002 and August 2019.[20] Several such murders have also been reported in New Zealand since prostitution was decriminalized in 2003 (White, 2015). Female, male, and transgender people in prostitution after the law was passed in Sweden described how johns became very careful, knowing they could be reported, while the prostituted persons could not be reported at all. This leverage strengthened prostituted persons' control, safety, security, and ability to defend their personal integrity.[21]

After ten years in effect, the Swedish government concluded that its law was working as hoped (Statens Offentliga Utredningar [SOU], 2010: 49, 120, 123, 128, 130 232). Survivors reported that the law had empowered them by stopping them from blaming themselves, shifting the responsibility to the johns for the mental scars and difficult memories they live with (SOU, 2010: 130). The stigma of prostitution more generally may be shifting to the buyers. Contrary to the lies being circulated, as the sex industry goes into panic mode, this model is the only legal approach to prostitution that has ever even partly worked against the sex industry in the history of the world.[22]

[20] A voluntary initiative counts known prostitution murders (and attempts) reported in the media or verified through other sources. *See* Sex Industry Kills (2019).

[21] Larsdotter et al., 2011: 98–99, 245, 260; National Board of Health and Welfare [*Socialstyrelsen*], 2004: 34 (reporting, inter alia, an informant who knew "several" prostituted women who had "dared to file rape complaints" against buyers because the new law was "a source of strength and support.").

[22] The law's critics sometimes say that other Swedish laws, including migration and housing, are applied to deny residence permits to prostituted persons and/or obstruct indoor prostitution. See, e.g., Vuolajärvi (2019). To remedy this, Sweden's laws must be strengthened, not revoked. To date, whether the prostituted person is an injured party with rights of a crime victim is considered case by case. The threshold is too high in practice. Many foreign prostituted persons in Sweden do not dare testify against pimps and traffickers, because they risk the charges being downgraded from human trafficking to procuring, which excludes them from rights to health care, housing, residence permits, and other crime victim support. See Swedish Police

When prostitution is legalized, by contrast, trafficking goes through the roof.[23] It makes economic sense. Once the women and children are installed, the profits from operating in the open are astronomical. Illegal prostitution also explodes under legalization, as visible in Australian venues.[24] Legal brothels require protections the johns do not want, so they go next door to the illegal brothels and pay more. This makes life even more dangerous for the often illegal immigrant women in those brothels, who are in more danger to begin with, and are typically paid less if at all.

Legalization, the sex industry's main goal, is a failed experiment. The German government has concluded that legalizing the sex industry there failed to deliver any of its promised benefits. It hasn't reduced crime, organized crime's hold, or trafficking; it hasn't made it easier to leave, healthier, or safer (Federal Ministry for Family Affairs, Senior Citizens, Women and Youth, 2007: 79). It does corrode law enforcement apparatus and leads society to think that there is nothing wrong with it. The New Zealand government committee inquiring into prostitution laws in 2008 similarly found that violence against women in prostitution and the social stigma surrounding the sex industry continued despite decriminalization (New Zealand Government, 2008).

One reason legalization doesn't work is that most women in prostitution do not want prostitution to be all their lives are ever going to be, and being legal means deciding that prostitution will be part of your official life story. Most prostituted women, even if they have to do this right now, have dreams. So they resort to the illegal prostitution that flourishes under legal prostitution, and receive few if any of its purported benefits.

In light of this evidence, the moral distinctions that structure law and policy on this topic emerge as ideological and confused, making more socially tolerable and endlessly debatable an industry of viciousness and naked exploitation. Most adult women in

Authority [Polismyndigheten] (2018: 70); Christina Halling et al. (2012: 10–16, 29–30, 40–41). All prostituted persons should be considered victims of crime.

[23] See, e.g., Sullivan (2007). [24] See, e.g., Sullivan & Jeffreys (2002); Sullivan (2005).

prostitution are first prostituted as girls and are just never able to escape. As they age out, they retain the vulnerabilities of class, caste, sex, and often race, combined with a criminal record and almost always psychological devastation. Sexually stigmatized, women are discriminated against so that sex is all they have to sell. Traffickers and pimps are incentivized to grab girls when they are most powerless, hence most desirable to the market; then, with each day that passes, their exploitation is more blamed on them. When used indoors, prostituted women are industrially accessible to pimps and johns and invisible to most everyone else. Legal and illegal regimes inflict the same harms and pathologies, many of which get worse with across-the-board legality. At the core of prostitution are forms and amounts of force that make it hard to believe that a free person with real options would ever voluntarily elect it.

Perhaps the deepest injury of prostitution is that there is no dignity in it. Calling it sex work when it is not sex in the sense of intimacy and mutuality, or work in the sense of productivity and self-support, can be a desperate grab toward that lost dignity, as well as a cooptation for the sex industry of the dignity that the exploited never lose.

An adequate law or policy to promote the rights of prostituted people has three parts: decriminalize and support the exit of people in prostitution, penalize the buyers strongly, and criminalize third-party profiteers. To promote equality, the violators have to be closed down, the world opened up to the violated. This is what they are asking for. Not one woman in prostitution I have ever met wants her children to have that life. What does that say, except that prostitution chose her?

Unlike sex industry advocates, prostituted women – those I work with and for – have no difficulty envisioning their lives outside of prostitution. They see real work, love, dignity, and hope.

REFERENCES

APNE APP Women Worldwide. 2015. *Red Light Despatch*, **VIII**(9). http://apneaap.org/wp-content/uploads/2012/11/RLD_September-2015.pdf.

Barry, Kathleen. 1984. *Female Sexual Slavery.* New York: New York University Press.

ECOSOC. 2002. Recommended Principles and Guidelines on Human Rights and Human Trafficking. May 20, U.N. Doc. E/2002/68/Add. 1, at 7 n.6.

Ekberg, Gunilla S. 2002. The International Debate About Prostitution and Trafficking in Women: Refuting the Arguments. Unpublished paper: Seminar on the Effects of Legalisation of Prostitution Activities, Stockholm, Sweden.

Farley, Melissa et al. 2004. Prostitution and Trafficking in Nine Countries: An Update on Violence and Posttraumatic Stress Disorder. *Journal of Trauma Practice,* **2**(3–4), 33–74.

Farley, M., Franzblau, K. and Kennedy, M. A. 2014. Online Prostitution and Trafficking. *Albany Law Review,* **77**(3), 1039–94.

Federal Bureau of Investigation. 2018. Table 43: Arrests by Race and Ethnicity. https://ucr.fbi.gov/crime-in-the-u.s/2018/crime-in-the-u.s.-2018/topic-pages/tables/table-43.

Federal Ministry for Family Affairs, Senior Citizens, Women and Youth. 2007. Report by the German Federal Government on the Impact of the Act Regulating the Legal Situation of Prostitutes. Publikationsverstand der Bundesregierung. www.bmfsfj.de.

Ghosh, S. N. 2011. Review: Anuja Agrawal, Chaste Wives and Prostitute Sisters: Patriarchy and Prostitution among the Bedias of India. *Indian Journal of Gender Studies,* **18**(2), 263–66.

Halling, Christina et al. 2012. Svårigheter och möjligheter i organiseringen av stöd till offer för människohandel för sexuella ändamål i Sverige. [*Difficulties and Potential in the Organization of Support to Victims of Human Trafficking for Sexual Purposes in Sweden*]. Malmö: Malmö University. https://perma.cc/6GV8-DZCB.

Henriques, Fernando. 1962. *Prostitution And Society: A Survey.* London: MacGibbon & Kee.

Hunter, Susan Kay. 1993. Prostitution is Cruelty and Abuse to Women and Children. *Michigan Journal of Gender and Law,* **91**(1), 91–104.

Kotsadam, Andreas and Jakobsson, Niklas. 2014. "Shame on You, John! Laws, Stigmatization, and the Demand for Sex. *European Journal of Law and Economics,* 37(3), 393–404.

Larsdotter, Suzann, et al. 2011. Osynliga synliga aktörer: Hbt-personer med erfarenhet av att sälja och/eller köpa sexuella tjänster [*Invisible Visible Actors: LGBT People with Experience in Selling and/or Buying Sexual Services*]. RFSL. https://perma.cc/X5PY-TSB3.

MacKinnon, Catharine. 2011. Trafficking, Prostitution, and Inequality. *Harvard Civil Rights-Civil Liberties Law Review,* **46**(2), 271–309.

2016. Rape Redefined. *Harvard Law and Policy Review,* **10**(2), 431–77.

2017. *Butterfly Politics.* Cambridge, MA: The Belknap Press of Harvard University Press.

Macleod, Jan et al. 2008. A Research Report Based on Interviews with 110 Men Who Bought Women in Prostitution. Women's Support Project. www

.prostitutionresearch.com/wp-content/uploads/2008/04/ChallengingDemandScotland.pdf.

Malarek, Victor. 2009. *The Johns: Sex for Sale and the Men Who Buy It.* New York: Arcade Publishing.

Moran, Rachel. 2015. *Paid For: My Journey Through Prostitution.* Dublin: Gill Books.

Mujaj, Endrit and Netscher, Amanda. 2015. Prostitutionen i Sverige 2014. En omfattningskartläggning [Prostitution in Sweden 2014. A Scope Survey]. Länsstyrelsen [County Administrative Board] Stockholm. https://perma.cc/2ML4-6LMR.

National Assembly, Fr. 2016. Texte Adopté 716 Proposition de loi visant à renforcer la lutte contre le système prostitutionnel et à accompagner les personnes prostituées [*Text adopted 716, Bill proposing to strengthen the fight against the prostitution system and to accompany prostitutes*]. April 6. www2.assemblee-nationale.fr/documents/notice/14/ta/ta0716/%28index%29/ta.

National Board of Health and Welfare [*Socialstyrelsen*]. 2004. Prostitution in Sweden 2003. Stockholm: SoS. https://perma.cc/0vWJVmQN1Ea.

National Criminal Investigation Department [*Rikspolisstyrelsen*]. 2003. Trafficking in Women: Situation Report no. 5. https://perma.cc/QXD7-DVMN.

2009. Lägesrapport 10: Människohandel för sexuella och andra ändamål 2007–2008. https://perma.cc/9ZAV-N8CQ.

New Zealand Government. 2008. Report of the Prostitution Law Review Committee on the Operation of the Prostitution Reform Act 2003. www.justice.govt.nz/policy/commercial-property-and-regulatory/prostitution/prostitution-law-review-committee/publications/plrc-report/report-of-the-prostitution-law-review-committee-on-the-operation-of-the-prostitution-reform-act-2003

Noorani, Tabrez. 2018. *Love Sonia* (film). Zee Studios.

Nussbaum, Martha C. 1998. 'Whether from Reason or Prejudice': Taking Money for Bodily Services. *Journal of Legal Studies*, **27** (S2), 693–94.

Parriott, Ruth. 1994. Health Experiences of Women Used in Prostitution: Survey Findings and Recommendations. Available from the University of Minnesota Digital Conservancy: http://hdl.handle.net/11299/205150.

Sex Industry Kills. 2019. Prostituiertenmorde in Deutschland. Last updated August 4. https://sexindustry-kills.de/doku.php?id=prostitutionmurders:de; https://perma.cc/8WPK-LQCR.

Swedish Police Authority [*Polismyndigheten*]. 2018. Människohandel för sexuella och andra ändamål: Lägesrapport 19 [*Human Trafficking for Sexual and Other Purposes: Situation Report 19*]. https://perma.cc/3CUX-YR7G.

Stark, Christine. 2019. Strategies to Restore Justice for Sex Trafficked Native Women. In John Winterdyk and Jackie Jones, eds., *The Palgrave International Handbook of Human Trafficking* 1. Basingstoke: Palgrave Macmillan, pp. 1–22. https://link.springer.com/referenceworkentry/10.1007%2F978-3-319-63192-9_123-1.

Statens Offentliga Utredningar [SOU]. 2010: Förbud mot köp av sexuell tjänst: En utvärdering 1999–2008 [*Prohibition Against Purchase of Sexual Service: An Evaluation 1999–2008*]. July 2. www.government.se/articles/2011/03/evaluation-of-the-prohibition-of-the-purchase-of-sexual-services.

Sullivan, Mary. 2005. What Happens When Prostitution Becomes Work: An Update on Legalisation of Prostitution in Australia. www.feministes-radicales.org/wp-content/uploads/2012/03/Mary-Sullivan-CATW-What-Happens-When-Prostitution-Becomes-Work...-An-Update-on-Legalisation-of-Prostitution-in-Australia.pdf.

2007. *Making Sex Work: A Failed Experiment with Legalised Prostitution.* North Melbourne, Australia: Spinifex Press.

Sullivan, Mary Lucille and Sheila Jeffreys. 2002. Legalization: The Australian Experience. *Violence Against Women,* **8**(9), 1140–48.

UN OHCHR. 1926. Slavery Convention, art. 1(1), Sept. 25. 46 Stat. 2183, 2191, 60 L.N.T.S. 253, 263.

1949. Convention for the Suppression of the Traffic in Persons and of the Exploitation of the Prostitution of Others, art. 1, December 2, G.A. Res. 317 (IV), U.N. Doc. A/1251.

2000. Protocol to Prevent, Suppress and Punish Trafficking in Persons, Especially Women and Children, Supplementing the United Nations Convention Against Transnational Organized Crime art. 3(a). November 2. G.A. Res. 25 (II), at 54, U.N. Doc. A/55/383.

UNAIDS. 2008. Inter-Agency Task Team on Gender & HIV/AIDS, Fact Sheet: HIV/AIDS, Gender and Sex Work 1. www.unfpa.org/hiv/docs/factsheet_genderwork.pdf.

Vanwesenbeeck, Ine. 1994. *Prostitutes' Well-Being and Risk,* 1st ed. Amsterdam: VU University Press.

Vuolajärvi, Niina. 2019. Governing in the Name of Caring – the Nordic Model of Prostitution and its Punitive Consequences for Migrants Who Sell Sex. *Sexuality Research and Social Policy,* **16**(2), 151–65.

Waltman, Max. 2014a. Assessing Evidence, Arguments, and Inequality in Bedford v. Canada. *Harvard Journal of Law & Gender,* **37**(2), 459–503.

2014b. The Politics of Legal Challenges to Pornography: Canada, Sweden, and the United States. *Stockholm Studies in Politics, 160.* Stockholm: Stockholm University. PhD thesis. https://papers.ssrn.com/sol3/papers.cfm?abstract_id=2539998.

White, Penny. 2015. Commentary, "Remembering the Murdered Women Erased by the Pro-Sex Work Agenda." Feminist Current, November 13. www.feministcurrent.com/2015/11/03/remembering-the-murdered-women-erased-by-the-pro-sex-work-agenda/; https://perma.cc/CS8A-JMPU.

CHAPTER 15

Gender, Revenge, Mutation, and War

Akbar Ahmed

MANY MUSLIM WOMEN – PARTICULARLY MUSLIM TRIbal women – face daunting problems in numerous countries today as a result of the "war on terror" era conflicts that have taken men away from homes and threaten the often-fragile security of the families left behind. Traditionally independently minded and distinct Muslim tribal societies who live by a code of honor and are governed by councils of elders, from West Africa to South Asia, have been locked in brutal conflicts with central governments that, for decades, have sought to control them and subsume them into a centralized system.

After 9/11, the US and other nations focused on the so-called "ungoverned spaces" of Muslim tribal societies on the periphery in hunting terrorists, allying with central governments and utilizing technologies such as the drone which have exacerbated center–periphery tensions. The turmoil of these brutal conflicts has led to the breakdown of traditional structures of Muslim tribal society and has resulted in a mutation of tribal codes. Wanton acts of violence have resulted which violate both traditional codes and Islamic custom and law.

American missiles, attacks by government security forces using helicopter gunships and heavy artillery, suicide bombers, and tribal warfare have traumatized populations over vast swathes of the world as millions seek shelter and flee their homes. Women have found themselves as destitute refugees in larger faraway cities, struggling to feed and protect their children, and are open to exploitation and harassment. The children they struggle to bring up in these diminished circumstances are particularly vulnerable to being recruited into violent causes. On top of this there is a horrifyingly high incidence of rape of women by government security forces.

As a result of this chaos, for the first time in history, women in Muslim tribal societies have adopted suicide bombing to avenge the wrongs they believe have been inflicted on them and their families. As Mignon Nixon argues in this volume, "War cements the social by exporting our destructiveness." The impact on women of the global fight against terrorism in Muslim tribal societies and how the situation might be improved has been a crucially significant, though rarely discussed, side of the conflict. Without understanding the role and importance of gender in the analysis, the full impact of the war on terror cannot be understood. Adapted from the book *The Thistle and the Drone: How America's War on Terror Became a Global War on Tribal Islam* (2013),[1] which examined forty case studies of Muslim tribal societies, this chapter will utilize many of these case studies to help us in understanding how the war on terror has become a war on women.

Each person in these tribal societies – from the Pashtun of Afghanistan and Pakistan to Yemenis and Syrians, from the Tuareg of West Africa to the Tausug of the Philippines – faces the same dilemma within their particular political and social contexts: attempting to reconcile Islam, with its categorical prohibition of suicide and the killing of innocents, and tribal identity, with its emphasis on honor and revenge, in the midst of such rapid turmoil and change. They are tilting to their much older tribal identity rooted in the code of honor, but even this code is now mutating.

In September 2012, for example, a female suicide bomber blew herself up with at least thirteen people at Kabul airport as "revenge" for an offensive American film attacking the Prophet

[1] This book was completed while the author was the Diane Middlebrook and Carl Djerassi Visiting Professor at the University of Cambridge Centre for Gender Studies, 2012.

of Islam. In Iraq between 2007 and 2008, twenty-seven suicide bombers in Diyala Province were women (Chulov, 2008). Similar incidents in other tribal societies illustrate the far-reaching impact of the mutation of tribal honor and revenge. Chechnya offers a prime example. In June 2000 two teenage girls, seventeen-year-old Khava Barayeva, the niece of a prominent Chechen rebel leader killed the previous year, and her best friend Luiza Magomadova, aged sixteen, became the first known Chechen suicide bombers when they drove a truck full of explosives into a Russian army base in their home village of Alkhan-Yurt. Khava's *cri de coeur* expressed her anger and frustration in a prerecorded video with Luiza, and could be that of any of the other female suicide bombers:

> Sisters, the time has come. When the enemy has killed almost all our men, our brothers and husbands, we are the only ones left to take revenge for them. The time has come for us to take up arms and defend our home, our land from those who bring death to our home. And if we have to become *shakhids* for Allah we will not stop. *Allah Akbar!* . . . Our forefather[s] would have killed anyone who tried to [touch] their women but today Muslim women are getting attacked and raped in front of those who claim to be men they have no sense of jealousy for their Muslim sisters honour to the extent that they sit and drink tea while listening to this appalling news!! Do you consider yourselves men? …. This life is not worth anything – every person will die and leave this life behind …. So why do we not choose the best way to die, martyrdom, the highest most eminent way? We have chosen this way for ourselves and hope you will choose this way too inshallah. (Murphy, 2010: 140; Larzillière, 2017: n.14)

THE CAUCASIAN CASE

Khava and Luiza's words demonstrate the place of women in *Nokhchalla,* the Chechen code of honor, which is the equivalent of other codes such as *Pashtunwali* among the Pashtun. The case illustrates how the code has mutated with the destruction of traditional society. Under *Nokhchalla*, if a man takes the life of a woman or rapes her, male members of her family have the right to kill two members of the offender's family. Khava and Luiza's anger is directed as much against the Russians, whom they accuse of rape, as against their own men, whom they blame for failing to defend their honor. The duty of men to protect the honor of women is illustrated in a Chechen story about a man who accidentally brushed his little finger against the hand of the woman in whose home he was staying as a guest. To protect her honor, the man cut off his finger.

The bloodshed that followed Russia's all-out attempts to crush Chechnya's bid to secede after the collapse of the Soviet Union threw Chechen society into ferment. In 1996, Chechens succeeded in expelling the Russians, but in 1999 the Russians returned with more than 90,000 troops and killed between 30,000 and 40,000 Chechen civilians. Entire families were decimated. Eleven close relatives of the Chechen leader Shamil Basayev, including his wife, daughters, and brother, were killed in May 1995 (Myers, 2006). In 2000 Basayev stepped on a landmine and needed to have his foot amputated. The operation, conducted under local anesthetic, was taped and televised with Basayev watching dispassionately. Undaunted, later that year Basayev challenged Vladimir Putin to a duel. "The choice of weapon we leave to you," he taunted. In spite of promoting himself as a macho man of action – with internationally circulated photographs of him shirtless, with rippling muscles and holding a rifle, or taking aim to shoot a tiger – Putin believed discretion was the better part of valor and did not take up the offer.

In all, Russian operations in Chechnya after 1994 killed about 100,000 Chechens out of a population of only a million. With the complete devastation wrought by the two Chechen wars, increasingly desperate Chechens such as Khava and Luiza sacrificed themselves to take revenge and terrorize the Russians, hoping to make them experience the pain the Chechens had felt. In September 2004, 30 men and 2 women wearing suicide bomb vests took more than 1,100 people hostage in a school in Beslan, North Ossetia, an operation that led to the deaths of 334 people, including 186 children. Basayev claimed responsibility. One member of the group was reported by a hostage to have said that a Russian plane from Beslan's airfield had killed his entire family, and now his sole purpose in life was to seek revenge, even if it involved murdering women and children (Leung, 2009).

A number of suicide bombers followed Khava and Luiza, many of them women. In November 2001, Elza Gazuyeva, a twenty-three-year-old woman who had lost sixteen of her relatives to the Russians, including her husband, two brothers, and a cousin, walked up to General Gaidar Gadzhiyev and asked, "Do you still remember me?" She then blew herself up, killing the general and his bodyguards. Before this incident, Gadzhiyev had personally summoned Elza to witness her husband's torture and execution, during which the general had slashed open her husband's stomach and forced Elza's face into the gaping, gory wound gushing blood. In October 2002, 19 Chechen women wearing explosive vests along with 22 men took 800 people in a Moscow theater hostage, with 170 people losing their lives. In August 2004, two Chechen women whose brothers had been killed blew themselves up on two separate airliners nearly simultaneously, killing ninety people, while the sister of one of them blew herself up at a Moscow metro station the following week, taking the lives of ten people. Out of a total of 110 Chechen suicide bombers between 2000 and 2005, 47 were women (Speckhand & Akhmedova, 2006: 63). Studies have shown that nearly all of these women had lost at least one relative in the war with Russia, some had been raped, and others had been kidnapped and tortured. While some were linked to groups and leaders such as Basayev and Dokka Umarov, the Chechen head of the insurgent group Caucasus Emirate, a great number had no organizational link at all.

When Rizvan and Muslimat Aliyev, a brother and sister aged twenty-three and nineteen, respectively, blew themselves up in the capital of the Republic of Dagestan, Makhachkala, in May 2012, killing 13 and injuring 101, they were signaling a similar breakdown to the one across the border in Chechnya. The instability and resulting violence in Dagestan began after Putin asserted direct control of the region in 2004, ending local autonomy. Dagestan, meaning the Land of the Mountains, is home to a number of segmentary lineage tribal societies,[2] including the majority Avars, Lezgins, and Dargin peoples. The region has a long history of violent resistance against Russian rule, particularly by the Avars under the famous Imam Shamil in the nineteenth century. Since 2004, suicide bombings have been a constant threat. They have targeted the police and other representatives of Russian authority in the region in acts of revenge for torture, humiliation, and the killing of family members. Many in the police force are now too frightened to even wear their uniforms as so many are being killed by unknown assassins who follow them for days before striking. Every traffic officer in the Dagestani capital is accompanied by a riot policeman in camouflage with a Kalashnikov. A thirty-year-old police officer told the *New York Times* that even when he and his colleagues stopped to help a woman who had fallen on the ground, she told them that she hoped all of them would be murdered (Barry, 2010).The Caucasian tribes, in the tactical manner of other peoples such as the Pashtun in their battles with central authority in history, have brazenly targeted top government officials. In 2004, after a number of failed attempts, the Chechens killed the Moscow-backed Chechen president, along with a number of other senior government officials, when they bombed a stadium ceremony commemorating Russia's victory in the Second World War. A Russian general was killed in Dagestan in 2008, while in 2009 the Avar minister of internal affairs for Dagestan, known for combating the rebellious groups and often employing the slogan "Take no prisoners," was killed by a sniper in

[2] Anthropologists described the "segmentary lineage system" as a type of social organization characterized by nesting attributes in which a smaller segment was part of a larger and larger group of segments, with the largest being the ethnic group itself (Middleton & Tait, eds., 1958).

broad daylight while attending a wedding party at a restaurant. In September 2011, the deputy director of the federal prison system in Dagestan was shot dead.

The Russian government subjected the other Caucasian republics to the same ruthlessness and was met by similar revenge attacks, not only on Russian security forces but also on anyone associated with the government, even imams and other religious figures. In June 2009 in the Republic of Ingushetia, a female suicide bomber critically injured the president of the republic and his brother, the region's head of security, while killing his driver and bodyguard. In 2010 the top cleric in the majority Circassian republic of Kabardino-Balkaria was murdered, and there were 108 attacks on law enforcement personnel that year, during which 42 were killed (Vatchagaev, 2011). In a February 2011 trial of fifty-eight terror suspects in Kabardino-Balkaria, a lawyer who worked with their families contended: "What these lads did came after months and years of provocations by the security services on the basis of their religion. They were beaten, they were sodomized with bottles. Some had crosses shaved into their heads. Some were forced to drink vodka" (Parffit, 2011). An Ingush suicide bomber in January 2011 blew himself up in Moscow's international airport, killing thirty-seven people. In October 2012, a suicide bomber detonated a bomb at a police checkpoint on the border between Ingushetia and North Ossetia Province, killing a policeman and wounding three others.

THE KURDISH CASE

On June 30, 1996, Zeynep Kinaci, a twenty-four-year-old Kurdish woman, walked into a group of Turkish soldiers singing the Turkish national anthem in a military parade in Tunceli Province of eastern Turkey. Masquerading as a pregnant woman, she blew herself up along with ten soldiers, thus becoming the first suicide bomber among the Kurds. Kinaci was married, had a college degree, and worked in a state hospital as an X-ray technician.

According to the Kurdistan Workers' Party (PKK), which she had joined the year before, Kinaci had conducted the suicide mission to "avenge" an attempt by Turkish intelligence to kill the head of the PKK, Abdullah Ocalan. Just before she took action, Kinaci had written a public message outlining the reasons for her action. She began by stating her name, village, and tribe, the Mamureki, and revealed that her husband had been captured by the Turks. She continued: "I believe that my support for the PKK and the liberation movement had its roots in the fact that my family was concerned to preserve their Kurdish identity."[3] Addressing the head of the PKK, she declared: "Your life gives us honour, love, courage, confidence, trust and belief .... I shout to the whole world: 'Hear me, open your eyes!' We are the children of a people that has had their country taken away and has been scattered to the four corners of the world" (Ozcan, 2006: 176).

Not long before her suicide, Kinaci's region of Tunceli, known as one of the least accessible areas of Kurdistan with its snow-capped mountains and deep ravines, and whose tribes had remained effectively independent from central government control for centuries, had been characterized as "Turkey's largest prison" (Bruinessen, 2000: 246). It had been the target of a Turkish military campaign in the late 1930s that left as many as 70,000 people dead in the face of burgeoning Turkish nationalism under Mustafa Kemal Ataturk, and tension continued to boil under the surface for decades afterward. In 1994 and 1995, the army carried out extensive operations in Tunceli Province to counter the PKK, which had emerged during the 1970s in opposition to ongoing "Turkification" of the Kurds. These operations resulted in the partial or complete destruction and forced evacuation of around one-third of the villages in the mountainous

[3] Zeynep Kinaci (Zilan). PKK Online. https://pkk-online.com/en/index.php/sehitlerimiz/103-zeynep-kinaci-zilan.

province. The pattern was repeated throughout Turkish Kurdistan, where some 200,000 troops were stationed. By 1999 Turkish policies and the resulting war with insurgents had left 35,000 dead and roughly 2.5 million to 3 million Kurds displaced.

In response to these operations, Kurds launched a wave of suicide bombings. Between 1996 and 1999, the PKK, which described itself as a "revolutionary revenge organization," carried out fifteen suicide bombings, with a further six bombers intercepted before they could detonate their bombs (Bruinessen, 2000: 239; Schweitzer, 2001: 81). It is notable that 66 percent of the bombers were women (Skaine, 2006: 81). In 1996 Ocalan, whose name in Turkish means "he who takes revenge," declared that "each and every Kurd can become a suicide bomber" (Biggs, 2006: 184). Although the PKK stopped its attacks in 1999, suicide bombings continued. Believing that Turkey was uninterested in peace, the PKK revived its campaign against the government in 2004. A series of suicide bombings followed throughout Turkey, including a suicide bombing in Ankara in May 2007 that killed nine people and an October 2010 suicide bombing in Taksim Square in central Istanbul that injured thirty-two. In October 2011 a female suicide bomber blew herself up near an office of the ruling AK Party in Bingol in eastern Turkey on the anniversary of the founding of the nation, killing two people.

THE SOMALI CASE

Late on a Friday night in June 2011, Haboon Abdulkadir Hersi Qaaf, a veiled Somali teenage woman, entered the Mogadishu home of her uncle, Abdi Shakur Sheikh Hassan Farah, Somalia's minister for the interior and national security. Nothing seemed out of the ordinary about the visit. Farah had been paying Haboon's tuition at the local medical school, and she was a frequent guest at his home. The guards knew her well, and this night, as on so many other visits, they let her pass by without so much as a second glance. But this visit was different. Strapped to

Haboon's body was a vest of explosives that she detonated after getting close to her uncle, blowing her to pieces and killing him. The Somali group Al Shabab claimed responsibility for the attack, calling Farah an "apostate official" and vowing to continue to target those who associated themselves with the US-backed central government in Mogadishu.

The Somali traditional code of honor and practice of Islam had begun to mutate by the time the country collapsed into civil war after the fall of General Siad Barre in 1991. The ensuing and unprecedented clan-on-clan bloodshed killed 25,000 people in Mogadishu in a mere four months. Somali tribal society mutated further with suicide bombings. Three months before an American-backed Ethiopian invasion in December 2006, the first Somali suicide bomber targeted the Somali president, missing him but killing five people, including the president's brother. Suicide bombings accelerated following the Ethiopian occupation and intervention of several other African countries. In March 2007, a suicide bomber named Adam Salad Adam drove his Toyota past a checkpoint at an Ethiopian military base in Somalia and detonated the explosives in his vehicle, killing sixty-three Ethiopian soldiers and wounding a further fifty. A Somali group called the Young Mujahideen Movement claimed responsibility for the bombing, saying it was in revenge for the rape and torture of a Somali woman named Suuban Maalin Ali Hassan at the hands of Ethiopian troops.

By the time Haboon decided to blow herself up, Al Shabab was regularly launching suicide attacks, often against innocent civilians. The twenty-five victims of a suicide bombing at a Benadir University graduation ceremony in December 2009 included three government ministers, while most of the others were graduating students. In July 2010 Somali suicide bombers killed seventy-four people watching the World Cup in Uganda, the week after Al Shabab had vowed to take "revenge" against Uganda for its military support of the Somali government and for committing the "massacres" of Somalis. An October 2011 suicide strike on a government building killed more than a hundred people, most of them students who had come to check examination results for scholarships to Turkey.

This suicide attack, declared the bomber in a video, "will be a big blow to the heart of the enemy" (USA Today, 2011). Those who go abroad to college, he said, "never think about the harassed Muslims. He wakes up in the morning, goes to college and studies and accepts what the infidels tell him, while infidels are massacring Muslims" (Associated Press, 2011). Al Shabab was ruthless with those it felt were collaborating with the government or spying. Ordinary people were petrified with fear. "We wake up with beheaded bodies on the streets every day," a Mogadishu resident told the Associated Press in August 2011. "They call themselves Muslims while doing what Allah banned! Everyone is trying to leave here because people are being killed like goats" (Guled, 2011).

As in the case discussed above, Somalis often targeted the highest possible officials, as seen by Haboon's murder of her uncle. In June 2007, a suicide bomber attacked the home of Somalia's prime minister, missing him but killing seven others. In June 2009 a suicide bomber killed thirty-five people at a hotel in central Somalia, including the Somali minister for national security and several Somali diplomats, one being the former ambassador to Ethiopia. In September 2009, two suicide bombers attacked the African Union military headquarters in Mogadishu, which also housed the offices of DynCorp International, a US military contractor supporting the Somali government, killing twenty-one people. Among those who died was a Burundian major general, the second highest ranking African Union commander. In April 2012, just as the prime minister of Somalia was beginning to address an elite Mogadishu gathering in the newly opened Somali National Theater, a female suicide bomber detonated her explosives, narrowly missing him but killing the head of Somalia's Olympic committee and the head of the nation's football federation.

THE NIGERIAN CASE

In January 2012, a female suicide bomber from Bauchi State in northeastern Nigeria attempted to gain entrance to the headquarters of the Federal Capital Territory Administration (FCTA) in Abuja, the capital of Nigeria. The FCTA runs Abuja, and its offices house the senior government ministers and thousands of government workers. Although she was stopped before she could detonate the bombs strapped to her body, the emergence of this female suicide bomber in Nigeria, Africa's most populous nation, again points to a breakdown in traditional society and the resulting mutation. Although suicide bombings had been frequent in the region, this was the first known example of a female suicide bomber. It was indeed a harbinger of things to come. According to one study, of the 434 suicide bombings carried out by the group popularly known as Boko Haram between 2011 and 2017, "at least 244 of the 338 attacks in which the bomber's gender could be identified were carried out by women" (Kriel, 2017).

Boko Haram struck fear into Nigerians with its ferocious attacks on both government and civilian targets. Many commentators translate Boko Haram in its literal sense as "book forbidden," implying a rejection of "book" or Western education. The group identifies itself as People Committed to the Propagation of the Prophet's Teachings and Jihad. It was founded by a Kanuri, Ustaz Mohammed Yusuf – "Ustaz" meaning teacher – in 2002 in Maiduguri, the capital of the northeastern Borno State, as a nonviolent microfinance Islamic organization opposed to what it saw as a corrupt government. Its members were drawn from the lower economic classes and students of Quranic schools. The group was dominated by the historically segmentary lineage Kanuri people, who previously had their own independent kingdom until British colonialism.

In July 2009, violence erupted when Boko Haram's meeting place in Bauchi State was raided by Nigerian national police and nine of its members were arrested. Within a couple of hours, reprisal attacks occurred against the police. Riots then erupted, eventually spreading to three other states in the northeast. The fighting lasted for five days. During this time, the military was filmed executing suspected members of the group in public. According to the Red Cross, 780 bodies were found in the streets of Maiduguri alone, with hundreds more killed throughout the northeast (PressTV, 2009). The government targeted the group's affiliated mosques for destruction. After the riots, Mohammed Yusuf, the founder of the group, was captured and shot, and his body was later found dumped in Maiduguri in full view of its residents, his wrists still in handcuffs. The government claimed he died while attempting to escape custody, an incident later cited by Boko Haram as provocation for revenge attacks against the security services.

After Yusuf's death, Abubakar Shekau, also a Kanuri, became leader of the group. To show solidarity with Yusuf, he married one of Yusuf's four wives and adopted their children. The group began to recruit other ethnic groups, such as the Fulani, another tribal people in northern Nigeria. The first suicide bomber in Nigerian history, who Boko Haram announced was Fulani, blew himself up in the national police headquarters in Abuja in June 2011. His target was the inspector general of the Nigerian national police, who the day before had declared in Maiduguri that "the days of Boko Haram are numbered" (Maiduguri, 2011). Another suicide attack followed a few months later, this time on the United Nations headquarters in Abuja, killing twenty-one people and injuring seventy-three.

Boko Haram also began to target fellow Muslims, particularly those associated with the central government. In September 2011, Babakura Fugu, Mohammed Yusuf's brother-in-law, was shot outside his house in Maiduguri two days after attending a peace meeting with the former president, Olusegun Obasanjo. In July 2012, a teenage suicide bomber blew himself up in the central mosque of Maiduguri, killing five and injuring a further six. His main targets, who escaped from the blast uninjured, were the deputy governor of Bornu State and the shehu of Bornu,

Abubakar Umar Garbai el-Kanemi, both Muslims (Al Jazeera, 2012). The previous year, the shehu's younger brother was killed by gunmen. The shehu is one of the main religious leaders of the Kanuri, and the position of shehu was also the former ruler of the Kanuri Kanem-Bornu Empire, which was absorbed into the British colonial government. The current shehu is directly descended from the shehus of the Kanuri Empire. One month later, a suicide bomber targeted the emir of Fika, another religious figure who had spoken against violence and in support of the security forces; this attack occurred during Friday prayers at the central mosque in Potiskum in Yobe State, missing the emir but injuring dozens of people.

In adopting an Islamic identity, the group was also concerned about matters outside the tribe such as the status of Muslims in Nigeria, a country largely divided between a Muslim north and Christian south. In January 2012, in the wake of the 2011 Christmas Day bombings in which several churches were attacked in Abuja, Jos, and in the northeastern Yobe State, Shekau, the leader of Boko Haram, announced, "We are also at war with Christians because the whole world knows what they did to us. They killed our fellows and even ate their flesh in Jos" (BBC News, 2012). Shekau was referring to several incidents in 2011 in which Christian Berom tribesmen ate the charred flesh of Muslims they had killed and roasted in the Plateau State of the Middle Belt region in Nigeria. In a widely circulated online video, voices can be heard telling a young man who is hacking apart a charred and headless body with a machete, "I want the heart" and "Did you put some salt?" as youths proudly hold up severed heads blackened by fire for the camera. Several policemen can be seen standing back and watching the cannibalistic feast. There is an air of festivity about the gathering, as if the revelers were enjoying a special celebration.

The volatile Middle Belt region, which serves as the border between Muslim north and Christian south and where different religious and ethnic groups live side by side, has been caught in a vicious cycle of attack and counterattack between the tribal communities. Revenge attacks between Christian and Muslim tribal groups remain a constant threat in the region, such as in Kaduna State, bordering Plateau State, where a number of assaults killed dozens of Christians in the fall of 2012, including a November suicide bombing of a military base church killing eleven.

Large-scale violence erupted in Plateau State on September 7, 2001, when the palpable tension between the communities led to the Jos riots in which more than a thousand people were killed over a six-day period. By 2004, nearly 54,000 people had been killed in Plateau State, according to a Nigerian investigative committee (Associated Press, 2004). At the heart of the conflicts are the nomadic Muslim Fulani herdsmen who moved south in increasing numbers and in the process clashed with other tribal groups in the area. Once again, the actions of the Fulani reflect the mutation of both Islam and *Pulaaku*, the Fulani tribal code.

Fulani migrations south accelerated as the grazing routes for their herds disappeared in the north, mainly because of the Sahel drought of the late 1960s and 1970s. The move was also encouraged by the development of new farming practices in the Middle Belt region from the 1970s onward that decimated the tsetse fly population harmful to their cattle (Waters-Bayer & Bayer, 1994). With the removal of the barrier that the tsetse fly formed, more and more Fulani began to move their grazing routes and their camps farther south, coming into conflict with the region's resident farmers over land use. The largely Christian farmers, especially the Berom who are the dominant ethnic group in the Plateau State, complained of the destructive presence of Fulani cattle herds on their land, and would often kill or steal them.

For the Fulani herdsmen whose very existence depends on cattle, these attacks were devastating, threatening not only their livelihood but also their identity in *Pulaaku*. The Fulani organization Miyetti Allah stated in February 2011 that herdsmen had lost about 8 million heads of cattle in the preceding decade (Iluyemi,

2011). The young Fulani boys who often tend the herds, an important way to demonstrate manhood in traditional society, frequently became the victims of ethnic hatred. Inasmuch as the Muslim herders and Christian farmers are both motivated by codes of revenge and honor, any violent act is certain to trigger a series of bloody counterattacks.

Just before dawn on Sunday, March 7, 2010, for example, a group of machete-wielding Fulani herdsmen descended upon the Christian Berom villages of Zot, Ratsat, and Dogo-Nahawa in Plateau State. The Fulani began to fire into the air in order to draw the Berom farmers out of their homes. As the Berom emerged into the streets, the Fulani hacked them to pieces. Most of the victims were those least able to run away: women, small children as young as three months old, and the elderly. The Berom villages were then set on fire with people still inside their homes. After a few hours of bloodshed, some 500 victims lay dead. These acts of savagery were perpetrated in revenge for attacks on the Fulani by Berom youth from the same villages earlier that year, when over 350 Muslims, mostly Fulani, were killed in riots that arose out of objections to the construction of a mosque in a Christian-majority neighborhood in Jos.

The Fulani are also subject to discrimination by the central government and risk being arrested, tortured, killed, and deported on the slightest pretext. The government of Plateau State, headed by a Berom governor, denied the Fulani any recognition as citizens and attempted to expel them from the region. In May 2009, it was announced that 20,000 Fulani had been expelled from Plateau State into other northern states (Jaafar, 2009). The state government often justified these actions on security grounds, referring to the Fulani herdsmen as "terrorists." Ahmed Idris, a representative from Plateau State in the Nigerian House of Representatives, referred to these deportations as "ethnic cleansing" (US Department of State, 2010). According to the Fulani leader of Miyetti Allah, "The race was facing extinction" (Iluyemi, 2011).

In July 2012, another case of ethnic violence in Plateau State hit international headlines, this one directly involving central government security forces. A Fulani herdsman had been accused of killing a member of the Nigerian security forces, the Special Task Force (STF), in Plateau State, and the STF responded by burning fifty Fulani homes to the ground. Three days later, Fulani herdsmen launched revenge attacks on nine Berom villages in Plateau State that they associated with the STF, killing at least sixty-three people, many in the home of a Christian pastor. During their funeral the following day, the Fulani again attacked, killing about twenty of the mourners, among them two senior Berom politicians, a Nigerian federal senator, and the majority leader of the Plateau State Assembly. The next day, Berom tribesmen retaliated by killing anyone they identified as a Fulani in the area, bringing the weekend's death toll to more than 200 (Garba, 2012). After these incidents, the Berom community called for the expulsion of all Fulani from Plateau State.

Farther east in Nigeria, the Fulani herdsmen have come into similar conflict over land with the Tiv farmers who are Christian and organized along the segmentary lineage system. The nomadic Fulani have also run into problems with farmers across West Africa as the Fulani ethnic group extends over half a dozen countries, where they are variously known as Fulani, Fulbe, Fula, or Peul. In Ghana as the Fulani shifted their herds south owing to changing environmental conditions, bloody battles erupted, pitting the Fulani herdsmen against local farmers and the security forces, as in Nigeria. One Ghanaian member of parliament reflected the mood against the Fulani when he publicly announced in December 2011, "If in the course of defending ourselves they have to die then it is justified. So killing them I personally support it" (Modern Ghana, 2011). In May 2012 deadly violence erupted along the Burkina Faso and Mali border, pitting Fulani herdsmen against Dogon farmers, a primarily animist ethnic group living in Mali.

EXTENT OF THE BREAKDOWN

The frequency of the suicide attacks and their geographical span, especially the advent of female suicide bombers, should have alerted the world that something has gone horribly wrong in tribal societies on the periphery, and that governments far from resolving the problems have exacerbated them. In response to these tribal actions, the central government has responded with unthinking force that routinely includes rape and, in some instances, even abets cannibalism. Despite their fearsome reputation throughout history, the tribes have traditionally associated revenge with satisfying honor and not with committing murder for its own sake. Revenge is a measured response meant to address an injustice – and not meant to lapse into excessive violence, which is considered dishonorable. Tribal elders seeking to maintain the code and the religious leaders appealing to Islam both work toward balance and stability. The actions of the suicide bombers in their indiscriminate killing are thus devoid of both tribal honor and religious compassion. The fact that many of the suicide bombings are conducted by women, whose protection is considered a matter of honor for the tribesmen, is further evidence of the devastation being wrought on the community, with too many of the women being raped and their husbands arrested, tortured, or killed. As Sara Ahmed has illustrated in this volume, willful women are "willing to put their bodies in the way," denouncing the status quo. Focusing on the issue of gender in this context of the war on terror can help us understand what is going wrong and the potential for the situation to be ameliorated.

The depth of the dilemma faced by individuals under such circumstances cannot be fully appreciated without measuring the suicides against Islam's ideals. Islam not only categorically prohibits suicide – only God gives and takes life – but it considers the idea of female suicide especially reprehensible. Women in the ideal have the highest possible status in Islam, both theologically and sociologically. The sayings of the Prophet and his behavior toward women confirm this position. When asked the best way to reach paradise, the Prophet thrice replied, "Under the feet of the mother," pointing to the importance of the elevated position of the mother as a child-bearer and role model. The Prophet's household provided some of the leading role models for Muslim women, which would have been known to each of the female suicide bombers mentioned here. Khadijah, Aisha, and Fatima – successful businesswomen, scholars, military commanders, and carriers of the sacred lineage – each of these extraordinary women embodies compassion, courage, and balance in her life and serves as a guide to Muslim women. By abandoning their example and taking her own life, the female suicide bomber is saying she is prepared to negate her Islamic heritage and duty. Yes, something has gone terribly wrong.

As the cases described above demonstrate, every member of a tribe faces a dilemma within a particular cultural, social, and historical context: each must weigh the Prophet's words against the unchecked desire for revenge. This dilemma is a product of the disruption of the relationship between state and tribe, center and periphery. In the ensuing mayhem, a new, cruel, and revengeful leadership has emerged bent on destroying whatever remains of the traditional model. It promotes bloodshed, ironically in the name of Islam. For the women who face this dilemma, the burden is even heavier, knowing that they need to preserve and perpetuate life. With the traditional models broken and without efforts to reconstruct them, these societies will find it difficult to emerge from the current state of pain, cruelty, and violence.

We have seen, as evidence of the breakdown discussed here, the Taliban's attempts in the Pashtun district of Swat in Pakistan to kill Malala Yousafzai. She persevered and has become a symbol of the desire of women and Muslim tribal women, specifically, to be educated. Her efforts and the ideals she promotes symbolize hope and also point the way to resolving these crucial and serious issues in the future. The most crucial first step then may be to acknowledge the importance of education in tribal society, where education levels for women in particular are woefully low.

Finally, tribal people must be treated as full citizens of the state with access to economic opportunity and democratic representation. They must be treated with dignity and honor – an absolute necessity in the context of local cultural gender roles and responsibilities – by central governments and their international allies. Indeed, understanding the gendered dynamics of traditional structures of Muslim tribal society is key to a better relationship between center and periphery and ultimately, in attaining political stability.

REFERENCES

Ahmed, Akbar. 2013. *The Thistle and the Drone: How America's War on Terror Became a Global War on Tribal Islam.* Washington, DC: Brookings Institution Press.

Al Jazeera. 2012. Suicide Bomber Targets Mosque in Nigeria. July 13. www.aljazeera.com/news/africa/2012/07/2012713153221739855.html.

Associated Press. 2004. World Briefing Africa – Nigeria: 53,000 Killed in 3 Years of Ethnic Conflict. *New York Times,* October 8. www.nytimes.com/2004/10/08/world/world-briefing-africa-nigeria-53000-killed-in-3-years-of-ethnic.html.

2011. Somali Bomber Who Killed 100 Slammed Education. Deseret News, October 6. www.deseret.com/2011/10/6/20221078/somali-bomber-who-killed-100-slammed-education#somalis-carry-a-wounded-man-at-the-scene-of-an-explosion-in-mogadishu-somalia-tuesday-oct-4-2011-a-rescue-official-says-at-least-55-people-were-killed-after-a-car-laden-with-explosives-blew-up-in-front-of-the-ministry-of-education-in-the-somali-capital-of-mogadishu-the-al-qaida-linked-militant-group-al-shabab-immediately-claimed-responsibility-for-the-attack-on-a-website-it-uses-after-more-than-a-month-of-relative-calm-in-mogadishu.

Barry, Ellen. 2010. With Breakdown of Order in Russia's Dagestan Region, Fear Stalks Police. *New York Times,* March 20.

BBC News. 2012. Boko Haram: Nigerian Islamist Leader Defends Attacks. January 11. www.bbc.co.uk/news/world-africa-16510929.

Biggs, Michael 2006. Dying without Killing: Self-Immolations, 1963–2002. In Diego Gambetta, ed., *Making Sense of Suicide Missions.* Oxford: Oxford University Press, pp. 173–208.

Bruinessen, Martin van. 2000. *Kurdish Ethno-Nationalism versus Nation-Building States: Collected Articles.* Istanbul: Isis Press.

Chulov, Martin. 2008. Violent Province's 27 Female Suicide Bombers Who Set Out to Destroy Iraqi Hopes of Peace. *The Guardian,* November 11.

Garba, Ibrahim. 2012. Weekend Clashes Kill 200, as Nigeria Struggles for Control. *Christian Science Monitor,* July 9.

Guled, Abdi. 2011. Somali Islamists Behead 11 Civilians in Capital. Associated Press, August 26.

Iluyemi, Victor. 2011. Fulanis Lament Loss of 250 People, 8 million Cattle to Jos Crisis. WorldStage Newsonline, February 8. http://worldstagegroup.com.

Jaafar, Jaafar. 2009. Nigeria Plateau Deports 20,000 Fulani – Fuldan Chairman. *Daily Trust Nigeria*, May 9.

Kriel, Robyn. 2017. Boko Haram Favors Women, Children as Suicide Bombers, Study Reveals. CNN, August 11.

Larzillière, Pénélope. 2017. On Suicide Bombings: Questioning Rationalist Models and Logics of Gender. *International Review of Sociology*, 27(1), 108–25. www.tandfonline.com/eprint/tQYKCc4RWyzg69flvHrw/full.

Leung, Rebecca. 2009. New Video of Beslan School Terror. CBS News, February 11. www.cbsnews.com/news/new-video-of-beslan-school-terror/.

Maiduguri, Ahmad Salkida. 2011. The Story of Nigeria's First Suicide Bomber-Blue Print Magazine. Sahara Reporters, June 26. http://saharareporters.com/news-page/story-nigerias-first-suicide-bomber-blueprint-magazine.

Middleton, John and Tait, David, eds. 1958. *Tribes Without Rulers: Studies in African Segmentary Systems.* London and New York: Routledge.

Modern Ghana. 2011. 'I Support Killing of Fulani Nomads' – PC Appiah Ofori. *Citi News (Ghana)*, December 16.

Murphy, Paul J. 2010. *Allah's Angels: Chechen Women in War.* Annapolis, MD: Naval Institute Press.

Myers, Steven Lee. 2006. Beslan Organizer Is Killed, Russia Says – Europe-International Herald Tribune. *New York Times*, July 10.

Ozcan, Ali Kemal. 2006. *Turkey's Kurds: A Theoretical Analysis of the PKK and Abdullah Ocalan.* Abingdon, UK: Routledge.

Parfitt, Tom. 2011. Islamists on Trial. *Foreign Policy*, February 24.

Press TV. 2009. Red Cross Finds 780 Corpses in Single Nigeria City. August 3. www.webcitation.org/5jcIg8G9P?url=http://www.presstv.ir/detail.aspx?id=102384§ionid=351020505.

Schweitzer, Yoram. 2001. Suicide Terrorism: Development and Main Characteristics. In The International Policy Institute for Counter-Terrorism, ed., *Countering Suicide Terrorism: An International Conference.* Herzlia, Israel: International Policy Institute for Counter-Terrorism, pp. 75–76.

Skaine, Rosemarie. 2006. *Female Suicide Bombers.* Jefferson, NC: McFarland.

Speckhand, Anne and Akhmedova, Khapta. 2006. Black Widows: The Chechen Female Suicide Terrorists. In Yoram Schweitzer, ed., *Female Suicide Terrorists.* Tel Aviv: Jaffe Center for Strategic Studies.

US Department of State, Bureau of Democracy, Human Rights, and Labor. 2010. 2009 Human Rights Report: Nigeria. Washington, DC, March 11.

USA Today. 2011. Somali Militants Warn of More Attacks after Bombing. October 5.

Vatchagaev, Mairbek. 2011. Rebel Attacks in Kabardino-Balkaria Skyrocket. *Eurasia Daily Monitor*, **8**(25), February 4.

Waters-Bayer, Ann and Bayer, Wolfgang. 1994. Coming to Terms: Interactions between Immigrant Fulani Cattle-Keepers and Indigenous Farmers in Nigeria's Subhumid Zone. *Cahiers d'Etudes Africaines*, **34**(133/135), 214–16.

CHAPTER 16

Bed Peace and Gender Abnorms

Mignon Nixon

WHY DOES GENDER MATTER FOR UNDERSTANDING the world we live in now, a time of continual war, resurgent militarism, and hyperbolic, "toxic" masculinity? It matters because war is social, and therefore gendered. "If we see war as a way of establishing society," Juliet Mitchell observes, then "peace has to be something we ... work for against our norms," beginning, I suggest, with our gender norms (Taneja, 2015: 266). As long as our war and gender norms align, we struggle to conceive of peace. But what might working for peace against our norms of gender and war look like? In this chapter, I focus on an iconic event that takes up this question, Yoko Ono and John Lennon's *Bed-In for Peace*, which the couple performed twice in 1969 to protest the American war in Vietnam (see Figure 16.1).[1] Ono and Lennon both actively embraced feminism, and the *Bed-In for Peace* was a feminist intervention in the gender politics of militarism, war, and the anti-war movement itself.[2] The event however is remembered rather differently, as a quixotic gesture with scant political import. This dismissive reception of the *Bed-In for Peace*, and its provocation to think about the place of everyday gender roles in peace politics, is, in itself, a gendered response, disavowing questions of gender that are fundamental to the problem of war.

[1] The first *Bed-In for Peace* took place at the Amsterdam Hilton Hotel, March 25–31, 1969. The event was reprised in Montreal, at the Queen Elizabeth Hotel, May 26–June 2, 1969.

[2] On Lennon's engagement with feminist politics in collaboration with Ono, see Kristine Stiles (1992).

Figure 16.1 'Bed Peace'. John Lennon and his wife Yoko Ono are having a week's love-in their room at the Hilton Hotel, Amsterdam. They will stay in bed for seven days – with fruit, flowers and peace signs. March 1969. *Credit:* Trinity Mirror / Mirrorpix / Alamy Stock Photo.

The position that gender matters for peace, espoused by Ono and Lennon in solidarity with women-led pacifist groups – in particular, Women Strike for Peace, one of the first groups to call out the incursion into Vietnam – is still exceptional in our own time of war. Writing in the late 1980s, in the aftermath of the American war in Vietnam, cultural historian Susan Jeffords underscored the regressive force of "re-masculinization" (1989). In this drive to restore male privilege, energized by hostility towards feminism and, more generally, towards women, Jeffords identified a "pervasive masculinism" in the Reagan era that resonates powerfully again today (1989: 116). Returning to the *Bed-In for Peace* now reveals why gender continues to be important in working for peace against our norms.

***

In March of 1969, the avant-garde artist, filmmaker, and composer Yoko Ono and the musician John Lennon announced that they would marry and then celebrate their honeymoon in a hotel in Amsterdam. They invited the press to join them. The wedding would be private, but the honeymoon would be public. The couple intended to talk with visitors about peace for a week. They called the event a *Bed-In for Peace.* Anticipating a titillating scene, a throng of reporters and photographers rushed in at the appointed hour, only to find the newlyweds lying propped up in bed side by side, dressed in chaste nightclothes and settled back onto snowy pillows, looking more like companionable convalescents than newlyweds. Installing themselves in the honeymoon suite with the prim seriousness of children, Ono and Lennon put their bodies on the line in a new way. "I like to fight the establishment by using methods that are so far removed from establishment-type thinking that the establishment doesn't know how to fight back," Ono once remarked (Ono, 1971). The *Bed-In for Peace* was a case in point. Staged first in Amsterdam, a youth capital, and then in Montreal, a Canadian haven for American draft resisters and deserters, the *Bed-In* expressed solidarity with nonviolent protest, conscientious objection, and draft evasion. It also suggested that working for peace might mean reinventing our everyday gender roles. Stretched out beside Ono, Lennon aligned himself with his partner, a Japanese avant-garde artist, war survivor, pacifist, and feminist. Defining his political role in alliance with a co-equal woman, he adopted a posture that was rare in the anti-war movement, which was still dominated by the same masculinist mentality that prevailed in the culture at large. "Bed Peace," proclaimed a handmade sign hung above the bed in Amsterdam.[3] To stage a *Bed-In for Peace* – a "piece" that anyone could choose to perform, like Ono's earlier "instruction pieces" – was to demonstrate in bed, for peace, but also to demonstrate for peace in bed, for bed peace.[4]

In 1969, the anti-war movement was in gender crisis. "The war presented a paradox," the feminist historian Alice Echols observed (1992: 181). While opposition to the war brought women and men

[3] This later became the work's alternate title, and the title of the film Ono and Lennon made from footage of it.

[4] For examples of Ono's event scores, see her *Grapefruit: A Book of Instructions and Drawings* (1970). See also Liz Kotz (2001).

together in a common political project that sought to level gender, class, and racial hierarchies, "building in the present the desired community of the future," the widening of the war in Southeast Asia and the intensification of violence against protesters at home by police and the National Guard created a climate in which "almost anything short of 'picking up the gun' seemed impotent," Echols recalled (1992: 173, 180–181). Divided between militant and nonviolent philosophies, the movement was also split along gender lines. Marginalized as "helpmates or worse," she observed, female activists increasingly refused to accept male supremacy (1992: 173). Their resistance to masculine authority, and to the implied claim that the anti-war movement was itself an extension of the traditionally masculine domain of war, exposed deep trends of misogyny in anti-war culture.

In one notorious incident, at the counter-inaugural protest staged by the National Mobilization Committee to End the War in Vietnam (Mobe) in January 1969, following the election of Richard Nixon to the presidency, men in the audience heckled two feminist speakers, Marilyn Webb and Shulamith Firestone. Jeering at Webb to "take it off," they demanded that she be removed from the stage, and threatened to rape her (Echols, 1992: 179–80).[5] War as a culture of sexualized violence had come to the anti-war movement in dramatic fashion. Meanwhile, Ono and Lennon were quietly preparing their *Bed-In*. "We worked for three months thinking out the most functional approach to boosting peace before we got married," Ono recalled, a timeline that places the genesis of the piece at about the time of Nixon's inauguration and the Mobe protest (Yorke, 1982a: 57). Counteracting the attempts by some men in the Movement to intimidate their female peers with threats of sexual violence, or by attempting to force them, even bodily, off the public stage, Lennon and Ono

[5] Echols added that when Webb returned home after the protest, "she received a phone call from a prominent SDS [Students for a Democratic Society] leader in Washington, D.C. who warned that if she or anyone else 'ever gives a speech like that again, we're going to beat the shit out of you wherever you are.'"

shared a bed, a world stage, a feminist politics, and a peace message. The *Bed-In for Peace* was a real-time performance of the proposition that "the restructuring of personal life and renunciation of male privilege" were integral to the process of ending this war and preventing future ones (Echols, 1992: 180). The event expressed, in Ono's terms, a "wish or hope" that changing the way we behave in bed might help bring an end to war. "Event," the artist wrote, apropos of her event scores, "is not a get-togetherness," but "a dealing with oneself .... It has no script as Happenings do, though it has something that starts it moving – the closest word for it may be 'wish or hope'" (Ono, 1970).

Staging their *Bed-In* at a moment of gender crisis in the anti-war movement, Ono and Lennon used the event of their marriage to demonstrate that gender equality was integral to the social process of ending the war and thinking toward future peace. Countering the view of some male anti-war activists that "women's liberation seemed not merely trivial, but dangerously diversionary," Lennon embraced feminism (Echols, 1992: 181). Distancing himself from the machismo of war and of militant anti-war activism, he publicly made his bed with Ono, presenting their relationship as a refuge from sexual posturing, a place to "get some peace," as he expressed it in "The Ballad of John and Yoko" (1969), including, implicitly, sexual peace.[6] "Bed Peace," the sign positioned over Ono's, the distaff, side of the bed in Amsterdam, in turn took on the significance of woman's equality with her male partner, of freedom from sexual violence, of reproductive freedom, and of feeling at home in a shared bed, as an integral dimension of peace. Adopting an earnest and affectionate tone, and dressing and styling themselves similarly, the couple played up their commonalities, revealing the egalitarian balance and reciprocity of their relationship, which they actively performed for the cameras, addressing their world audience together. In a stream of

[6] "Being ourselves is what's important. If everyone practiced being themselves instead of pretending to be what they aren't there would be peace." Lennon quoted in Cott and Doudna (1982: xviii).

interviews, they patiently articulated the aims of the protest, and strove to ameliorate by example the gender divisions and sexism of the dominant culture, but also of the anti-war movement, in which women and men played separate and unequal roles. Appearing side by side, physically supporting each other, and taking it in turns to converse with the press, they demonstrated that theirs was a relationship in which intimacy and equality, the personal and the political, were intrinsically connected.

Getting married, as performed by Ono and Lennon, was a political act. "We decided that if we were going to do anything like get married," Lennon explained, "we would dedicate it to peace" (Yorke, 1982a: 57). Their marriage was, by any definition, an event. Vilified for mesmerizing Lennon and breaking up The Beatles, Ono – avant-garde Japanese Conceptual pacifist artist – was multiply "other." The couple's response to the climate of hysteria that surrounded their partnership was to use the fascination and hostility it aroused to provoke thinking about hatred and war, the war in Vietnam but also war at home, in America and everywhere. Inviting the world at large to their honeymoon, the couple made this conventionally private ritual the occasion for public reflection on war but also on the warring in everyday life, on the social rituals and structures, including marriage, which sustain war and inhibit peace.

Ono and Lennon's decision to marry for peace highlighted the nexus of war and marriage as social institutions. War cements the social by exporting our destructiveness, sending it elsewhere to rid us of it and to stop us from killing our own, the Italian psychoanalyst Franco Fornari argued in *The Psychoanalysis of War*, published in 1966, amid the escalating violence of the American war in Vietnam. From this perspective, America's war was an extreme instance of finding, or if necessary making, an enemy to destroy ([1966] 1974: xvi). War is exogamous. We kill outside the group. Marriage (an institution Fornari's theory does not encompass) is also bound by exogamous rules. We marry outside the family, but traditionally inside a prescribed social group. Lennon and Ono were members of historically hostile groups, former enemy nations, and bore different ethnicities. Their marriage, put on public display in the *Bed-In for Peace* at the height of a war stoked by racialized hatred against an Asian people, summoned another war energized by racism, and a taboo of miscegenation. The atomic bombings of Hiroshima and Nagasaki in 1945 hung over the war in Vietnam not only politically and militarily but also psychically, symbolizing the "pantoclastic prospect" of destruction on a planetary scale (Fornari, [1966] 1974: xxvii). Nuclear war, Fornari suggested, posed an existential threat to war and, by implication, to other social arrangements, including marriage, that underpin a society structured by war. By transgressing the cultural and historical norms of marriage and war, the *Bed-In* laid bare their mutually reinforcing architecture, as a provocation to reflect upon alternative ways of "establishing society."

Juliet Mitchell considers war and marriage together, as Ono and Lennon do. Both she and they trace a lateral line between the family and the social group (Mitchell, 2003). Working for peace against our norms calls for "thinking siblings." It also means being alive to the potential for change that is latent in social play. The social prohibition on killing one's own, Mitchell points out, "might produce enemies," as Fornari maintains, but it might instead promote "a kind of play." To propose play as an alternative to war might be idealistic, she concedes, but "it's a place to look" (Mitchell, quoted in Taneja, 2015: 265). Ono and Lennon looked to play as a strategy for working for peace against our norms.[7] "They adopted the 'bag of laughs' as a motif symbolic of a peaceful and joyful attitude of resistance to the Vietnam War," Kristine Stiles observes (1964: 164). Bagism, the term they coined to describe their political work, was a play on Ono's *Bag Piece* (1962), which calls for a performer, or two, to crawl into a muslin bag, disrobe, and nap. Ono demonstrated it as an anti-war work in a Trafalgar Square peace protest before the couple

[7] For a reflection on the use of play in artistic resistance to war, see Rosalyn Deutsche (2017).

began performing it together, to the bemusement of the press, which on one occasion responded by pointing microphones in the direction of the bag. Asked how their peace campaign began, Lennon recalled that he and Ono were "in different bags, as we call it." Getting "these two egos" into one bag was the starting point of the couple's peace campaign, which was pitched in the discursive space of the media image, a place to try out ideas about what working for peace against our norms might look like (Yorke, 1982a: 70).

We fight and play with our siblings and peers in childhood, Mitchell observes, and in war, we kill and rape our contemporaries, not our parents. "But ironically, it is in societies based on the social contract of brotherhood that these activities are not laterally controlled. Our social imaginary can envisage only vertical authority" (Mitchell, 2003: xv). Looking cross-culturally to kinship systems in which lateral relations are more complexly articulated, she argues that our submission to vertical authority in war is culturally contingent, and therefore susceptible to change. Ono and Lennon also explore this idea. *Bed-In for Peace* embodies a social imaginary that attends to the lateral dynamics of everyday life, including intimate relationships and friendships. They act as individuals, "two egos," but from the group, not apart from it, linking the individual, the couple, and the group in a fluid and free-associative dynamic. Like Mitchell, they suggest that by reshaping our norms we might begin to engender a politics of equality, restrain our violence, and "give peace a chance."

In her classic study "On Violence," Hannah Arendt described the rebellion of the young, "the first generation to grow up under the shadow of the atom bomb," against the patriarchal authority of the warmongers as belonging "among the totally unexpected events of this century" (1970: 116, 130). A case in point was the prevalence of "fraternization" between "enemy" groups, including, by 1969, students and National Guard within the United States. Arendt offered the example of the People's Park Protest in Berkeley, California, where on May 16, 1969, then-governor of

California Ronald Reagan ordered 2,000 armed members of the National Guard to quash demonstrations that erupted after a young man was shot in the back and killed by police during a protest at a local community park. She drew attention to one hopeful sign: "some guardsmen fraternized openly with their 'enemies'" (1970: 131). As this vignette attests, the social imaginary of the late 1960s was expanding through protest, as well as through draft evasion, peace strikes, and even desertion. "We truly believed that what would stop the war was if the soldiers stopped fighting it," one veteran recalled.[8] Soldiers in the ranks joined the anti-war movement, defying military dress codes by growing their hair and wearing peace signs on their uniforms, publishing alternative newspapers, and refusing to fight. In 1967, veterans of conscience founded Vietnam Veterans against the War and began lobbying Congress to end the war, bearing witness to its uncommon brutality, its pattern of atrocity, and its tacit policy of genocide. When Ono and Lennon proposed staying in bed for peace, they therefore expressed solidarity with draft avoiders, draft resisters, and deserters whose refusal to go to war, or to serve out their tours, had driven some underground, or across the border to Canada. They also reminded their audience that this pronounced shift toward "lateral control" found its origins in women-led pacifist politics, which raised consciousness about the role of gender hierarchy in Cold War militarism, about the calculated maiming and killing of civilians in Vietnam, and about a war culture of escalating sexual violence.

In April 1968, at the Paris Conference for Women to End the War in Vietnam, Vietnamese representatives bore witness to the systematic use of sexual atrocity by American forces. Sexual violence was "an everyday feature of the American war" (Turse, 2013: 165).[9] Sexualized torture, gang rape, and rape-murder were also

[8] This is the testimony of an interviewee in the documentary film *Sir! No Sir! The Suppressed Story of the G.I. Movement to End the War in Vietnam* (Zeiger, 2005).

[9] The extent of sexual assault in Vietnam became more public with the testimony of returning veterans in the Winter Soldier Investigation. See Richard Stacewicz (2008); Daniel Lang (1989).

common in the war's "atrocity-producing situation," as the psychiatrist Robert Jay Lifton described it (1973). Atrocity, Lifton observed, is classically explained as an aberration of war, exonerating the military hierarchy at the expense of the individual, whose war crime is portrayed as a personal excess. In the atrocity-producing situation of the war in Vietnam, he argued, a vast pattern of war crime exposed the fallacy of this conception. Through his extensive work with veterans in "rap groups," Lifton came to consider atrocity as an effect of soldiers' socialization, which, from the moment of induction, exploited racism and misogyny to dehumanize the enemy and normalize the killing of civilians. Histories of the war, including Lifton's groundbreaking psycho-histories, however are mostly silent on the subject of sexualized atrocity, despite the graphic testimonies of survivors and perpetrators. That war rape is universal, Mitchell argues, is the necessary starting point for any effort to prevent it: "How do we account for the rampant sexuality of war, the seemingly inevitable rapes and gang rapes that accompany killing," for the fact that "sexual violence seems to 'automatically' accompany war violence?" (2000: 129). Indeed as Jacqueline Rose argues in this volume, "violence against women is not an aberration, an outlier in relation to the conventional arrangements" (see also Akbar Ahmed in this volume). In Vietnam, the rapes and gang rapes that accompanied killing were not the actions of rogue actors, as the military falsely claimed, but part of a social order in which, to take one example, soldiers who raped and then murdered women and girls were referred to by their peers as "double veterans," signifying their elevated status in the group (Turse, 2013: 170). For some women in the American peace movement, these revelations of systematic rape and rape-murder deepened a sense of solidarity with, and responsibility to, Vietnamese women, who were, in the words of one participant, "subject to the greater burden in the war because of their sex" (Swerdlow, 1993: 221).[10] This culture of

[10] Witnesses reported "American troops thrusting bayonets into the bellies of pregnant women" and placing poisonous snakes in the trousers of girls and tying the ends so that the snakes "wriggled into the internal organs of the girls."

"fraternization" between putative enemies, Vietnamese and American women, while ignored in most contemporary reports as well as in later war histories, underscores the role gender played in anti-war resistance, bringing women together in community with one another against the "atrocity-producing" logic of Cold War militarism.

Rather than address the problem of war rape directly, the *Bed-In for Peace* instead countered military socialization, and the inculcation of an atrocity-producing culture of misogyny and racial hatred, by offering a model of gender and racial equality between individuals. Ono had addressed the sexualized character of war violence in a previous work, *Cut Piece,* which she first performed at the Yamaichi Concert Hall in Kyoto in July of 1964. Taking the stage in formal attire and carrying a large pair of scissors, she invited the audience to cut pieces of fabric from her clothing. Kneeling on the floor in the traditional posture of *seiza,* she placed the scissors before her. While she sat motionless, members of the audience mounted the stage one by one. Immobile and silent, Ono surrendered to the will of the chance strangers who approached her. Subsequently performed from 1964 to 1966 in Tokyo, New York, and London, *Cut Piece* instigated the audience to step into the shoes of one who, by instruction, violates another in the presence of onlookers, or stands as witness to such an act. Some participants stooped or squatted alongside Ono, placing their bodies on the same level as her own, approaching the task with silent reverence. A few exulted in a public display of sexualized sadism. But *Cut Piece,* one scholar remarks, "does not unmask the audience as merely sadistic" (Bryan-Wilson, 2003: 103). Rather, it invites an active reflection on war, including war rape, and our complicity in it, as part of how we "establish society."

After the *succès de scandale* of the Amsterdam *Bed-In,* Ono and Lennon had planned to reprise the event in the United States. "We tried to do it in New York," Lennon later recalled, "but the American government wouldn't let us in. They knew we'd done it in Amsterdam; they didn't want any peaceniks here, which is what we heard the Department of whoever controls that said" (Peebles, 1981: 22–23). When Lennon was denied permission to enter the United States, the couple moved the second *Bed-In* to Montreal. Canada was "right next door to the other place."[11] Circumventing the Nixon administration's travel ban, the couple gave broadcast interviews that reached over the border to American audiences. In one, conducted during the People's Park protest in Berkeley, they warned demonstrators against provoking armed police and National Guard to even wider violence. "Make love, not war. That's all we're sayin'," Lennon implored the crowd.[12]

"I'm cheering the police," announced conservative cartoonist Al Capp, arriving at the Montreal *Bed-In* in the midst of the crisis. Introducing himself to Ono and Lennon and their assembled visitors as "that dreadful Neanderthal fascist," Capp, sporting a crisp blazer and silk handkerchief, had come at the invitation of the Canadian Broadcasting Service, which was making a television programme about the event, to act as a foil. Meanwhile, Ono and Lennon were making their own film, *Bed Peace,* to document the events. In it, Capp's performance as the avatar of masculine supremacy and established power captures the regressive drive for "remasculinization" in all its manic intensity. A syndicated newspaper cartoonist and a familiar figure on late-night television, Capp was a throwback to the 1950s, attempting to keep a grip on a media career as cultural mores rapidly shifted. By 1969, his vitriolic attacks on the counterculture, the anti-war movement, and students had earned him the reputation of a crank, and he was being eased off high-profile shows. He "saw all hippies as layabouts and slobs. He hated their hairiness .... Laziness especially incensed him," one critic summarized (Theroux, 1999: 45). His response to the *Bed-In,* with its scattering of handmade signs–"Stay in Bed!" "Hair Peace," and "Grow Your Hair" strategically

[11] Lennon quoted in Peebles (1981: 23).

[12] Ono and Lennon, 1969. This and further quotations from dialogue in *Bed-In for Peace,* where cited without another source, are from this film.

positioned for a television audience – was predictably "square." To Lennon's invitation to "sit on the edge of the bed here, Mr. Capp," he declined, declaring his preference "to sit on something *hard*." A folding metal chair was produced. Settled onto this perch, Capp launched into his prepared questions. "What about during World War II," he began, apparently intending to probe the limits of the couple's pacifist stance, before veering in a direction no one probably anticipated: "What," Capp mused, "if Hitler and Churchill had gotten into bed? Which Hitler would clearly have enjoyed." "What about Churchill?" Lennon gamely interjected, before venturing that "if Churchill and Hitler had gone into bed, a lot of people would be alive today."

Capp's primary association to the *Bed-In for Peace* was sleeping with the enemy, a culturally debased form of fraternization, and he was quick to appreciate its subversive power. The theme also echoed the racial prejudice surrounding Ono and Lennon's union. When Ono interrupted his *mano a mano* with Lennon, Capp erupted: "Simmer down, woman!" he commanded, adding in a loud stage whisper to Lennon: "Good god, you've got to live with that? I can see why you want peace." For Capp, who at another point in the interview referred to himself as "just normal," the *Bed-In* stimulated thoughts of seduction between dominant men. Confronted with a woman and a man of different ethnicities lying in bed talking of peace, he, being "just normal," responded by voicing homoerotic fantasies of power and an undisguised misogyny. In *Bed Peace,* his rant proved the couple's proposition that the work of peace lies in part in exposing the irrational kernel of established, masculinist power. "You just did a great deal for peace, Mr. Capp," Lennon summed up.

"What would you do in case of a war?" another questioner demanded of Lennon – as if there were no war, as if they were not "doing anything." "I'd die of fright," he replied. Maintaining his stance alongside Ono, he aligned himself with her, refusing the provocation to man up and shunning the possessive attitude to war often displayed by male anti-war activists. Relinquishing the myth of heroic masculinity, he implied, was a path to psychic relief, a refusal with the potential to expand political and social consciousness. "You talk as if something's going to happen outside of us," Ono interjected, addressing the interviewer, taking up the question that is not addressed to her, a woman, who has no obvious role to play "in case of a war." "We're all in this you see," she continued. "We are all in the same society, and in the world, and everything that happens to us is our responsibility." Speaking with frank simplicity at a time when "lying in politics" had become a new form of art, the couple drew attention to the reality, and the potential, of a continuous nuclear and media world (see Arendt, 1972: "Lying in Politics"). Implicit in Ono's observation that "we are all in the same world" was the Cold War nuclear legacy of the atomic bombings of Hiroshima and Nagasaki in 1945. By enacting a public ritual of peace in the celebration of a marriage between citizens of former enemies, Britain and Japan – one that crossed barriers of nation, culture, ethnicity, race, and class – Ono and Lennon offered their union as a symbol of hope for the nuclear world.

The purpose of war is to rid ourselves and our group of destructiveness by providing us with enemies to kill, Fornari contended, but nuclear weapons, he claimed, had precipitated a crisis of war. To the extent that war now encompassed the prospect of destruction on a planetary scale, the social institution of war seemed in danger of becoming obsolete. This threatened loss of war, Fornari argued, demanded unprecedented psychic and social adaptations ([1966] 1974: chapter 5). To confront the realization that, in Fornari's terms, war was no longer a viable solution to the problem of destructiveness meant that we faced "a dealing with oneself." Arguing that it was possible, and pressing, for individuals to begin to accept responsibility for war at the level of the unconscious, Fornari underscored the role of psychic work – what Ono called "dealing with oneself" – in Cold War politics ([1966] 1974: xviii). His theory is radical in its attention to the unconscious of the group, but it ignores the place of gender in the group mind of the nuclear society. Ono and Lennon foregrounded it. In *Bed-In for Peace*, they performed solidarity, equality, and reciprocity in an intimate relationship between members of former enemy groups as, in effect, a psychic and social shift that is critical to the long-term survival of society. As survivors of total war in Europe and Japan, bearing witness to the past effects of patriarchal mythologies of marriage, family, and nation, they embodied the potential, and urgency, of resocialization in a nuclear world. Their individualistic, do-it-yourself, free-associative protest techniques operated on the principle of assuming responsibility for war at the level of the unconscious, while also suggesting that in order for embracing responsibility to have political import, we need to approach it as group-work, as psychic labor performed as part of the group, and therefore as work in which gender plays a pivotal role.[13]

This was an argument feminist peace activists had also been making for some time. Histories of the anti-war movement typically relegate women to a supporting and belated role in opposing the war, reproducing the masculine supremacy of the anti-war movement itself, a mindset the *Bed-In for Peace* actively challenges. But in reality, women played a pivotal role from the start. At the height of the Cold War, in November of 1961, picketers in sixty cities across the United States walked off their jobs and "out of their kitchens" to demand an end to nuclear testing, calling their action a Women's Strike for Peace (Swerdlow, 1993: 15). Playing up the era's prescribed feminine role of mother, in contrast to the anti-war strikes of the Vietnam era soon to come – including *Bed-In for Peace*, with its invitation to "stay in bed" and "grow your hair" for peace – WSP protests displayed a conspicuous conformity to gender and social convention fashioned for the McCarthy era, a time of rigid social conservatism and rampant anticommunism.

[13] I am using an invented term, group-work, to gesture toward psychoanalytic theories of the unconscious – from Freud's dream-work, joke-work, and work of mourning to J. B. Pontalis's death-work – and to suggest that the anti-war work of Ono and Lennon was engaged in a specific analysis of what Mitchell calls "the importance of laterality for understanding the interpenetration of violence, power, and nonreproductive sexuality" (2000: 225).

Demonstrating at the United Nations in the midst of the Cuban missile crisis, hatted and gloved WSP protesters carried hand-lettered placards urging President Kennedy to "be careful, and let the U.N. handle it" (Swerdlow, 1993: 89–90). Called by the House Un-American Activities Committee (HUAC) to testify on charges that WSP was a Communist front, the witnesses mocked the absurdity of the charges, eliciting laughter and applause from a hearing room packed with women, an episode that inflicted fatal damage on the fearsome reputation of HUAC. Adopting a "motherist" peace rhetoric, they couched calls for multilateral nuclear disarmament under international control in an exaggerated feminine politesse, effectively disarming the political establishment and attracting widespread, appreciative press attention that galvanized public support for nuclear disarmament (Swerdlow, 1993: 141). Staging photogenic events that appealed to the press as novelties, WSP successfully circumvented the filters that excluded pacifist voices from mainstream reporting, as Ono and Lennon would later do on a global stage. The group's tactics were gently subversive, but the effect, as WSP historian Amy Swerdlow observed, was to help "legitimize a radical critique of the Cold War and U.S. militarism" (1993: 3).

In June 1963, at its second international conference, WSP pivoted from its successful push for a nuclear test ban treaty to early opposition to the war in Vietnam, pledging "to alert the public to ... the specific ways human morality is being violated by the U.S. attack ... on women and children" (Swerdlow, 1993: 129). WSPers, as they called themselves, exploited their protected social position as a self-described "housewife brigade" to form networks for draft counseling, advising conscripts on tactics for avoiding the draft.[14] The group's internationalist perspective, and focus on women, also brought a distinctive person-to-person culture of female solidarity to the broader anti-war movement. In 1965, WSP activists visited Hanoi. "We travelled half way around the world to enemy country, and to me it felt like coming home to

[14] On WSP's antidraft work, including draft counseling, see Swerdlow, 1993: 158–86.

family and friends," remarked one woman of the experience of meeting the leaders of the North Vietnamese Women's Union (Swerdlow, 1993: 217). Women leaders of the Vietnamese revolution also visited North America. In 1969 – the same year of Ono and Lennon's Canadian *Bed-In* – Women Strike for Peace joined with other women's peace groups, including Canada's Voice of Women and the Washington, DC-based Women's Anti-Imperialism Collective, to invite Vietnamese revolutionaries, barred by their enemy status from visiting the United States, to attend a peace conference in Canada, where American women could meet them by crossing the border, as other Americans did to evade the draft. "We are sisters together; we will help each other; we wish neither Vietnamese nor American loss – it was instant love," wrote one participant in the WSP journal *MEMO*.[15] This idealized image of sisterhood is contradicted by other accounts, which exposed the tensions in the peace and women's liberation movements of 1969, "coming out of factionalism, racism, liberalism, and other movement maladies," as a contributor to the women's liberation journal *off our backs* reported (Swerdlow, 1993: 229). With the encouragement of the Vietnamese to work "collectively with love for one another," women of different generations and histories however did begin to examine the conditions of their own oppression, and that of their sisters at home and in Vietnam, as the core of what needed to be analyzed and transformed to bring an end to the war (Swerdlow, 1993: 229).

Recalling the WSP script, which might have been summarized as "fighting the establishment by using methods that are so far removed from establishment-type thinking that the establishment doesn't know how to fight back," Ono and Lennon declared their refusal to accept outdated solutions to the world's conflicts. They encouraged others to follow their own inclinations. They echoed the WSP's proposition that "every woman has a personal responsibility to achieve a peaceful world now." Their audience, however, was global. "Publicity is our game," Lennon explained. "The

[15] Cora Weiss, quoted in Swerdlow, 1993: 227.

Beatles' thing was that. And that was the trade I've learned" (Yorke, 1982b: 67). By staging an event the press dismissed as a stunt, and portrayed as a celebrity lark rather than a serious news story, the couple succeeded in garnering front-page headlines in every major Western newspaper. Even the perceived frivolousness of the *Bed-In* did not detract from reporting on it. On the contrary, derision only seemed to amplify the coverage. Through a canny use of media, they exploited antagonism toward their alliance to overcome a situation of de facto censorship of international criticism of the war in Vietnam, rendering the mass media an active zone of public protest. Picking up on the legacy of the WSP's distinctive form of individualistic, "structureless," "unorganizational" anti-war politics, they resisted totalizing solutions to war (Swerdlow, 1993: 19, 3). Instead, embracing a similar do-it-yourself ethos to WSP, with its determination to disarm and outwit the state, they improvised ways to work for peace against our norms. Recoding internationalist-feminist politics for a global countercultural movement, they drew extensively on their own histories as artists. From its beginnings, Ono's avant-garde work had been involved with the performance of everyday gestures. Adapting Ono's scripts and props to their double act, and exploiting Lennon's grasp of the social imaginary – or, as he put it, publicity – they deconstructed the apparatus of the media, using their avant-garde and popular bona fides to conduct peace "research" into the most "functional" contribution art could make to the aim of peace.

"Imagine," the Lennon song that would become an anthem of the international peace movement up to the present day, borrows directly from Ono's avant-garde project. "The lyric and the concept," he explained, "came from Yoko ... it was straight out of *Grapefruit*, her book." Published in 1964 (and reissued in 1971 in a mass-market edition), *Grapefruit* is a compendium of works in which, Lennon explains, "there's a whole pile of pieces about imagine this and imagine that" (Peebles, 1981: 43.)[16] The idea of

[16] Lennon acknowledged that "in those days I was a bit more selfish, a bit more macho, and I sort of omitted to mention her contribution .... I have given her credit long overdue."

the instruction piece, as Ono revealed in the catalogue of her 1966 exhibition at the Indica Gallery in London, where she and Lennon famously met, "derives from as far back as the time of the Second World War when we had no food to eat, and my brother and I exchanged menus in the air" (Indica Gallery, 1966). *Painting to Construct in Your Head,* Ono's talismanic work, exemplifies her principle of imagination as a mental discipline by which to keep alive the possibility of change. When she and Lennon embarked on their peace research, they embraced this principle. The radical aim of pacifism, they suggested, is to imagine peace.

The Bed-In for Peace attempted to revive "the personal, prefigurative politics of the early 1960s," a politics predicated on the idea of "building in the present the desired community of the future" (Echols, 1992: 181). By inviting visitors to bear witness to a relationship in which what is "normal" is gender equality, Ono and Lennon offered a concrete demonstration of what working for peace against our norms might look like. The timing was significant. By 1969, prefigurative politics had waned with the intensification of the war and the expansion of state violence against anti-war protesters at home. The inexorable escalation of the war exacerbated gender divisions in the anti-war movement, which the Movement's male leaders treated as an extension of war, as much as an alternative to it, while also presuming the prerogative to direct it, just as their counterparts, also men, prosecuted the war itself. This, together with the pervasive trivializing of feminism's role in anti-war and peace politics, alienated female activists from the anti-war movement, but also divided them from one another. Some now declared masculine supremacy "the enemy," and argued for a radical, separatist feminism. Others saw women's liberation as an integral part of anti-war politics, however resistant some male activists might be to social change that touched them "where they lived" (Echols, 1992: 180). While WSP had obliquely resisted the antifeminist orthodoxy of the Cold War, revealing a "latent political power" in maternal morality, by 1969 it had also exposed the limitations of motherist politics, including self-sacrificing acceptance of women's subordinate position (Elsthain & Tobias, 1990), cited in Swerdlow (1993: 234)). It was in this environment of gender division in the anti-war movement that Ono and Lennon took to their bed, calling for "peace at home." The *Bed-In for Peace* in Vietnam was also a *Bed-In for Peace* in America. What we do in bed, the couple proposed, matters for what we do in war, and about war, at home and abroad.

"It is a queer experience," Virginia Woolf remarked, near the end of her life, "lying in the dark and listening to the zoom of a hornet, which may at any moment sting you to death. It is a sound that interrupts cool and consecutive thinking about peace. Yet it is a sound – far more than prayers and anthems – that should compel one to think about peace." Not to "think peace into existence," she warned, would condemn "millions of bodies yet to be born" to "lie in the same darkness and hear the same death rattle overhead" ([1941] 2009: 1). Both Ono and Lennon had lain under the "zoom of a hornet." As a child of twelve, hunkered down in the family bunker on the outskirts of Tokyo, Ono survived the firebombing of the city in March of 1945, when American B-29s dropped bombs, gasoline, and napalm on the city, burning it to the ground. Five years earlier, on the night of October 9, 1940, John Lennon was born amid German Luftwaffe bombing raids on Liverpool. The *Bed-In* echoed Woolf's appeal to us – and, as Jacqueline Rose explains in the volume, also Arendt's appeal – not to act, but to think. Ono and Lennon "stopped." The stillness of their marathon conversations with visitors offered pacific resistance to the mania of war. For Woolf, thinking peace into existence was a psychic labour, an effort to "drag up into consciousness" that which "holds us down," namely, "the desire for aggression, the desire to dominate and enslave" ([1941] 2009: 3).

In pacifism, Ono and Lennon suggested, desire – wanting – plays a vital role. Politics "needs to have a real purchase on people's desires and fantasies to move us," the political theorist Chantal Mouffe has written. It needs to take fantasy seriously. Only by offering "identities which can help people make sense of what they are experiencing" and give them "hope for the future," she maintains, can politics work (2005: 25). By comparison with the vivid social imaginary of war, and the powerful identifications it mobilizes, peace is unthought, unimagined, even undesired. Its "affective dimension," in Mouffe's terms, is eclipsed by the excitements, intensities, and idealizations of war (2005: 25). The *Bed-In for Peace* responds to this incipiency, or latency, of peace by offering the couple's relationship as a tangible fantasy – a gender fantasy – that begins at home. With humour, tenderness, and evident pleasure in each other, Ono and Lennon embodied a sensual continuity between their intimate relationship and the ideals of social transformation, between the "*jouissance* of the body" and "social fantasies" of gender and racial equality (Mouffe, 2005: 27). Ministering to desire, to hope, and to the idealism of youth that war also courts, the *Bed-In* affirms desire as an intrinsic dimension of political subjectivity. It also exhibits the way in which gender features in the *work* of peace: the psychic, artistic, and intellectual labour that thinking peace into existence against our norms demands.[17]

REFERENCES

Arendt, Hannah. 1970. *On Violence*. New York: Harcourt Brace Jovanovich.

Arendt, Hannah. 1972. *Crises of the Republic: Lying in Politics, Civil Disobedience on Violence, Thoughts on Politics, and Revolution.* New York: Harcourt Brace Jovanovich.

Bryan-Wilson, Julia. 2003. Remembering Yoko Ono's Cut Piece. *Oxford Art Journal,* **26**(1), 99–123.

Cott, Jonathan and Doudna, Christine. 1982. *The Ballad of John and Yoko.* London: Joseph.

Deutsche, Rosalyn. 2017. Louise Lawler's Play Technique. In *Louise Lawler: Receptions,* Exhibition catalogue. New York: MoMA.

Echols, Alice. 1992. "Women Power" and Women's Liberation: Exploring the Relationship between the Antiwar Movement and the Women's Liberation Movement. In Melvin Small and William D. Hoover, eds., *Give Peace a Chance:*

17 "We try to be non-serious about things, but we are very serious about being not serious," Lennon remarked in one interview, to which Ono added: "We may be too serious, even. We try to have a sense of humour and we try to smile at everyone . . . from the bottom of our hearts .... But it's very difficult for our generation to genuinely smile . . . we're trying" (Williams, 2010: 28).

Exploring the Vietnam Antiwar Movement. Syracuse, NY: Syracuse University Press, pp. 171–81.

Elsthain, Jean Bethke and Tobias, Sheila, eds. 1990. *Women, Militarism and War: Essays in History, Politics and Social Theory*. Towtowa, NJ: Rowman and Littlefield. Cited in: Swerdlow, Amy. 1993. *Women Strike for Peace.* Chicago and London: University of Chicago Press.

Fornari, Frano. [1966] 1974. The Psychoanalysis of War. Alenka Pfeifer, trans. Garden City, New York: Anchor Books.

Indica Gallery. 1966. Yoko at Indica: Unfinished Paintings and Objects by Yoko Ono. Exhibition pamphlet. London: Indica Gallery, n.p.

Jeffords, Susan. 1989. *The Remasculinization of America: Gender and the Vietnam War.* Bloomington, IN: Indiana University Press.

Kotz, Liz. 2001. Post-Cagean Aesthetics and the "Event" Score. *October,* **95** (Winter), 54–89.

Lang, Daniel. 1989. *Casualties of War.* New York: Pocket Press.

Lifton, Robert Jay. 1973. *Home from the War: Vietnam Veterans: Neither Victims nor Executioners.* New York: Simon & Schuster.

Mitchell, Juliet. 2000. *Mad Men and Medusas: Reclaiming Hysteria and the Effect of Sibling Relationships on the Human Condition.* London: Allen Lane.

2003. *Siblings: Sex and Violence.* Cambridge: Polity Press.

Mouffe, Chantal. 2005. *On the Political.* London and New York: Routledge.

Ono, Yoko. 1970. *Grapefruit: A Book of Instructions and Drawings.* New York: Simon & Shuster.

1971. Letter to the Editor. *The Post-Standard,* October 9.

Ono, Yoko and Lennon, John. 1969. *Bed Peace,* accessed August 13, 2018. http://imaginepeace.com/#videos.

Peebles, Andy. 1981. *The Lennon Tapes: Lennon and Yoko Ono in Conversation with Andy Peebles.* London: BBC Books.

Stacewicz, Richard. 2008. *Winter Soldiers: An Oral History of the Vietnam Veterans against the War.* Chicago, IL: Haymarket Books.

Stiles, Kristine. 1964. Bag Piece 1964. Catalogue entry in Alexandra Munroe, ed., with Jon Hendricks, *Yes Yoko Ono,* exhibition catalogue. New York: Japan Society/Harry N. Abrams.

1992. Unbosoming Lennon: The Politics of Yoko Ono's Experience. *Art Criticism,* **7**(2), 21–54.

Swerdlow, Amy. 1993. *Women Strike for Peace.* Chicago and London: University of Chicago Press.

Taneja, Preti. 2015. How Can We Live with Ourselves: An Interview with Juliet Mitchell. In Robbie Duschinsky and Susan Walker, eds., *Juliet Mitchell and the Lateral Axis: Twenty-First-Century Psychoanalysis and Feminism.* New York: Palgrave Macmillan.

Theroux, Alexander. 1999. *The Enigma of Al Capp.* Seattle, WA: Fantographics Books.

Turse, Nick. 2013. *Kill Anything that Moves: The Real American War in Vietnam.* New York: Henry Holt.

Williams, Richard. 1969. *Melody Maker,* December 6, 13, 20. Reprinted as: 2010. People Prefer a Dead Saint to a Living Annoyance Like John and Yoko. *Uncut: The Ultimate Music Guide,* 3, Lennon special issue.

Woolf, Virginia. [1941] 2009. *Thoughts on Peace in an Air Raid.* London: Penguin.

Yorke, Ritchie. 1982a. Boosting Peace: John and Yoko in Canada. In Jonathan Cott and Christina Doundna, eds., *The Ballad of John and Yoko.* Garden City, NY: Doubleday and Company/A Rolling Stone Press Book.

1982b. John, Yoko, and Year One. In Jonathan Cott and Christina Doundna, eds., *The Ballad of John and Yoko.* Garden City, NY: Doubleday and Company/ A Rolling Stone Press Book.

Zeiger, David. 2005. *Sir! No Sir! The Suppressed Story of the G.I. Movement to End the War in Vietnam.* Los Angeles, CA: Displaced Films.

Index

CPSIA information can be obtained
at www.ICGtesting.com
Printed in the USA
LVHW090122171121
703555LV00005B/167